SCARE TACTICS

Rugge claimed that he never saw Nick's mouth being taped up, but he said he heard Hoyt pulling out some duct tape, ripping it off and doing something with it. To his ear, it sounded like duct tape was being applied to Nick, and later he mentioned it being placed around Nick's mouth.

Rugge would claim later that he still believed that Ryan Hoyt was only trying to scare Nick into not talking—until the next few unforgettable seconds. Rugge said he was sitting on a rock nearby when Hoyt raised the shovel and whacked Nick in the head with it. The sound was very distinct in the otherwise silent night. The boy tumbled over, and Rugge presumed that Nick had been knocked out.

According to Rugge, "Hoyt picked Nick up and dragged him over to a hole. He was holding him under the arms and was dragging him faceup." Rugge said he couldn't see where Hoyt placed him, but that it was probably in the hole that Pressley had dug earlier that night.

Then, under the twinkling stars and pale moon, Ryan Hoyt raised the pistol and pressed his finger down on the trigger.

MOST
WANTED
KILLER

ROBERT SCOTT

PINNACLE BOOKS
Kensington Publishing Corp.
http://www.kensingtonbooks.com

PINNACLE BOOKS are published by

Kensington Publishing Corp.
119 West 40th Street
New York, NY 10018

All Kensington Titles, Imprints, and Distributed Lines are available at special quantity discounts for bulk purchases for sales promotions, premiums, fund-raising, and educational or institutional use. Special book excerpts or customized printings can also be created to fit specific needs. For details, write or phone the office of the Kensington special sales manager: Kensington Publishing Corp., 119 West 40th Street, New York, NY 10018, attn: Special Sales Department, Phone: 1-800-221-2647.

Pinnacle and the P logo Reg. U.S. Pat. & TM Off.

ISBN-13: 978-0-7860-1885-7
ISBN-10: 0-7860-1885-2

First Printing: April 2010

10 9 8 7 6 5 4 3 2 1

Printed in the United States of America

Acknowledgments

I would like to thank Debbie, Connie, Jennifer and Rene for all their help on this book. I would also like to thank my editors at Kensington, Michaela Hamilton and Mike Shohl.

Ryan Hoyt told me, "I want a hole seven feet by two feet and as deep as you can dig it. Just dig, if you know what's good for you."

—Graham Pressley

1

ABDUCTION

It was a typical morning in the West Hills section of Los Angeles on a warm summer afternoon. Pauline Mahoney was returning from church with her two boys and one of their friends, and as she approached the intersection of Platt and Ingomar Streets, she suddenly witnessed a sight that ripped apart the tranquility of the day. At least two young men, and possibly three, were beating and kicking a young teenager, who lay on the ground, trying to defend himself. As Pauline recalled later, "The boy they were beating was a young man. They were really beating the crap out of him!"

Mahoney would recall that it was four young men beating up the lone individual, when, in fact, it was two or three against one. Nonetheless, despite her error in numbers, she witnessed a severe beating in progress. Mahoney recalled, "The lone boy was lying on the ground, so I couldn't tell if he was thin or heavy, but he was not an overweight boy. He was lying down against a wall, and the others were kicking and beating him. It was all happening as I was driving by. I observed all of this for about twenty seconds, and then they threw him into a white van. The young men who were beating him were all white, and all of them had short hair. The victim was also white.

"My vehicle was only about four or five feet away from them. I drove up to a stop sign, and instead of making a right-hand turn, which I would normally do to go home, I continued forward in order to get the license plate number. I drove by slowly and got the license plate number, and then continued on slowly, looking in my rearview mirror just to kind of see what was going on. The van started to drive away, and it left one of the attackers on the street. It stopped to let him get in, and I was trying to look inconspicuous. Then I made a right at the next block and went home.

"My two boys in the car with me were six and nine years old. I wasn't able to write down the license plate number right then, so me and the boys stated the number out loud as we saw it, and continued repeating it until we got home. Then I wrote it down before I made a phone call. It was only about a minute from the time I saw the boy being beaten until I got home and made the phone call."

Mahoney's voice was excited as she called 911 at around 1:00 P.M. on August 6, describing the beating and what appeared to her to be a kidnapping. As far as things she observed, the boy who had been beaten did not voluntarily climb into the van, but rather was thrown in against his will.

Amazingly, there was a second phone call that went to a 911 dispatcher about the same incident. It was from a woman via her cell phone, and though she refused to give her name, the information she gave was similar to that of Mahoney. The caller described young men beating a boy as he lay on the sidewalk near a wall. Then the attackers threw the young man into a white van and drove away.

Despite such good information, especially from Mahoney about the van's license plate, nothing would go right from that point forward. The dispatcher who took the call from Mahoney reported it to the Los Angeles Police Department (LAPD) as "an assault with a deadly weapon with subjects still on scene." In fact, it should have been labeled as a more urgent dispatch—"an assault still in progress."

When LAPD officers Brent Rygh and Donovan Lyons arrived on the scene at Ingomar and Platt, there was no assault in progress by that point; there were no assailants, no victim, no van. Officer Rygh said later, "I thought it was some high-school kids just slap fighting, or horsing around, the way high-school students tend to do."

Officer Rygh did call Pauline Mahoney on his own cell phone, but he never went to see her in person. When he took the information she had given about the van's license plate, he ran the numbers, but mistakenly thought the address of the van's owner was a long distance from the scene, rather than close by. Officer Rygh and his partner did not go to the van owner's address to check up on the whereabouts of the van. Nor did they pass on the information they had to other nearby police agencies.

Further mistakes were made on the second 911 call by a dispatcher. This dispatcher labeled the call as an "information-only broadcast," instead of the correct labeling as a "kidnapping in progress." Officers Rygh and Lyons never got any information about this second message at all, since it was deemed to have such low priority.

Little did the LAPD know at the time that the white van was now traveling out of the county, eventually heading for Santa Barbara. Inside, it held four young men, three of them kidnappers: twenty-year-old Jesse Rugge, twenty-year-old William Skidmore and nineteen-year-old Jesse James Hollywood. Their victim was fifteen-year-old Nick Markowitz, and his half brother, Ben, had once been Hollywood's pal and fellow drug dealer. But on August 6, 2000, Ben was no longer Jesse Hollywood's friend, and the feud that had gone on between them for six months now took a dangerous turn for everyone involved.

2

BEN AND NICK

Ben Markowitz was a handful from an early age. He was headstrong and willful; trouble seemed to be his constant companion. His father, Jeff, tried almost everything he could to get Ben back on the right path, but nothing seemed to work. Jeff related, "The first (bad) thing Ben ever did, he slashed some tires, and from there it escalated into an assault with a deadly weapon, which was brass knuckles. He thought he was protecting a girl. Little things like that. 'Little' big things that just kept going on and on. Ben was living with his mother, at twelve years old, and he started getting into trouble. So he moved in with myself and my new wife, Susan, and basically, we kind of got him on track for a while. He got involved in karate, baseball and a lot of different sports. He was doing okay for a while.

"Ben was a good athlete. Exceptional. He was a national champion in karate, he was in all-star baseball, he was an unbelievable little athlete. And a real joy to watch, to be honest. The other stuff—we kept hoping it was going to get better, but at fourteen he brought a weapon into the house and my wife, Susan, found it. She actually found a clip to a weapon, a nine-millimeter pistol. We traced it down, found out whose it was, and what it was all about.

"From that point on, Benjamin was in karate, and we actually had him move in with his sensei (karate teacher). His sensei said, 'Let me have him for a while. I'll take him to school.' So we tried that route. And after about eight months, Ben came back home and I took the three-car garage and we turned it into his bedroom. But he and I got into an argument over painting it. He wanted to go out and not help paint, and it was a knock-down, drag-out fight with my son. I had to hold him down and tell him that we were going to finish the project. He actually attacked me.

"We painted that night, and I got him to stay. I told him that if he finished painting, he could go out. The next day we went to counseling. Ben had been in counseling since he was four years old. At counseling I kind of blew up with Ben, and the counselor said that there was no way I could get into physical confrontations with my son. So I said to Ben, 'You can either do it my way, or the highway.'

"I got home from the counselor, and we were going to finish a few things in his room, and he disappeared. I didn't hear from him for six months after that. Well, actually I heard from him, but I couldn't get ahold of him. He would call and say, 'I'm fine. I'm fine.' And I was thinking that sooner or later he's got to come back, and he did. But he came back tattooed from his shoulder blades down to his ankles. He had moved in with a tattoo artist. And he had a real hard-core attitude, including an SFV tattoo."

SFV stood for a gang from the San Fernando Valley. It was, in part, a white supremacist gang, which Jeff and Susan Markowitz, being Jewish, found incredibly offensive. In fact, one of Ben's tattoos was a swastika. Ben was fifteen years old.

"He came home with two pit bulls and said, 'Well, I want these dogs.' And we had a giant argument over those two dogs. We already had two dogs, and I said, 'No, we can't have any more dogs!' And he disappeared again.

"Maybe a month later I got in touch with him at a friend's house. This family had always been interested in helping out. Always been there for him. They took him to school and he went to continuation school next to his old high school, and he was doing okay at his continuation school.

"But some kind of confrontation happened in the school between him and another student. I was at work and I got a phone call from the principal of the continuation school to get down there. They had black gang members from one end and they had white supremacist gang members at the other, and Ben was the one who instigated the whole thing. All turned out fine and well, everybody ran away, and it all dissipated, but again, Ben . . ." Jeff left the rest of the sentence remain unspoken. "This thing escalated into something of unbelievable consequence.

"Through all of this period, Ben was working for me. I was picking him up, bringing him to work, and he was taking the bus. I was trying to do whatever I could do to try to bring him back. The assault with a deadly weapon was when he was fifteen. He was at the beach and he ran into a guy that had raped a friend of his, and Ben thought he had to be her protector. He walked over to this guy, had his hand in his pocket, and he also had brass knuckles. The guy came at him when Ben confronted him, and Ben took a swipe at the guy. Actually cut the guy on the top of the head.

"The police happened to be right there, because these boys had sneaked onto the beach, and the police had been called to go after them. So the police happened to be right there when Ben confronted this boy. Ben was arrested, and he was in for about eight months.

"When Ben got to be eighteen, I got him into an apartment, and he and a group of guys, well, it turned into a fiasco. Actually, before that, I moved out with him, and personally moved into his apartment. Just he and I. I took him to work every day, back and forth, and I visited with my wife on the weekends. Just to try something. Just to make him regroup and understand the ethics of work. It was the only thing I thought might work.

"In the meantime Ben, well, he's probably the most lovable guy you'd meet. And he's very caring and very considerate. I can't tell you how many friends and how many enemies he has. It's probably fifty-fifty. Anybody would do anything for him, and at the same time, he has people that really dislike him. Ben was an urban legend in our town, because he would defend himself. He would fight for what . . . well, a lot of times it wasn't for what he believed, a lot of times it was because he had been drinking. Which is probably, like, a lot of people's downfall. But if backed into a corner, he'd come out on top. It's just the way he is. In juvenile hall there was a guy after him that was two times his size. The guy finally cornered him in the shower, but Ben came out smelling like a rose. That's just the way he is.

"He knew karate, but beyond that, even before that, you could throw him up in the air and he'd land on his feet. He's a cat with nine lives. The problem is what he left in his wake behind him."

Ben Markowitz had a friendship with another young man from the area—Jesse James Hollywood—and Ben had played in the same baseball league with Jesse. Although years older than Jesse, Ben and Hollywood hit it off, and in time Ben moved into Jesse's residence, and was part of his party scene. Because of Ben's tough image, some people even came to view Ben as Hollywood's "enforcer."

As one reporter put it later, "Jesse James Hollywood was a wannabe bad boy. Ben Markowitz was a real bad boy." Ben recalled later, "I'd known Jesse for years. He was younger than me, but we played the same sports. Later I sold marijuana for Jesse Hollywood. He would just front me so much at a time and I would pay him back when I got the money. He was supplying me with about two pounds a week. It cost about four thousand two hundred fifty a pound. I'd sell that and I'd get, like, fifty-two hundred. I was turning two pounds a week. Jesse was getting it from his dad. I knew from the beginning that his dad was in the drug-dealing business. We would not really talk about it, but Jesse let it be known.

"There were about four or five other people dealing for Jesse Hollywood. There was a guy named Brian, John, Ryan, Jake and a guy named Josh. As for Ryan Hoyt, I used to go out with his sister when I was young, like, twelve years old. I met Ryan then. Jesse, he had a way of picking on everybody, but I guess he picked on Ryan more than anyone. Just making fun of him."

A *Los Angeles* magazine writer named Jesse Katz, who later studied this world of Jesse Hollywood and his buddies, wrote: *Jesse Hollywood was a businessman. The people around him were basically lost souls. Jesse James was kind of the center of their universe. None of these kids would stand up to him, but Ben Markowitz just didn't seem to care, and he was probably the only member of that crew that didn't kowtow to Jesse James Hollywood.*

Hollywood might have made fun of the others, but Ben would not take very much of a ribbing from him or anyone else. He had a volatile temper, was extremely strong, proficient in karate, and most people knew not to mess with him. Ben had one more thing—a younger half brother named Nick, whom he liked very much, and whom Ben took steps to keep from following down the path he had taken.

Jeff and Susan Markowitz were recent divorcees when they met in San Fernando Valley in 1982. They hit it off, and about a year later they were married. Susan's only son, Nicholas, was born to them in 1984. Susan recalled that Nick was a happy baby and a very quick learner. By the age of two and a half, he could identify Snow White and all of the seven dwarfs.

The family eventually moved to a housing tract in the West Hills section of Los Angeles, which was on the edge of the San Fernando Valley. Originally the area had been the site within the domain of the Spanish San Fernando Mission. The valley remained mostly agricultural, with picturesque orange groves, until the early part of the twentieth century, when Los Angeles obtained water from the Owens Valley, which allowed new housing in the San Fernando Valley. After that occurred, the days of agriculture were over, and the Valley became a vast suburb of Los Angeles. The mid part of the Valley over time became somewhat run-down, but by the year 2000, West Hills was still one of the "tonier" areas of the San Fernando Valley.

Growing up in one of those suburban homes, Nick took piano lessons, enjoyed drama, read Shakespeare and studied martial arts. He and his mother were very close and even wrote in a journal together. It contained notes on the day's events, funny stories and depictions of how they were feeling at the time. Susan later told a reporter, "He was the funniest person on earth. He just had so much energy. I don't know what was going on in his head, but he would do anything to make us laugh."

Nick wasn't just a "mama's boy." He studied Tae Kwon Do and was very proficient at it. Jeff Markowitz later said of his son Nick, "He had a lot of friends. He had a funny personality. He was full of life. He was a jokester. He was in drama, and he just loved to use that on everybody, and he could play it up. He had awards for drama, and did it three years running, from junior high into high school."

Longtime friend Laura Milner knew Nick from the time they went to elementary school together, and she was interested in the theater as well. She said, "We were both theater geeks. Nick had a way of lighting up a room. He was silly and you could talk to him. He liked to mess around with the guys, but could hang out with the girls. That's why girls liked him."

As tough as he could be, Nick was also very sensitive. Alireza Hojati, his teacher at the Academy of Karate, in West Hills, said of Nick, "In the first ten minutes, you could see that he was sensitive. He sparred, but you knew that he was a very gentle soul. He had a very hard time bringing himself to hitting anyone."

At his Bar Mitzvah, Nick chose to speak about Moses, near the end of his days, and his admonition to the people of Israel to follow a path of justice. It was a speech about fair play and doing what was right. In many respects the things Nick talked about covered the area of witnesses and trials, ironic in light of what was to happen later to him and those around him.

Yet, despite all his good qualities, by the time he was fourteen, Nick was starting to drift. His dad noted, "He was very articulate, a quick learner and intelligent kid, but he didn't push too hard. If he would have studied, he would have been unbelievable, but he didn't. His grades became average, nothing great. Instead of staying home, he would go out with his friends and started doing that more and more. And after karate he'd say, 'I'm going to so-and-so's house.' We knew the parents, we knew the families, but we never collaborated with them. Never found out what they were doing."

In fact, by the end of the 1990s, the West Valley was no longer a haven of peace and tranquility, untouched by drugs and violence. A friend of Nick's named Brandie Rosa told a reporter that it didn't matter where you lived in the Valley, you could get booze, drugs and sex there at an early age. She said, "I found it just as easy to get drugs in Agoura Hills or West Hills, as anywhere else. Kids there are rich and bored and it was always easy to get pot and blow (cocaine)."

Brandie hung out with Nick and his friends, smoked cigarettes with them and sometimes smoked dope as well. She said that Nick in some ways was unique—in that he fit easily into groups of people who had nothing to do with each other, the slackers and dopers, as well as the straight-A students who never got into trouble. By the time he turned fourteen, it was hard to tell exactly how Nick was going to turn out, or who he was going to be.

Even Jeff and Susan realized this. Jeff later said, "He was just picking everything apart. He was deciding which way he'd go."

One thing not helping matters was that Nick idolized his older half brother, Ben. He admired Ben's tough-guy ways and seeming fearlessness. Jeff recalled, "Ben's relationship with Nick—the urban-legend idea—we knew the 'older brother/younger brother' thing filtered into Nick. There was no stopping it. There was no way. They loved each other, and it was genuine. And to try to stifle him would have been even worse. In fact, I did. I tried to put a stop to the relationship, because I knew where it could lead, the possibilities. And I hoped that Nick, my younger one, would see the damage Ben had caused to himself and to others. But he didn't see that. All he saw was some slight amount of glory—something that you read about, you see on TV, you see it in the news. The tough guy that the movies are all about. You feel for the tough guy—Captain Hero.

"Nick was falling into that same kind of category. I found out that Ben was getting involved in drugs, and it just so happened that Nick started to do the same on a small scale, but it could have escalated into something. The first thing we found out about Nick, he had a very small amount of marijuana on him and he was caught at school with it. It was just a bag with some remnants, but it was still known that it was there. Then one day he had some Ritalin on him. (Ben had taken Ritalin as a child, and Nick was curious what effect this had on Ben.) Nick had it for recreation. He said, 'Well, I always wanted to try it.'

"Anyway, we had a New Year's party in the year 2000, and Nick was on something. We didn't know what it was. For some reason Ben felt it was his place to find out what it was. I wasn't aware of this at the time, but Ben confronted Nick to find out what it was, and I think it was that Ritalin again. It was funny how Ben was trying to protect Nick from all of this. And Ben actually confronted him, physically shook him and shook the information out of him, trying to protect Nick and keep him from that possible life—the life he was leading. But it was almost too late. At that time Nick had a real taste for it.

"Nick ran away more than once. The first time he went to Ben's place and stayed with Ben and Ben's girlfriend without telling us. But they called right away, so we knew Nick was safe. Ben told me, 'Just leave it alone. I'll take care of it.' Which meant he kept him overnight and brought him home.

"Another time Nick disappeared for a day. There had been an argument. I think it was related to Ben. Nick went to visit Ben in Malibu and Ben was living there at the time with a cousin. So Nick came home again after one night."

In the summer of 2000, Nick Markowitz was at a real crossroads of who he was going to become. Jeff recalled, "Nick was getting bored and I asked if he wanted to come to work, and he jumped at the chance. We just started having some good talks. The life he was deciding to choose or not to choose—his brother, his and my relationship. We were talking about a lot of little things. Little/big things."

One of the places Nick liked to hang out with his friends was on a hill near Pomelo School, in West Hills. In this secluded spot they would smoke dope, talk and watch the sunsets. They brought an old table up there, along with bits of carpet and a bench, and it became a regular hangout. The site was nothing to look at, but at least it was private, and it was theirs. One person who visited the hillside spot was a girl named Jeanne, and Nick began to have a crush on her. It was his first real romance.

Perhaps if there had been more time, Ben, Jeff and Susan could have swayed Nick away from the lifestyle he was dabbling in. But things were on a collision course, because of who Ben Markowitz was, and who Jesse James Hollywood was. Had the Markowitz family never had any contact with the Hollywood family, chances are good that Nick would not have found himself being shoved into a white van on the corner of Platt and Ingomar Streets, on August 6, 2000. Chances are good he would have had his fling with marijuana and drugs and moved on to a very different life. In that neighborhood, in the year 2000, however, Jesse James Hollywood was a very real factor, and as much an urban legend as Ben was.

3

JESSE JAMES HOLLYWOOD

No doubt about one thing, Jesse James Hollywood had a very memorable name. His name not only conjured up an image of the famous nineteenth-century outlaw but Tinseltown and the film industry as well. Yet, according to his grandmother Virginia Hollywood, Jesse was not named for the famous outlaw, but rather for an uncle named Jesse James, who had passed away. And Hollywood was Jesse's real surname and not some movieland conceit.

Almost everyone who would talk about Jesse James Hollywood recalled what a great athlete he was as a boy, especially in baseball. Jesse's father, Jack, was a coach in the Westhills Baseball League, where a lot of the neighborhood boys played, including, at various times, Ben Markowitz, Jesse Hollywood, William Skidmore and Jesse Rugge. Robin Leduc remembered Jesse Hollywood playing on a team with her son, Ray. She said, "He was a great little athlete. We lived for watching those boys play baseball." Leduc and other parents spent time volunteering in the snack shack and rooting on their kids from the stands. Many of the boys were good at baseball, but Jesse Hollywood really stood out for his talent.

Even though Jesse was short in stature, he had lots of energy, charisma and drive. Peter Gunny, who played baseball with Jesse, recalled, "He was a real popular kid. Everyone knew him and wanted to be friends with him." And as far as his talent went, Jesse's old coach at El Camino Real High School, in Woodland Hills, remembered him as being "agile and focused, a good player who took his sport seriously."

Even though Jesse was a great baseball player, he also had a temper and an attitude. He had a run-in with a teacher at El Camino Real High School in his sophomore year, cursed out the teacher and was expelled. Principal Ron Bauer later said, "It was a fairly serious incident." A teacher added, "Let's just say his behavior was very extreme and out of line."

In 1992, Jesse and his family moved to the Colorado Springs area of Colorado, where his dad managed a sports bar. While in the area, Jesse continued playing baseball, and made friends easily, as usual. One of his friends was Chas Saulsbury, who regarded Jesse Hollywood as a very good baseball player. Chas also related one more thing, "Jesse, by the age of fourteen, was already smoking dope."

Jesse Hollywood's friend, William Jacques, who also lived in the area, would agree with this statement later. William said, "I first met Jesse when he was fourteen years old. He sold marijuana even then."

Despite his yen for marijuana, Jesse remained an excellent ballplayer. In fact, Richard Dispenza, his baseball coach, became his godfather. Dispenza liked Jesse, despite the boy's sometimes volatile temper, and he had a real respect for Jesse's talent on the baseball diamond. Dispenza, in his own right, was well regarded, not only for helping kids around the baseball field, but in the community as well.

By 1996, the Hollywood family was back in southern California, and Jesse began attending Calabasas High School. He was so good a player that even though he was so young, he played on the varsity team—a team that won the championship that year. Coach Rick Nathanson remembered, "Jesse had an uncanny knack for getting on base."

The following year it seemed that Jesse Hollywood would only get better in baseball, but in a preseason accident, he injured his back and leg and didn't get on the team. Nathanson recalled, "I think he got a little depressed because he'd been looking forward to a very competitive season."

With his baseball dreams shattered, Jesse Hollywood turned in a very different direction—one of fast cars, cute girls and fast times. Eventually one girl from high school would become Jesse James Hollywood's girlfriend. Her name was Michelle Lasher, and her life would become inextricably tied to later events in his life stemming from the rash kidnapping of Nick Markowitz on August 6, 2000.

Michelle was a short girl, barely five feet tall, with luxuriant dark hair and exotic dark eyes. Her family was Jewish, which was unexpected, since Jesse Hollywood was starting to hang around white guys with racist attitudes. These attitudes did not seem to be a part of Jesse's makeup, and he often went over to the Lasher home on Jewish holidays and celebrated with them, as Michelle did with his family at Christmas and Easter.

Michelle later said, "He was respectful of me. He didn't say anything bad about Jewish people." Michelle also related later that she and Jesse started dating in high school, and when she graduated, she took the summer off and went to Europe. When she came back to the United States, she moved in with Jesse Hollywood. By this point, even though he was only eighteen years old, he had started living in his own home in Reseda, on Elkwood Avenue.

Even though Jesse was listed as graduating from Calabasas High in 1998, the fact was he had been suspended from school the week before graduation. Administrators at the school would later not say why. Jesse did some work laying hardwood floors, but that was definitely not his main occupation as the months progressed.

Jesse was not only smoking marijuana, but he had begun dealing it as well, using his buddies as distributors. Among these friends were his old baseball buddies Ryan Hoyt, William Skidmore and Jesse Rugge. By the time Jesse Hollywood was nineteen years old, he bought a three-bedroom house on Cohasset Street in the San Fernando Valley. According to court records, he took out a $164,000 first mortgage for a $205,000 house, which, in essence, meant he paid $41,000 up front toward the purchase. This was a large amount for someone who had no full-time job and was only nineteen years old. Jesse did work part-time for Lee Esh as a carpenter, helping finish floors, but that did not garner him a huge amount of money. Even Jesse's neighbors suspected that Jesse and his buddies were dealing drugs. One person who later claimed never to have seen Jesse actually dealing drugs was his girlfriend, Michelle Lasher. When asked this by police, a grand jury and at several trials, she was consistent in her statements—if Jesse did deal drugs, he never did it in her presence.

One neighbor, however, later told a *Los Angeles Times* reporter, "Everybody knew it was drugs. I mean, all the nice cars. He didn't really go to work or nothing. It was kind of—run in for a second, and drive off." Other neighbors spoke of luxury cars always stopping by Jesse's house, and Jesse's own black Mercedes and a blue tricked-out Honda in the driveway. It was fairly obvious to most of the neighbors that something fishy was going on—but they didn't pry into what the young man was up to, other than to take note that a lot of young people were always hanging around Jesse Hollywood's house, and people were coming to his door at all hours of the day and night.

Lee Esh later told a reporter that he knew that Jesse and his buddies were smoking dope, but he didn't know that they were also selling it. Esh recalled, "As far as I was concerned with these kids, they all smoked pot. I basically didn't see a problem. I would've trusted Jesse to give my kids a ride to the park. I thought he was a responsible kid."

Responsible or not, Jesse and his buddies were always hanging out around his house and in the yard. One neighbor recalled Jesse and his pals in the front yard, wearing tank tops, smoking cigarettes, while Jesse's two pit bulls scampered around in the backyard. And the neighbors were also aware of the parties that took place at Jesse James Hollywood's house—most of these were loud and boisterous, and full of young people.

Jesse had a big-screen TV in the living room and a wave-shaped bubble lamp. The kitchen had a built-in microwave and there was a gas barbecue grill on the patio. And Jesse's 1995 Honda Accord DX Coupe was something to behold. He eventually got an article about it, along with photos, in a European car magazine. The car had fluorescent lights, hydraulic switches, Niche Gefell rims and an impressive sound system. Jesse's car alone could make heads turn.

Just what one of the parties at Jesse's house was like was captured on videotape by Ryan Hoyt. Hoyt pointed the camera at Jesse, who held a Heineken beer in one hand and smoked dope from a long yellow bong. Jesse wore baggy jeans, a blue Dodgers cap turned backward, and a T-shirt from Serial Killer Inc. On the front of the T-shirt was a scene from the movie *Heat,* Robert De Niro and Val Kilmer making a getaway in a shoot-out from a bank heist. One word was etched on the T-shirt: *money.*

Rap music was thumping in the background as Jesse began speaking to the camera: "One time I was walking down the street, cuz. Some nigga hit me up, cuz. I'm like, 'What up, cuz?' Nigga straight ran my ass over! That's why I'm a little fucked-up right now, cuz." Then he spoke straight to Ryan and said, "Get the camera away from me, cuz! Before I have to bust yo' lip, cuz."

A short time later, Ryan Hoyt's voice can be heard asking Jesse, "You been drinking tonight?" as if Hoyt were a policeman.

Jesse yelled back, "Fuck the police!"

Ryan continued to follow Jesse around with the camera, and began singing lines from the television reality show, *Cops*.

Things soon took a turn for the worse, as far as Hoyt was concerned. Jesse took the video camera away from Hoyt and started mocking him. Jesse asked him, "Now, how much money you got in your bank?" He was asking because Ryan Hoyt owed him $1,200 for dope that Hoyt hadn't sold, but rather had smoked himself.

Hoyt answered, "Enough to pay you some money."

Jesse asked, "What's gonna be there tomorrow, Hoyt? I'm serious, man! I can see it's gonna be like nothing!"

"It's not gonna be nothing!" Hoyt responded.

"What's it gonna be then? Just tell me!"

In fact, it was going to be nothing. By now, Ryan Hoyt was virtually Jesse James Hollywood's indentured servant. To help pay off his dope debt, Jesse made Ryan come over to the house every day to clean the house, do garden work, paint and clean up after the pit bulls, Dublin and Brooklyn. It was laborious and demeaning work, and Jesse and his friends often mocked Hoyt as he went about his chores. They called him "Hoytie, asshole, faggot," and a lot worse. Sometimes they referred to Hoyt as Hollywood's "bitch."

A man who got to know Jesse James Hollywood very well later was screenwriter Michael Mehas, and he told the *Ventura County Reporter,* "He (Jesse) was generous in a controlling kind of way. He would give you what he wanted you to have and kind of bring you in, and it was a kind of controlling mechanism. These guys had nothing better in their lives to do. They didn't have ambition, they weren't incredibly intelligent, so they just hung around Jesse."

In fact, Ryan Hoyt was very much less than intelligent—and tests later would prove that he had a low IQ. In the years to come, Jesse James Hollywood's fate would become intertwined with that of Ryan Hoyt more than he might have wished. If Hoyt was his "bitch," as many of Jesse's other friends declared, it was this unhealthy relationship of master and servant that would in many ways be Jesse James Hollywood's downfall.

Victoria Hoyt, Ryan's mother, left a vivid account of what young Ryan's life was like. She recalled, "I met Jim Hoyt, Ryan's father, when I was fifteen years old. Jim is approximately ten years older than me. We moved in together when I was seventeen years old, and a month later he began physically abusing me. One day we were supposed to go to Disneyland with his family, and I was not able to take the day off work. This upset Jim and he threw me against a wall and beat and pounded on me with his hands. Several neighbors saw what was happening and did not intervene. I had black eyes and bruises all over my body. The woman living in the front unit helped me inside and gave me a sedative. We did not call the police.

"Jim Hoyt was also verbally abusive. He would often say, 'Fuck you, you worthless piece of shit!' to me and the kids. Jim would get angry easily and would yell and fly off the handle for no apparent reason.

"We married on June 4, 1977, when I was nineteen years old. I was pregnant with Kristina at the wedding. Kristina's biological father was not Jim Hoyt. My mother is the only one who knew that Jim was not Kristina's father. When I was six months pregnant with Kristina, I was serving dinner and dropped a baked potato on the floor. As I bent over to get it, Jim kicked me in the stomach and slammed my head against the wall. The day before Kristina was born, Jim smacked me and threw me on the bed.

"There was an incident when I was eight months pregnant with Ryan. I was in the driveway and arguing with Jim. Suddenly he kicked me in the lower stomach/groin area, pulled my hair and threw me against the car. I then fell on my back. My father came running and attempted to get Jim off of me. Jim did not come home for a week after that. I had cramps and pains in my stomach. I was afraid to go to the hospital because I did not want to get Jim into trouble and upset him anymore, so I rested at home until the pains stopped. Ryan was born a few weeks later.

"When Ryan was approximately four months old, I was carrying him up the aisle of a home improvement store. I tripped over a piece of fishing line that was strung across the aisle and dropped Ryan on his head. We took him to Tarzana Medical Center, where a doctor told me that he was fine. Several months later I was with Ryan at the beach. He had a slight ear infection. Later that night he had a high fever and went into convulsions. We called 911 and he was taken to the hospital.

"At the age of two, Ryan had a viral infection. He was vomiting and had diarrhea and could not keep anything in his system for weeks. I took him to the doctor and he was admitted to the hospital for a week. He had to get a spinal tap. The doctor thought it was a viral infection, possibly meningitis or pertussis. Ryan lost fifteen pounds, but he was never tested for neurological damage.

"These beatings and abuse on me happened at least once a week. The kids would be there to see and hear it. Jim then began abusing the kids. He would yell at them horribly and tell them how worthless they were and would smack them. Jim is an alcoholic and would drink in front of the kids and would often smoke marijuana in the house. So I would often take Ryan and the kids to the park, to the beach, anywhere just to get them out of the house and away from Jim. We would be at my mother's house a lot.

"I was afraid what Jim would do if I divorced him. I was not working and had no money. He filed for divorce first and just told me one day, 'You're not taking the kids, so get out or I'll run you over with my car!' I believed him and walked out, leaving my kids at the door crying and begging me not to leave them. I walked outside and Jim pushed me to the ground and held a pipe wrench over my head, threatening to bash my head in. Ryan and the kids watched this. I left Ryan, Kristina and Jonathon with him.

"I moved in with my parents, and Jim had the kids. Shortly after, Jim began dating Robin Deschaine, and they were married. They had a son, Ryan's half brother Austin. Kristina told me that Jim would come into her room in the middle of the night and would hit her legs for no reason while she was sleeping. She would pretend that she was still sleeping and did not wake up so he would stop and leave her alone.

"When Jonathon was around seven years old, he asked me to take him to school so that he could report Jim for hitting him. Ryan was very protective of Jonathon and Kristina and would often take the blame for things he did not do. Ryan often took the beating for them.

"Kristina was twelve or thirteen years old when she found out that Jim Hoyt was not her biological father. Up until this point, no one knew, including Ryan. This devastated Kristina and she began running away from home all of the time. She turned to drugs and prostitution to survive. She would often be seen in front of a McDonald's in Hollywood, panhandling. Kristina attempted suicide several times. This devastated Ryan.

"When Ryan was fourteen years old, Jim separated from Robin and moved to Topanga Canyon, with Ryan and Jonathon. Things were going well for the three of them during this time, and Ryan seemed to be doing well. However, Jim eventually reconciled with Robin, and things were then worse than ever.

"Ryan began spending more and more time at the

home of my mother, Carol Stendel. I would meet them there, and this was our second home. He was fed, clothed and supervised there. He went there almost every day. During this time I had substance abuse problems. I never spent time with Ryan while I was intoxicated. Unfortunately, this sometimes meant he would not see me at all. I recall one Christmas when Ryan, Kristina and Jonathon were at my mother's house for the day. I was supposed to come over and spend the day with them. I didn't show up or call because I was intoxicated."

Of all the friends hanging around at Jesse James Hollywood's house, Ryan Hoyt had endured the most chaotic childhood. The rest had led fairly normal suburban lives—up to a point. Despite all the drug activity going on at Jesse Hollywood's house, he was never arrested for using or dealing. Jesse Hollywood was arrested for minor disturbances, such as being underage and possessing alcohol, and on another occasion for resisting arrest while being disorderly. His buddies also had a few scrapes with the law, but nothing major. William Skidmore was arrested twice for being under the influence of a controlled substance, and once for resisting arrest. Jesse Rugge had been arrested for carrying a concealed knife at school, and in the year 2000, for driving under the influence. Ryan Hoyt, unlike the others, had no arrests at all.

Ben Markowitz, the toughest of Jesse Hollywood's friends, later had a take on all the other guys in Hollywood's orbit. Ben said, "As far as I was concerned, they were just a bunch of punks that couldn't fight worth a lick." Ben especially had an opinion about William Skidmore, and it wasn't very flattering. He said, "He was a crackhead. He was just the type of person, whoever he's hanging out with right at the moment, he's friends with. If all of his friends decide to jump somebody, he's going to jump in. Then if he sees the guy the next day, when he's not with his friends, he's going to try and patch things up."

Court documents would allege later that Jesse James Hollywood was getting the marijuana from his father, and that it came from British Columbia in Canada—a potent strain known as "BC Bud." Jack Hollywood, however, would deny ever distributing marijuana to Jesse, and said that Jesse got it elsewhere. BC Bud was considered to be top-quality marijuana by users, and generally cost more than lower-grade pot. And British Columbia would become an important factor in the years to come in Jesse's life.

Ben Markowitz eventually had problems with money owed to Jesse Hollywood, as Ryan Hoyt had. Ben, however, was not the type to be turned into an indentured servant or mocked, and this debt would turn into a deadly feud with an unexpected victim—Ben's half brother, Nick.

4

FALLING-OUT

There are various versions of what went wrong between Jesse James Hollywood and Ben Markowitz, but the one as reliable as any comes from Ben. He said later, "Someone owed Jesse money, and I knew the person, and instead of Jesse going over there and doing something to harm him, I said, 'I know him, let me take care of it.' And I went over there (San Diego) and he didn't have the two thousand that he owed Jesse, so he gave me two hundred E pills (Ecstasy), which is about what it's worth when you buy a lot of it. It's ten dollars a pill. And I sold some of it, and it ended up not being good. It was fake. So I still ended up owing Jesse the money, because I took it upon myself to take it. I was the one that wanted to take it into my own hands to try and make money off of it."

Ben's original plan had been to sell the Ecstasy at raves, where he could earn $20 for every pill that had cost him $10. Even though Ben often owed Jesse money, he said he was "clean" in all debts, until the fiasco of the fake E pills.

According to one document, Ben eventually paid Jesse

$600, and when Jesse demanded the rest of the money, Ben tossed him the remaining Ecstasy, which wasn't good, and an additional $200. Furious at the shortfall, Jesse told Ben, "Go fuck yourself and pay me the money!"

Ben recalled saying, "I told him, 'All right, whatever!' and just kind of walked away."

Jesse James Hollywood wasn't about to take this lying down. It was as much a matter of pride as about the money. If he let Ben Markowitz slide on this, he would lose face with the others. Jesse apparently used William Skidmore as a go-between, making Skidmore phone Ben in the middle of the night and harass him about the debt. At least that is what Skidmore said later. Ben, who had little respect for Skidmore, recalled, "I got a couple of phone calls from one of Jesse's friends, William Skidmore. He'd call me late at night and say, 'What's going on? I thought we were friends. Why don't we work this out?' By then, I wasn't friends with Jesse, or hanging out with him." And Ben certainly wasn't friends with Skidmore, whom he called a "punk." Ben would say later that the phone calls were threatening in nature.

Things might have cooled off eventually, but Jesse just wouldn't let the debt go, even though $1,200 was not a great deal of cash in the operations he ran. One night Jesse and his girlfriend, Michelle, went to a restaurant, BJ's Microbrewery, where Ben's girlfriend, Eliza Voita, worked as a waitress. They ran up a tab of $50, but instead of paying, Jesse skipped out without paying anything, telling Voita that Ben could pay the tab and take it off from what Ben owed him. In fact, in one version, according to Ben and others, Jesse Hollywood actually wrote this down on the bill for the meal and it stated that she could charge the meal to Ben.

This infuriated Ben, and he decided to up the ante. According to Ben, Jesse Hollywood had recently scammed an insurance company on his supposedly stolen Honda. The fact was, Jesse had sold his Honda Accord to a chop shop, and then reported it stolen to the AAA Insurance company for $36,000.

As Ben recalled, "Since Jesse did that to my girlfriend, I decided to go to his insurance company and tell them that he had his car stolen to get the insurance money. It was thirty-six thousand dollars. I was there when he had gone to get forms from the insurance company." Because of his actions, Ben believed Jesse never saw a dime of the insurance money and that really made him furious.

Apparently, Ben told Jesse what he had done, but the feud did not stop there. Ben let Jesse know that he carried a gun around a lot. Ben related later that he knew that Jesse also had guns, including a semiautomatic rifle, a shotgun and a TEC-9 handgun. The TEC-9 was a semiautomatic, which Ben said that Jesse altered to make it fully automatic. "It was like in the movies," Ben recalled. "Like you'd think an Uzi would look like."

Through the spring and early summer months of 2000, the feud ratcheted up a notch when Ben phoned Jesse and left a message: "I know where you live, buddy!" From that point on, the messages—according to Jesse James Hollywood, his buddies and Michelle Lasher—became even more threatening.

Michelle said, "Ben left many threatening phone messages. On one of them he said that he was going to kill Jesse, his family and me."

Jesse knew how "crazy" Ben could be when irritated. Jesse decided that it was becoming too dangerous to live in his house on Cohasset Street.

Jesse Hollywood borrowed a white van from a longtime family friend named John Roberts, and Jesse and his buddies started moving furniture out of the house to a storage locker across town. According to Michelle Lasher, she and Jesse were going to move into a house in Malibu and not tell anyone where they lived. "We just wanted to get away from the whole scene," she said later.

The house on Cohasset Street was almost empty in the

first week of August, when Ben decided to ante up once again. Ben went over to Jesse's house and broke out several windows with a pipe or baseball bat. According to Skidmore, he and Jesse were sleeping on the floor near the windows when the attack occurred, shattering glass onto their sleeping bags.

They didn't know at the time who had done it, and their first thoughts were that it was some local gang members who had broken the windows. But it soon became evident who the assailant was. Ben left a message on Jesse Hollywood's answering machine saying, "This is Li'l Shooter." (That was Ben's nickname.) He let it be known that he was the one who had broken the windows, and he was still after Jesse Hollywood.

The broken windows really set Jesse Hollywood off. According to some sources, he went to Santa Barbara on August 5, 2000, to recruit Jesse Rugge, who was now living with his father and stepmother there, to help in exacting revenge upon Ben. Rugge would have a different take on why Jesse Hollywood came there that day, saying that it was only to make plans about Fiesta—but by the time Rugge was relating what had happened, he was in plenty of trouble and might not have been telling the whole truth about things.

Jesse Rugge noted, "Jesse Hollywood came up to Santa Barbara on the fifth, and Will Skidmore was with him. They had come up for Fiesta. Hollywood was ranting and raving about Ben Markowitz. Said that [Ben had] broken out his front windows and left a verbal voice mail on his pager. Jesse played that message for me."

Rugge also gave a description of Jesse Hollywood at that moment. "If you could picture a five-foot-four man with an attitude! He was in the hallway, just pacing and saying, 'Listen to it. Can you believe that fucking shit! Can you believe it!' He was getting all ranted and raved. As I remember the message from Ben, it was 'This is the beginning, bitch! This is just the beginning. This is Li'l

Shooter. You're fucking dead, you little midget! You're fucking dead! I know where your family lives. And I know where you live!'"

One more person in Santa Barbara at the time, according to Rugge, was sixteen-year-old Kelly Carpenter. Rugge couldn't remember for sure, but he thought that Kelly heard Hollywood ranting and raving about the message from Ben as well. Kelly would also relate later that she had seen Jesse Hollywood prior to August 6, and she had a very negative reaction about him. She thought he was sleazy and not someone that a person would want to be around.

Jesse Rugge would eventually deny that Hollywood recruited him to go back down to West Hills so that they could smash the windows at Ben Markowitz's parents' house. (However, Kelly Carpenter recalled that Rugge went there for that very reason.) Rugge related that they left Santa Barbara around 7:00 P.M. on August 5, just to go to Hollywood's house to smoke dope and drink. Rugge said that the plans had changed about Fiesta, because their friend Brian Affronti was going to go with them on August 6. Rugge noted that when he got to Jesse Hollywood's house, there was no furniture left inside, and he recalled, "He showed me the front windows, where they were axed out."

On the morning of August 6, 2000, Jesse Rugge said that he, Hollywood and Skidmore got up fairly late, after a night of drinking and smoking dope; then they rolled up their sleeping bags and put them away. Rugge related that he heard Jesse Hollywood, who was on the phone to Brian Affronti, say, "Are you ready? All right. I'm coming to pick you up, late." Hollywood was in the midst of still moving items out of his house to a storage unit, and he had John Roberts's white utility van. There were some boxes and crates inside the van, and since Hollywood didn't want to drive, he handed the van's keys to Rugge.

Rugge later remembered very well the route they took

that morning from Jesse Hollywood's house. He said, "We came out of Cohasset Street, made a right on Woodlake, and came to a stop sign. We made a left on Saticoy and came up to a stop sign right there, at the corner of Platt where it meets Ingomar. Across the street was Taxco Trails Park."

Rugge started the van forward again and Jesse Hollywood spotted a boy walking up the street. Rugge recalled, "Hollywood shouted, 'That's Ben Markowtiz's brother! That's Ben Markowitz's brother! Pull over!'"

Rugge pulled over as instructed, about one car length in front of Nick, and as he did so, Jesse Hollywood jumped out of the passenger door and opened the side door so that Will Skidmore could get out. According to Rugge, Hollywood was shouting, "Let's beat him up!"

Even though Pauline Mahoney thought she saw four young men beating up Nick on the sidewalk, it may have been only three or even just two. Rugge claimed emphatically later on that he never left the driver's seat, but only watched Hollywood and Skidmore confront Nick. And Rugge would also claim that neither Hollywood nor Skidmore threw Nick into the van, but rather that Nick got in under his own power. Of course, if Nick had just been beaten up and ordered to get in by Hollywood, it wasn't a matter of getting into the van because he wanted. It was because he was under severe duress.

Once Nick Markowitz and Skidmore were in the van, Jesse Rugge was so rattled that he stepped down on the gas pedal, and the van began moving forward. He later recalled, "I freaked out. I didn't know what was going on, so I peeled away." According to Rugge, it was Nick, not Skidmore, who said, "Hey, you left Hollywood back there!"

A very shaken Jesse Rugge put the van in reverse, backed up to where Hollywood was, and as Hollywood climbed in, he called Rugge a "fuckin' idiot." Once in the van, at least according to Rugge, Jesse Hollywood made him drive in a very peculiar direction. Rugge related, "Usually going to Affronti's, we kept on going straight down Valley Circle and then onto March. But Hollywood made me drive by the Markowitz house. And right around there he laid into Nick. I mean, verbally. He started talking about the threats Ben had made to him. To his family. I guess he (Hollywood) knew about Jeff Markowitz having been an Olympic ringster (boxer) and he started talking shit. Hollywood said stuff like, 'Your brother is a fucking piece of shit!' And 'Your dad's a pussy!' Skidmore and I were just looking at each other. Skidmore looked stunned, 'like what the hell.' I was scared."

It was a fateful string of events that had led to Nick Markowitz being on that street at all on Sunday, August 6. On the day before he was beaten up and tossed into a van, Nick Markowitz had been having a rocky time with his parents. Jeff Markowitz recalled, "Saturday night, Nicholas went out with some friends to CityWalk. CityWalk is a place where they have restaurants, movie theaters and the like. Kids go there, it's a hangout. Nick went up there with some friends and his curfew was midnight. He came home at eleven-thirty, and as he walked in the door, my wife and I, we were right there. I'm not sure why we were right there, but we were, and as soon as we saw him, we knew there was something wrong. You could see it in his face, his eyes were droopy, and I said, 'What's going on? Why are you home so early?' And he said, 'Oh, it didn't go so well.'

"And as I turned, he had on a pair of baggy pants, with a large pocket in the back, and I noticed something bulging in the back of his pocket, and I said, 'What's in your pants pocket?' And he kind of put his hand back there and said, 'It's nothing. Nothing, Dad.'

"My wife and I confronted him, because we wanted to know what was going on, and as we got closer, he pulled away and ran out of the house. And we figured here we go again. Another overnight trip. A runaway night again.

"Forty-five minutes later he came back, and he walked up the driveway, and Susan was there to meet him, and I met him inside the house. Susan was there to meet him with a hug and a kiss, and the first thing he said was 'I hate it when you talk to me about smoking.' Basically just to say to her it was just cigarettes in his back pocket, and that's why he left.

"He came into the house and we sat down in the living room, and I could tell he was hungry. So we got him—well, he likes a bowl of cereal late in the evening, and he got a bowl of cereal. We started to talk and Susan said, 'Why don't we just wait until the morning?' And I said, 'Okay.' I figured he'd be sleeping in."

It was later determined that the bulge in Nick's back pocket was not a pack of cigarettes, but rather a small pouch he carried, which often contained a pipe for his marijuana and Valium pills. Jeff surmised that Nick returned these items to his hillside hangout and then returned home, claiming that he'd only been carrying a cigarette pack in his back pocket.

Jeff continued, "I got up in the morning and did my usual Sunday-morning tennis match, came home, expecting Nick to be in bed asleep. Susan was downstairs making breakfast and I said, 'Well, I guess we have a job ahead of us.' She said, 'Yeah.' She was making breakfast, and I said, 'Well, why don't you go ahead and wake him up and bring him down.' She answered, 'I was up there about nine, because his grandmother called wanting to know a phone number, and he was pretty out of it.' (In other words, very sleepy.) Then I said, 'Well, why don't you wake him up now.'

"She went back up there and she let out a profanity. He wasn't in his room. The profanity was basically to say, 'How could he leave again without telling me!' Because we had a good conversation the night before, thinking we were going to get to the bottom of things. But he took off.

"I didn't think anything of it at the time, because, like I said before, he'd taken off at times. And we also knew that he had taken something the night before and maybe he was going back out to recover it, or do something, but he figured he'd better get out while the getting was good.

"This was about eleven A.M. That's when it started. That's when hell started."

Ironically, Nick passed his cousin and uncle that very morning as he walked home. His cousin Jennifer Markowitz was riding in her father's vehicle that morning, just having been picked up by him after a workout at the gym. Jennifer spotted Nick walking near Taxco Trails Park, and had her dad pull over to where Nick was. Jennifer rolled down her window and asked if Nick wanted a ride home. Since he was only a few blocks away from his house, he said no. Jennifer and her dad drove off.

Jeff related later, "My brother Monty saw Nick walking across the street that morning. He figured Nick was just going home from a friend's house. I wonder what would have happened if Nick had taken a ride home with them."

From the moment Nick Markowitz was thrown into the van, his journey, and those of the others, would take a random, almost surrealistic course. There seemed to be no rhyme or reason to the odyssey, and if Jesse James Hollywood was the ringleader, he also seemed at a loss as to what to do with Nick once he had him. Since Hollywood and Skidmore and Rugge had been on their way to Fiesta Days in Santa Barbara, ostensibly after planning to smash out the windows at the Markowitz home, Jesse Hollywood had Rugge drive on in that direction.

As the van moved along the highway, Nick's pager began to beep. It had been given to him the week before by his parents, with instructions from them that he was to respond to it immediately when it went off. If not, they would take it away. Jesse Hollywood ordered Nick not to answer it, but Nick's mom kept punching in the number, and Hollywood eventually took the pager away from Nick.

Brian Affronti was scheduled to go with them to Fiesta Days, and he lived in Chatsworth on the northwestern side of the San Fernando Valley. When they arrived at Affronti's residence, Hollywood walked up the driveway to his door and asked him if he was ready to go. Affronti said that he was and they walked down the hill to where Affronti could see the white van. He knew that Hollywood was using it to move some furniture from his house to a storage unit.

Rugge would later give an account of what was going on in the van while Hollywood was talking to Affronti. Rugge said, "Jesse Hollywood was up there about fifteen or twenty minutes. William and I kept looking at each other and shaking our heads. Nick talked to us a little, but didn't really say too much. And when Affronti got down to the van, I saw he had a sack of pot. He had a giant bag of it. It was just rolled up. And he had duct tape." Rugge did not like the advent of the duct tape being brought on the scene. It made everything seem more ominous. What was strange was that Rugge's version about the duct tape coming from Affronti's house was different than what several other people would recall about the next stage of the journey to Santa Barbara.

Jesse Hollywood got in and sat down in the passenger seat, while Affronti got in the back. He immediately recognized William Skidmore and Jesse Rugge, but he didn't recognize the boy who was also in the van. At the time Affronti thought that the kid was just another friend of Hollywood's, Rugge's or Skidmore's, who would be going to Fiesta in Santa Barbara.

They drove to William Skidmore's residence in Simi Valley, because Skidmore was a diabetic and needed to take his daily injection of insulin. Rugge recalled on the way there that a pipe full of marijuana was lit up and passed around. Once at Skidmore's residence, William ran into his house and it only took him about two minutes to do his task with the insulin.

Everything seemed to be just a normal day for Brian Affronti, but then on the ride to Santa Barbara, Hollywood turned around and suddenly lit into the boy. Hollywood said, "If your brother thinks he's going to kill my family, he has another thing coming! Your brother is going to pay me my money right now. If you run, I'll break your teeth!" Affronti was shocked by this confrontation. Up until that moment, he thought that the boy was just another one of Jesse's friends.

Somewhere near Oxnard, on the 101 Freeway, traffic slowed down because of congestion, and Jesse Hollywood ranted at Nick once more. According to Rugge, Hollywood wanted Nick to give him all his personal possessions. Nick handed over a small address book, a wallet that contained $80, seven small Baggies of marijuana and some Valium pills. Hollywood also took Nick's ring, which was an heirloom. According to Rugge, Hollywood said, "'Give me the fucking ring, too!' Nick didn't want to take it off, and then Hollywood made him take it off."

This upset Rugge, and it was the only time during the kidnapping or drive to Santa Barbara that he spoke up and objected to something that Hollywood did. Rugge said, "Jess, just give him back his ring, man." Surprisingly, Hollywood did. And this ring would play an important factor in developments a week later.

Jesse Hollywood wanted Nick deposited at Jesse Rugge's father's house in Santa Barbara, but Rugge did not want to take him there. According to Rugge, he started trying to think of where else Nick could be taken, and he related later, "It just popped into my head to take him to a friend's house, Ricky Hoeflinger, who lived on Modoc Road in Santa Barbara."

Rugge used Jesse Hollywood's cell phone, but Hoeflinger wasn't there at the time. Another person, Emilio

Jerez, was, however, and Rugge spoke to him. Rugge said, "I asked him if I could stop by, and he said, 'sure.'" Rugge didn't tell Jerez that other people would be coming over to the house later, along with a kidnapped boy.

At least that was his version. Emilio Jerez would later state that when he talked to Rugge on the cell phone, the topic of a closet being in the house was mentioned, and the possibility that someone might be stuffed inside of it came up during the conversation. Jerez, who had just moved into Hoeflinger's house in the previous week as a housemate, wondered what all of this was about.

Rugge said later that when he pulled up near Hoeflinger's house, he parked the van on a corner, left the others inside the van and walked to that residence. When he rang the doorbell, a friend of Hoeflinger's, Gabriel Ibarra, answered the door. Rugge recalled, "I said, 'Is Emilio in?' And he says, 'No, he's taking a shower.' So I wasn't going to go in without anybody's permission. When I walked away, I was walking back around, and I could hear Ricky Hoeflinger's music from his car. He was coming down Modoc in his Altima. He's got a good sound system in that car, and I knew it. So I turned around and started walking toward where he was coming from. He made a right into his driveway, parked, got out, and we shook hands and gave each other a little hug. I said to Ricky, 'There's a little problem going on.' I didn't give him too much details about it. He asked, 'Who's up with you?' And I said, 'Hollywood, William, couple of other people.' He said, 'All right, come on in.'"

Rugge didn't mention it later, but two girls were also with Richard Hoeflinger that day. They were Hoeflinger's cousin Shauna Vasquez and her friend Jaymi Dickensheet. All of these people would have many things to say about what occurred at Hoeflinger's house over the next few hours. But that was all in the future.

Rugge continued, "So when I went back to the van, I

said let's go. And Hollywood said, 'All right.' They all came out. Hollywood walked in first, then it would have been Brian, Will, Markowitz and myself. Immediately inside the house, Hollywood started to act, like—well, he was running around, pacing, pacing up and down the hallways, checking closets, and, frankly, just talking shit. I knew he had a gun in his waistband at the time."

According to Rugge, Hollywood seemed to be very upset that Hoeflinger's closets were full and there was nowhere inside them to stash a kidnapped boy. Rugge also said that Hollywood was running around the house as if he owned the place. Rugge said, "The rest of us were all in the living room, just stalling there, confused. We didn't know what to do. I didn't know what was going on. None of us did." Rugge's story of not going immediately to the back room with the others would be contradicted by almost everyone else later.

Nick was taken to a back bedroom, and Rugge did not join the others there for two to three minutes. At least that's what he said later, although others in the house would put him in the bedroom with Nick, right from the beginning. Rugge said that when he did enter the room, he was surprised to see Nick taped up with duct tape. Rugge recalled, "Nick was taped up and smoking a bong." (Apparently, it was held by someone else so that he could smoke it.) "There was a blindfold over his eyes and his feet and hands were taped up. There was like a white sock around his eyes. I believe the sock was from Nick's foot."

Brian Affronti also went into Hoeflinger's bedroom and was surprised to see Nick Markowitz, hands and ankles bound with duct tape. As he said later, "The whole scene freaked me out!"

Rugge, at least, thought the whole duct tape incident was ridiculous. According to his later statements, "I looked at Hollywood and said, 'I'm going to go get a knife and cut him out. I went to the kitchen and grabbed a knife and cut the binds. William and Brian Affronti were right there.

Hollywood didn't say anything, because I think he kind of realized that all these people were around."

Yet, Rugge would change details of this story as well, and in another version Rugge said, "We all thought the duct tape was kind of absurd. Ricky, everybody. So Ricky went and got a knife from the kitchen, brought it back, put the knife in there and cut it out."

Hoeflinger was on his way to a barbecue, and he said later, "I saw that stuff in the bedroom before I left for the barbecue, but I didn't make it obvious to anyone at the barbecue. I didn't say anything, because I didn't know what was going on."

By this point Brian Affronti was becoming more and more freaked out by the whole situation and asked Jesse Hollywood for the van's keys so he could go home. Hollywood answered, "Well, first I'm going over to Jesse Rugge's house to take a shower and change my clothes." At that point Hollywood and Rugge left, leaving Nick with Affronti and Skidmore.

Rugge related that he and Hollywood went to Rugge's father's house in Santa Barbara, probably around 4:00 or 4:30 P.M. Since there was only one shower upstairs, they took turns taking showers. Rugge recalled that Jesse Hollywood still had a gun, and he took it with him into the bathroom. They spent anywhere from a half hour to forty-five minutes at the Rugge residence; then they went back to Hoeflinger's place.

Meanwhile, William Skidmore and Brian Affronti had been left with Nick Markowitz at Ricky Hoeflinger's place, while Hoeflinger and the two girls went to one barbecue, and Ibarra went to another. In fact, Skidmore and Affronti weren't guarding Nick as much as they were smoking dope, drinking and playing video games with him. When Hollywood and Rugge walked back in, they were greeted by an amazing sight. Nick Markowitz was playing a 007 video game with these older guys and beating them.

Rugge said later that Nick had been sitting around with

Skidmore and Affronti, drinking Tanqueray and smoking dope. As far as the video game went, Rugge related, "Nick was on a roll for a good hour. He was being treated like everyone else in that house."

Eventually Skidmore and Affronti left in the white van, heading back home to the Los Angeles area. Rugge noted that Hollywood made several phone calls before leaving, but whom he was calling, Rugge couldn't say. Rugge also noted that things were better now between Hollywood and Nick. They even sat down on the same couch, playing video games and talking. Hollywood was not threatening Nick at that point. What was even more strange, to Rugge, was that Jesse Hollywood was not making a concerted effort to find out where Ben was at this juncture, nor trying to resolve the situation with Nick.

At around 9:00 P.M., Richard Hoeflinger and the two girls came back to his house, and they were surprised to see Rugge, Nick and Jesse Hollywood still there. At least all of them would agree that things had cooled off, as far as Nick and Hollywood went. Nick was not duct taped, and he was free to roam around the house and even into the backyard, where he smoked several cigarettes. In fact, Nick could have taken off from the backyard at that point, and nobody would have known for several minutes.

Before Jesse Hollywood left to return to Los Angeles (and there would be multiple versions later of how he did that), according to Rugge, Jesse told him to keep an eye on Nick until it was decided what to do with him. As Rugge would say later, the plan was just to keep him up in Santa Barbara until Hollywood decided what his next move would be. Rugge was under the impression that Jesse Hollywood would contact Ben Markowitz and come to some kind of agreement with him in exchange for the release of Nick. In essence, Ben was going to hand over money on his debt to have Nick released, according to how Rugge understood the situation.

Later asked why he didn't just tell Nick to get up and

leave at this point, Rugge answered that he didn't know why he didn't, although he was certain that Jesse Hollywood was carrying a weapon around with him at the time. In fact, neither he nor the others were exactly rocket scientists. They spent their days smoking pot, drinking and hanging out. Holding down a steady job and decision making were just not part of their world. Even though Rugge did not want Nick with him, he did not make any plans at that point to send him on his way. And for his part, Nick did not get up and leave, either. He had his own agenda, and it seemed to have been that he didn't want to cause waves for his half brother, Ben.

Rugge and Nick stayed for at least another hour and a half at Hoeflinger's place after Jesse Hollywood had left. At least that's what Rugge said later. Since Hoeflinger and the others were going to bed soon, Rugge and Nick took off for Rugge's residence, where he was living with his dad and stepmom in Santa Barbara. Since Rugge didn't have a car, they walked nearly two and a half miles to Baron Rugge's residence. It was late at night, and Rugge noted that Nick was stumbling along, having smoked a great deal of pot and having drunk quite a bit of Tanqueray. It took them a long time to walk the two and a half miles.

When they got to the Rugge residence, Jesse Rugge related, "My father, stepmom, a guy named Doug and a friend of Doug's were there. We walked in, and they were in the kitchen smoking cigarettes, 'cause we don't smoke cigarettes in the rest of the house. I came into the kitchen, and Nick stood right there by the door, and I said, 'Dad, Melissa, this is a friend, Nick. Nick is going to be staying for a day for Fiesta.' And I asked Nick if he wanted a beer, and he said no. So I got myself a beer, and from there we went right out into the living room.

"I drank my beer, we watched some TV, and that was it. As far as sleeping arrangements, I gave Nick some options—my bed, the floor or the couch downstairs. He took the floor, so I had a bunch of blankets in my closet, and pillows, and that's how I made up the bed. We eventually fell asleep, watching television."

The next morning, Monday, August 7, 2000, Jesse Rugge awoke first and went downstairs and called his friend Graham Pressley. Then he paged Jesse Hollywood and asked that he give him a call back. Rugge noted that Nick got up about 11:00 A.M., and was watching TV upstairs, when Rugge was through talking to Hollywood. Neither Rugge's dad or stepmom were there, because they had gone to work, it being a Monday morning. Jesse Rugge took a shower, and Nick could have easily walked out the door, but he didn't. Asked later if he was worried that Nick would bolt, Rugge answered, "I really didn't care if he did or did not."

On Monday, August 7, seventeen-year old Graham Pressley went over to Jesse Rugge's house. Not unlike Skidmore and Rugge, Pressley would become intertwined in events surrounding Nick Markowitz. Pressley was born in 1983 in Santa Barbara to Charles and Christina Pressley. Charles worked as a maintenance man, and Christina was a real estate appraiser. Christina described Graham as a happy baby and youngster who got along well with his parents and others. He was in a Gifted and Talented Program in the second grade, and as a boy he participated in Scouting and was active in sports, especially soccer. In fact, he was so good at that sport that he was even invited to try out for the Olympic Development Program.

Friends who knew Pressley at that time said that he was a tremendous soccer player, but very modest about his abilities. One friend said that Graham always took time to praise other players' abilities.

In the long run the talent on the soccer field was more of a curse to Graham than a blessing. Dr. Rahn Minegawa, a psychiatrist, who later spoke with Graham, said, "Graham's interest in soccer waned as a result of the pressure and anxiety he experienced at a higher level of play, and his growing resentment toward his father for putting pressure on him to play. He quit playing altogether at the age of thirteen, much to the disappointment of his father. It was also the time that Graham first began to use marijuana."

Because of his marijuana use, Graham became bored and restless in high school, even though he was very bright. In his freshman year he was expelled from San Marcos High School when drug paraphernalia was found on him there. Graham enrolled at La Cuesta High School, in the Independent Study Program, where he easily passed the California High School Proficiency Examination. Soon after, he took seven credits' worth of courses at Santa Barbara City College, even though he was only seventeen years old, and technically would have still been a junior in high school that year.

Since Graham Pressley was a frequent guest at the Rugge residence, he walked right into the house while Jesse Rugge was taking a shower. Rugge recalled later, "When I got out of the shower, Graham and Nick were talking in my living room. We smoked some pot, hung out, watched TV and listened to music. Later me and Graham watered the backyard."

Another person arrived at Rugge's house that afternoon— seventeen-year-old Natasha Adams. She related later, "I lived in Santa Barbara my entire life. I'd known Graham Pressley for about eight years by 2000, but I really only started hanging out with him about 1998. I first met Jesse Rugge in 1999, but only really started to hang out with him in June 2000. Me and him and Kelly (Carpenter) and Graham hung out just about on a daily basis.

"I went over to Jesse Rugge's house on Monday in the late morning, probably around eleven A.M. (It may have been a little later.) I'd seen Jesse (Rugge) on the previous Saturday night, and he didn't tell me specifically, but I overheard him talking to his friends and he said that he was going to go down to L.A. He originally had lived down there, but he moved up to Santa Barbara."

There was one more person at Rugge's house that morning besides Graham Pressley and Jesse Rugge—it was Nick Markowitz, whom Natasha had never seen before. At some point, according to Natasha, Pressley told her about Nick, "They (meaning the others) had kidnapped this kid and brought him back up here to Jesse Rugge's house."

Whatever the time this information had been given to Natasha, she and Rugge, Pressley and Nick, all went over to her house to hang out. Natasha recalled that this was sometime in the afternoon of August 7. Another person joined them there, Natasha's friend, sixteen-year old Kelly Carpenter. Kelly had known Natasha and Graham since elementary school, and Jesse Rugge since October 1999.

Kelly recalled, "I went over to Natasha's house about two P.M. I didn't know one boy who was there. Jesse Rugge didn't stay very long, and there wasn't anything unusual about the other guy, except I didn't know him. As far as I knew, he was just another friend."

When Kelly talked to Nick, she recalled later, "He was very sweet, pretty quiet, but really a nice guy."

Sometime late in the afternoon of Monday, August 7, Jesse Rugge did have contact with Jesse Hollywood by phone. According to Rugge, he told Jesse to come up to Santa Barbara and get Nick out of there. According to Rugge, Hollywood agreed to come to Santa Barbara, and showed up there late that afternoon. Rugge didn't say what vehicle he had, but related later, "I left from Natasha's house and picked Hollywood up down the street, and we ate at the shoreline, East Beach. He liked that place on the beach, so he decided to take me there. Michelle, his girlfriend, was with him. She's got fake breasts, and she's tiny. Really short. Kind of past my elbows, maybe. Anyway, she and Jesse ate, but I didn't. We were there maybe thirty-five minutes."

Later Rugge would say that he spoke right in front of

Michelle Lasher to Jesse Hollywood about getting Nick Markowitz out of Santa Barbara. Rugge's exact words, according to him later, were "'Aren't you taking him home?' And Jesse didn't give a response. He gave me, like, a shrug and started talking about something different."

Michelle Lasher would later deny ever having gone to lunch with Jesse Hollywood and Jesse Rugge that day in Santa Barbara. It was hard to tell by that point who was lying and who was telling the truth, because they were all in a great deal of trouble.

After Jesse Rugge had left Natasha Adams's house, she spoke to Nick about his predicament, and she asked him why he just didn't leave, now that Rugge was gone. According to Natasha, "Nick said he was going to stick around because he was going to help out his brother and that he was fine."

It may also have been here that Nick told her, "When this is all over, it will be a story to tell my grandkids," although there was also a version that he spoke these words later on August 8.

Natasha recalled, "He had a scrape on his elbow, and he asked for some rubbing alcohol, so I gave it to him." Kelly Carpenter also remembered this incident by saying that they gave him some alcohol and Neosporin. She didn't remember the cuts and bruises as being very bad.

At this point Kelly Carpenter had no idea that Nick had been brought to Santa Barbara against his will, at least not at first. Later, however, she recalled, "We were at Natasha's house and she leaned over to me and whispered that he'd been kidnapped." Soon they began referring to Nick as the "Stolen Boy."

Later that same day Kelly, Natasha, Graham and Nick returned to Jesse Rugge's house in Santa Barbara. Kelly recalled, "It was probably around four P.M. I walked out to the back patio, and Jesse Hollywood and his girlfriend, Michelle, were there. Nick immediately went upstairs in the house. I had met Jesse Hollywood maybe a week before."

Kelly related later that she knew that Jesse James Hollywood dealt drugs and that Jesse Rugge was working for him. She said she also knew that Graham Pressley bought marijuana from Rugge and sold it, though she never spoke of a direct link between Pressley and Hollywood. Asked to describe how much marijuana they were dealing, she said, "A fair amount."

As to her impression of Jesse James Hollywood, Kelly responded, "He liked to talk. He gave me a bad impression. He didn't make me feel very comfortable." As for Michelle Lasher, Kelly said, "His girlfriend, she was a very petite girl. She had fake breasts and dark hair. And a high-pitched voice. I asked her where she was from and she told us about the Valley. But I really didn't talk to her much."

Natasha Adams also had a fairly similar reaction to all of this as Kelly had had. Natasha remembered, "I had seen Jesse James Hollywood before. I didn't like him. He seemed like an unkind person, just kind of sleazy. The wrong kind of person to hang out with."

As for Michelle Lasher, Natasha recalled, "She sat on Hollywood's lap and called him, 'Jess.' They were acting like they were in a relationship." Natasha would also note later that Michelle spoke about her breast augmentation procedure, something that Natasha referred to as a "boob job."

Natasha recalled Nick going upstairs as soon as he realized that Jesse James Hollywood was there. Since Natasha knew about the kidnapping, she surmised it was the reason why Nick did not want to be around Jesse Hollywood. And according to Kelly, she heard Jesse James Hollywood say one very ominous thing as he and Michelle were leaving Rugge's residence. According to Kelly, Jesse Hollywood said to Rugge, "'Well, we'll just tie him up and throw him in the back of the car and go to the Biltmore and get something to eat.' Something like that. He said it in a joking manner, but it made me really uncomfortable."

Rugge also commented on this time frame later. He said, "We were not even there for, like, fifteen minutes back from the restaurant, when Natasha, Graham, Kelly and Nick showed up. Nick went upstairs. He didn't like being around Jesse and Michelle, so he jumped up and split. Hollywood didn't say anything to Nick. The rest of us hung out a little bit. Before Hollywood and Michelle left, we talked a little about Nick. He told me he was going to come up later, pick him up and take him away." Apparently, Rugge didn't object to this "later" period of time when Nick would be taken away, although the exact time was never specified. And Rugge still believed "taken away" meant "taken home." Rugge also learned that Jesse Hollywood still had not been in touch with Ben Markowitz. There was one more thing that Rugge was not divulging at the moment, that would come back to haunt him later. In his version of his meeting with Jesse James Hollywood, he would talk later of being offered $2,500 to kill Nick.

Natasha recalled leaving Rugge's house around 5:00 or 6:00 P.M., and Kelly Carpenter left with her, but not Graham Pressley. Pressley stayed at Rugge's house with Jesse Rugge and Nick. Even though at that point, Natasha Adams and Kelly Carpenter were pretty sure that Graham Pressley had told them the truth, that Nick Markowitz had been kidnapped and was being held in Santa Barbara on the orders of Jesse James Hollywood, neither one of them told law enforcement or even their parents about what was going on. At this point they knew nothing about the $2,500 that Rugge said that Jesse Hollywood had offered him to kill Nick.

Eventually Jesse Rugge did tell Graham Pressley about

this supposed offer. Just when he did that would be a bone of contention amongst many later on, although it seemed to have been after Natasha and Kelly left. Rugge assured Pressley that he was not going to follow through on the offer.

5

THE LEMON TREE

Jeff and Susan Markowitz had growing concerns about Nick since the evening of Sunday, August 6, when he didn't come home. Jeff recalled, "We made phone calls that evening to Ben because Nick had seen Ben both times before (when he'd left home), seeking his brother for help. Nick really didn't go far from home when it came to running away.

"So we were making phone calls Sunday night to Ben, and he said Nick wasn't with him. We called every one of Nick's friends, and nobody had seen him. He had been paged time and time again, and all of his friends had been paging him and they all said that he would have called them back, because he called all of his friends back right away.

"He had just gotten his pager the week before, and Susan made sure that he knew that if he didn't call back, he'd lose it. So we started getting frantic that he was not returning the messages. I got home from work and I was thinking, well, he had some new friends, maybe it was a different group of friends that he'd been associating with, and he stayed with them. I got ahold of Ben, started tracking down everybody and driving all over town. We started doing a little of our own investigating, and nothing turned up.

"Ben knew he had some enemies out there, and the first person he wanted to call was a boy by the name of Jesse Hollywood. Ben told me I had met him, or saw him, parked out in our front yard one time. Ben said Jesse had been to our house, and Ben said Jesse brought Nick home on one occasion. So the first call was to this Hollywood guy. Ben made the call. And I didn't get any indication that Ben had any real trouble to a great extent, at the time. I knew that Ben lived with Jesse Hollywood for a while and he owed some money to him.

"But there was another character that Ben had involvement with that he was also concerned about. Henry Chang. In fact, that particular character, supposedly a drug dealer, had attacked Ben the night after he and I had gotten together to look for Nick. Which, in our mind, kind of cut him out of the equation, because there was no way he would . . ." Jeff's thoughts drifted off, but the implication was that Chang would not have drawn such attention to himself if he'd kidnapped Nick.

"So now, Ben was looking back at this Hollywood character again, and we were trying to make some kind of contact. There was a boy who had left his driver's license at our house, and we tracked him down. We asked if he knew where Nick or Jesse Hollywood was, and he said no. We were about to give his license back to him and he said, 'I don't think he (Jesse Hollywood) did something.'

"Susan did a spreadsheet of all Nick's friends, and within probably a couple of hours of Sunday night, she was already on that. She got every name and number, every address, and made contact with every parent, or everybody we could, to try and track this thing down. I had inadvertently run into one of the boys that Nick was out with the night before, at a park. I went to various parks on Monday. By Monday we got frantic, and Monday night I went to all the different parks where these kids hung out, and it was there I ran into a boy who had seen Nick on Saturday night. And I gave the boy Nick's pager number. I said, 'Page him. Don't tell him why and call me, and let me know.'

"By Tuesday morning we knew that there was something wrong. I went to the police station and made a missing persons report. Friends started contacting friends, and it started escalating. Everybody was searching for him. Friends or foes, everybody wanted to find Nick."

There was one foe, however, not looking for Nick, because he knew exactly where Nick was. That, of course, was Jesse James Hollywood.

On Tuesday, August 8, Rugge said that Nick got up before he did, and once again Nick could have easily walked out the door and away from the whole scene. By Tuesday, as well, Natasha Adams had become so worried about Nick that she had Graham Pressley walk with her to a park near Jesse Rugge's house so that she could talk with Pressley away from the presence of Rugge.

Kelly Carpenter also came along with them. As Natasha recalled the conversation, "I expressed my concern about the fact that Nick Markowitz was still here and that he wasn't supposed to be. And I asked Graham what they were going to do about it. He told me that they had no idea, but that they weren't going to hurt him in any way and that they were just waiting to get a call from Jesse Hollywood. Graham Pressley also told me that Jesse Rugge had been offered money to kill Nick Markowitz. And I remember being shocked and appalled. I said, 'What are you going to do?' And he said, 'Of course, we're not going to do that. But now we don't know what to do, because we're in danger. All of us are!'

"And I asked him if we could tell somebody, and I told

him we were in over our heads and that I didn't know how much longer I could not tell Nick. Graham told me not to say anything, that something could happen to Jesse Rugge, that something could happen to him, that something could possibly happen to us. And he said to act like I didn't know and I wasn't involved and not to worry about it."

As to whether Natasha promised not to tell anyone, she said later, "I was crying, so I don't think I answered him."

Kelly Carpenter also had a recollection of talking to Graham Pressley about Nick's status, but it's not clear if this was at the same time in the park. What Kelly recalled of talking to Graham was "He told me that Nick, well, that the guys that had been down there were looking for Nick's brother, and they were not able to find him (in West Hills). They found Nick, and they beat him up and they put him in the van, and they brought him up to Santa Barbara. Graham said he wasn't one of them who did this. I was aware that Jesse Rugge was down there, and it was him and Jesse Hollywood and Will Skidmore who had done it."

As far as what was going to happen to Nick now, Kelly said, "Graham didn't seem to know the answer to that question." Pressley seemed to be just about as confused about the situation as Kelly and Natasha were.

Natasha later thought that the whole conversation with Graham Pressley took about fifteen minutes. As soon as they walked back to Jesse Rugge's house, Natasha confronted Rugge about the situation. She said later, "He told me that he didn't know what to do, but that he knew he was going to get Nick home, and that he would put him on a Greyhound bus that day. He was worried, though, because he didn't know if Nick would say anything to anybody when he got home. This happened while both Nick and Graham were present."

Natasha added, "Nick said, 'I'm not going to tell anybody. I'm cool.' And he was pretty easygoing about the whole thing."

The one thing Natasha didn't bring up in Nick's presence

was the fact that Jesse Rugge had been offered money by Jesse Hollywood to kill him. The offer was later stated as being either $2,000 or $2,500. Even Rugge would later mention these amounts. If she had uttered these few words to Nick at the time, he might have had a very different outlook about his present circumstances.

Kelly Carpenter recalled of this conversation, "Jesse said that he was sick of it, and that he wanted to give Nick fifty dollars to get him on the train to go home that night because he didn't want to deal with it anymore. And he asked Nick, 'How do I know that I'm not going to have cops knocking on my door tomorrow?' Then he told Nick, 'I just better not have cops coming to my door tomorrow!' This was about one-thirty in the afternoon when he said it. Nick didn't have any response to this, but he seemed to be more relaxed now."

Jesse Rugge's recollection of all of this was somewhat different than the others, and he did not bring up anything about having been offered any money by Jesse James Hollywood to kill Nick. What he did say was "Graham, Kelly and Natasha left for their walk, and when they came back, I noticed Natasha had been crying. Her eyes were puffy, and so when I started talking to her, asking her what's wrong, she said, 'You know he should go home!' And I said, 'I understand. He's got to go home. He is going home.' Nick was right there, sitting on the couch. So I told him he was free to leave. I'd give him fifty dollars to get on the train. I didn't want him in my house anymore. I was tired of the whole concept of [Jesse Hollywood] putting myself, my friends, my family—let alone Nick—in jeopardy. But Nick didn't really give me a response at first. And I said, 'If I give you fifty dollars, I won't have the cops come knocking on my door.' He said, 'Don't even worry about it.' After that, the whole cloud lifted. Like we were back to doing the normal routine."

Pressley would later recall of this exchange that everyone felt better after the conversation. He said, "We all breathed a collective sigh of relief."

About that exchange Kelly Carpenter recalled, "We started to watch a video, and Jesse Rugge said that maybe we should all go to a hotel and go swimming. It wasn't uncommon for kids to go to a hotel to use the swimming pool. It was a really hot day, and it didn't seem too unusual for me. Jesse Rugge kind of had a conversation with himself about which hotel. He got out the Yellow Pages and was looking for one in particular. Then he said, 'Well, how about the Lemon Tree Inn?'"

Rugge said of the process about picking the Lemon Tree Inn, "It was just a sporadic thing. It was between three and four P.M. when we started talking about it. Graham and I were talking about it, going over there to have a good time with the girls, and with Nick, and the swimming pool just popped in. It was just like, 'Let's go swimming.' And I asked Nick if he wanted to go swimming, and he said yes. So we all decided to go find a place with a pool, and the Lemon Tree had a pool."

Although the facts aren't clear, Rugge had to have called Jesse Hollywood around this time, because Hollywood would soon know that Rugge and Nick were going to the Lemon Tree Inn. Either Rugge called Jesse Hollywood about this, or mentioned it to him when Hollywood called Rugge around that time.

Natasha had to go home for a while, and left the others at Rugge's house. She did some errands and was away from Nick and the others for at least an hour and a half. During this time, however, she did not tell anyone else about Nick's plight. As far as the others getting to the Lemon Tree Inn, Kelly recalled, "Graham's mom came and picked us up from Jesse Rugge's house and took us to the hotel."

On the trip over to the Lemon Tree Inn, Kelly said, Nick didn't say anything to Mrs. Pressley, but Christina Pressley would remember things differently. Christina had been

on her way to a five-thirty yoga class, but she agreed to
swing by Jesse Rugge's house to pick up Graham, Kelly,
Jesse Rugge and a boy she didn't know. When Graham got
into the car, according to Christina, he introduced Nick by
saying, "He's staying with Jesse Rugge for a few days."
Christina swiveled around to get a good look at Nick because of her concerns with some of Graham's friends. She
had taken Rugge and her son out to lunch a few months
earlier and had been put off by Rugge's extensive tattoos.
As she put it later, "Graham was going through a rough
period" right then, and she didn't think Rugge was a good
influence on her son.

The boy Nick, however, seemed okay. Christina said to
him, "Nice to meet you," and he replied, "Nice to meet
you, too. Thanks for the ride."

Christina later said that she had no inkling that this boy
was in any kind of trouble. He seemed to be just another
friend of Graham's, Jesse's and Kelly's. It seemed as if
they had plans for a swim party on a hot August afternoon,
and nothing was out of the ordinary.

Even before Nick and the others were heading to the
Lemon Tree Inn, Jesse James Hollywood went to contact
Stephen Hogg, a lawyer who was a friend of the family.
This occurred during the late afternoon of August 8, 2000.
Hogg had represented Jesse on two previous criminal
charges—resisting arrest and being a minor in posses-
sion of alcohol. Jesse went over to Hogg's residence and
was very antsy. He smoked one cigarette after another
while there. Just what Jesse said would have variations
later, but the gist of it was always the same.

Jesse Hollywood told Hogg that some friends of his
were holding a boy hostage. Jesse asked, "What do I do?"

Hogg replied, "You've got to go to the police."

Jesse said, "I can't."

"Jesse, you have got to!" Hogg replied.

Jesse then asked what kind of trouble his friends might be in.

Hogg responded, "If they ask for a ransom, they can get life."

According to one set of details about this, Jesse immediately bolted from the backyard. Hogg later would say that Jesse did not bolt right then, but kept on talking about other things. Many more details would come out about this pivotal moment, but those details would not be revealed for years. Whatever the circumstances, all references to this incident have Jesse Hollywood being at Stephen Hogg's house for no more than ten to fifteen minutes. And Hogg was certain that the holding of the unnamed boy was not some past event, but something that was occurring right then, and Jesse Hollywood was involved, to some degree. To what extent he was involved was going to have grave consequences for Jesse Hollywood and his friends.

Stephen Hogg began to worry about this episode and wondered how much more deeply implicated in it Jesse might be than he let on. Hogg began paging Jesse, but Jesse did not call him back. Someone else did, however—it was Jack Hollywood. At the moment Jack Hollywood was at the luxurious Ventana Inn in Big Sur, on the rugged California coast, below Monterey, about 150 miles north of Santa Barbara.

As Jack Hollywood stated later, "It was I who contacted Steve Hogg first on an unrelated matter. It was about a case in Ventura for a DUI case that he was handling for me. I received information from Mr. Hogg about a problem involving Jesse. Just vague information."

There were some in law enforcement later who believed Stephen Hogg contacted Jack Hollywood first, and not about his DUI problems, but rather about the situation with Jesse.

Jack Hollywood later said, "I tried to get ahold of John Roberts and I talked to him. I tried to get ahold of Jesse, but the cell phone number I had for him didn't work."

Jack Hollywood would not relate later if Stephen Hogg told him exactly what kind of trouble Jesse was in. In fact, Jack would claim that Hogg did not want to say over a phone what the nature of the trouble was. One thing Jack Hollywood did was tell Steve Hogg to get in touch with John Roberts, a longtime friend of Jack's. It was Roberts's van that Jesse and the others had used to kidnap Nick, and this whole mess was involving more and more people as time went on.

Along with the van, John Roberts came with a lot of baggage, as far as the present predicament was concerned. Roberts was a sixty-eight-year-old retired wiseguy who'd had dealings with the Chicago mob. Roberts made no bones about his Chicago "tough guy" years, and later spoke openly about it to newspaper reporters.

Stephen Hogg did get in touch with Roberts by phone, and Roberts recalled saying, "'Am I in trouble?' Is Jack in trouble? And Hogg said, 'No.' So I said, 'Who's in trouble?' And he said, 'The kid.' And I thought, 'I don't even know what the hell you're talking about.'"

Later, Roberts would say of this that he knew that Stephen Hogg was Jack Hollywood's lawyer for a number of years prior to August 2000. Roberts then related, "Hogg was a close friend of the Hollywood family for a long time. He (Hogg) contacted me and he asked me to come out to his house and I told him I would, but I'd have to meet him in some kind of a place where he'd lead me to his house. I wasn't sure I'd know how to get there, so we met at a McDonald's in Simi Valley." (This happend sometime on the night of August 8.)

"So, after that, he led me to his house, and that's where the conversations became real. When we got to his house,

I asked him, 'What are you talking about?' And he said, 'Jesse. There's been a kidnapping.' It floored me. And I said, 'Well, let's talk.' And the gist of the conversation was extremely strong. First of all, to find out where Jesse was, because he would not let anybody know where he was at that point. Not even Steve. And then to find out where the child was who was being held and get him out of there and back to his family. But the most important thing was to find out where Jesse was.

"I don't think Steve went into the conversation that he had with Jesse other than to tell me that there had been a kidnapping and Jesse was involved. And that was enough. So, first of all, we wanted to find the boy. The child. And I'm sixty-eight years old and I'm from Chicago, and I remember Chicago. I was going to go out and find where the child was, and I'm going to do my Chicago act in front of these twenty-year-old boys. And I'm going to grab the kid and I'm going to give him some money to keep his mouth shut. Which, of course, is ridiculous, because there's no such thing as a fifteen-year-old keeping his mouth shut. But the whole thing was to get the child out. And the idea of the money, that's old-fashioned 1950s gangster talk.

"When I talked to Hogg about the money he said, 'We can't do that.' And I said, 'Well, I don't care. We're going to find the boy, but we have to find Jesse first,' and we didn't know how to do that. When I left Hogg's house, the basic understanding was we would both try to find out where the boy was, but not in cooperation with one another.

"I didn't have any of Jesse's numbers, his pager or his cell phone, but I believe that Steve constantly was calling those numbers and got no reply. Basically, at the time I just knew the kidnap victim was a young kid. I didn't know his name or what the thinking was of the boys who took him. After that evening I had no more conversations with Mr. Hogg."

* * *

When Jesse Hollywood had taken off from Stephen Hogg's residence on the late afternoon of August 8, he and Michelle Lasher went to a friend of Jesse's named Casey Sheehan. Sheehan said later that when he got home from work a little after 4:00 P.M. on August 8, Jesse and Michelle were already at his house. Even though Jesse had come to Sheehan's house in Michelle's BMW, he now asked Sheehan for the car keys to Sheehan's old Honda Accord. Sheehan gave Hollywood the keys without asking why Jesse wanted to borrow his car, rather than just using Michelle's BMW. Michelle later would give the reason for Jesse leaving Sheehan's house, because he wanted to return to his home on Cohasset Street, shower and change clothes. But one key player in what was about to happen had a very different story of why Jesse Hollywood went there. And that person was Ryan Hoyt.

The person Jesse Hollywood went to see at his house in West Hills, sometime around 5:00 P.M., August 8, was the same Ryan Hoyt who had cleaned up around his house and scraped up all the dog crap around the yard. The same Ryan Hoyt that he and the others had constantly made fun of. According to Ryan, Jesse asked him if he wanted to erase his debt. Ryan recalled, "He said there was a mess that needed to be cleaned up. He said I needed to go take care of somebody."

As Ryan Hoyt pondered this, he would say later, "Imagine how Jesse would treat me if I had told him to 'just fuck off!'"

Ryan also saw this as an opportunity to be seen in a different light by Jesse Hollywood and his buddies, to be seen as a guy who could take care of things and was more than just the butt of everyone's jokes. For once to be seen as the tough guy of the group. And Ryan would later have two versions of what he was about to do. In one version he was taking Jesse Hollywood's TEC-9 up to Santa Barbara to "take care of Nick." In another, later version Ryan had a very different tale to tell. But by then, he was sitting behind bars and in lots of trouble.

At this point stories would also differ as to Jesse Hollywood's TEC-9 semiautomatic pistol. According to Ryan, Jesse gave him a duffel bag with the TEC-9 inside. This pistol had been modified to be fully automatic—able to fire twelve rounds per second. Ryan was given instructions to go pick up Nick Markowitz at the Lemon Tree Inn and take care of him. At least that is what Hoyt would say later in one version of events. As Ryan took off, Jesse phoned Rugge at the Lemon Tree and said that someone was on the way there to "take care of Nick."

Jesse Hollywood and Ryan Hoyt drove back to Casey Sheehan's house in Sheehan's old Honda Accord. It's not apparent if Casey and Michelle saw Ryan at all. Most likely, Jesse Hollywood got out of the car and gave Ryan the keys before he went inside Sheehan's house. Ryan Hoyt took off, heading up to Santa Barbara.

Since it was Michelle Lasher's birthday, Jesse took her and Casey Sheehan out to dinner at the Outback Steakhouse in Northridge. It was Michelle's twentieth birthday, and besides being a nice birthday present, it would also give Jesse an alibi concerning Nick. Jesse, Michelle and Sheehan sat down and had dinner, and the tab came to $108.98. And to pay the bill, Jesse Hollywood used a credit card, something he rarely did, since he generally paid for things with cash. But a credit card bill would prove that he was in Northridge in the crucial evening/night hours of August 8, 2000, and not anywhere near Santa Barbara.

Sheehan recalled being with Jesse and Michelle from around 9:00 P.M. to almost midnight. He also recalled one more thing—Jesse Hollywood had told him that "the thing with Nick is being taken care of." At the time Sheehan said he didn't know what Hollywood was talking about.

* * *

While this was going on, Kelly Carpenter, Jesse Rugge, and Graham Pressley would all have slightly different versions of what occurred when they reached the Lemon Tree Inn and the subsequent events that occurred there. Kelly recalled, "Jesse Rugge paid for the room while me and Nick and Graham sat in the lobby. Then we all went up to a room on the second floor."

Jesse Rugge recalled, "We went into the office, and Nick was standing next to me, and then he went and sat down next to Kelly. This was near the front desk, where you check in. I paid cash. And right about then, Graham left and went down to see his friend Nathan Appleton on State Street. I gave Graham a hundred bucks to get us a quarter ounce of marijuana. So then, me and Kelly and Nick went up to the room on the second floor."

According to Kelly, once inside the room, they all tried to figure out how to make the video recorder on the television work. Kelly added, "Nick said he'd taken some Valium. He'd had trouble sleeping the night before, and he kind of needed it to sleep."

Rugge commented later about the television set. "We kept fiddling with everything, trying to figure it out, and couldn't figure out how to work it. So we left, went downstairs, took the elevator off the hall and went to Ralphs market to buy a pack of cigarettes."

While Rugge went inside the market, Kelly and Nick stayed outside, and he definitely could have taken off at that point. Kelly asked him why he was staying and, according to Kelly, "he told me that he didn't want to rock the boat, so to speak. That he believed that he was going home and that he didn't want to try and mess it up and have them angry at him and have everything change."

In another conversation then or later, Kelly said, "Nick said he just couldn't wait to go to a—he mentioned some hill that's by his house. He liked to watch the sun set there, and that he would go there and call his friend and just kind of lay low and just be happy that he was home." By his "friend," Nick most likely meant Jeanne, the girl he was starting to consider to be his girlfriend.

Jesse Rugge got the cigarettes, and as the three of them arrived back at the Lemon Tree Inn, Graham Pressley and Nathan Appleton were just pulling into the parking lot. They all went back to the rented room and watched television and smoked dope. Kelly said later, "We went out onto the patio. Jesse Rugge wanted to go get us all food and he went downstairs to get food. The rest of us just sat outside, talking. Nick was sitting on the patio talking with Natasha and myself." (Natasha Adams had joined the others, although just when is not exact.)

Rugge went down the street to a place called Chubbies, and he recalled, "I bought everybody a dinner-type thing. Three cheeseburgers, fries and Cokes. When I got back, Kelly didn't eat her cheeseburger, because she's a vegetarian. So I split it in half, and me and Nick ate it. And we gave Kelly extra fries."

After they had eaten their meals, "we smoked a blunt," Rugge recalled. "A blunt is a cigar—well, you hollow out the center of tobacco and break up your pot and put it inside there, and it's like a big joint. It's called a blunt. We sat around a table on the patio-type thing in back.

"There was this black man standing next door. He was in his late forties, and once we lit up the first blunt, he was like, 'What are you guys smoking?' So I proceeded to carry on a conversation with him. There were, like, pillars between the balconies, separating them, and I was leaning up against the balcony, just shooting the breeze with him. Smoking a blunt and passing it back and forth to him. Nick, during this time, well, there were two blunts going around, and he was out on the balcony, too."

Kelly would remember of this period, "The man in the next room, he was on the patio next to us, and there was a wall that separated the patios. But there was, like, holes in it that you can hear people and see people through. It was very easy to hear people next door. The man had a conversation with Jesse Rugge and they were passing a joint back and forth between one another and just having a conversation. I didn't hear what they said. They were just talking."

Natasha Adams would have her own take on what she recalled about the Lemon Tree Inn that evening. Natasha said, "When you walked in the door of the room, you could see directly to a patio. There was a bedroom to your right, and it was just a room with two beds and a TV and a phone. The others were in the room when I got there. We drank, we smoked and hung out in the hotel room."

Natasha said that at some point Graham Pressley and Nick went swimming in the Lemon Tree Inn's pool. She did not mention the man from next door talking with Jesse Rugge or smoking dope with him. However, in time, a "person of interest" would come forward and talk about having been in the next room and his recollections of the young people at the Lemon Tree Inn.

As far as Graham's and Nick's trip to the pool, Rugge recalled that they both went swimming, and no one else could see the pool from the room or the balcony. He also said he really didn't care if Nick took off at that point or not. When Nick and Graham got back, Nick told him about the girls that he and Graham had met at the pool. Nick seemed to be in a good mood at that point.

Graham Pressley spoke of the girls as well. He said, "We stayed in the Jacuzzi with them for a while." Asked later why he and Nick left the pool area when they did, Pressley commented, "No more girls."

At 8:20 P.M., Rugge had a phone conversation with Jesse James Hollywood, and Hollywood was down in the Los Angeles area. Rugge's recollection of the call was, "Hollywood said, 'Nick's going home. Somebody is coming to pick him up.' And I said, 'It's about time.' The call only lasted about thirty seconds."

The only person that Rugge told about this short phone call from Hollywood was Graham Pressley. Rugge said later that Pressley reacted with a smile when he heard the news that Nick was going home. Both the girls and Nick were out on the balcony at the time of the conversation.

Besides smoking blunts on the balcony, everyone drank Jack Daniel's as well. Because of all the dope and booze, Rugge said, Nick lay down on a bed and fell asleep fairly early. What happened next comes in various versions.

According to Natasha Adams, at around 11:00 P.M., Jesse Rugge announced, "I'm sorry, but you ladies have to leave. Someone is going to come and pick up Nick." This remark seemed to include Nathan Appleton, but not Graham Pressley. According to Natasha, "Graham got up to leave, and Jesse said, 'Aren't you going to stay back?' And Graham said, 'Okay,' so we left."

Kelly Carpenter's recollection of these events was different. She said, "We had seen earlier that the hotel rules stated that you had to be out by, I can't recall whether it was ten-thirty or eleven P.M., and at that point we just wanted to go. Nathan Appleton, Natasha Adams and I left." When asked later if Jesse Rugge told them they had to leave, she didn't recall this. Nor did she recall Jesse Rugge saying anything about somebody coming to pick up Nick.

Jesse Rugge's version of this was different than the other two. He said later, "There was a list of rules and regulations for the room, and I think the list was movable. It ended up by the TV. I read it out loud, and I was joking around when I was reading the rules because we were smoking pot and drinking. It said hotel guests were prohibited in a room after ten P.M."

Pressley also remembered that Rugge told the others they had to leave, and he made a joke about the Lemon Tree rules, since they were all drinking and smoking dope.

Whatever the circumstances, Nathan Appleton, Kelly Carpenter and Natasha Adams left the room sometime between 10:30 and 11:00 P.M. Graham Pressley stayed behind with Nick and Jesse Rugge. As the others left, someone else was indeed on his way to the Lemon Tree Inn.

The someone else was, of course, Ryan Hoyt, but he got lost on the way there and had to call for directions to the Lemon Tree Inn. When Hoyt finally arrived, the only inhabitants of the motel room were Nick Markowitz, Jesse Rugge and Graham Pressley. Just what occurred next is a matter of debate on whether someone believes Ryan Hoyt, Graham Pressley or Jesse Rugge. When Hoyt spoke of the events of that night, two years later, his story was absolutely different than the ones Rugge and Pressley had told of the events.

In Rugge's version there was a knock at the door around 11:20 P.M., and when he opened the door, his heart sank. He was expecting Jesse Hollywood to be standing there. Instead, it was Ryan Hoyt, who carried a small blue bag. Rugge said that Nick was asleep on the bed, and Graham Pressley was sitting on a chair, watching television. Rugge claimed, "The first thing that Hoyt said when he came in was 'Why isn't Nick taped up?' I said, 'He doesn't need to be taped up. I don't know what you're talking about.' Then he just gave me a look. He was carrying a blue bag, like a Dodger bag. It was zipped up, and he put it down on the floor. The weight of it, when it hit the ground, you could hear it. There was a noise, like two metals rubbing together. My stomach dropped. I thought there was a gun in there.

"He told me to follow him into the bathroom. The first thing he said in there was 'You done fucked up! You're fucking up!' That's when he pulled out a gun and popped a clip into it. I felt like it wasn't real. The whole scene wasn't real. I was frightened beyond belief. I walked out and looked at Graham, and Graham just caught my look."

Graham's take on this was different than Rugge's. He recalled being surprised by someone coming to the door who was not Jesse James Hollywood. The person was carrying a duffel bag and seemed to be surprised that Pressley was there. This person went into the bathroom, but he did not close the door all the way. When Pressley went to wash his hands at a sink near the bathroom, he looked inside and was startled to see a gun poking out of the duffel bag, and the person was wiping down a clip of bullets.

Rugge continued with his tale: "Hoyt was still holding the gun, and Nick was asleep. I believe Graham saw the gun. He looked like a ghost. I recognized the gun as being Jesse Hollywood's TEC-9. Then Hoyt just told me, 'Let's go.' I wasn't going to argue. We walked out the front door, him behind me, with the gun still in his hand. Walked to the elevator, opened it up, and got in the elevator together. And that's when he just opened, like, his belt and then shoved the gun down his pants.

"I was scared. I didn't think this was real. I thought he was crazy. When we got down, he pointed me to his car and we got in. He drove down State Street and said we were going to my house. I looked at him with a freakish look. But what was I going to say to him? When we got to my house, he asked me where my shovels were and told me to go get them, but I said no."

According to Rugge, he didn't go get the shovels, but he told Hoyt that there were some by the side of the house. Hoyt went out, leaving Rugge in the car, and soon returned with a flat-head shovel and a pointed shovel. The handles were long, but instead of putting them in the trunk of the car, Rugge said, Hoyt put them inside the vehicle lengthways. After that, they drove back to the Lemon Tree Inn, and Rugge claimed that on the way to the elevator, Hoyt wanted to know if Rugge knew the area around Santa Barbara very well. Rugge said that he didn't. Then Hoyt asked him, "Does Graham?" Rugge said something to the effect that Graham had lived there all of his life.

When they got back inside the room, Nick was still asleep, and according to Rugge, Graham was still watching the TV, as if he were frozen in place. According to Rugge, Hoyt said three words, "Graham, let's go." The TEC-9 was still in Hoyt's waistband. Pressley got up without a word and followed Hoyt out the door.

Ryan Hoyt eventually would have a lot to say about his trip to the Lemon Tree Inn. But that was years in the future, and by that point he was fighting for his life.

6

THE LIZARD'S MOUTH

Graham Pressley contended that Ryan Hoyt forced him to come along on a ride out to the mountainous area around Santa Barbara. Graham was aware that Hoyt had a gun, and he had no idea if Hoyt was ready to use it or not. According to Graham, Ryan Hoyt wanted him to find a nice isolated spot out in the Santa Ynez Mountains, and Graham thought that a spot he knew might fit the bill. It was called the Lizard's Mouth, because of a rock formation there that did look like a lizard with its mouth open as if to catch its prey. The Lizard's Mouth was a party spot for teens, and Graham had been there before.

Graham and Ryan traveled up Highway 154 toward San Marcos Pass, then went onto narrow, winding West Camino Cielo Road. This small road ran along the side of the Santa Ynez Mountains in snakelike curves, with beautiful views of the ocean and Santa Barbara by day. But now, it was near midnight, and the road was enveloped in darkness with no other vehicles on its pavement. Graham guided the car up to an area near a gun club, which was at a distance from any dwellings, and then he and Ryan got out and hiked through the brush toward the Lizard's Mouth. Ryan had Jesse James Hollywood's TEC-9 and a shovel with him, and Graham also had a shovel. According to Graham, once they reached an area near the Lizard's Mouth, Ryan Hoyt forced him to start digging a hole.

According to Graham, Hoyt told him, "You'd better start digging, if you know what's good for you." The ground was rocky and hard near the Lizard's Mouth, so Pressley and Hoyt moved about five hundred feet away to where the ground was softer. Even then, Graham only managed to dig a hole about a foot and a half deep, and six to seven feet long. He said later that he wasn't sure if he was digging his own grave. Graham recalled, "I thought maybe this person wanted to get rid of me, because I'd become a liability."

It wasn't perfect, but Ryan decided it was deep enough to hold the body of a fifteen-year-old boy. When he told Pressley to quit digging and to come along with him back to the car, Pressley said he felt a rush of relief wash over him that he wasn't going to die at that moment. He knew that the hole he had just dug was not intended for him.

Probably around 1:00 A.M., August 9, Ryan Hoyt and Graham Pressley returned to the Lemon Tree Inn. Incredibly, Ryan left Pressley in the car by himself, and even though Pressley guessed what was coming next, he didn't bolt. According to Pressley, Ryan Hoyt even left the TEC-9 in the trunk of the car at that time. Pressley would say later that he was too afraid to tell Nick what was going to happen, or even leave himself, certain that if he did, Hoyt would track him down and kill him and his family.

At least that's what Graham Pressley said later. Rugge, who was still in the room with Nick, had a very different story. He said, "Graham walked in first, with really rosy cheeks, like he was holding back his emotions. I just looked at him, and he looked at me, and we just caught each other's eyes. It's hard to describe. At that point Hoyt came in and shook Nick's feet and woke him up. It was hard to get him up. When he got up, we went outside, and I was in front, Graham behind me, Nick behind Graham and then Hoyt. I saw Hoyt had the blue bag in his hand at that time. He pointed to where his car was parked, and we all went over there. It was real quiet at that time. I was scared and didn't know what to think.

"We got in and Ryan Hoyt drove, because I couldn't drive a stick. I sat shotgun, Graham was behind Hoyt, and Nick was behind me. I asked Hoyt where we were going, but he didn't say anything. Then I asked Graham. At first he didn't answer me. So I said again, 'Graham, where are we going?' Graham turned to me like he was crying, and he said, 'We're going to Lizard's Mouth.' Then everything went dead again. Just quiet." Rugge added that Nick didn't say a word on the ride, and that he "looked scared."

Graham Pressley also commented later about the drive up to Lizard's Mouth, and remarked on the unearthly quiet in the car. He said there was an incredible tension within the vehicle, but that neither he nor Rugge warned Nick about what was going to take place. As far as he knew, Nick was still under the illusion that someone was coming up there to take him home to West Hills. Graham even held the slim hope that the hole he had just dug was only intended to scare Nick into remaining silent about what had happened to him.

After they reached the parking spot near the gun club, there would be various versions of what happened next, and depending on which version was true, it would have grave implications for Graham Pressley later. What came to light, years later, is most likely what occurred, and by then, even Pressley would admit to it. He said that he guided the others up the trail until they heard a young man and woman off in the distance. These two seemed to be having a good time up there. As the couple walked back toward the road, they passed Pressley, Nick, Rugge and Hoyt, who had moved off to the side of the narrow trail. The couple said "good-bye" to the four young men and moved off down the trail. At that point "I was sitting on a rock and just lost it. I refused to move any farther. They just left me there, and went on without me," Pressley said later.

In Jesse Rugge's version of events, it was Graham Pressley who led the others over the rough and broken ground, sometime between two-thirty and three A.M., in the early-morning hours of August 9, all the way to the grave. Rugge said, "Hoyt just told us, 'Let's go,' and Graham took the lead. Then it was Nick, myself and Hoyt behind me. Only Hoyt had a flashlight." But even though Rugge swore to this version, Pressley's seems to be the most accurate, where he sat on the rock near the trail and refused to go up to where he had dug the hole.

Rugge estimated it took anywhere from five to ten minutes to get to where Hoyt wanted them to go. Rugge said of the area, "We sat down on these plane of rocks for a while. Nick sat down on a rock, Graham sat down on a rock and I stood facing Graham. Hoyt was behind me, looking at Nick. I believe the gun was in the bag then, and he was holding the bag at all times.

"Hoyt turned to me and told me to tape up Nick, and I said no. He looked at me with an angry look. Nick just sat there quietly, with his head down. Graham was lying on a rock, and then he just disappeared like a ghost." (Rugge seems to have confused the time line. Pressley was on that rock before making it all the way to the grave site.)

"Hoyt told Nick to put his hands behind his back, and Nick did. Then Hoyt taped him up. After that, Hoyt told him to get up and to walk. Hoyt walked him over, on a flat rock, and the rock dropped out onto a flat dirt area and he walked out on this dirt."

Rugge claimed that he never saw Nick's mouth being taped up, but he said he heard Hoyt pulling out some duct tape, ripping it off and doing something with it. To his ear, it sounded like duct tape was being applied to Nick, and later he mentioned it being placed around Nick's mouth.

Rugge would claim later that he still believed that Ryan Hoyt was only trying to scare Nick into not talking—until the next few unforgettable seconds. Rugge said he was sitting on a rock nearby when Hoyt raised the shovel and whacked Nick in the head with it. The sound was very distinct in the otherwise silent night. The boy tumbled over, and Rugge presumed that Nick had been knocked out.

According to Rugge, "Hoyt picked Nick up and dragged him over to a hole. He was holding him under the arms and was dragging him faceup." Rugge said he couldn't see where Hoyt placed him, but that it was probably in the hole that Pressley had dug earlier that night.

Then, under the twinkling stars and pale moon, Ryan Hoyt raised the pistol and pressed his finger down on the trigger. It sprayed nine bullets into Nick's body, and only stopped at nine because it became jammed. Nick was hit in the stomach, neck, chest and chin—dying almost instantly.

After the thunderous roar of the fusillade, there was an eerie silence. According to one version, Hoyt ordered Rugge to throw dirt onto Nick's body, but Rugge only managed to throw one shovelful on the boy before getting sick and vomiting nearby. Seeing that Rugge wasn't up to the task, Hoyt started shoveling dirt into the grave. He did one more odd thing as well—he threw the TEC-9 into the grave with Nick. Then Hoyt shoveled more dirt into the hole and piled some branches and twigs there. It was a shoddy job at best, with parts of Nick's body still exposed, but at 3:00 A.M., in the dark, it might have seemed okay to Ryan Hoyt.

Jesse Rugge and Ryan Hoyt walked back down the trail to the car, and Rugge was almost in a daze. Once again,

Pressley could have taken off on his own during the time the other two were gone, but he did not. He was still there when the other two returned, minus Nick Markowitz. Hoyt had been very quiet on the trip down the hill to the car, but once he reached it, he seemed pleased at what he had accomplished. Pressley remembered him saying, "That's the first time I ever did anybody. I didn't know he would go so quick." Graham Pressley was speechless.

Rugge would remember Hoyt joking about him vomiting and mocking him in front of Pressley. "Then he lit a cigarette, and that was it. We just drove away."

Hoyt drove back to the Lemon Tree and Graham Pressley went inside the room without comment. He was told to pay for the room when he checked out the following morning. And Pressley's mom, having fallen asleep earlier in the night, didn't even realize he'd missed his 11:00 P.M. curfew and wasn't home. She had no idea that he wasn't there until Graham phoned her the next morning, at six o'clock, from the Lemon Tree, asking for a ride home.

When Christina Pressley picked him up, Graham was very quiet in the car and looked pale. She asked him if he was all right, and Graham responded that he didn't feel well and he hadn't slept much that night. Christina would recall later, "He was clearly sick or shaken, or something was very wrong."

As far as the others went, Rugge said, "Hoyt drove me to Los Angeles. It was quiet in the car. Lots of smoking cigarettes. We didn't talk about the killing of Nick. It was about seven forty-five A.M. when we got to my mom's place. I told him to drop me off there."

Rugge said later that there weren't any plans made to throw law enforcement off track. No contingency plans to leave the area or hide out. No plans at all. Rugge said Ryan Hoyt just let him off and drove away.

When Rugge went in the door, he said that his stepdad, Scott, was there. "I was really quiet. I walked to the room I stayed in, waited until he was done with his stuff, and when he left, I just drank a lot of water. A lot of fluids. I was sick, man. I was scared. Scared of Hoyt. Scared of going to prison. Scared for what someone else had done."

According to Kelly Carpenter, she spoke in person with Graham Pressley at around 11:00 A.M. on Wednesday, August 9, and he lied to her, saying that Jesse Hollywood had come to the Lemon Tree Inn after she, Natasha Adams and Nathan Appleton had left, and scared Nick with a gun to keep him quiet. Pressley told her it was a TEC-9 and that it "was a really gnarly gun and shot, like, three bullets at a time." Carpenter added, "Graham told me that he drove Jesse Rugge, Nick Markowitz, Jesse Hollywood and a friend down to L.A., and so we were completely clear now."

Natasha Adams was nearby, and either she or Carpenter asked Pressley how he had taken them home, since he didn't have a car. Carpenter said, "What he told me was that Jesse Hollywood had purchased a van for five hundred dollars for this use, only to drive down to L.A. and drive back up." She didn't ask Graham why Jesse Hollywood would rent a van in Santa Barbara if it had to be brought back there and not West Hills. Nor did the name Ryan Hoyt ever come up in the conversation with Pressley or anything about Lizard's Mouth. She recalled, however, about Pressley's demeanor that morning. "He was very tired and very flustered and overwhelmed."

Ryan Hoyt would later relate what he did after his return from Santa Barbara. By that point, however, Hoyt was telling a story in which he did not even accompany Pressley and Rugge to Lizard's Mouth, much less murder Nick. Though that is at variance with what Rugge and

Pressley said, some topics Hoyt did speak about in the days after Nick was murdered seem to be valid. Hoyt recalled, "Jesse Rugge and I drove out of Santa Barbara and took Highway 101 straight back. We stopped at a McDonald's in the Valley to get something to eat. I was starving. Then I dropped Jesse Rugge off at his mom's house and returned to my grandmother's place. I still had Casey Sheehan's car. I showered, shaved and relaxed. About two hours later, I called Rugge to see how he was doing."

Even before Kelly Carpenter had her talk with Graham Pressley, or Hoyt and Rugge made their way back to Los Angeles, Jack Hollywood had been trying to contact Jesse Hollywood on the night of Tuesday, August 8, and into the early hours of Wednesday, August 9. His quest to find Jesse was still occurring around the time that Nick was being led to his death up at Lizard's Mouth.

Jack recalled, "After driving back from Big Sur, I got ahold of my son by phone when I got really close, and he finally said that he was at Michelle's house. I called him from some city between Santa Barbara and Ventura. I didn't go into specifics, I just said, 'I want to talk to you.' He said, 'Okay, but it's kind of late.' I said, 'Well, you know, I want to talk to you.' So he just told me that he was at Michelle's house and how to get there, since I'd never been there. Her house is in Calabasas.

"It took me about an hour to get from where I called to Michelle's house. It was, like, one in the morning when I got there, and Michelle was sleeping. My wife was out in the car sleeping, and Michelle's parents weren't there. The conversation I had with Jesse was in the living room. He was kind of evasive. He seemed scared and confused. He indicated that some of his friends were holding a kid, and he was worried that they were in some kind of trouble. But he said the kid was just up there having ribs and drinking beers with some of his friends. And he wouldn't tell me who they were. And that was pretty much it. He was kind of acting like, 'How come you're here? I don't want you involved in this!' But he seemed pretty shook-up."

It's not certain at that point if Jack Hollywood believed his son. Asked later in court if he thought Jesse was involved in some kind of criminal activity, Jack answered, "Yes."

Jack continued, "I said, 'What happened here?' I really didn't have a lot of information. I just got a kind of vague picture that these guys had gotten involved in something, and I didn't know exactly what it was. I was trying to find things out, and he was scared, and he was evasive. He was kind of ticked off that I found out, and he didn't want me to know. He said things were probably all right now, and the kid had probably been let go, but he (Jesse) could possibly get into trouble because he was somehow involved when they took the kid.

"I was pressing, and saying, 'Where is the guy? Let's get him out of there. Let's make sure nothing happens.' And Jesse said that he'd tried all night to get ahold of them at the place where the guy was, and they must have gone somewhere else, or else they just let him go and they just took off. At that point I didn't know who they were.

"It was, like, two o'clock now, and I said, 'I've got to get some sleep.' So I said, 'I want to see you in the morning. I want to come over in the morning and let's make sure that everything is okay. That we can help this guy out.'

"I dropped my wife at home and then drove over to John Roberts's house. I asked him what he thought. He said the same thing that I'd heard. That some friends of Jesse's had taken some kid, because, I guess, they had some kind of beef with the kid's brother. He said the kid was somewhere at someone's house. He gave me the same picture about them up drinking and partying, but they were worried that when they let the guy go, that they were all going to get arrested. Roberts said he got this information from Steve Hogg. He was kind of the position of 'let's make sure that he's let go.'"

John Roberts would later recall of this visit with Jack Hollywood that not only was he there, but Laurie Hollywood was as well. Roberts said later, "They drove up to my house, about two in the morning. And they were in pieces. Absolute pieces. Emotionally—they just couldn't handle it. Jack was crying. She was crying. 'Upset' would be a word that was kind of the low scale to what they were.

"I told them I'd been to Steve's house and told them that we had to find Jesse in order to find where the kid was. Steve Hogg had said that if we got the boy, the child, safely away quickly, before any damage was done to him, that he might be able to get Jesse off with a short-sentence prison term. But he was going to have to go to prison."

Later on in the morning of August 9, Jack Hollywood and John Roberts went to see Jesse Hollywood in person at Michelle's parents' house. As Jack recalled, "Michelle was in the house and Jesse and I were out on the back porch. It was around eleven A.M. I wanted to know where the kid was at, and how do we get ahold of him. Jesse wouldn't say anything with John there, but he gave me a pager number. Jesse told me, 'This is Ryan Hoyt's number, and he'll know where the guy is, and you guys can go get him.'"

What John Roberts recalled of this meeting was that he went to Michelle Lasher's residence with Jack Hollywood and "she let us in. Jesse was somewhere in the back of the house. And Jesse and Jack and I went way out in the back-yard patio to talk. Both of us confronted him, and our whole argument was, number one, we had to know where the child was, and number two, that we wanted him to go to Steve Hogg and have Steve Hogg walk him into the police department. But he wouldn't do it. He was afraid. He didn't think it was that consequential. He gave us no information. No conversation of any kind. It was almost like he did not at the time regard it as being a terribly serious thing."

According to both John Roberts and Jack Hollywood, they got nothing useful out of Jesse, and they both left. Jack Hollywood said later, "I went to a pay phone at Gelson's Market, right down the street. I paged Ryan Hoyt from there. I waited for about a minute or two and he called back. I said, 'What's going on?' He said, 'Oh, how are you doing?' And I said, 'Well, let's get together. Why don't you come over and we'll sit down and talk.' He didn't say where he was, but I asked him to meet me at a park that was near to where I was, Serrania Park in Woodland Hills.

"I got there first, and then he arrived. The first thing I said was 'What the hell's going on with this thing? And where is the kid? Show me where he is, and John and I will go and get him.'"

Apparently, Ryan Hoyt lied, since Nick was already dead and buried. According to Jack, Hoyt said, "I don't know how to get in touch with him."

Jack added, "I sensed that he was pretty rattled. Again I said, 'Let's find out. Call whoever it is that you need to call, and you can just leave, and John and I will go and get this kid and take him home.'

"And Ryan was kind of, I don't know how to say it, very agitated and rattled and said he couldn't. So I said, 'Here,' and gave him my home phone number. I said, 'If you find out, call me. Leave a message or I'll be there, but you need to find out where this guy is, and we need to let him go. Whatever the consequences are from there, that's part of the deal, but that's what needs to happen.'

"And then he just said, 'Okay, I'll do that.'"

According to Jack Hollywood, at that point Ryan Holt gave him the impression that Nick Markowitz was still alive, when, in fact, he had been dead for several hours. Ryan Hoyt would later have his own take on his conversation with Jack Hollywood. Hoyt said, "I found it unusual that Jack Hollywood was paging me. He paged me maybe once or twice in the whole time I'd known him. I went to meet him at a park, and he was there waiting for me. We greeted each other in a roundabout way and he told me that Benjamin Markowitz's brother had been taken. I was taken aback by that. I just said, 'What are you talking about?'"

Hoyt's whole story line later would be that he was the fall guy for what others had done, especially Jesse James Hollywood and Jesse Rugge. It was they, not he, who had been instrumental in Nick Markowitz's murder. In fact, according to Hoyt, he would later say that he never saw Nick Markowitz at all when he went to Santa Barbara on the night of August 8.

Hoyt added, "He went on to ask me where the boy was, who did it, and so on and so forth. I replied I didn't know. I mean, even if I did know, it was kind of out of my hands, anyway. I was kind of mad he brought me into the whole thing, but he asked me to find out what I could, and I said that I would. I was aggravated when he left. Very aggravated.

"From the park I proceeded to try and get ahold of Casey Sheehan and Jesse Hollywood. I did get ahold of Casey, and I told him I had his car. He told me the key to his house was under a cooler, so I took the car back there and went into his house. I got to his house about four-thirty P.M. After I got there, Jesse Hollywood showed up, along with Michelle Lasher and William Skidmore. I asked Jesse, 'What is your father doing paging me?' He just looked at me, with a smug look, and told me not to worry about it."

On August 10, 2000, Jesse James Hollywood and Michelle Lasher went to a car dealership and Jesse leased a new Lincoln Town Car. Ryan Hoyt would not speak of this at all later, and probably didn't know at the time that this was occurring. Ryan also related later that he was drinking a lot of booze and smoking a lot of dope on this day. All through these days after the murder of Nick on August 9, various people connected to Jesse James Hollywood would have different stories about what was occurring. And all of their stories had to be viewed in the light of how they were trying to distance themselves from what had occurred.

August 11, 2000, was Ryan Hoyt's twenty-first birthday, and he seemed to have gained new status within Jesse James Hollywood's hierarchy. There was a party for Ryan at Casey Sheehan's residence, attended by about thirty people. During all the drinking and smoking of dope, in one version Ryan confessed to Sheehan what he had done in regard to killing Nick Markowitz. At least that is what Sheehan said. Sheehan recalled, "Ryan didn't show me that much emotion as far as . . . like he had a lot of guilt on his conscience or anything like that. I was still in disbelief about what had happened, what he had said to me. He said he had killed Nick Markowitz. I didn't know whether to believe him or not."

Later, Ryan would tell a very different story about events at the party. In his version there was no mentioning by him of killing Nick or even seeing him in Santa Barbara. Ryan did say, "At the party Jesse Hollywood gave me four hundred bucks for my birthday, and he told me, 'We're straight. No more debt.'

"During my party we were all drinking and smoking heavily. I was kind of drunk at the time, but not severely drunk. Casey Sheehan asked me why Jack Hollywood had talked to me. I said, 'I believe he was looking for Jesse and [was] kind of flustered.' Then it kind of came up in a roundabout way—I kind of looked at Casey and said, 'Do you think they killed him?'" (This meant Nick.)

Obviously, Ryan was talking about Graham Pressley and Jesse Rugge killing Nick Markowitz. Ryan added, "I thought Jesse Hollywood was involved. Jack had used the words 'Ben's brother had been taken.' And I automatically assumed when somebody is taken—well, only one person can't take another person. So I assumed it was more than one."

Sheehan was concerned about things that had transpired because it had been his car that Nick had been driven in by the others up to where he had been killed. Sheehan confronted Jesse Hollywood about this, and Hollywood told him, "Just don't worry about it!"

That was easier said than done. Casey Sheehan was indeed worried that Nick's body would be discovered, and there would be a link back to him. Even though the others partied on, as if nothing had happened, Sheehan was no longer in a partying mood. As things turned out, Casey Sheehan had good reason to be concerned.

Ryan Hoyt, however, partied on as if nothing of consequence had happened. He had Sheehan take him to a skateboard and clothing shop called the 118 Board Shop. Here, Hoyt bought several items of clothing, which surprised Sheehan, since Hoyt was almost always broke.

In fact, Hoyt was so unconcerned about the events of the previous days that he related later, "On August twelfth, Brian Affronti, William Skidmore, myself, Stephen Lightfoot and a couple of other people, we all played, drank all day and went swimming in Casey Sheehan's pool. And that day Skidmore told me that Nick Markowitz was dead." (This was related by Hoyt when he was trying to distance himself from any part of the murder, pretending this was the first time he ever had confirmation that Nick was dead.)

"Skidmore said that Nick had been murdered. At that point things started to click together for me, what with Jack Hollywood, Jesse acting the way he was, and Casey not being surprised when I told him about my conversation with Jack Hollywood. Things just started coming together that Jesse Hollywood was involved."

For journalists, law enforcement and everyone else looking at the events of the days after August 9, it became a maze of contradicting stories. Obviously, some people were lying, but the trick was to try and discern who was lying and who was telling the truth. Or at least parts of the truth.

What had looked like a good enough grave for Nick in the dark early-morning hours of August 9 was in fact a very slipshod affair. A few shovelfuls of dirt and branches on his body were not enough to keep away insects and flies from congregating at the area. On August 12, three days after Nick had been killed and buried, a group of hikers went up to the Lizard's Mouth area. One of the hikers was twenty-six-year-old Darla Gacek.

It was the first time Gacek had ever been there, and she and the others scrambled around the unusual rock formations and admired the views of the city of Santa Barbara and the Pacific Ocean in the distance. Gacek was a resident of Santa Barbara who managed a dental office while studying philosophy and history at Santa Barbara City College. She and the others were amidst the rocks when they heard what they thought was the buzzing of bees. Going to investigate, they saw that it wasn't bees but rather hundreds of flies buzzing around something that was dead.

Gacek recalled, "At first, we thought it was a dead raccoon or deer. We went there and kicked the sand [off of it] and uncovered blue jeans and part of a T-shirt. Then we knew it was a body. The whole time we were hoping it wasn't a kid."

Even though the stench was awful on that warm day, Gacek guarded the body while one of the hikers went for help. That hiker came upon a group of student filmmakers in the area and borrowed a cell phone from them. Then he called 911.

About being there with the body, Gacek recalled, "I was surprisingly calm. You'd think that you would freak out with a situation like that. We couldn't see a face or hands, so we hadn't really seen anything to humanize it."

Interestingly enough, Gacek knew almost immediately that the body was put there because of a murder. She said later, "This was not an accident." She knew not to touch the body or disturb the area, because her brother was a police officer in Downey and she watched television crime shows, such as *NYPD Blue.*

Gacek said later, "We knew we had a crime scene on our hands and we had already messed with things a little bit. We didn't want to make it any harder on the police. And there were lots of kids hiking in that area that day, and I didn't really want a little kid to see that."

Gacek would also recall that as she stood guard over the body, she saw families hiking, heard the filmmakers playing music and saw butterflies flitting around. It should have been a beautiful summer day in the Santa Ynez Mountains. Instead, she was standing watch over a human body, which smelled terrible in the summer heat, with a myriad of flies buzzing around. She recalled, "It was totally surreal. It was the weirdest thing. I was thinking, 'The world is so beautiful, but yet there's this body that someone put here.'"

According to one account later, one of the film students actually went over and videotaped Nick in his grave. This person supposedly did that so that he could hand it over to law enforcement to show what he had viewed that day up near Lizard's Mouth.

What had started as a supposedly one-hour hike, at around 10:30 A.M., turned into an all-day ordeal for Darla Gacek and her friends as they answered questions of Santa Barbara County Sheriff's Department (SBCSD) detectives who arrived on the scene. The first deputy didn't even arrive at the remote location until two hours after the initial call to the sheriff's office. It would be another two hours before detectives arrived on the scene. Finally as Gacek and her friends drove home, she and the others tried to make light of the situation, because it was, in fact, "scary and creepy," as she put it. She hoped the victim would turn out to be a "bad person," and not some kid. "Maybe someone who got what they deserved." In the end it wouldn't be that way at all. Nick Markowitz did not deserve the fate he received.

Among the detectives on the case was David Danielson, who'd been a detective for four years on the force. Working with Detective Galante, he booked into evidence all the bullets, cartridge casings, live cartridges and the gun into evidence. The "projectiles"—the actual bullets that had been fired—were 9mm in caliber. Danielson noted, "All of those were in a very short distance of the actual grave site." Of cartridge casings found near the grave site, nine were recovered on the first day of investigation. Two unspent bullets were still found within the TEC-9 semiautomatic pistol. The breech area of the gun was full of dirt, and there was one unfired live round in the chamber. Danielson noted, "Another round was jammed up in the breech area." Eventually the TEC-9 was delivered to the Department of Justice (DOJ) criminalists in Goleta, California, near Santa Barbara.

Time and the elements had not been kind to Nick. His eyes, nose and wounds were filled with the larvae of insects, and the summer heat did not help any. It took two days for Santa Barbara homicide detectives to even figure out who he was. They were aided in this by a fingerprint that matched Nick's arrest record for when he had been busted with marijuana.

* * *

While the detectives were at work, Casey Sheehan had another conversation with Ryan Hoyt, on Sunday, August 13, about the events that had occurred in Santa Barbara in the previous week. As Sheehan recalled, "We were just talking on the way out to see my father at the beach in Malibu, and Ryan seemed kind of scared. He just kind of brought up, 'We took care of Nick.' He said, 'We took him to a ditch and shot him and put a bush over him.'"

Hoyt added that Jesse Rugge had been with him at the time, though Hoyt didn't say who had actually pulled the trigger of the murder weapon. Sheehan and Hoyt spent the afternoon at Sheehan's father's house in Malibu. On the drive home Hoyt voiced his concerns with Sheehan about whether he should stick around the area or leave.

Hoyt would later have a different story about this day. He said, "Casey and I went to Malibu to his father's house. On the way there I told Casey what Skidmore had told me the night before. We talked about the gist of it, but I never mentioned details about any murder to Casey."

On Monday, August 14, Santa Barbara detectives drove to West Hills and pulled up near the Markowitz home a short time after 6:00 A.M. Jeff peeked out the window and told Susan that men in dark suits were at the door. He recalled later that even though they were in a daze, they gave the detectives Nick's eleventh-grade portrait photo. The detectives showed Jeff a distinctive belt buckle, and Jeff said it was Nick's. They showed him a ring, and Jeff said, "On my sixteenth birthday it was given to me by my parents. On Benjamin's birthday I gave it to him, and when Nicholas was bar mitzvahed, Ben gave it to him. Nick wore it constantly. He never took it off."

Susan would later say that the moment the detectives came to the door, she knew that Nick was gone. For all intents and purposes, the life she had lived up to that point was also gone.

Even before Nick's body was found, Jesse James Hollywood had gone down to Palm Springs with his mother, Laurie, in his new Lincoln. It would be a while before all the details came out about this, but Jack Hollywood had some things to say about this set of days. Jack said later, "I knew that Laurie and Jesse were going to go out to lunch, and she called me and said that she was going to ride there with him. She wanted to talk to him because she had seen that he was pretty shook-up. She had talked to him on the phone previously and she knew that something was up. I still believed there was a kid missing, but I had not told her.

"Jesse drove her there in a car he had just leased. A brand-new Lincoln LS. He leased it from a dealership where a person I know, named Chris, worked. Jesse went to Palm Springs because his girlfriend Michelle was staying there. He was staying with his girlfriend, who was at some modeling convention or something. He had lunch with Laurie and dropped her off at a hotel, and then I came and picked her up. We stayed overnight and then I drove her home. I didn't see Jesse when I was up there. Laurie and I left at six in the morning, because we have another son that we had to come home to. So I guess Jesse wanted to spend some time with his girlfriend, and I didn't track them down."

As to why Jack didn't stay in the hotel where his son was staying, he later said, "I think it was booked. And Jesse was just staying in the room that Michelle already had." Jack said he phoned that room while he was there, but no one answered the phone. (Many law enforcement officers later believed that Jack had actually seen Jesse in Palm Springs, or at least had spoken to him by phone there. They also believed Jack was helping Jesse to escape the area at that point and that he knew that Jesse had helped plan the murder of Nick Markowitz.)

On August 14, Ryan Hoyt still did not seem overly concerned, even though he knew that more and more people were aware of Nick's death. Ryan said later, "I had met a female on my birthday, and I went out with her. We wound up back at Casey Sheehan's house on Monday, the fourteenth. The next day I hung out with my brother most of the day."

On August 15, a short article about the dead boy named Nick Markowitz was finally in the *Santa Barbara News-Press*. One of the people reading the article that day was Natasha Adams and she saw a photo of the boy she had known as Nick at Rugge's home. Natasha was so shocked by this sudden revelation, she burst into tears. Graham Pressley had obviously lied to her about Nick Markowitz making it home safely from the motel. She soon phoned Jesse Rugge and he told her, "It's not what you think!"

Not to be put off, Natasha headed to Rugge's house and confronted him there. Rugge wasn't wearing a shirt or T-shirt at the moment, and she recalled, "I could see his heart beating through his chest."

Natasha was no fool, and she knew she had been spending two days with a boy who had been murdered after she and Kelly left the Lemon Tree Inn. Natasha went to the attorney's office, where her mother worked, and told a lawyer there what she knew. Before going to the authorities, the lawyer drew up an immunity statement for Natasha and presented it to the Santa Barbara District Attorney's (DA) Office. The DA's office got in touch with law enforcement, and a grant of immunity was given to Natasha Adams to see what she could tell them. In fact, she could tell plenty, and at 4:00 P.M., August 15, 2000, she was sitting down with Santa Barbara homicide detectives giving dates, places, addresses and names. The names included Graham Pressley, Jesse Rugge, and Jesse James Hollywood.

7

ROUNDUP

Because of things that Natasha Adams said, Graham Pressley was brought in for questioning by Santa Barbara detectives on the evening of August 15, 2000. Pressley told SBCSD detective Cornell that at the Lemon Tree Inn he had asked Ryan Hoyt and Jesse Rugge for a ride home in the early-morning hours of August 9, 2000. According to Pressley, those two had taken him and Nick Markowitz up to West Camino Cielo Road and told him to wait in the car. Then Rugge and Hoyt escorted Nick up a trail into the brush and hills. Pressley said he waited in the car for about fifteen minutes, at which time he heard a rapid series of gunshots. When Rugge and Hoyt came back down the trail, Nick was not with them. They then drove Pressley back to the Lemon Tree Inn without saying anything about what had happened. Pressley denied being at a grave site or digging a grave.

Graham's dad was with him during the interview, but detectives thought that Graham was withholding information and might be nervous discussing certain details in front of his father. Detective Bruce Cornell and Detective Legault told Charles Pressley about their concerns, and after a discussion he agreed to wait outside the interview room but could return at any time. The interview continued with Charles watching and listening to the rest of the interview on a television monitor from an observation booth.

A lot of the things Graham said just didn't add up, and a later police report stated: *By the end of the evening, detectives offered Mr. Graham Pressley a polygraph because they had two concerns. One concern, was that he was present at the time and location of the killing. The other was that Jesse James Hollywood was the mastermind of the plot to execute Nick Markowitz, and had been present in Santa Barbara when it happened.* Whether they surmised this from what they'd learned from Graham Pressley or heard from Natasha Adams, the report didn't state.

Graham told his father and the detectives he would pass a polygraph test based on those two questions and he wanted to take a test. It was agreed Graham would return the next morning to take the polygraph exam.

On the morning of August 16, Graham Pressley did return to the Santa Barbara County Sheriff's Department, along with his mother, Christina, to take the polygraph test. In the presence of his mother, Graham waived his Miranda rights, but he wanted his mother to be with him during the exam. Graham was told that polygraphs were taken without anyone else being present, since other people in the room could distract the subject. Graham agreed to take the exam without his mother being there.

Polygrapher Wayne Smith came into the room and explained the process to Graham and told him the questions that would be asked. One of the questions would be whether Graham had dug the grave up near the Lizard's Mouth. Graham had previously denied having been to that location at all, but for some reason now, he told Smith that he had been there, and that, in fact he had dug a grave. Because of this admission, the polygraph test was canceled, and Graham was returned to the interview room, along with his mother.

According to another police report about this situation: *Mr. Pressley initially asked for his mother, and then changed his mind and elected to proceed without her. During the interview he told detectives that he had actually taken two trips up to West Camino Cielo. He told detectives that Hoyt and Rugge knew of the area called Lizard's Mouth, but did not know how to get there. Pressley knew that area and agreed to take Hoyt there, and he and Hoyt brought shovels and dug a shallow grave.* Pressley stressed that he had been forced to dig a grave on Hoyt's orders, and Hoyt had a gun.

The report went on to say that after digging the grave, Hoyt and Pressley returned to the Lemon Tree Inn. They were there for about twenty minutes; then Hoyt, Rugge, Nick Markowitz and Pressley all returned up to West Camino Cielo Road. Pressley again gave directions as Hoyt drove, until he parked the vehicle near the trailhead. Pressley said that Rugge was the front passenger, and he and Nick were in the back.

Graham declared that he did not return up the trail with the others, but only waited in the car. After twenty to twenty-five minutes, he heard gunfire, and about twenty-five minutes after that, Rugge and Hoyt returned to the car, minus Nick Markowitz. Once Rugge and Hoyt were back at the car, Hoyt drove away quickly and commented that this had been his first killing, and he had no idea that Nick Markowitz would go so quickly. According to Pressley, Rugge told him not to tell anybody.

In light of Graham Pressley's statements, and those of Natasha Adams, detectives started fanning out across Santa Barbara and Los Angeles Counties. Jesse Rugge was soon arrested on August 16, and was tackled by police and pushed to the ground. Things were even more dramatic at William Skidmore's arrest, around 4:30 P.M. on August 16. A Los

Angeles SWAT team surrounded Skidmore's residence, where he lived with his parents, in Simi Valley. A telephone call was placed by a negotiator into the house, and Skidmore eventually surrendered peacefully. One of the neighbors told a reporter at the scene, "We're freaked out! Very scared!" Another neighbor called the Skidmore family, "The perfect family." Other neighbors were less flattering about Will Skidmore. One said that he was a troublemaker and malcontent.

One of the first people involved in the initial abduction of Nick Markowitz to really start spilling everything he knew was William Skidmore. Skidmore sat down with the Santa Barbara sheriff's lieutenant Drew Standley and sheriff's detective Bruce Cornell. Cornell started things off by saying to Skidmore, "You look familiar." Skidmore replied, "I might have seen you before." Then Cornell asked him if he knew why he had been arrested, and Skidmore replied, "Suspicion of murder—that's all they told me."

Cornell corrected him, "Kidnapping and suspicion of murder, and the murder aspect of it, I don't think you went out and shot or killed anybody."

"No."

"Okay, I know you didn't, but some things that they're implicating you in, well, that's why we have the murder charge there. I don't know you other than what I've heard over the last three or four days, so I want to read you your rights." Cornell read Skidmore his rights, and then asked, "You've been arrested a few times?"

"Yeah," Skidmore replied.

Cornell laughed at Skidmore's expression, then said, "A lot?"

"Not too many times. Just a coupla months ago, I was arrested for a parole violation."

"Well, I just wanna see what I can do. See where we can

get to on this. So you wanna talk to me about this, so we can get down to what's going on here?"

Skidmore laughed nervously and replied, "I really don't know much. I heard what happened and I didn't get on with his older brother and—"

"Whose older brother?"

"Nick's. The rumor was going around that my buddy beat him up or took his brother, and that I took him, too."

"Who's your buddy?"

"Huh, my buddy Jesse."

"You talking about Jesse Holiday." (Cornell had the last name wrong at this point.)

"Yeah."

"Hollywood. I call him Holiday every time," Cornell responded.

"Yeah. I guess guys beat up Nick's brother a coupla nights ago."

"Who beat up his older brother a couple of nights ago?"

"A coupla older guys. Some Valley guys. I guess they beat Ben up at a Friday's (T.G.I. Friday's). Some peckerwoods and some other guys."

Cornell asked, "Henry Chang, maybe?"

Skidmore said, "Yeah. I know a lot of people don't like him." (He meant Ben.)

Cornell wanted to know if Skidmore knew what had happened to Nick, and Skidmore replied, "Yeah, sure. My girlfriend told me. I saw the newspaper."

Cornell responded, "Well, a lot of things have been goin' on. We've been doing a lot of investigation and we haven't stopped for a week now. You know we've come up with a lot of information. I wouldn't have you here if I didn't have enough to get to have you here, okay. Like I said, I don't think you killed anybody, so I don't want you to think that, but I do want you to understand [about the] kidnapping. Now from what I've been told, the kidnapping was a real violent kidnapping."

"I know."

"I want you to be real honest about it. Because if you lie about things, you know how that works."

Skidmore said that he did know.

Cornell added, "If you lie, it just makes you look like you're more involved than you really are. I think your involvement was picking up the kid off the street and taking him up to Santa Barbara."

Skidmore agreed. "That's pretty much the way it was. The only involvement was when he got in the van. He didn't say nothin'. In the van he gave us some bud."

Cornell was surprised by this and said, "Oh, really!"

"Yeah, he gave me some pills, and then I left that night 'cause we got drunk at Fiesta and Nick was drinking a little with us. And then I left that night and never went back."

Cornell asked, "He was up at Fiesta in Santa Barbara? Was that on a Sunday night?"

"One of those days. We went up in the middle of the day, and we saw him walkin', and I guess his older brother had bashed out my friend's windows. So we were gonna go over there to his parents' house and see if Ben was there, but we saw his younger brother, and we pulled up. We said, 'Hey, what's up? Get in the van!' He's like why? 'We're gonna talk to ya,' we said. So he jumps in the van, and we talked with him for a little bit. He said, 'I've got some drugs.' We all started smoking weed with him, and we went up there (to Santa Barbara). Then I ended up going home, and I don't know . . . I guess he stayed up there."

Cornell replied, "Yeah, he ended up getting killed. So it's kind of nasty stuff. Okay, when you say you saw your friend, you were driving around lookin' for Ben? Who was your friend? Was that Jesse?"

"Yeah, Jesse. We were just gonna go for Ben and—"

"So what happened? Why did it go wrong?"

Skidmore replied, "I have no clue."

Cornell asked where they had been when they picked

Nick up, and Skidmore replied, "It was right off Sati. It was like Saticoy where it turns to Ingomar, and right by the Apple Market. It was like a block from there." Then Skidmore laughed and said, "He came willingly."

Cornell replied, "He really didn't want to be there, though."

Skidmore laughed again and said, "He jumped in."

"So you were up by Saticoy and Ingomar, and you were gonna go over to Ben's friend's house?"

Skidmore corrected him and replied, "Ben's parents' house. And we saw Ben's brother walking, so we pulled over."

Cornell wanted to know who was in the vehicle with Skidmore, and he said that Jesse Hollywood and one other guy had been with him. Asked who the other guy was, Skidmore responded that it was "Jesse Rugge." Skidmore added that they had been in a rental van because Jesse Hollywood had been moving that day. (He didn't say anything about it being John Roberts's van.)

Cornell asked who else had been involved in all of this, or had seen anything of Nick, and Skidmore replied that his friend Brian Affronti had seen Nick. Then Skidmore added, "We picked him (Affronti) up on the way and he came in the van."

"So you went up there and picked Nick up. Did you go straight to Fiesta after you picked him up, or did you take him anywhere else?"

"Uh, we went by my house 'cause I had to take my insulin, 'cause I'm diabetic and I thought we were gonna stay out for the night. I did my shot for the day and then we just headed up there."

"You stay up there overnight?"

"Nah. We came . . . well, we started drinking Tanqueray, and it's like a strong sort of drink. And we ended up coming back that night . . . me and Jesse Hollywood and Brian."

Cornell wanted to know how long they had been at

Skidmore's house, and he answered they were only there for about two minutes while he gave himself a shot for diabetes. He also said that neither Nick nor any of the others went into the residence with him. They just stayed in the van. Skidmore said after that "we went to one of Jesse Rugge's friend's houses."

"Do you know who that was?"

"It was, like, the first time I ever met him. He was a Mexican guy. He had a little hair on his chin."(It was probably Emilio Jerez or Gabriel Ibarra.)

Cornell then asked, "Was Nick nervous about things?"

"Oh, yeah."

"He say anything about it?"

"No, he just said, 'Oh, my!' 'cause Jesse Hollywood asked him . . . well, about the broken window, and he (Nick) said his parents would pay for it. And he and Jesse were talking about that."

"Okay, so you leave Nick at his (Rugge's) friend's house? How long did you stay there?"

"About an hour and a half," Skidmore replied.

"Get buzzed?"

"Yeah."

Some of this didn't add up and Cornell said, "You dropped Brian Affronti off at his house?"

"Um, you mean Jesse Rugge? We left him in Santa Barbara and we came back and dropped Brian off at his house, and then I went back to Jesse Hollywood's house and spent the night there with my girlfriend. Well, she almost spent the night. She stayed a little bit and left."

"Okay, so when you left Nick at this guy's house, what'd you tell this guy?"

"Told him (Rugge) to hold Nick. Just hold him, because his brother owed money, and just hold him there."

"Jesse Hollywood was telling this?" Cornell asked.

"Yes."

"Did he say how long to hold him there?"

"No."

"Say he'd come back for him later?"

"Yeah, he'd be back." Then Skidmore asked, "Have they taken anybody else into custody for this, or am I the only one?"

Cornell responded, "We're getting everybody. We want to find out what happened. Did you guys tell Nick, 'Hey, everything is gonna be okay. All we want to do is get in touch with your brother'?"

"I was expecting nothing like what happened!"

"Yeah. I think a lot of people were. I think it was one of those things that . . ." (Cornell did not want to finish this sentence, but rather let Skidmore explain things at his own pace.) "What did Hollywood tell Jesse Rugge?"

"Just told him, 'Buddy, do you have any friends just to watch him for a little bit?' And Rugge said yeah."

Cornell wanted to know if Rugge or anyone was supposed to be paid $2,500 for holding or killing Nick. Skidmore said that he didn't know anything about that, and added that he never was offered any money.

Then Cornell asked if Skidmore didn't like Ben. This brought a surprise response from Skidmore. "I used to be good friends with him. I used to live with him."

"You did?"

"Yeah, sort of. He used to live on Ventura, out in the Valley, and I used to stay there every night, and we used to do a lot of drugs together."

"That was back when he was selling through Jesse Hollywood?"

"Yeah, that's when he was. He jacked them, five or six different guys, for, like, ten thousand dollars. A lot of people." (It was not clear who these people were.)

Cornell asked if Ben had stolen things out of Jesse Hollywood's house, and Skidmore answered that he didn't know. Cornell also wondered if Ben had stolen some dope from Hollywood, and Skidmore said, "Maybe some dope. 'Cause he stole from everybody, even his good friends. That happened a couple of months ago and I guess Ben owed Jesse, and Jesse went to the place where Ben's girlfriend worked and got a free meal. He said to take it off the tab. And Ben said, 'Oh, fuck you! I'm gonna come over there and sweat you. And I'm gonna beat your ass and shoot you! I'm gonna do this and that.' And then he came over to Jesse's house with an ax and he axed out the front windows, about three weeks ago. Then he left a voice mail, 'Yeah, buddy. This is Li'l Shooter.' He used his own gang name."

Cornell said, "So Jesse was a little bit upset with Ben for damaging his house. He likes his house a lot, doesn't he?"

"Yeah."

"He likes his cars, too. I hear he's got some pretty nice cars."

"Yeah. He's got a nice car."

"He doesn't even work, does he?" Cornell questioned.

"Uh, he does flooring for a little bit, off and on."

"More makin' money off of other things?"

Skidmore only laughed at that, knowing that the answer was yes.

Cornell wanted to know where Nick had been taken after being at Hoeflinger's house, and Skidmore responded, "That's where you got me."

"You don't know at all?"

"Nah."

"Okay, so when's the last time you talked to Jesse Hollywood?"

"Might have been yesterday."

"Where was that?"

"At my house."

"Do you know where he's at now?"

"I have no clue. He doesn't return pages." Skidmore laughed.

"Think he knows what's going on?"

"You might have a better clue than me."

Cornell wanted to know if Hollywood had told Skidmore anything about Nick on the previous day, and Skidmore said that he hadn't. Then Cornell wondered if Skidmore had asked Hollywood why Nick had been killed, and added, "To be honest with you, I don't think you're the bad guy. Jesse had this done, that's why we're after Jesse. I mean, you're in trouble for this, but I'm after Jesse. Jesse put . . . well, we know who the guy is that did the shooting. I mean, if he took Ben out and shot him, that's between those two, because they did something to each other. But they took a fifteen-year-old boy and executed him, and that's wrong."

"Yes."

Once again Cornell wanted to know what Jesse Holly-wood had spoken about to Skidmore. Skidmore said that Hollywood hadn't said much. In fact, Hollywood had originally told Skidmore a different story about what had happened to Nick, and had said he was still alive. Skidmore's girlfriend, however, had shown Skidmore a newspaper article about Nick being dead, so he knew Hollywood was lying.

"Did you ask him about it?" Cornell wanted to know.

"When Jesse came over, I said, 'Yeah, man, I seen it in the newspaper.' And he said, 'I'm outta here!' and just left. Just left his cigarette pack right on my table in the front of my house. I think he was with his girlfriend. He just scatted."

Cornell wanted to know what Hollywood's girlfriend was named, and Skidmore told him Michelle, but he didn't know her last name. Cornell asked if Michelle lived with Hollywood, and Skidmore said that she lived with her parents up in a gated community in Calabasas.

This was interesting to Cornell, who told Skidmore that he'd heard Jesse James Hollywood had another house in Calabasas, and might be hiding out there. Skidmore replied that he didn't think Hollywood had another home there, and that someone had probably mixed up Hollywood's girlfriend's house as being another home that Jesse owned. To this, Cornell responded, "That's good to know. Because if that is his girlfriend's house, and we go barreling in there . . . well, it's nice to know that." Skidmore laughed about that and agreed.

Cornell added, "There might be some people in there to be careful with. You know, you're friends with a guy that did this, and Jesse's just as bad as the guy who shot Nick. Can you imagine having a fifteen-year-old . . . walk him out to the boonies when the kid has knowledge of what's goin' on, and then to shoot him?"

All Skidmore said was "No."

"I mean, would your friend do that, just 'cause he works for Jesse Hollywood? I mean, I don't understand that. Did you talk to him about it?" (Cornell was referring to Ryan Hoyt in these suppositions.)

"Not really."

"What did you say to him about it?"

"I couldn't believe it happened."

"Do you know where he's at?" (Cornell again meant Hoyt, who had not yet been apprehended when Skidmore's interview began.)

"Um, no."

"Did he make any money off this?"

"I don't know if it cleared a debt or something," Skidmore answered.

"Did he tell ya it cleared a debt?"

"Uh-huh."

"Tell how much?"

"No."

"Do you know where he's at?"

"No."

"When he (Hoyt) said to you, Jesse told him to do it, did Jesse tell him how to do it?"

"No, he just told him find a spot."

"Why did Hollywood say he had to do it?"

"Um, 'cause they didn't trust Nick if they let him go," Skidmore replied.

"They thought he might snitch?"

"That was the reason."

"You know, I can see where a guy that does that—I can see him bragging about how he did it."

Skidmore replied, "The word got around."

Cornell asked how Hoyt had killed Nick, and Skidmore told him, "I guess he walked him up the hill, got him off a trail, took him out, told him that he was gonna give him to somebody else, or something like that. Brought him up there, and I guess hit him with a shovel and then shot him in the hole that he dug prior to that."

Cornell wondered if the shooter said what the shovel blow had done to Nick, but Skidmore said that hadn't come up. Cornell wanted to know if the guys up at Lizard's Mouth had buried Nick or just had left him in the hole. Skidmore said that they'd buried him.

Cornell made more of a statement than a question when he said, "It was Jesse's gun, wasn't it?" (Cornell was referring to Hollywood.)

"I guess he had two or three guns."

"I think he (the shooter) told you how he did it, because I think he probably showed you how the gun went. From that, you probably know which gun it was. Which gun do you think he used?"

"I think he probably used the TEC or the AR (assault rifle)."

"What's a TEC?"

"TEC-9."

"Did he tell you how it went? How the bullets hit the body?"

"Nah. Though I think he said Nick was lying in the hole already when he shot him. Something like that."

"Tell you who was with him?"

"No."

"Do you know who was with him?"

"No."

"A couple of scared people. I think they probably crapped their pants," Cornell observed.

"Yeah."

"You know, one of them threw up. So what did you think when he was telling you that? Do you think he was bragging about it?"

"Could have been, yeah," Skidmore agreed.

"Did he tell you how many times he's done this before?"

"Nah, he's never done it before."

Cornell wanted to know what had happened after Nick was dead, and Skidmore heard that they'd just left Santa Barbara. Asked where they went, Skidmore said they went home. Cornell asked how many days after the killing it was before he saw the shooter again, and Skidmore replied, "A couple of days."

"After you saw the newspaper?"

"I think it was two days ago. I saw him the day before that. I seen him a couple of times and just hung out."

"But before you saw the newspapers, what did you start talking about? Did he tell you anything before that?"

"Right before, but I didn't believe him. I mean, before that, he told me what happened, but he gave me a little story about it. It was set up in the mountains."

Cornell asked if the "gunman" said that he'd met Rugge, Nick and others in downtown Santa Barbara. Skidmore said that he hadn't heard that, and that Hoyt hadn't given much in the way of details about where they met or where in the mountains the killing had taken place, other than it was a quiet area.

Cornell inquired, "He didn't know that area, did he?"

"I don't think so."

"Did he tell you who showed him around?"

"It must have been one of the guys that was in Santa Barbara."

"He didn't tell you who?"

"No."

"Did he tell you how the others reacted?"

"He said someone threw up, but I think it was only two of them (at Lizard's Mouth). He said he was nervous, too."

"He tell you how the hole got dug?"

"Nah, I think it was dug earlier in the day."

"Did he bring those things to dig with, or what?"

"I don't know."

Cornell asked, "What happened to the gun?"

"I thought he buried it with him."

"Did he say what he did with his clothing or anything afterward?"

"Nah. I think he got new clothes."

When Cornell asked what kind of vehicle Hoyt drove up to the killing site, Skidmore said, "That's a good question. He might have gotten someone's car. Because the van, we already . . . well, Rugge got rid of it." (Actually, it had been taken back to John Roberts's residence.)

Cornell asked what kind of cars they had access to, and Skidmore said they had access to a white van and a rental car from a Van Nuys Mercedes dealership because Hollywood's Mercedes was in the shop. Skidmore also said that Hollywood might have access to his girlfriend's car, which was a blue BMW. Then Skidmore added that his friend Casey Sheehan had an older red Honda Accord. Skidmore said that Casey Sheehan lived in Reseda, not far from the San Fernando Mission, and was a friend of Jesse Hollywood's. Cornell wondered if Hollywood might have used that car, and Skidmore said that he might have.

Back to Hoyt, Cornell wanted to know if he'd said anything to Nick before shooting him, and Skidmore didn't know. Skidmore continued that "his friend" (meaning Hoyt) had said Nick was scared as they took him up the trail toward the Lizard's Mouth. Cornell then said, "You haven't asked Jesse Hollywood much about this, have you?"

"No."

"Can I ask you a question without getting you riled up? Are you afraid of Jesse Hollywood?"

"Yeah . . . no, I'm not afraid of him, but . . ." Skidmore didn't complete his thought.

"Afraid he could do some damage to you?"

"Yeah."

"It seems like a lot of people are afraid of him. Does he really have (inaudible word)? I've never talked to the guy."

"He's a nice guy. Just, ah . . ."

"Just doesn't take things from too many people."

"Yeah, I could beat him up, but he'd probably have a gun."

"He'd shoot ya. Okay, I know the name of this guy who killed Nick. I haven't asked you the name of the guy because I'd really rather you just say it. There's a lot going on here, and I need you to tell what it is."

This brought a question from Skidmore: "Is it Ryan?"

"What's Ryan's last name?"

"Hoyt," Skidmore replied. (He had not said Ryan's last name until this point.)

"And he's the guy who shot Nick?"

"Yeah. Uh, have my parents been contacted yet?"

"Your mom's here."

"Oh."

Cornell said that she was being talked to by detectives and they needed to find out what she knew. He asked if Skidmore had told her anything, and he responded, "Not really, no."

"She know what happened that night?"

"No."

"She guess?"

"No."

At that point Cornell showed Skidmore some photographs and asked if he recognized anybody in the set of photographs. Skidmore said that he thought he knew the one at the bottom left, and said it looked like Ryan Hoyt. Shown another set of photos, Skidmore said that Jesse James Hollywood was at the middle bottom. Viewing another set, Skidmore said, "That's me at the bottom right"; then he laughed.

Cornell said, "The reason I'm asking you is—you see how we picked you up?"

"Yeah."

"I mean, this was dangerous stuff. I'm glad you just walked out like that." (Cornell meant when Skidmore was arrested.)

"I didn't know what was happening. I thought at first I was in violation of probation."

Cornell laughed at that and said they wouldn't have sent a SWAT team in to get him on a probation violation. Then he added, "You know you were described to me by some people as kind of crazy, but you seem okay to me." Then Cornell asked, "This didn't have anything with Nick being Jewish, did it?"

"No, no! That's the first time I ever heard that."

"So you know where Hoyt is at?"

"I got a call the other day. He wanted to see what I was doin', me and my girlfriend, and I just told him we weren't doin' much. I told him to page me later."

"What's his page number?"

"I have it at home. I just wrote it down today."

Cornell wanted to know if Skidmore's mom could get to that pager number, and Skidmore said he'd written the pager number down in a phone book at home. He had written it in the *H* section of the book.

Cornell next wondered if Skidmore knew where Jesse James Hollywood was. Skidmore said he knew his pager number, but not where Hollywood was at the present time. Skidmore gave Cornell the pager number and Hollywood's cell phone number.

Cornell said that he appreciated Skidmore being honest. At this point, for some reason, Skidmore said, "My aunt went to school with Nick's father twenty years ago and did gymnastics with him."

Cornell replied, "You know that it didn't just kill Nick, they killed the family. If you lose a kid like that, you never are the same. You're never happy, so you know that these guys need to go away. 'Cause if a guy like Ryan can go out and shoot a fifteen-year-old, he can go out and shoot anybody. That's why I'm kinda worried about him. I'd like to find out where he's at so we can be a little more controlled and not have some officer stop him on the street and get killed."

Skidmore said that he understood, and Cornell added, "I know you wouldn't want Ryan to get killed. I don't like to see people get killed."

Skidmore said, "He has no weapon."

Cornell was surprised by that and said, "What did he do with it?"

Skidmore said, "I thought he said they buried it with Nick."

Cornell wondered if Hoyt might have an assault rifle, but Skidmore said that the AR-15 belonged to Jesse Hollywood. Realizing that Hollywood seemed to own all the guns, Cornell asked, "Did Jesse Hollywood tell him to do it?"

Skidmore replied, "They just told me what happened and they got rid of the little gun. That's the only gun I know about."

Cornell wanted to know where Hollywood was when the killing took place, and Skidmore responded, "He came back with me when I came back that night." (Skidmore, at that point, was speaking about August 6, not the early-morning hours of August 9, when Hollywood was at Michelle Lasher's parents' house.) "I came back and slept at his house. The next day I got picked up by my mom. I went back to my house and I didn't talk to him for two days. I think maybe three days. And he showed up at my house with his new car."

Cornell asked if Skidmore had heard anything about a Colorado connection concerning Jesse James Hollywood, and Skidmore said that Jesse Hollywood used to live there. Asked if Hollywood might go back there now, Skidmore laughed and said, "Probably."

Cornell told Skidmore, "I don't know what's gonna happen, but like I said, I think your involvement ended when you took Nick up there to Santa Barbara. I don't think you really took him up there to be shot or anything. And I know what you've been saying here is the truth because everybody else is telling the same thing." (Everybody else, at that point, equaled Graham Pressley and Kelly Carpenter.) "Whether you're leaving some things out about the van, or if you guys picked on Nick or treated him a little bit bad. Did Jesse Hollywood treat him bad, a little bit, on the way up there?"

Skidmore said that Hollywood had been yelling at Nick, and Cornell wanted to know what Hollywood had been yelling. Skidmore said, "'Your fucking brother owes me money!' and Nick would say, 'Oh, yeah, but my parents will pay.' And Jesse said, 'No, your parents won't give me shit!' Just stuff like that."

"Jesse never called Ben?"

"No."

Cornell asked,"Then why take Nick if he didn't call Ben or anything?"

"Yeah, that's what I was wondering, 'cause I thought they were just gonna—well, he was gonna call him and say, 'Give me my money or we're gonna beat up your brother.' Then they shot him." Skidmore laughed nervously.

Cornell replied, "My lieutenant sometimes says, 'Why didn't you ask him these questions?' and, damn, I knew I should have asked this or that certain question. So, is there something I'm not getting here that's important—I mean, you gave me all the information, but is there something you didn't give me that I didn't ask? It'd be nice so I don't have to worry about my lieutenant asking if I asked you."

Skidmore replied, "I can't think of anything. You pretty much asked everything."

Cornell did have more questions, however, and asked what color the van was that they had been in. Skidmore said that it was white. Asked if he knew what rental company it had come from, Skidmore said that he didn't know. As to how old the van was, Skidmore answered that it was an older model, not a minivan. He called it a "gardener's van."

Cornell wanted to know what had occurred between Ryan Hoyt and Jesse Hollywood after Nick was killed. Skidmore said, "He just came back and he said his debt was cleared."

At that point there was a knock at the door and Lieutenant Drew Standley popped his head in and said, "Hi." There was a brief conversation between the two detectives and then Standley left. Cornell turned to Skidmore and said, "Remember I told you my lieutenant may ask me questions, and he was right there listening and asked me a bunch of questions." Skidmore responded by laughing.

Cornell started asking questions that Standley had posed. "What is Brian Affronti's pager number?" Skidmore didn't know that, but he gave him Affronti's cell phone number. Cornell wanted to know what kind of car Jesse Hollywood had now. Skidmore thought it was a silver Lincoln Town Car. Cornell asked what had started everything in the first place, and Skidmore replied, "Ben just broke the windows. He just came up to Jesse [Hollywood's house], and me and Jesse were sleeping right on the floor in the living room, 'cause his furniture had already been moved out, and the windows were just bashed right in on us. We didn't think it was Ben at the time, but then he called later that night and left a message, saying, 'What's up?' We knew his voice. And he was all like, 'This is Li'l Shooter.' And he's all, 'Yeah, motherfucker!'"

Cornell wanted to know if anyone else was involved that the police didn't know about at the present time. Skidmore said, "No. Well, Brian. I called him and told him what happened and he was just 'Oh, shit! I can't believe that!' He was scared, too."

Lieutenant Standley came in at that point and began to ask Skidmore questions directly. Standley said, "It's kind of hard to believe all of this started out as one thing and it kind of ended up as another. It all seemed to kind of overlap. When you guys got out of the van, there's this little discrepancy about what you're saying transpired and what we've learned from interviews that we did with some witnesses. Can you explain to me what you did when you got out of the van?"

Skidmore replied, "We got out, we just said to the kid, 'Get in the van.' Jesse Hollywood grabbed him by the back of the shirt and then Nick said, 'I'm getting in the van.' And he jumped right in."

Standley said, "Imagine—a couple of guys pull up. He's fifteen and scared. You said something about this van and someone moving. Who was moving?"

"Jesse Hollywood was moving. He moved all his stuff to storage. Right off Canoga and Roscoe, between DeSoto. There's a big storage place there. It was furniture from his house—the Cohasset house."

Standley wanted to know if Jesse Hollywood usually carried guns around with him, and Skidmore said that he didn't that often, unless he thought the place he was going might have an enemy with a gun there. Skidmore said that the guns were under a blanket in the van on the day of the kidnapping, but that no one had taken them out and shown them to Nick.

Standley replied, "Detective Cornell told me that you were saying that Hoyt admitted to doing it."

"Yeah."

"To killing Nick?"

"Yeah. So he had to have been the one to go back to Santa Barbara."

"Did he go alone or did Jesse Hollywood go, too?"

"I don't think Jesse Hollywood went, but there was somebody else there."

"And who do you think the somebody else was?"

"It could have been a couple of different people."

"Who do you think?"

"Ah, I don't know. It's hard to say," Skidmore replied.

"Come on. You've come this far."

"Couple of friends. I mean, it's hard to say. Jesse (Hollywood) has a couple of friends that would probably do it. It could have been one of the guys up in Santa Barbara."

Standley wanted to know how close Skidmore was to Jesse Rugge, and Skidmore said that he'd known him for a while and that he'd played sports with him. Standley continued, "All right. How did they get this fifteen-year-old kid all the way up in the mountains and on this hiking trail in the middle of nowhere?"

"You got me there. 'Cause they just told me they took him to a spot, and they were like, 'I don't think anybody's gonna find him for a while.'"

"Who else have you talked to about this?"

"I talked a little to Jesse Hollywood about it. He was like, 'Oh, man. It went bad. Don't say nothing!'"

"Who's responsible for all this?"

"When it first started, Jesse Hollywood. Then we went away from there, and I have no idea. I was there the first day, and that's all."

"You're responsible."

"Responsible for going over there to break windows and then that not happening," Skidmore said.

"Yeah, but you got Nick in the van. So you're somewhat responsible, right?"

"I don't know. If you consider me being there, then okay. But Nick and Jesse were right there smoking weed in the van, and me coming home and not knowing what happened the next couple of days, and then finding out what happened."

"Yeah, all right. So if Jesse Hollywood's the ringleader, he's more responsible, right?"

Skidmore laughed and said, "Yeah."

"So the initial plan was just to break windows, and not try to get Ben?"

"It was to break windows."

Wanting to know what other relatives Jesse Hollywood had in the area, Skidmore said that he had an aunt in Reseda or Saticoy. Asked if he knew Hollywood's girlfriend's last name, Skidmore said, "I don't know. She has a weird last name."

"What's she look like?"

"She's short, has curly black hair. Real thin. She works, I think, at Nicky's Gymnastics. I think that's on Ventura in the Valley."

Wanting to know if Hoyt had a girlfriend, Skidmore said he didn't think so. Then Skidmore said that Hoyt had a brother in Tehachapi State Prison and he thought the guy was doing six years for armed robbery. As far as where Hoyt might be at the present time, Skidmore thought he might be at Casey Sheehan's house in Reseda.

Once again the question came up as to why Ryan Hoyt would shoot Nick to death. Skidmore said, "I don't know. It might have been to clear his debt. That's what I'm guessing, 'cause he owed Jesse money. Twelve hundred dollars."

"So you think he would do something cold-blooded like that to a kid?"

"You never know. You see people on the news doing bad stuff."

"He's your friend."

"If he was intoxicated or something."

Asked if Ryan Hoyt might still be in town, Skidmore said, "Maybe. I don't think Jesse Hollywood is, though. He probably went to Colorado. He had a lot of money. He said he could go to Puerto Rico if he wanted to, or Costa Rica."

"Was he scared?"

"He was yesterday, because he bolted out."

Then Skidmore asked, "Is my mom still here?"

"I think they took her back home. The warrant for you is no bail, so what that means you stay in jail until you go to court in a couple of days. Then they decide whether you should have bail or not. They'll have more information on the case by then."

"Who do I tell I'm diabetic? I take insulin."

"We'll do that in jail."

By August 16, Ryan Hoyt knew something was in the wind. Still, he did not make any concrete plans about leaving the area. Hoyt said later, "I made a phone call to speak with William Skidmore, but I reached his sister. She said that he'd been arrested. Then she told me to be careful. I was pretty shook-up. I started making phone calls and paged Casey Sheehan. He contacted me and told me he didn't want me at his house, but I went there, anyway.

"When Casey got home, we discussed the article that had been in the newspaper. While I was there, I got a page and it was an unfamiliar number. At first, I didn't think anything of it, but it got very repetitive, and it seemed that every time it stopped beeping, it beeped again. That's when I thought the police were trying to page me. I asked Casey if I could use his phone, but he said no, because he thought his phone was tapped. So I told him to take me to a pay phone."

Sheehan recalled of these events that "Hoyt phoned me, and I said, 'My house is hot.'" (He meant it was under surveillance.) "He came over to my place, and that's when I really, really found out what was going on. Ryan was very worried. He was scared. He kind of repeated himself, and said, 'We did something bad.' I called my aunt, and I called a cousin, because I felt that my car was involved in this murder. And when Ryan came over, he was getting pages—well, I believe the sheriff's office paged him quite a few times. The events that had occurred, [they] really started making sense now. Two and two was going to equal four. Earlier it wasn't equaling four."

Hoyt got Casey Sheehan to drive him to a phone booth down the street. Hoyt later would say that he was going there to phone law enforcement. Others believed he was going to the pay phone to try and make arrangements to flee the area. Whatever the circumstances, Sheehan drove him to a pay phone, and Hoyt barely stepped out of the vehicle before he was tackled by officers, pushed to the ground and hand-cuffed. Casey Sheehan was also taken into custody because detectives didn't know at the time how much he was impli-cated in everything that had transpired. At this point detec-tives were pulling in everyone even remotely involved in the case so that they could try and make some sense of what had occurred in the abduction and murder of Nick Markowitz.

8

"I'M DYING FOR SOMETHING SO STUPID!"

William Skidmore had been very cooperative with authorities during his questioning, but with Jesse Rugge, it was more like pulling teeth without an anesthetic. Santa Barbara sheriff's office sergeant Ken Reinstadler and detective Mike West spoke with Rugge in an interrogation room, and West said, "Ken is my sergeant. We just wanna talk about some activity that's been goin' on here in Santa Barbara during the past two weeks. That's the reason we're here. When deputies contacted you a little while ago, what did they tell you?"

Rugge answered, "When they tackled me, I didn't know what was goin' on. It freaked the hell out of me. I'm shaken up."

West wanted to know if Rugge worked or went to school, and Rugge answered, "I'm pretty much just waiting for school to come around. I scored myself a DUI here actually, that's why I'm staying up here right now. If I wasn't, I'd be livin' with my mom."

West wondered if Rugge had to live in Santa Barbara because of the DUI, and Rugge answered, "No, I was working with my uncle as an electrician and that fell through because my car kind of broke down. I got it fixed up and went to drive three of my buddies home, and got pulled over. I got a DUI, but didn't pay the fine, and just did the jail time, and ever since, I've been trying to find work right up here. I've been looking for landscaping or gardening. Back in the day I was working at a gas station, and stuff like that."

West asked Rugge where he had been during the day of Sunday, August 6, and Rugge replied, "I was over at my buddy Ricky Hoeflinger's house. And my friend Adam drove me home." Asked if he had seen anything in the news about the murder of Nick Markowitz, Rugge responded that he had seen something in the Santa Barbara newspaper. At that point Detective West said that he was going to Mirandize Rugge. He asked him if he knew what that meant.

Rugge said that he didn't. "I'm totally spaced. I'm just freaked out. I'm blank right now, sir."

West went ahead and gave Rugge the Miranda warning, and asked him if he understood what he had been read. Rugge replied, "Yes, sir." Then Rugge added, "I'm spooked out how you guys just came upon me on this. I mean, where did this come from, and how did this happen?"

Reinstadler jumped in and said, "We're questioning you in relation to your participation or being a witness in a homicide."

Once again Rugge wanted to know how the police had gotten their information, but Reinstadler answered, "Do you want to talk to us, yes or no? We can't talk to you unless you waive your rights. And we can't ask you questions. You can stop answering anytime you want."

"Wait. If I waive my rights, what happens then?"

"We're gonna ask questions of you."

"Do I go home or anything like that?"

"No, sir. You are under arrest."

"I'm under arrest?"

West replied, "You've been arrested, and we would like to talk to you about this homicide."

Rugge finally said it was okay to go ahead and question him, and he signed the waiver of his rights to ask for a lawyer. After it was signed, Rugge was asked if he'd been arrested before, and he said he had been for the DUI. Then West asked him if he had any idea of why they wanted to talk to him, and Rugge replied that he had no idea.

West began, "This young man, well, the body was found up in the hills of Santa Barbara, off of Highway 154. His name was Nicholas Markowitz. Do you recognize the name?"

"Yeah, I've heard of his older brother down there, where I used to live."

"Did you go to school with Ben?"

"No, just knew him through parties and things. Through the Valley scene."

"Okay, Nick was found up here. Do you know anything about this?"

"No, sir."

"But you said you saw it in the newspaper?"

"Yes, sir."

"Did you read the article?"

"Not really. I just looked at it and just briefly—well, just tripped out."

"What do you mean by 'tripped out'?"

"I was surprised. I just looked at it, and it said 'Woodland Hills.' It's from the same area as me."

"Have you been down to that area recently? Is that where your mother lives?"

"Yeah. I just came back from there, actually. Came back Sunday during the daytime. I came from a wedding."

"Did you ever know Ben to come up here to Santa

Barbara? Why do you think Nick would be up here in Santa Barbara?"

"Go figure. I don't know."

West asked what Rugge had been doing all summer long, since he hadn't been going to school or working very much. Rugge answered, "Well, I've been transferring kinda like from my mom's to my dad's place. Kind of hanging out. Not doing anything. Kind of lopping it. Working around the house with my dad, and the front yard or whatever. I mean, you guys scared the hell out of me. I thought you guys were someone like . . ." He didn't finish the rest of sentence but laughed nervously instead.

West wanted to know who Rugge hung around with in the Santa Barbara area, and he said his friends were John and Graham. The name Graham rang a bell with West, and he said, "Graham who? What's Graham's last name?"

"I don't know Graham's last name. I just met him through a buddy of mine from up here."

"And John's last name?"

"Ziegler. Johnny Ziegler. Occasionally I just talk to him every once in a while. I don't associate with a bunch of kids up here."

"Okay. So when you go down to L.A.?"

"I hang out sometimes over there at a house."

"Are you dating anyone now? Hanging out with any girls?"

Rugge laughed and said, "Nope. Striking out pretty much right now."

Reinstadler chimed in. "You have no female acquaintances at all?"

"Uh, a girl named Kelly. I don't know her last name. I just met her through my friend Graham. She has blond hair. Very short."

"You don't know Kelly's last name?"

"No, sir. I do not, sir."

"You met her through Graham?"

"Yeah. I stopped going to party scenes when I was, like,

nineteen. I stopped doing that shit. All there is, is chaos, and no point in it. So I've pretty much just been hanging over at my mom's house. Kinda around the neighborhood."

West wanted to know if Rugge had been contacting people he knew from his high-school days, and Rugge said that he hadn't done that very much. Then he added, "All of them are just doing their own things. Everyone grew apart. You know, just slouchin'."

West asked why Rugge knew Ben Markowitz, and Rugge said he knew him from the party scenes that he used to attend. Asked if he'd talked to Ben at those parties, Rugge answered, "I just ran into him. I think he knows who I am. I met him through a buddy named Johnny down there."

"A different Johnny? Not John Ziegler?"

"No, a different Johnny, but I don't know his last name, either."

West then asked Rugge to name off as many people as he could from his days in West Hills, and Rugge rattled off some first names: "Loren, Rick, James, Bear, Chris, Justin, Andy, Rebecca, Courtney, Jason and Jeremy." They were all people around his age.

West said, "Did you say Jesse?"

"No, Jason," Rugge replied nervously.

Reinstadler jumped in. "Let's rephrase that question. Do you know any Jesses?"

"Jesse? Um."

Reinstadler added, "And keep in mind, you're not sitting there because we're stupid."

Rugge responded, "Yeah, but I know a bunch of kids, dude."

"Tell us about Jesse."

"About Jesse? What?"

"About Jesse from West Hills."

"I used to play baseball with this kid named Jesse."

"What's Jesse's last name?"

Rugge lied and said, "I don't know Jesse's last name."

West broke in. "What does this Jesse do now?"

Rugge replied, "I think he's working, like, for a wood floor company. I don't know what he's doing right now. I haven't seen him in a while."

"What does he look like?"

"I don't know. He had long hair. I think."

"A white guy?"

"No, brownish."

"You mean Hispanic?"

"No, not really. I mean tan. I haven't seen him for a while—like, probably a month and a half ago," Rugge lied.

West wanted to know how many years Rugge had known this Jesse person, and Rugge replied that he had played baseball with him on a Little League team when they were young. West jumped Rugge on the fact that he'd played on a team with this Jesse person and that he'd seen him only a month previously, and yet, "You don't remember his last name? Do you realize how that sounds?"

"Well, it sounds awkward, but you guys puttin' me in this situation where it's like you're just asking me all these questions where I don't even get—"

"I'm just asking you names of people and associates."

"Look, I know the kid from playing baseball when we were younger. That's the only way I know the guy. I have no association. I've probably seen him by running into him on the streets or at a party. That's the only thing I have, all right!"

"Okay, okay! Well, you're obviously nervous about why you're here. And I told you, we're investigating a homicide."

"I'm freaking out by this point!"

"I'll ask you the freakiest question in the world. Did you have anything to do with this?"

"No, sir."

"Anything at all. I mean, I'm not asking you necessarily

if you killed the kid. I'm just asking if you had anything to do with it."

"No."

"Did you have knowledge of it? How it happened? How it was set up?"

"Where did you get that idea? I don't get why you guys are even asking me this! This is ridiculous, sir!"

"I'm trying to see how sure you are of your answers and the fact that you don't know too many last names. Let's say you took a polygraph test. Would you be willing to take a polygraph test? We can't use that against you in court."

"I guess . . . but I'm telling you the truth. I mean, this is ridiculous!"

Reinstadler said, "We have talked to a lot of people. And we know what happened."

Rugge responded, "What happened?"

"You know what happened! Look, we don't know what your involvement was in this, all right. I don't think you're a stone-cold killer. I think you got into something that's gonna haunt you for a long time. I understand that. We all make mistakes. Do you understand where I'm coming from? I made a bunch of them in my life. Sometimes we make mistakes 'cause we drink too much. Sometimes we make mistakes 'cause we treat our wives or girlfriends bad. Sometimes we make mistakes by hanging around people we shouldn't. I think you hung around and got involved with somebody that walked down that path. It got awful black and dark and something happened. Maybe you were told it wouldn't happen, and now it's our job to piece the puzzle together. Of course, we're not gonna tell you everything we know, because obviously we'll have to prove it in court. But this is your opportunity."

Rugge was still claiming that he didn't know anything about what either Detectives West or Reinstadler were talking about. So Reinstadler got Rugge speaking about Fiesta Week in Santa Barbara, instead. Rugge admitted that he had attended events on De La Guerra Street, and that he had been there with his friend Will, cousin Autumn and her boyfriend. Rugge said he had hung out there with the others until midnight and then had gone home.

West asked him if he went out on the evening of August 5 and Rugge answered, "I think I probably went out around eight P.M. Something like that. I walked to upper State Street and took the bus all the way down. I met up with Graham later on that night, I think. I did meet up with Graham. Nah, I didn't even see Graham. Excuse me."

"We're talking about Fiesta night, the fifth." (This was when Rugge had been visited by Jesse Hollywood, who wanted to recruit him to break out windows at the Markowitz residence.)

"I was up there and just hung around State Street and came home and pretty much went to bed. I didn't really do anything, 'cause I don't really have that many friends up here. I just know a coupla kids."

"Are you saying you didn't see Graham then?"

"I did not."

"Did anyone come over to your house on Saturday the fifth?"

"No."

West and Rugge went around and around about whether Rugge's parents were home on August 5 and how long Rugge stayed at the residence that day. His stories kept changing as to times he was at home and when his dad and stepmom had been there. And as far as Sunday the sixth went, he'd stayed home all day long and no one had come over to his house. Asked if he had gone down to the Los Angeles region at all around that time, Rugge lied and said, "I went Tuesday over to my mom's house, and pretty much hung out there all day. I did some chores for her, went over to my friend Jack's house and hung out over there. Just went swimming and then came back to my house. I spent the whole time there, pretty much three days. And then my sister came up with me and with my niece."

West got back to the article in the newspaper, and Rugge's stories kept changing on that as well. He said that he hadn't read it, or that he had read part of it, and finally, "I don't really read newspapers. I just briefly go through them when I'm pretty much on the pot."

West asked, "So you know anything about how he was killed?"

"No, I do not."

"Have you ever had a gun?"

"No, sir."

"Have you ever used a gun?"

"No, sir."

"Have you ever seen a gun?"

"Yeah. I've seen a gun."

"What do you know about guns?"

"Shit. Ah. My brother-in-law and my dad had twenty-twos."

"Is there any ammunition in your house?"

"Nope. It's nothing like that, sir. My dad's never been like that. We've never been that type, you know."

Reinstadler wanted to know if Rugge's dad, stepmom or mom knew of Rugge's friends down in the Valley. He answered, "Oh, a little bit. They don't really like my friend Ricky."

"Do they like Jesse?"

"Jesse—well, they always had no problem with him and the guys I played baseball with when I was a younger kid."

Reinstadler asked, "Now, Jesse that you played baseball with. It's Jesse Hollywood, right?"

"Probably. I think so."

"He's the same Jesse Hollywood that both your stepmom and father saw at your house that weekend, right?" (The lieutenant was referring to August 5.)

"I don't know. I doubt that."

"Your mom and dad are sitting out in our lobby. We're

serving a search warrant at your house. That's why the guys tackled you there on the three-yard line. We've been talking to your dad and stepmom for about an hour and a half. They make it real clear that Jesse Hollywood was up that weekend. You know, the guy you really don't know. You're thinking now, aren't you?"

Rugge replied, "What am I thinking?"

"I think you're thinking about should you tell us the truth or not."

"I have no clue what I'm supposed to do here. I mean, go to jail for the rest of my life. That's where I'm headed!"

Reinstadler responded, "Hey, we're not saying that!"

"Well, that's the way it's lookin' to me. I'm getting accused of something I did not do!"

"Then, buddy, you'd better start talkin' to us!"

"Why? 'Cause I don't have no idea what you're talking about."

"You don't have any idea? No idea at all? All the people that you've been with during that period of time? Do you have any idea that they wouldn't talk to us and tell us what happened?"

"Well, you obviously know as much as I do."

"We know a little."

Rugge replied, "Why don't you brief me?"

Reinstadler answered with disgust, "No. I'm not gonna tell you! I want you to tell me, 'cause that way I know that you are telling the truth. You've already started off a little rocky here."

Rugge replied, "Obviously."

"You tell me that there's this Jesse baseball player, who you don't really know, and I'm telling you he was with you that weekend. You need to start tellin' the truth. We know about Jesse. We know about what happened Monday, Tuesday and Wednesday. We know you were with them, and they burned ya."

"Who?"

"I'm not gonna tell ya! You're gonna tell me! Show

me that you want to tell me the truth. We know how everything happened. We also know that you're supposed to be upset over this. So maybe things didn't happen the way you wanted them to happen."

West chimed in, "What if somebody told us that they saw you with Nick Markowitz? How do you explain that? Are you saying that you not only knew Ben, but you really know Nick, too?"

"I don't know."

Reinstadler said, "Is there some reason why you would be with Nick other than having something to do with his death?"

West added, "If so, please explain to us, because we could clear this all up, but somebody saw you with Nick. What would be the reason?"

Rugge replied, "I don't know why. I don't know why, sir. I don't get this at all, right now!"

Reinstadler retorted, "I'll go you one further, okay. I'll ask you if anything unusual happened, and if you went to places, maybe motels, maybe you wouldn't normally go to, between that Sunday of Fiesta and, let's say, Wednesday. Would that help you remember anything? I would like to give you the opportunity to let us know what happened so that someone will think that Jesse (Rugge) isn't a cold-blooded killer. Jesse, like I told you before, you got caught up into something you didn't think would turn out this way. I know this isn't easy to talk about and there's a lot of unknown factors out there. You're worried about your future."

Rugge responded, "Whatever. I'm dead, no matter what, so I don't get what you're saying. I'm sitting here, and I'm goin' to jail. I'm goin' to jail for about six, seven or eight years. I'm seeing death, no matter what."

Reinstadler asked, "Why do you say that?"

"Because this is bullshit, man!"

"Did you pull the trigger?"

"No. I don't know what you're talking about."

"You do know what we're talking about! You're not talking like some guy who doesn't know what we're talking about. I'm asking you, did you pull the trigger or did somebody else? I think somebody else is responsible for this, and I hate to see you make a bad decision."

Rugge replied, "I guarantee you, if you think Jesse Hollywood and those guys are the ones you're thinkin' about, I doubt it's him."

"Well, the bottom line is you know who it is. Jesse is involved. He's involved up to here, okay. Other people can make bad decisions besides yourself and Jesse. Other people are comin' from different places than you are. Maybe you didn't know what was going to happen. Maybe you thought this was to scare somebody and it turned into something else. Between this man (West) and myself, we have about fifty-five years as cops. We've seen it all. We work homicides. It's never a clear-cut thing. A lot of mistakes are made, and all we're trying to say is, we took a puzzle, we took a couple of pieces out, but you can still see the puzzle. We have all that, and it's lookin' to us like you're definitely involved. In fact, buddy, you were around when it happened. You were there!"

"No, I wasn't."

"You were right there, Jesse!"

"I don't know what people have been telling you, sir."

"Tell us about the Lemon Tree, then."

"Who was at the Lemon Tree?"

Reinstadler laughed and said, "I know you were at the Lemon Tree."

"Do ya?"

"Yeah. I also know that you were there renting a room, and I can prove it. People are gonna pick out pictures I have and you're one of them. And guess who one of the pictures is of?"

"Who?"

"The dead guy. Now, isn't that a coincidence? Don't you

think that's a coincidence, Jess? I mean, what would you think?"

"It's some shit!"

West jumped in and said, "What I see is that you're a little scared. And that's okay."

Rugge laughed nervously at that.

"I know that Jesse Hollywood is a dangerous guy. He's a dangerous guy, isn't he?"

"I don't know what you're talking about. Jesse Hollywood is not a dangerous guy."

"Are you afraid of what Jesse Hollywood is gonna do to you?"

"No. I'm afraid of what jail's gonna do to me, sir. That's one fuckin' thing I'm scared about!"

"Well, we can make sure that Jesse Hollywood is not going to see you."

"You don't understand. That's not the point. I'm going away for a very long time. I'm gonna get hurt inside there, man. I'm light, man."

Reinstadler asked, "Who do you think determines how long you need to stay inside there?"

Rugge answered, "You guys do."

Reinstadler laughed and replied, "Nah. You think cops determine that? Who are the guys that say you have X amount of years?"

"A judge."

"Exactly."

Rugge replied, "Still, no matter what, I'm goin' to jail, because somehow I'm a part of this because I know people."

"No. You're a part of this because you went along with the program. I personally believe getting the story right."

"Can I have a cigarette?"

"No. Sorry. This is important. You were with Nick for a couple of days. People saw you. People will testify about that. You've made comments to people about what happened."

"To who? Never mind."

Reinstadler said in disgust, "We're right back to where we were. Don't blink your eyes. You know I'm right. If you truly are afraid of just going to jail, a judge will look at you and see what kind of a person you are, and did you or not show remorse."

"I have nothin' goin' in my life you can look at. I look like a burn to everyone else."

"A couple of thousand bucks looked pretty good there, didn't it?"

Rugge was surprised by that comment and answered, "What couple of thousand bucks?"

"I know you got offered a couple of thousand bucks."

"I didn't get any money!"

"I'm not saying you did, but you got offered it, because some people have a lot of money. They've got a lot of juice. Sell enough weed and you can have all the money in the world, or at least it seems that way."

West added, "It was supposed to be just to teach this guy a lesson, and it all went bad. And all of a sudden you found yourself kind of being forced into this, didn't you? 'Cause all of a sudden, Jesse Hollywood was making you do this, and you were starting to realize that things are getting out of hand. Because if it's not that, then the only thing we can assume is you're a cold-blooded killer. So which is it? Are you a cold-blooded killer of a fifteen-year-old young man, or did you get caught up in something that seemed so simple and then just very quickly got very dangerous?"

Reinstadler reminded, "The judge won't know anything but that you were right there."

Rugge replied, "Yep. So he's gonna stick me."

"He's gonna stick all of you, bro! He's not just gonna stick you. He's gonna stick all of you for the exact same thing!"

"For what?"

"How about capital murder and torture?"

"Torture?"

"Capital murder, torture, kidnapping. Yeah. Let me tell

ya. If somebody gets, and I'm not gonna tell you how, but he gets bound up and he gets shot nine times with an automatic weapon in his own grave. I can tell right now you're not a cold-blooded killer. But you know who is, Jess, and all we're asking is for your help to show a judge that you were not that person."

"I'm not a killer! I don't know who was."

"You do. I know who was in the car. I know where you went. I know what you brought, and unless you start telling us how it went down, it won't matter who pulled the trigger. Because of your silence, a jury will think you did it."

"I'll be the only person sitting there."

"No, you won't!"

"Who else is gonna be sitting there? So it makes me look like I'm a rat. I get my ass stabbed in jail, no matter what."

Reinstadler said, "I thought you were just afraid of jail."

"I am afraid of jail."

"You're not afraid of Jesse Hollywood?"

"No."

"You're not afraid of Ryan?"

"Who's that?"

"Yeah, right! You didn't know him, either."

West chimed in, "You don't have to be a rat. Just tell us what you did. The others will remember *your* last name."

Rugge piped up, "That kid Adam, the guy you arrested me with, he had nothing to do with this."

Reinstadler said, "We sort of know that, but we're talking to him to see what you talked to him about."

"Nothing."

"Nothing, huh. I guess we'll find out. Can we go day by day, Jess? You be honest with us and tell us just what happened. Starting with the day that Jesse Hollywood came up and talked about this crap and you got sucked into it."

West said, "It will eat away at you, Jess, until you get it out."

Reinstadler added, "It's not going to get any better. The only way it can get better is if a judge can at least see that you are willing to cooperate enough to tell us what happened."

Rugge was still very worried, however, and replied, "I have to stand there in front of a judge and jury and I have to sit there and look at everyone across the courtroom. And you know what, all I did was hold the kid. Didn't hurt him. Acted like his best friend. That's all. I didn't do anything, all right!"

West said, "That's something good."

Reinstadler asked, "He (Nick) didn't see it coming?"

Rugge answered, "No one, I think, knew anything."

"Well, you knew a bunch of bullshit, right? You were handed a line."

Rugge replied, "Ben Markowitz is a . . . I just don't know the whole situation. I don't know. I'm freakin' out."

West declared, "If you were holding Nick, maybe that helped him some to know that somebody was there. What did you do? Can you tell us?"

"Nothing. I didn't do anything to him."

Reinstadler asked, "Ben Markowitz is a what?"

Rugge replied, "Ben Markowitz is a dead guy!"

The detectives got nowhere with questioning about Ben, so Reinstadler asked about Nick again. "What did Nick think was happening?"

"I don't know."

"Come on, Jess. I think he went along with the program to a point. Ben's a shithead, right? Everybody knows that. I mean, you don't understand that we just spent the last three days in the Valley. We talked to more kids, more stoners, than I've met in a lifetime. I've talked to Ben Markowitz. That's what this was all about, right?"

"I don't know. I was never briefed with anything."

"Tell me what Jesse Hollywood told you when he came up and talked to you and got you to go with him."

"Go where?"

"Ah, come on, Jesse! This is getting to be a little ridiculous! You're playing their game with us every time you get backed into a corner. You know the truth. The more you play like you don't know about anything, the more it looks like you know about everything. Because we can prove it. We can prove you were there. You need to fill in certain details about how the murder happened. That's the only thing we're asking for you to help us with. You acknowledged that you held Nick. I know Nick was walking around doing chores. What was up with that? Why did you ask him to do that?"

Rugge replied, "He was helping me out. I was doin' the stairs. I didn't hurt him. I said, 'I got the top of the stairs, you've got the bottom of the stairs.' He said all right. I did not hurt that kid. You gotta get that point!"

Reinstadler replied, "Jesse, then you need to tell us who did. I need to hear it from you, because if you don't, it doesn't matter."

Rugge still hemmed and hawed and worried that he would be sitting in jail with the others who had been involved. Reinstadler responded that Rugge would not be in any position of danger in the county jail. Rugge replied, "That isn't the point. There are people in other places, where everyone knows."

And then Rugge said something that would become hotly contested later on in proceedings: "I'd like to have an attorney at this point. I don't know who I'm gonna pay for anything like that. I don't know what's goin' on."

West told him that he had the right to an attorney, and Rugge added, "I'm goin' down the tubes, no matter what! You guys know as much as I do."

For whatever reason Rugge kept on talking rather than remaining silent, which he also had the right to do. He said, "I'm fuckin' scared, dude! Where am I going to be sitting when I go to jail? Where? L.A. County? I'd get ripped up there in a second."

West replied that he understood Rugge's fears and that he would be protected.

Rugge asked, "By who?"

Reinstadler chimed in and said, "Do you wanna talk to us? You just asked for an attorney. The law says we have to stop talking to you." Then Reinstadler added, "I get the impression you wanna talk."

Rugge said, "I do wanna talk. I don't want to be the person—"

Reinstadler cut in. "So, are you asking for us to continue to talk?"

Rugge replied, "Yeah, I guess so. Look, all I know is any prison I go to, I know there's someone else who's gonna know."

Reinstadler stated again, "You afraid of Jesse Hollywood?"

Rugge answered, "I'm not afraid of Jesse Hollywood. I'm afraid of someone else."

"You afraid of Ryan Hoyt?"

"I'm afraid of someone else."

"You afraid of Skidmore?"

"No, no. Skidmore has nothing to do with this."

"So you're telling me there's someone besides Ryan and Jesse Hollywood involved in this?"

Rugge answered, "Just tell me all the stuff as much as you know, and then I'll fill in the blanks for you."

Reinstadler laughed and replied, "We can't do that, man."

West tried a new approach. "This is what I know. You put Nick in the car, took him up to West Camino Cielo, and you put bullets into him. Is that what you want us to put on the report and send to the judge?"

"No!"

"Then tell us what happened. If you sit there and held him, if you helped Nick out, if you thought he was gonna go back to L.A. after this was all over, if you were there, and you were feeling like you were forced into doing something you really didn't want to be involved in, and you were gonna be killed if you didn't cooperate or whatever, tell us. If you're afraid of somebody, we've gotta know who it is or we can't protect you."

Reinstadler said, "People are goin' down, anyway, man. You might as well help yourself out by letting us know the details."

Rugge was still frightened, though, and replied, "And I just meet up with them in the transfers."

"No, you don't. I mean the jail isn't stupid. We can't do that. We can't put you in harm's way."

"So where do I go?"

"I can't tell you right now, 'cause I don't run the jail. You'll be put somewhere that you won't be in contact with these people."

Rugge replied, "But you see, the rumors get around. Other people inside there don't like the situation."

West responded, "Jesse, there's a lot of people in jail far worse than you. And they live long lives. This is not an issue. The issue here is how long are you gonna be in jail, because if we go to a judge with what we know, you're goin' down for first-degree murder."

Reinstadler added, "You saw guns. You saw shovels, you saw duct tape, you went up the hill with another person. And you came down, and Nick wasn't there anymore. This is a capital murder case. Do you understand what that means?"

"I don't know, sir."

"That means you could be sentenced to death. Unless we start gettin' information better than it looks. You took him up the hill and you killed him. You put him in his own grave. You shot him multiple times with an automatic weapon while he was trussed up. So it isn't gonna matter who you're afraid of. I'd be afraid of the needle! Is that spin a little different? Jesse, I saw you a second ago, with tears welling up in your eyes because you knew that Nick

Markowitz shouldn't have died. You thought that this was just a way to get Ben to pay a debt."

Rugge started moaning. "Ah, shit! Oh, shit! You know who killed him. I know you guys know."

Reinstadler replied, "I need to hear it from you because of what I don't know."

Rugge asked, "How many people are goin' to death for this?"

Reinstadler answered, "I want the guy who pulled the trigger. That's what I want. What do you want?"

West added, "I think from seeing this kid lying there in the dirt, the ones responsible for it should get what they deserve. If it means Jesse Hollywood contracted this whole thing, then he should go."

Rugge responded, "No one contracted anything. It just happened."

West replied, "Tell us how it happened. Because if you're not the one . . . you better tell us."

Rugge moaned, "I wanna die. I'm gonna die, anyways. Fuck!"

West continued, "Our guys are out there gettin' that little maroon car, whatever you wanna call it. It's gonna have evidence in it. We're gonna get the guy who did it. So you tell us if you want to help yourself, you have to tell us. It's the only way."

Reinstadler added, "Why do you think it just happened?"

Rugge responded, "He just . . . I don't know what to say. I don't know how to put this until I hear what other people's stories are."

"We can't do that, bro. We gotta hear your story. You know that, and you wanna tell a story."

West chimed in, "The only way to get rid of all the agony that you're feeling right now is to get the story out."

Rugge was still very scared about telling what happened in court, especially about who the "triggerman" was. Rugge said, "And then I gotta tell the story four more times in front of everyone else."

Reinstadler shot back, "Don't you think it doesn't really matter at this point what you say? You gotta think of yourself, man."

"I'm dead. Is anything happening to my parents? Please tell me."

Reinstadler said that nothing was happening to them. "They're not under arrest. We've been talking to them. They're probably still here."

Rugge groaned. "I'm dying for something so stupid! So fuckin' stupid! I should never have done it. Look, all I did was hold the kid, all right. I didn't even know what was goin' on. I went to a place up there and all I know was a person was supposed to come up and take him away."

West asked, "Are you saying that's what they told you?"

"Yeah."

"Right off West Camino Cielo, someone was supposed to meet you up there? Or down at the Lemon Tree?"

"Down at the Lemon Tree."

"That was supposed to be Jesse Hollywood, right?"

"No, sir."

"Then tell us who it was."

"Fuck, man! I gotta point them out to the jury in a courtroom, don't I?"

"Not necessarily. You know what you're doing? You're protecting him. Think how quickly he's gonna give you up. This is somebody that used you. He thought you were nothin' but a pawn in his game. And he used you and then tossed you after he got what he wanted."

Rugge asked, "What's gonna happen to me after this? I go to jail for how long?"

Reinstadler said, "Don't worry about that. You should worry about what we've started here."

West added, "That's gonna make a big factor in the determination of the final outcome of this."

Rugge said, "I can't believe this! I can't believe it came down to this."

"You made a mistake, man. You just have to make the

best of the situation. Which means you need to answer our questions."

Rugge nearly cried. "I feel so bad, man."

"Who do you feel bad for?"

"I feel bad for Nick. I'm so going down. For capital murder. But I did not pull the trigger."

"Prove it by telling us what happened. Prove it, Jess!"

"I don't know where to start, man."

"Why don't you start at the beginning."

Rugge asked, "Lemon Tree Inn?"

"No, that's not the beginning. Come on. When did you first . . . well, will you answer the questions truthfully as I ask them?"

"Yes, sir."

"Okay, when was the first time you were supposed to hold Nick Markowitz?"

"I think after the second day. He slept over my house."

"Who brought him over?"

"He got picked up."

"Who was there?"

"I was there. This guy tells me to jump out of the van and grab this kid, and I said, 'No!'"

"Who was this guy?"

"A guy."

"Can you say it? Jesse Hollywood?"

Trying to get Rugge to say that Jesse Hollywood had told him to grab Nick was like pulling nails.

West jumped in and said, "I thought you said it was a van."

"It was a car, I think."

"It was a van, wasn't it?"

"Yes, sir."

"Whose van was it?"

"I don't know."

"Yes, you do!"

"No, I don't!"

"I'm not asking you who killed him, I'm asking whose van it was."

"I don't know whose van it was."

Reinstadler asked, "Who was drivin' it?"

"Jesse Hollywood was driving the van," Rugge lied. "All I know is, I didn't wanna grab that kid. They made him get in the car. They ended up making me drive and I said, 'I'm not keeping this kid over at my house.'"

Reinstadler tried calming Rugge down. He said, "Look, the hard part is out of the way. Jesse Hollywood, okay." Rugge had obviously slipped up by saying that Jesse Hollywood had been at the initial kidnapping, although for some reason he lied by saying that Hollywood had driven the van.

Rugge was still "freakin'," as he put it, and exclaimed, "I didn't touch the fucking kid!"

"Okay. I believe you. How do you get down to the Valley from here?"

"I take the train."

"What day was it that you took the train?"

"Nah, I got picked up."

"Why are you lying about trains and stuff?"

"I'm just scared, man."

"Look, Jess. I know you're scared. The hardest part is out of the way."

"Jesse Hollywood didn't kill him!"

"Have we been mean to you? Are we trying to treat you with respect?"

"I don't know where I'm goin'. All I know is I'm a rat. And all I know is I'm fuckin' going down. I know the way I look. Like a fuckin' bitch!"

West got back to the point that Rugge had been holding Nick, and Rugge replied, "I just held him at my house. That was all I did. I didn't touch him. I didn't hit him. I let him walk around freely. I let him use my bath."

Reinstadler asked sarcastically, "He walk his own self

up to Lizard's Mouth? Look, what happened after you got up there? What went wrong?"

Rugge replied, "He was taken to his grave and got shot."

"Who was up there besides you? Once you get it out of your system, you'll feel a lot better, man."

"I'm going down, man. I'd rather stay in Santa Barbara than go to any other prisons. Anywhere else I go, there's brothers in there. You guys know who killed him. It wasn't Jesse Hollywood. You know that."

"You have to tell me. I'm not gonna tell you."

"So it's me who goes down for the murder?"

"You have to tell me, or that's what's gonna happen."

"I didn't even touch the gun. There's no fingerprints on it."

"I know it got wiped down."

"What happens to me now? Do I spend the night?"

"Don't worry about that. Let's finish this."

"If I say his name, I'm finished."

"Listen. You say you held Nick. That can be interpreted as kidnapping. You told us that he got grabbed and put in a van. Jesse Hollywood is the one who told you to do that. You wouldn't do it, so somebody else did. And then you ended up driving the van."

Rugge once again said, "Jesse Hollywood had nothing to do with this."

Reinstadler uttered one word in response, "Ugh!"

So around and around they went, until Rugge said, "This kid got pulled up a hill, over to his grave and got shot. I might as well have died with the kid."

Reinstadler shot back, "You helped dig the grave, didn't you?"

"I didn't dig no grave! Fuck no! You know who dug the goddamn grave!" By now, he really was freaking out.

"Jesse!"

"You guys are givin' me the third-degree burn. All I know is I'm dead! So you might as well take me in for murder. I'm goin' in for capital punishment. I sit there for six months and then go sit on death row!"

"That's what it's gonna be, unless you tell us what happened and who did it. That's the way it works. It's not our fault that you're in this spot, man."

Rugge asked, "You guys talk to Natasha?"

"We're not gonna tell you who we talked to."

"Graham?"

West wondered, "Is that why you don't want to tell us his last name?"

"Graham, Nathan and Kelly were in the hotel room that night. I never hurt the boy. Never, never even laid a finger on him. Don't get any wrong impression of me. I'm not a fuckin' killer. He could have run. He just obeyed everything. He just sat there and helped me out on a few things."

Reinstadler said, "Somebody had to be with him all the time."

Rugge responded, "Everyone was with him all the time. He wasn't tied down. He sat there and watched TV. I even left him alone with the phone and he could have made a phone call."

"Okay, so what was the plan then, to try and get this money?"

"I don't fuckin' know! I was never told about it!"

"Why did Jesse Hollywood want him picked up?"

"Look, we were driving down the street and this guy goes, 'Isn't that what's-his-name's brother?' All I did was watch the kid get put in his grave and get shot." (Rugge still would not say Hollywood's name knowingly.)

West asked, "What did the killer get out of this? Enjoyment?"

"I don't know."

Reinstadler asked, "Money?"

Rugge answered, "I don't know. My conscience has been eating away at me for the last week and a half."

West said that it was going to continue until Rugge

started telling the whole truth, but Rugge kept saying he was going to die if he told. The detectives answered that he could be protected, and around and around it went. They tried working on his sympathy for Nick. West said, "The only person that can help Nick now is you. Nick is dead, but you can do the right thing and it's gonna put you in a good place."

To this, Rugge asked, "Where is Graham?"

Reinstadler was getting to the end of his wits on all of this, and said, "I'm not gonna tell ya. We have no control of whether this is a capital case or not. We don't know if they'll file it as that or not. But for the district attorney and judge and jury to know what is appropriate, they need to know from you what happened and who did it. Because without that, it sounds like you're just trying to cover your ass and you shot him."

Trying a different tack, West asked, "Was Graham your buddy?"

"He's a friend of mine."

"Do you think he's still your friend?"

"I don't know, man."

"What did Graham get out of this?"

"Jack shit! He was a pawn. And I didn't take any money. I didn't take fuckin' diddly-squat!"

Reinstadler said, "But they offered you two thousand dollars."

"Nope."

"What? Then why were you telling people that?"

"Me? Nah. You just want the killer's name. All you want is the killer's name. All right! Fuck! I'll be running if they don't kill me."

"Come on!"

"It's so hard to say, man. I'm dead both ways. It doesn't matter. I was there—an accessory to murder. I can still go to the death chamber. I'm the one who fuckin' kept the kid with me. You guys know that from speaking to people, people who obviously thought this kid was gonna die. I treated this kid like my friend. Just 'cause I have tattoos and shit, I'm not a fuckin' liar!"

West jumped in and said, "I can see you're really agonizing over it, because it's placed you in a bad place. The only way you're gonna get out of there is by—"

"Ratting! Ratting!"

"No. Saying what happened."

Rugge was begging for a cigarette at this point, but they wouldn't give him one. Rugge also said that he knew the name of the one who had pulled the trigger, but once he said it, he'd be a marked man.

Reinstadler replied, "You're the guy who needs to prove you're not the cold-blooded killer. You keep repeating that you didn't do anything, but we know that you did go up the hill, and we know you and two other guys went up the hill, and we know that only two of you came back, and we know that there were gunshots."

"Two of us?" This comment made Rugge's ears perk up—they were excluding Graham Pressley in these equations. Rugge asked, "You haven't talked to Graham? Graham didn't say anything about what he did, did he? Obviously not."

This was also an opening for the detectives. Reinstadler kept saying, "What did I tell you?" meaning that Graham Pressley was protecting himself. And West said, "You're gonna protect him. I can see you wanna say it real bad. It's that part of you that's wondering what will happen afterward."

Rugge answered, "Nah, I know what's gonna happen."

Reinstadler countered, saying, "I just keep hearing this sad song. It sounds like a killer trying to cover his butt. Because I'll tell you this much, unless you want to give us details, we have no alternative."

"I didn't dig that hole."

"Then who dug it?"

"You already spoke to him."

"You telling me Graham dug that hole?"

"Yeah." (This was the first time any detective heard of this.)

"Is that what you're tellin' me? Don't give me any bullshit! I don't wanna talk in codes anymore."

"Look, I held the kid, took the kid up the hill, but I didn't stick no bullets in him. I didn't dig no fuckin' hole. I didn't drive the kid there. I didn't do anything with the kid. All I did was look at him when he was dead. And Graham dug the hole, but didn't kill the kid."

Reinstadler once again asked who pulled the trigger, and Rugge once again wouldn't tell him. Reinstadler was getting fed up with all the tap dancing around the issue and said, "We need to hear it from you, because if we don't hear it from you, I'm gonna do everything I can to get you juice, 'cause I think you killed him." Rugge kept denying he knew more than he'd already said, but West asked him what Graham had been doing up on West Camino Cielo. Rugge answered, "Graham sat by the car. The guy pulled the trigger. I helped the guy."

Reinstadler said, "You helped bury the kid, though."

"I only put like two shovel digs on him. I got sick. I couldn't do it."

"What was Nick saying, man? Was he making any noise?"

"No."

"What was the guy tellin' him before he did it?"

"I don't know."

"You heard what he said."

"No, I don't know what he said."

"You were standing right there!"

"Yeah, but half the time I was standing over at the rock, pretty much worrying about my whole entire life flashing in front of me. I didn't know what the fuck I was gonna do."

"Why didn't you run?"

"I was scared."

"You better be scared if you don't tell us who pulled the trigger."

West added, "Who bound and gagged him?"

Rugge answered, "I don't know who tied his arms. Probably the same guy who shot him."

Reinstadler asked, "Was Nick goin' along with the program? He wasn't screaming and yelling? After all, he wasn't gagged when he got up there."

"Exactly."

"So how did it happen? It took more than one dude. Were you gonna scare him? Was that the deal? What was the plan?"

"There was no fucking plan!"

"So what happened? You were at the Lemon Tree."

"All of us got into a car. Myself, Ryan and Graham." (This was the first time that Rugge mentioned Ryan's name.)

Reinstadler asked, "What's Ryan's last name?"

This freaked Rugge out once again, and he exclaimed. "I don't know! I really don't know."

"What did Jesse Hollywood call him?"

Rugge kept saying over and over that he didn't know, so Reinstadler asked him what kind of car they had been in, and Rugge said that it was a dark-colored Toyota. Even getting him to say what color it was, or if it was old or new, was a trial for the detectives. Reinstadler then said, "If I come up with a last name for Ryan, will you confirm it?"

Rugge answered, "If I know his last name."

"Well, do you know his last name or not? I think you do, because this guy has been hanging around with Hollywood for a while. He deals with Hollywood, and you know all about that. I'm not asking you about Hollywood's dealing, okay. We're talking about something entirely different here. Tell me his name."

Rugge once again wouldn't say Ryan Hoyt's last name, but he did say that he'd played baseball with him in West

Hills on a team named the Pirates. He also said that Ryan was a "bum-ass kid." Then Rugge told the detectives to ask his dad what Ryan's last name was.

In exasperation Reinstadler said, "I don't wanna hear it from your dad! There's a billion Ryans out in the world. I wanna hear it from you. This is what we're going to do, Jesse. We're gonna prove that you know Ryan's last name, just like we proved you were at the Lemon Tree. Once you tell me his last name, we can move on. We won't have to play this game for hours. I will make sure you're not in any kind of contact with him or anyone he knows in jail."

Rugge said, "I don't mind Santa Barbara, but anywhere else, I'm gonna die. I'm a rat, man. Do you know what they do to people like me?"

"Listen. I think you're just worried about yourself. You're not worried about Nick, who rotted in that hole with maggots all over him. You're not worried about anyone but yourself. Prove me wrong."

There was more questioning about the initial kidnapping and Reinstadler asked, "What was Jesse Hollywood saying why they needed to kidnap someone?"

Rugge replied, "He wasn't kidnapped."

"What do you call it?

"Okay. I guess it was a kidnapping. All right, this kid was brought up." And then the moment the detectives had been waiting for, Rugge added, "Hoyt came up."

Reinstadler jumped on that and said, "Ah, slip of the tongue!"

Rugge said, "It's all good. I'd already wanted to say it."

Reinstadler replied, "Tell me his name again," and Rugge responded, "Ryan Hoyt."

After all of this, Rugge admitted that he was afraid of Ryan Hoyt's brother. Rugge said, "His brother is locked up in prison. His brother did strong-arm robbery against some lawyer-type guy."

Reinstadler breathed a sigh of relief and said, "Okay, now

the easy part starts. Now we can just get to the business of figuring it out, okay."

Detective West wanted to know why duct tape had been placed around Nick's wrists and mouth, and wondered if he'd been screaming. Rugge replied that Nick hadn't been screaming, and that he'd only put tape around Nick's wrists on Ryan Hoyt's orders. Rugge added, "Nick didn't say anything. He was cooperating. He didn't fight. I just told him to put his hands together, and I said, 'I'm not gonna hurt you.' And he said, 'I know you're not,' and put his hands together like this. I put tape around his hands." Rugge added that it was Hoyt who had put tape around Nick's mouth.

As to who had gone up the trail on the way to kill Nick, West put it in a different way that implicated Pressley even more. West said, "So you're walking up this trail—you, Ryan, Graham and Nick, and you're carrying shovels and tape and this bag with a gun in it."

Rugge did not correct him by saying that Graham Pressley had not gone up the trail to Lizard's Mouth with the rest of them. All Rugge said was "I don't know what the bag looked like. Black duffel bag."

Reinstadler asked, "Did Graham wait down at the car on the second trip?"

Rugge answered, "He had to walk us there."

Another important point came up when the detectives asked who carried the shovels up to the hole that night. Rugge said that the shovels and the hole were already there, and continued, "Premeditated murder. It sounds like premeditated murder, but it wasn't. It was so sporadic."

Reinstadler wanted to know what Rugge thought was going to happen when they marched Nick up the hill. Rugge answered, "I thought all I was doing was holding the kid for a day and a half, and then letting this kid go back down to where he lived. . . . I've ruined my life! I've ruined this kid's life! I ruined the kid's family's life!"

Rugge explained that before shooting Nick, Hoyt had

propped him up on a rock and told him, "Sit here." Then Rugge said, "He (Hoyt) pulled him into the hole. I didn't care to look. Right then, I knew he was gonna die."

Reinstadler wanted to know who had called him at the hotel and said that someone was coming up from the L.A. area. Rugge said it was Hoyt who had phoned him, and not Jesse Hollywood. Then Rugge counteracted this statement that maybe it had been Jesse Hollywood, after all. Pressed on this point, Rugge finally admitted that it was Jesse Hollywood who had phoned and said that someone would be coming up to Santa Barbara.

What was strange to the detectives, and to Rugge as well, was that no one ever did phone Ben Markowitz about the debt. Rugge explained, "They said nothing to me at all about money situations with this guy. I was holding the kid, and that's all. You can talk to anyone up here, dude. All I wanted to do was fuckin' let him go. Someone was supposed to come up to the Lemon Tree, and I'd let him go. But then Hoyt showed up, and that's when I knew everything went sour. I was expectin' Jesse Hollywood, at least to show his fuckin' face. I let them use my house to hold this kid, and they killed him in my neighborhood!"

A lot of what happened didn't make sense, and Rugge agreed with the detectives on that score. "They kept saying, 'Don't worry, just keep Nick there. Just make him like your best friend,' and that's what I did."

West asked, "And they didn't offer you anything for that? Just use your house?"

"Yeah."

West wanted to know why Hoyt confided in Pressley, but kept Rugge in the dark about his intent to kill Nick. Rugge answered, "Because Graham had to dig a hole." And Rugge added that Graham Pressley had been used, because he had been up around Lizard's Mouth in the past. Detective West finally pinned down all five co-conspirators when he said, "Graham, Skidmore, Ryan,

Jesse Hollywood and you." Rugge did not argue with that assessment.

West wanted to know what both Ryan Hoyt and Rugge had said after the killing. Rugge answered, "I didn't say anything. I puked my guts out. And Ryan didn't say anything. I just kept lookin' at him. I kept lookin' at him. I couldn't believe it."

Then, out of the blue, Reinstadler asked, "Was there any sexual contact between you and Nick, or anyone else involved in this?"

Rugge was shocked and said, "Fuck no!"

As the grueling session finally wound down, Rugge kept repeating, like a mantra, "I'm a rat! I'm a fuckin' rat!"

When it was all over, Detective West and Sergeant Reinstadler probably felt like taking Excedrin Extra Strength. It had been an interview from hell.

9

LOOKING FOR HOLLYWOOD

Of all the people Ryan Hoyt could have called, he contacted his mother from the jail. In a disjointed conversation, in which her voice went from a whisper to a scream, Victoria Hoyt basically asked if he had murdered Nick Markowitz. She was very agitated and upset. She not only cursed emphatically, but she invoked the Lord's Prayer as well. Ryan insisted that he hadn't killed Nick, and there must have been something about the call that made him change his mind about talking to detectives. He had adamantly refused to do so, up until then, but after the phone call, it was he that sent a message through authorities that he did want to talk.

Hoyt had gotten wind somehow about what had been said in a news conference about him, and he wanted to "straighten things out," as he put it. Ushered into an interview room with Mike West and Ken Reinstadler, Hoyt was read his Miranda rights, and the detectives made no bones about what they thought he had done. The interview soon took an unexpected turn, however, and Ryan Hoyt was about to give them more than they had bargained for. In a news conference Hoyt had been portrayed as digging Nick's grave, and Ryan didn't want that to stand.

Hoyt: I came up here to tell you that the picture everyone is painting of me is not me.

Detective: Tell us who you are. Tell us how this went down.

Hoyt: I can't do that. Do you mind if I go back to my cell and think about it tonight and talk to you guys tomorrow, 'cause I know my arraignment is on Monday.

Detective: Once you're arraigned, we can't talk to you. That's the bottom line. If you want to tell us something, I'm being honest with you, this is the opportunity to do it. This is it.

Hoyt: There's no way I can talk to you tomorrow?

Detective: No. You know why?

Hoyt: Why?

Detective: Because somebody is going to get to you and tell you not to talk to us and play the games that we know people play. We know Jesse Hollywood. If you're afraid of him, you should be more afraid of what could happen to you if he is choreographing something about you without an explanation to a jury of twelve people or a judge. One thing we do want you to understand, is we have interviewed dozens of people. We know you're involved in this killing. Let's not play games. We know exactly who we're talking about, and

Hoyt:	I don't see how I can be placed at digging the kid's grave and killing him.
Detective:	You didn't dig the grave. That's a little misunderstanding, but you've been identified. You need to start telling the truth!
Hoyt:	I didn't dig the grave. All I did was kill the kid!

For whatever reason Hoyt had just told the detectives something much worse than digging the grave. Just why he thought that killing Nick was less egregious than digging a grave is unfathomable.

Hoyt must have still been afraid of Jesse Hollywood at this point, or protecting him. He told the detectives he didn't know who had given him the gun to take to Santa Barbara. Reinstadler asked him, "Did you meet someone before you got to the Lemon Tree?"

Hoyt answered, "No."

Reinstadler continued, "Okay, so what happened?"

Hoyt replied, "I think you guys know what happened," and he wouldn't use Jesse James Hollywood's name.

As it turned out, Jesse James Hollywood was just as mobile and resourceful as his friends in the crime had been slothful and inept. All of them had stayed at or near their residences and had been apprehended easily, but that was not the case with Hollywood. To fund his escape plan, Jesse began calling in old debts.

According to later documents, Brian Affronti owed him $4,000. At this point Affronti was very afraid of Hollywood. According to Affronti, William Skidmore had told him that he heard "something might have to be done about Affronti, if he becomes a liability."

Jesse Hollywood went by Affronti's house and collected

the money, as well as a shotgun wrapped in a sleeping bag. Also around this time, and it appears that he did so in Palm Springs, Jesse got more money from his bank, to the tune of about $5,000.

Much of what occurred from the time that Jesse Hollywood and Michelle Lasher left Palm Springs was learned later from Michelle. The trouble with her account was that it kept changing in some details. The most reliable "facts" seemed to go in the following vein: Michelle said that Jesse was extremely agitated all during the days in Palm Springs, and then suddenly he wanted her to go with him to Colorado. According to Michelle, later, Jesse told her she was either coming with him, or he was going to drop her off by herself in a bad part of town. Michelle went with him.

Many in law enforcement believed that Michelle knew exactly why she and Jesse were heading to Colorado. But through thick and thin, in years to come, Michelle would claim that she never asked Jesse the reason why. She said that she didn't want to upset him any more than he already was.

Whatever her knowledge of why they were heading east, Jesse and Michelle ended up in Las Vegas on the first part of their journey. Jesse gave her cash, and Michelle did the actual booking into the luxurious Bellagio hotel. Their stay in Vegas was of short duration, and soon they were on the road again, to Colorado Springs, Colorado. Once they got there, other old friends of Jesse Hollywood's would add bits and pieces of what Jesse did there, along with Michelle Lasher.

Out of the blue on August 16, 2000, the very day that Hoyt, Rugge and Pressley were being arrested, Jesse Hollywood and Michelle Lasher showed up at William Jacques's residence in Colorado. Jacques hadn't seen Hollywood for some time, and this visit to Jacques was totally unexpected. Jacques recalled later, "Jesse told me he was on vacation. He had gone by my parents' house, and my mom told him where I lived. I lived in an apartment about eight miles from where my parents lived. I knew his girlfriend from when I had visited Jesse in California. I spoke with her a little bit now.

"Jesse gave me a couple of guns he had and said that he didn't want them anymore. They were a shotgun and a rifle. I knew a little bit about guns, but not much. The weapons were in a black vinyl bag. There might have been bullets and shells for them, but I don't remember. I eventually gave the guns to my father."

Jesse and Michelle didn't stay long at William Jacques's apartment. From there, they went to the house of Jesse's old baseball coach, Richard Dispenza. Jesse still referred to Dispenza as "Coach."

Because the body of Nick Markowitz had been discovered, and many of Jesse's friends had been arrested, Jack Hollywood paged Jesse, only to receive a phone call in return that Jesse was on his way to Colorado. Jack Hollywood called Richard Dispenza, in Colorado Springs, and, according to Jack, told Dispenza over the phone, "I think my kid is in some kind of trouble. I'm not sure how involved he is, or what's going on, but the last I heard, he was headed that way." Dispenza had just been named Woodland Park High School "Teacher of the Year," and the last thing he needed was Jesse Hollywood showing up at his door. Nonetheless, he was Jesse's godfather, and he felt he had to do something.

When Jesse Hollywood and Michelle Lasher did show up at Dispenza's residence in Woodland Park, a community about fifteen miles from Colorado Springs, they stayed for most of the evening. According to Dispenza, Jesse did not reveal exactly the nature of why he was in trouble. In fact, Hollywood made up a tale about why he was there, and Dispenza seemed to go along with it.

William Jacques and his girlfriend, Crystal, went over to Coach's house that evening. Jacques recalled later, "I knew Coach from when Jesse lived in Colorado Springs. Crystal and I didn't spend much time there. I think Crystal, Jesse, Michelle and I went out to eat. Then we dropped Michelle back at Coach's house. After that, Jesse and I went to my place and watched some movies. One of them was *The Karate Kid*. It was just me and Jesse and Crystal there. We drank some beers and smoked some dope. This went on until about nine P.M. Then Jesse asked for a ride back to Woodland Park. I dropped him off in front of Coach's house."

According to Michelle, she and Jesse did not stay at Coach's house on the night of August 16. Instead, she booked them a motel room, while Jesse stayed in the car. Michelle booked in under a fake name—Sue Michelle.

Jacques recalled, "The next day, I met with Jesse again. It was probably in the morning and then we went to lunch, to a place called the Hatch Cover. Jesse paid for lunch. He had a thick wad of cash in his wallet. After that, we went to my parents' place in Fountain, Colorado. We drank some more beers and hung out. Jesse seemed just his usual self. He wasn't agitated or anything."

That same day, August 17, Michelle flew back from Colorado to Los Angeles, California. She originally had not told her place of employment about her sudden decision to go with Jesse to Colorado. Once in Colorado, she phoned the place where she worked: "I arranged to have someone replace me. I think her name was Misha or Nuisha. I didn't know her very well. She agreed to do it."

Michelle caught a flight from Colorado to Burbank, California, via Phoenix, Arizona. Once back in California, Michelle got a taxi ride home to her parents' residence in Calabasas. She was in for the surprise of her life. Michelle barely had time to get out of the cab before she was surrounded by law enforcement. Whenever talking about this experience later, Michelle would become very upset and spoke of it as being traumatic in the extreme.

Michelle said later, "As soon as I got to my parents' house, I was met by the police. I lied and said that I had been down to San Diego with my girlfriends. I was protecting Jesse." It's not quite clear as to which date, but Michelle also lied and said the Jesse had recently gone by her parents' home. She seemed to indicate that this had been on August 16 or the morning of August 17. Jesse Hollywood, of course, was in Colorado on those dates.

Meanwhile, in Colorado, Jesse did spend much of the day with William Jacques on August 17, and he was still hanging out with Jacques on August 18. Jacques recalled of that day, "We went over my brother David's house and hung around and drank beer. I drank quite a few beers, maybe six or seven. Jesse was drinking about the same. We both got a pretty good buzz. It was about that time he said that he was running from the police. He didn't say why, and I didn't ask why. At that point I wanted to distance myself from him. So in less than an hour after he said that, I asked him where he wanted to go. He said the Ramada Inn, and I took him there. We went to the Ramada Inn on Interstate 25 and Fremont Street in Colorado Springs. I just dropped him off and didn't see him anymore."

Jesse Hollywood wasn't through visiting friends in the Colorado Springs area, however. He drove to Coach's house and things become somewhat unclear at this point. Jesse may have even been there, but had gone out for a pack of cigarettes. When he started walking back to Coach's house, he spied law enforcement vehicles out front. Jesse immediately turned around and started walking in the opposite direction, leaving his car behind him.

Momentarily at a loss of what to do next, he remembered his old friend Chas Saulsbury in the area. Jesse started hitchhiking to the residence where he remembered that Chas lived.

Chas Saulsbury would have plenty to say about Jesse Hollywood in the years to come. As Chas recalled, "Jesse just kind of showed up. He said that he had been hitchhiking to get to my place. The reason why was, he said he had gone to Las Vegas and been robbed there. Someone had stolen his wallet and credit cards. I hadn't seen him in a long time. This was an unexpected visit.

"He was at my mom's house, and I walked in and there he was. He was sweating, and in a white T-shirt and jeans. He didn't have a car. At first, I didn't even recognize him. He looked so different. We walked outside and he said that he'd walked nearly ten miles to get to my mom's house. Since I didn't live at my mom's house anymore, we went out, and went to dinner and kind of caught up on things.

"Initially he said he was in trouble of some kind, but I didn't ask why. We ate at the Macaroni Grill, and Jesse paid with cash. He took money out of his pocket. We went to a friend's house later and got a small amount of marijuana. Then we went to a friend of mine's place, named Jeremy.

"We went there to see if Jeremy could make fake IDs for Jesse. Jeremy was good at doing computer stuff. Jesse told me at some point that his girlfriend, Michelle, had been with him, but she'd flown back to California. After Jeremy's, I rented Jesse a room at a hotel. I think it was there that there was a news report that the police were looking for Jesse." Later this story would change, and Chas thought he might have seen something about Jesse on the computer screen at Jeremy's house.

"Jesse told me he had brought some weapons out with him, an AR-15 rifle and shotgun. But he didn't have them anymore. He said he'd given them to Bill Jacques. Then he told me he had a Lincoln LS, but when he'd gone out to get some cigarettes near Coach's house, he'd seen the police there. He just walked away from his car and left it there. That's when he'd gone to my mom's place.

"After two days with him in the area, I left with Jesse, because he said he wanted to go back to at least Las Vegas. It was a bad decision on my part, but I was trying to rescue him. He requested that I drive him to Las Vegas, and I did, and we went in my 1990 Audi Quattro. We just left hastily, even though I was scheduled for work the next day.

"Jesse had vaguely told me about the problem at that point. And I'd kinda seen a little bit about it on the Internet. Just kind of glancing at the screen. It took us twelve hours to drive from Colorado Springs to Las Vegas. We had a conversation on the way there about what was happening, but it was a disjointed story. We stopped over in Las Vegas.

"We stayed for the night at the Mandalay Bay and then, I think, at the Hilton. I got to the Mandalay Bay at about two A.M. on August twenty-third. I paid with cash that Jesse had given me. I don't think we stayed even eight hours at the Hilton, when Jesse said that he wanted to go see his father in Los Angeles. So I agreed to drive him there. I had a misguided loyalty to Jesse at that time.

"There were hours of silence on the road, and at other times he would talk. The story just kept coming out, in bits and pieces. Jesse said that a friend of his was named Ben Markowitz, and they used to hang out together. But a feud developed between him and Ben. Ben made phone call threats to him and broke out the windows of his house. The situation got so bad, Jesse decided to move to another house. But while moving stuff there, Jesse saw Ben's little brother, Nick, walking down a sidewalk. On a spur-of-the-moment decision, Jesse decided to grab Nick."

Chas later admitted that he and Jesse smoked marijuana on the trip back to Los Angeles. And he also later admitted some details that he may not have told Jesse on the trip. Chas phoned a couple of different lawyers to see how much trouble he was in for transporting Jesse Hollywood to Los Angeles. Chas apparently didn't reveal to Jesse or anyone else just what they told him, until much later.

One thing of huge consequence did occur on that trip, somewhere between Las Vegas and Los Angeles. According to Chas Saulsbury, Jesse started telling him the reason why Nick had been killed. And then, Chas said, Hollywood explained about the role lawyer Stephen Hogg had played in the whole affair. Saulsbury later testified, "[Hollywood] talked to his lawyer to find out the implications of kidnapping and whatnot. At that point, from what he told me, the lawyer said that he was in enough trouble already and they should get rid of the kid."

That was Saulsbury's take on what Jesse Hollywood had said. Hogg would deny this statement emphatically and say that he had told Jesse Hollywood to "release" Nick and let him go home. "Get rid of the kid" had a much more sinister tone, and the only one who spoke of that scenario was Chas Saulsbury.

Meanwhile, authorities in Colorado became aware that Richard Dispenza had been less than truthful with them at their interview in his house. Lieutenant Mike Burridge, of SBCSD, told a *Los Angeles Times* reporter, "On the night Mr. Dispenza was being interviewed, he claimed he had no idea where Hollywood was. But we find out that he wasn't completely forthcoming. He was clearly deceiving us."

Burridge told a reporter for the *Colorado Springs Gazette,* "From what the detectives are telling me, at the time they were interviewing him, Mr. Dispenza knew Hollywood was in a hotel."

Knowing he was in a lot of trouble, Richard Dispenza obtained a lawyer, Dave Kutinsky, and turned himself in to authorities. Dispenza was booked on suspicion of harboring a fugitive, which was a felony, and was released on a $5,000 bond.

Kutinsky tried putting the best face on things by saying,

"Mr. Dispenza had absolutely no information at any time that this kid was wanted by police when he got a motel room. For police to imply that is totally irresponsible. Mr. Dispenza thought Hollywood was just looking for a place to stay and for some help. He didn't know. If he knew he was in trouble, he wouldn't have registered him under his name. He's certainly going to plead not guilty."

Nonetheless, Dispenza could have told authorities where Jesse James Hollywood was on August 18, if he had chosen to. Instead, he told them that Hollywood had left the area, and the manhunt went on. In fact, that was as close as authorities would come to capturing Jesse James Hollywood for a very long time.

Family and friends in Colorado were startled when they learned of Richard Dispenza's arrest for harboring an individual connected to a murder. His mother, Katherine, said, "He hadn't seen Jesse in four or five years. The kid said he was in trouble, but didn't say what kind of trouble. My son is innocent. He's in total shock right now."

Bob Graf, the school district's activities and athletics director, said, "Rich is a good teacher and motivator. He's got the support of a lot of people."

Reid Slaughter, whose son played football at the high school, added that Dispenza was like a second father to his son. "He's one of the best guys out there that I know. He'd do anything for all the kids—not just coaching, but in their personal lives and their academics. He was just a real good mentor."

Even a neighbor told a reporter, "He's a wonderful person and has a huge heart. He's a great neighbor. He minded his own business, but played ball with the kids, too. I just think he was at the wrong place at the wrong time."

That seemed to be Jesse James Hollywood's MO—causing terrible trouble for people who happened to be in the wrong place at the wrong time. Chief among these, of course, was Nick Markowitz, who paid with his life for being in the wrong place at the wrong time.

* * *

By now, Colorado Springs police, neighboring sheriff's offices, Santa Barbara sheriff's detectives and even FBI agents were looking for Jesse James Hollywood in the Colorado Springs area. They chased down more than thirty leads, but none of them helped in capturing Jesse. Lieutenant Skip Arms, of the Colorado Springs Police Department (CSPD), told a reporter about the frustration of Richard Dispenza lying to law enforcement: "Our contention is that had he been truthful with us, detectives would have been able to go to that hotel and make the arrest. Instead, we have this armed and dangerous man who is still out on the streets."

The next day more leads came in, but Arms noted, "Nothing has panned out." Fox Network's *America's Most Wanted* sent a film crew out to the area and they interviewed Lieutenant Arms. He told them in part, "We continue to follow any leads that we get. We've received a lot of calls into our call center and Crime Stoppers."

Lieutenant Burridge, of the Santa Barbara sheriff's office, added, "It's possible that Hollywood has left the Pikes Peak area. If you look at where he went, he went to a place where he knew people and had a knowledge of the area. The only places that he feels like that is in Los Angeles and your neck of the woods (Colorado). Hopefully, there's not another place we don't know about."

Detective Susan Payne, of the CSPD, told a reporter, "The longer this goes on, the more dangerous he becomes. The concern would be, anyone who crosses his path could be in danger. Each hour that goes by, he becomes more dangerous, because he's that much closer to being caught."

One lead pointed to a theft in the area of various weapons and a pickup truck, but this was later discounted. Detectives spoke with various people who had known Hollywood when he had gone to school in the area. One teacher, Marcia Hanning, remembered Jesse Hollywood as a difficult student in her seventh-grade geography class. She said, "He was not a good student. He was not at all positive about school."

There were still Hollywood sightings in the area, but by August 28, Santa Barbara sheriff's detectives had tracked down the Chas Saulsbury lead, and were pretty sure that Jesse Hollywood was either on his way back to the Los Angeles area, or was already there. In fact, they were right—Hollywood and Saulsbury had made it to the Los Angeles area as far back as August 23.

Chas Saulsbury's story would change over time, but the thread of truth seemed to have been that he and Jesse arrived on the north side of Los Angeles, where Saulsbury checked them in to a motel called the Country Inn. While there, Jesse set up a meeting with his father at the Sagebrush Inn, which was nearby. But instead of going there himself, he sent Chas. For whatever reason Chas and Jack Hollywood never met. At least that was both their stories later. And, apparently, Jesse Hollywood did not meet his father in the area then.

What did occur was that after Chas's abortive trip to the Sagebrush Inn, he returned to the motel room to find Jesse Hollywood looking at local television news. In a moment of surreal surprise, Chas said, "Jesse was looking at the television screen and his photo was on the screen. The news was about him being the ringleader of the killing of Nick Markowitz." This term "ringleader" would cause a lot of contention in the years to come, but right then, Jesse had more pressing things on his mind. He asked Chas to take him to John Roberts's house, and Chas complied.

Jesse Hollywood was not through using his connections to evade the law. He went to visit John Roberts at his residence, and Roberts would later testify that he heard someone at the door, went to the doorway and unexpectedly saw Jesse Hollywood standing there. Roberts said, "I got up and went to the door and grabbed him, pulled him into the house and shut the door. It was a very emotional meeting for the both of us."

While there, Jesse learned something important that Roberts had done in his absence. Roberts had thoroughly washed the van and wiped it down with solvent to erase evidence and fingerprints. Roberts added that when Jesse asked him to get a fake ID, he declined. Roberts later said, "I couldn't have him stay at my house."

The meeting between Jesse James Hollywood and John Roberts was very short, and according to Roberts, and later Jack Hollywood, Jesse did not contact his father or mother on this return trip to the area.

One other important thing happened there. Chas Saulsbury was supposed to wait for Jesse to come back outside of Roberts's house. Instead, he took off as soon as Jesse went into the house. Later, Chas would say, "I'd had enough!"

Chas drove back along the route he and Jesse had taken. Chas even stopped a few hours at a hotel in Las Vegas to get some rest. When he got back to the Colorado Springs area, he was met by detectives and willingly told them all about the trip out to California with Jesse. Saulsbury said they had reached Las Vegas on August 22, and had spent the night at the Mandalay Bay. The next day they drove to southern California and stayed at the Country Inn in Calabasas, north of Los Angeles. Then he had left Jesse Hollywood off in West Hills. On the trip west, Chas said, Jesse had shaved off his goatee.

Saulsbury also had some other important things to tell detectives:

Q: Did they (Hollywood, Rugge and Skidmore) ever find Ben?

A: They didn't find Ben, but just by a chance encounter, they saw his little brother walking down the street and they grabbed him in hopes that Nick would tell Jesse where Ben was.

Q: And did he?

A: No. Jesse said that Nick didn't say anything. Didn't tell him where he was. So they got him in the van and Jesse said one of the guys was pointing an AR-15 at Nick and they put a bag over his head.

Q: Were there already weapons in the van?

A: Jesse said they were driving around with an AR-15 and a shotgun, for sure, and some other stuff.

Q: He didn't say how he was related to the guns?

A: Just that they were his.

Now things got to a very important part, which helped fill in for the detectives why Jesse James Hollywood would have wanted Nick dead.

Q: Do you know where they went after they picked Nick up?

A: He didn't say specifically, but they went to some gangster's house that either Jesse or Rugge knew. (Chas may have mistakenly been referring to Richard Hoeflinger as a gangster.) They just had him there and at that point Jesse said he contacted his attorney to find out the ramifications of what he was into by just kidnapping this kid.

Q: Are those Jesse's words?

A: Yes.

Q: Okay, what did he say?

A: Jesse said he was talking to the attorney, and that the attorney said that he was in deep enough trouble already, that he might as well, I'm kind of unclear on this, but I was under the impression that Jesse was kind of spurred into action pretty much by the words of his attorney.

Q: And what do you mean, "spurred into action"?

A: Well, they had Nick, and he was captive, and Jess said that his lawyer said to him that kidnapping is a big enough offense. It's already life in prison. That if he were to get out and let any of the authorities know, that he'd be in hot water. (Chas was referring to Nick possibly escaping and telling on his captors.)

Q: And that's what Jesse told you his attorney told?

A: That's what Jesse said his attorney said.

Q: So what did Jesse do?

A: Jesse, then after talking to his attorney, gets in contact, I don't know if it was over the phone or in person, with Hoyt and Rugge, and pretty much of what I understand is that they decide to go ahead and kill the kid and bury the body.

Q: Who decided that?

A: Um, the group. Jesse, Hoyt and Rugge.

Q: And did anyone in particular decide to do it?

A: Um, Jesse said that Hoyt said, "I'll do it," quote, unquote.

Q: And did Hoyt have any expressions about him when he did that?

A: Jesse said he said it without batting an eye.

Q: What did Jesse do then? What did he tell you he did?

A: Jesse said that after talking with Hoyt and Rugge about following through with the murder, he got in touch with his girlfriend and they left L.A. I'm not sure what the time frame was, but he stayed in Palm Springs for a little while and they stayed at the Bellagio in Vegas.

A short time later Saulsbury recalled that Jesse James Hollywood's lawyer was named Steve or Stephen. It would take a while, but eventually law enforcement would surmise that this "Steve or Stephen" was Stephen Hogg.

Knowing that Jesse James Hollywood had communicated with his dad, Jack, Detective Mike West sought and obtained a search warrant for Jack Hollywood's house. In part, the search warrant allowed him and other detectives to search Jack Hollywood's residence in West Hills, California, and the surrounding yard. The house was described as a two-story white residence with an attached garage. The warrant allowed the search of all rooms, attics, basements, storage rooms and garages.

The warrant also included the seizure of any identifications of Jesse James Hollywood, and any false names he might be using, as well as all computer systems, floppy disks and CDs. Along with those, detectives were to seize all writings to and from Jesse Hollywood that seemed relevant, and to intercept incoming telephone calls that might occur during the search.

There was a huge litany of items seized by various detectives in the residence. Detective Williams got a Pacific Bell phone bill in the name of Jack Hollywood, found in the master bedroom, as well as a receipt and matchbook from a place named Cambridge Farms. Detective Bruce Cornell found phone numbers written on pieces of paper on the nightstand in the master bedroom. He also collected two Baggies of marijuana from the upstairs bathroom. In the kitchen Cornell seized an address book with phone numbers.

Detective Johnson found various identification papers with the name Jesse James Hollywood on them in the office, as well as miscellaneous school papers. Detective Reicheck seized a brown cardboard box on the left floorboard of a vehicle, and there was $7,600 within the box.

Detective Olmstead found various paperwork documents in the name of Jack Hollywood in the same vehicle, in a green camera bag and in the glove compartment. He also picked up sheets of paper from the southwest bedroom, while Detective Reicheck got a pad of papers from the northwest bedroom. Various written items on paper were found in the kitchen and on a sofa table, and Detective Flaa seized 1999 tax documents found in the drawer of a kitchen table.

Detective Flaa also seized surveillance equipment from a walk-in closet of the master bedroom, and Sergeant Walton got a letter from a table in the master bedroom. Receipts were obtained by Sergeant Willis from a trash can, and he grabbed check stubs and mortgage statements found in the den as well. Two letters to Jesse were seized, a Nokia cell phone in the garage, and a two-page letter from Jesse's mom to him found in the garage. One of the most intriguing items of all was found by Detective Williams inside a book from the living room. In the book was an airline boarding pass.

A second search-and-seizure operation garnered a black address book, which was taken, as well as miscellaneous phone numbers, receipts, bills and papers. Two glass vials with a white powder were seized, along with a digital scale and two small zip Baggies. Weapons seized were a black-powder pistol, a black-powder derringer, four boxes of ammunition, and one can of black powder. Found in the nightstand was United States currency, including fifteen 100-dollar bills. Additional items that appeared to concern drugs were a box containing white powder, a black round case containing white powder, one razor blade, and a perfume snifter containing a white powder.

Sheriff's detectives got a tip that Jesse Hollywood might be at John Roberts's residence. A Los Angeles county SWAT team was put together and surrounded Roberts's home on McLaren Avenue, at about 4:15 P.M., on August 28. Using a bullhorn, they spoke to Roberts, who was inside the house, and persuaded him to come outside, but there was no response from Jesse James Hollywood.

Believing Hollywood was still holed up inside, the SWAT team started firing tear gas canisters into the house. Over a three-hour period, almost three hundred pounds of tear gas were fired into the house, while police helicopters buzzed overhead. When John Roberts later assessed the damage done to his house, he said, "The whole interior of the house was destroyed." The SWAT team entered the house at seven-fifteen P.M., but didn't announce that Jesse Hollywood was not in there until eight forty-five P.M. John Roberts had just become the latest person to have his life turned upside down by Jesse James Hollywood's rash decision to kidnap Nick Markowitz on August 6, 2000.

Some of the neighbors were disgusted by the disruption of their lives by the siege and clouds of tear gas drifting in the area. Many of them had to hide in their homes for the entire time. Terri Carrera said, "We moved here five years ago, thinking this was a good neighborhood to raise our kids. And here we are in the suburbs and this happens!"

Another neighbor added, "This is nuts! Just nuts!"

More and more was now starting to come out in the area newspapers about Ben Markowitz, Nick Markowitz, Jesse James Hollywood and his friends. Santa Barbara County sheriff Jim Thomas told reporters, "This is one of those things that you just shake your head at. They were boyhood friends who used to play baseball together."

Barron Rugge, Jesse Rugge's dad, told a reporter, "It's a nightmare. Jesse (Rugge) had said (up at Lizard's Mouth), 'What are you doing?' and Hoyt just plugged him. It was Hoyt and Hollywood that put him up to it. I'm emotionally crushed. He's been a great kid, he just got messed up with the wrong people. I knew them when they were together in West Hills, when they were twelve or thirteen."

William Skidmore's mother told reporters, "We are in shock. Just in shock. It's all very, very upsetting. We love our son."

Perhaps the most crushed, and also most self-deluding, was Victoria Hoyt. She told a reporter that when she spoke to Ryan after his arrest, he was laughing and saying he did not do the crime. "Ryan is loving, sweet and kind."

George Cliffords, who had coached all the boys in baseball, except Graham Pressley, related, "It's on everybody's lips, but no one can say what happened after they were about twelve or thirteen years old. If you're asking if there was something that indicated things would go this way, I have to say no."

Frank Leonor, a league official, added, "I remember Skidmore the most. He was the nicest of the whole group. I would say that Hollywood was extroverted. He was a leader. Skidmore would be more of a follower. These boys are the same age as mine. I'm looking at this situation and counting my blessings."

Ryan Hoyt, William Skidmore, Jesse Rugge and Graham Pressley came before Santa Barbara Superior Court judge Deborah Talmage for their arraignment. Asked how they pled, each and every one of them pled, "Not guilty."

As a grand jury was put together, Santa Barbara County deputy district attorney (DDA) Ron Zonen began compiling a large witness list, which included many detectives and also civilians connected to parts of the case. These included, in part, Brian Affronti, Stephen Hogg, Jack Hollywood, Laurie Hollywood, Gabriel Ibarra, Michelle Lasher, Pauline Mahoney, Ben Markowitz, Jeff Markowitz, John Roberts, Chas Saulsbury, Casey Sheehan and Natasha Adams.

In a hearing between DDA Gerald Franklin and DDA Ron Zonen, and attorney James Blatt, for Jesse James

Hollywood's parents, Jack and Laurie, a deal was hammered out where they would have immunity while testifying to the grand jury.

One of the most important pieces of the puzzle on this list of witnesses concerned Jesse James Hollywood's attorney, Stephen Hogg, and what had transpired between him and Jesse on August 8, 2000. Hogg cited attorney/client privilege to keep what was said between him and Hollywood private. Whether he would be compelled to testify would make a huge difference in whether the prosecutors could make a case against Jesse James Hollywood as to motive for the killing of Nick Markowitz.

Of all the names of people on the list, including those behind bars, such as William Skidmore, Jesse Rugge, Ryan Hoyt and Graham Pressley, one name stood out for its glaring absence—Jesse James Hollywood.

10

A FUNERAL AND AN INDICTMENT

Santa Barbara had always been perceived as an upscale community spared violent crime, but when the first news articles of the kidnapping and murder made their way into the newspapers, it was like a bombshell exploding in the seaside town. Under the headline ANATOMY OF A KIDNAPPING, the *Santa Barbara News-Press* stated: *During the two days that fifteen-year-old Nicholas Markowitz was held in Santa Barbara before being killed by his kidnappers in early August, more than two dozen people learned of his plight and yet did not call police.* The article went on to relate that Hoyt, Pressley, Rugge and Skidmore had all entered not guilty pleas, and that Jesse James Hollywood was on the run and the subject of a nationwide manhunt.

The article stated that a host of young people, Jesse Hollywood's father, a friend and a lawyer had all heard parts of what was going on before Nick was murdered, and yet none of them had contacted authorities. Prosecutors called the abduction "a continuous ongoing sort of party with an edge," where friends of the kidnappers dropped in to smoke dope and take Valium.

The article also related that Nick had first been taken to a home on Modoc Road, where Richard Hoeflinger and another young man lived. Hoeflinger knew that something was wrong, but he stated, "I didn't want to get involved. I did not want to know what was going on."

Citing further evidence, newspapers reported that Gabriel Ibarra had been at Hoeflinger's house and had seen Nick with duct tape on his arms and legs. Supposedly, Jesse Hollywood had threatened Ibarra if he ever told anyone. Of this threatening nature of Jesse Hollywood, DDA Ron Zonen said, "He has a kind of aura about him where he just walks in and the whole atmosphere chills."

Articles told of Nick being taken to the home of Jesse Rugge's father, and being allowed to walk around freely there, as well as at Rugge's girlfriend's house. By this phrase they probably meant Natasha Adams's home. It was there that Natasha and Kelly Carpenter had cleaned Nick's wounds and first learned of his abduction. One of the young women there even told a detective later, "The atmosphere was mostly light and fun," but she started to have second thoughts about the atmosphere by the second day.

It came out in a report that when Natasha Adams found out what the consequences could be, she confronted Nick about his situation and said, "I asked Nick if they were going to kill him. And he said, 'Oh, no, of course not.'" Yet, around this same time, she heard that Jesse Rugge had already been offered $2,500 to murder Nick, an offer that Rugge refused. Nonetheless, Natasha said, both Rugge and Pressley were afraid of Jesse James Hollywood.

Natasha told authorities, and this got into the newspaper, that she had confronted Rugge and told him to take Nick back home before something terrible happened.

According to the report: *"Rugge looked me in the eye and he swore to me that he was going to take Nick home, and he said it a number of times that afternoon."*

Ben Markowitz had also spoken to detectives, and it was reported that he said: *"Up until what happened, as far as I was concerned, they (Jesse Hollywood's buddies) were a bunch of punks that couldn't fight worth a lick. I never seen them doing anything like I heard what they did."*

Articles reported that Nick's body had been found lying facedown in a shallow grave—bound, gagged and shot nine times. By the time a grand jury was being empaneled, prosecutors already had surmised the reason Jesse James Hollywood had ordered Nick Markowitz killed. Ron Zonen stated to reporters, "It appears that Jesse Hollywood consulted with an attorney and possibly learned what the penalty was for kidnapping, particularly kidnapping and extortion. Hollywood became spooked by it, and the decision was made that they weren't going to return Nick, but rather they would kill him."

Also talking to authorities was Casey Sheehan, and he said that on Wednesday afternoon, August 9, after the murder had occurred, Jesse James Hollywood, Michelle Lasher, Will Skidmore and Ryan Hoyt had come to his house. Supposedly, at that time Hoyt had told Sheehan that he had "taken care of a problem" with Nick Markowitz. When Sheehan asked what the problem was, Hoyt had told him, "It's best you don't know."

An indictment was in the early stages of being drawn up concerning Jesse James Hollywood, Ryan James Hoyt, William Robert Skidmore, Jesse Taylor Rugge and Graham William Pressley. The first paragraph stated that the above named *were accused by the grand jury of the County of Santa Barbara of the crimes of Murder and*

Kidnapping for purposes of ransom or extortion. As far as the murder went, Count 1 of the indictment stated that the perpetrators had with malice murdered Nicholas Samuel Markowitz, with special circumstances of the murder taking place during the commission of kidnapping. Special Allegation 1 alleged that a TEC-9 handgun had been discharged by Ryan Hoyt, which caused the death of Nicholas Markowitz. Special Allegation 2 stated that the others, with Ryan Hoyt, had been in league with Ryan Hoyt when he murdered Nick. Special Allegation 3 said that Graham Pressley was over the age of fourteen and *committed an offense which if committed by an adult would be punishable by death or imprisonment in a state prison for life.*

Count 2 dealt with kidnapping for purposes of ransom or extortion. It related that the conspirators forcibly detained Nick for the purpose of ransom and extortion of money from him. (In effect, he was being held as ransom to make his brother pay a debt.) Special Allegation 1 of this count stated that Nick had suffered death while in the commission of the kidnapping.

The newspapers, by now, were also giving a more indepth look into the world that Jesse James Hollywood and his friends had inhabited. The *Santa Barbara News-Press* called it a "suburban underworld," and related, *Ryan Hoyt arrived at the home of Jesse James Hollywood every morning at 10 AM. He would pick up the beer cans strewn around from parties the night before. Then he would go outside to clean up the backyard. The twenty-year-old Hoyt behaved like a modern-day indentured servant to pay off a $1,200 drug debt that he owed Hollywood.*

Even as the investigation into Nick's death and the hunt for Jesse James Hollywood continued, Nick Markowitz was laid to rest at Eden Memorial Park in Mission Hills.

It was a bright sunny day, in contrast to the somber mood that engulfed hundreds of mourners, including Nick's parents, Jeff and Susan. At least three hundred people packed the memorial service, half of them teenagers who had known Nick.

Rabbi James Lee Kaufman told the gathering, "There are deaths such as this when we can't shake an angry finger at God and say, 'Why?' We can only look to ourselves." Some of Nick's friends also spoke, including sixteen-year-old Zach Winters, who said, "You were always a call away when I needed you. Things aren't going to be the same without you. All I can say is, I love you, man. We'll always be friends for life."

After the memorial service six young pallbearers carried Nick's casket up a grassy slope to the grave site. Three of the pallbearers were openly weeping. One of Nick's friends said later, "He always made me laugh. Even when I was mad at him, I couldn't stay mad for long."

Another friend added, "You wake up and realize all the drug dealing has to stop."

One person who did not attend the memorial service and funeral was Ben Markowitz, out of respect for Susan. He told a reporter for KNBC that if he showed up, he wouldn't have blamed Susan if she wringed his neck. Then he added, "I wish I was the one who was gone. I can't even fathom anyone doing that to him, especially people that I grew up with, laughed with and cried with. I mean, these were my friends."

Even before the funeral, Jeff and Susan Markowitz had created a candlelight memorial in their front yard. They had set up large photographs on poster boards with photos of Nick during various stages of his life. They also made a short comment to the public: "Nick was a very smart, charismatic, compassionate person. He loved nothing more than participating in activities such as drama and karate. He loved drawing and video games. Nicholas

Samuel Markowitz's memory will be in the hearts of his immediate family."

Adding to the theme of disbelief, which pervaded the community of West Hills, was an individual named Ryan, who had played baseball with Jesse James Hollywood on the El Camino Real team. Ryan said, "Jesse was always mellow. It's weird, because I know the victim, and though I'm not going to lose any sleep over it, I'm not going to ever forget it, either. It will always be in my head. It's just too weird."

In fact, Ryan had seen Jesse Hollywood just days before the kidnapping. Ryan recalled, "He was cool as usual. He was always cool with me. He wasn't like some guy plotting a murder."

Into the autumn of 2000, attorney Stephen Hogg was fighting the prosecutors' contention that he was going to have to testify as to what his conversation had been with Jesse Hollywood at his residence. Hogg not only asserted attorney/client privilege, but also asserted the privilege against self-incrimination. To override these contentions, DDA Zonen put together a Motion to Compel document and submitted it to Judge William Gordon, who was presiding over the case. In laying out his Statement of Facts, Zonen wrote that on August 6, 2000, Nick Markowitz had been abducted by Jesse James Hollywood, William Skidmore and Jesse Rugge. After Nick was being held at Rugge's residence, Hollywood had gone to attorney Stephen Hogg's residence, sometime on the late afternoon of Tuesday, August 8. Hollywood told Hogg that someone he knew had kidnapped a boy and they were holding him. Hogg, in turn, told Hollywood that such an action could get the kidnappers life in prison. It was after this conversation, Zonen contended, that Jesse Hollywood had hired Ryan Hoyt to kill Nick Markowitz.

It was the conversation between Jesse Hollywood and

Chas Saulsbury on the road back from Las Vegas that had tipped authorities off to this Hogg/Hollywood connection, and Zonen emphasized this in his motion. Saulsbury told detectives during testimony that Hollywood mentioned that the attorney's name was Steve.

Chas Saulsbury, in part, had these things to say about the subject of Jesse and an attorney:

> Q: What did he (Hollywood) say about the conversation with the attorney? What did he tell you?
>
> A: They had grabbed Nick and they were trying to get Nick's older brother, and in the hopes of finding him, they grabbed his little brother just on a whim on the side of a street, and they took him to some-body's house. And Jesse called his lawyer, I believe, because of what he told me. Jesse talked to his lawyer to find out implications of the kidnapping and whatnot. At that point, from what he told me, the lawyer said that he was in enough trouble and they should get rid of the kid.

Zonen stressed to the judge that Code 912 stated, "Attorney/client privilege is waived with respect to a communication protected by such privilege if any holder of the privilege, without coercion, had disclosed a signif-icant part of the communication or has consented to such disclosure made by anyone." Zonen also cited a case en-titled *National Steel Products Co.* v. *Superior Court.* The relevant part of that stated, "The privilege is waived even if the conversation is overheard by an unintended but known third party." Since Jesse Hollywood had willingly told Chas Saulsbury what his conversation between Stephen Hogg and himself had supposedly been, the attorney/client privilege was no longer valid, at least ac-cording to Zonen.

The reason Zonen was pushing so hard on all of this

was, as he stated, "Hollywood's conversation with his attorney, Hogg, was the pivotal point of the kidnapping. It was the moment Hollywood decided that Nick Marko-witz should be killed, rather than risk a lifetime in prison. It is a statement that not only furthered the conspiracy, but raised it to a higher level—one of murder."

Trying to tie the name "Steve," which Chas Saulsbury had mentioned coming from Jesse Hollywood, to Stephen Hogg, Zonen had evidence of things that John Roberts and Jack Hollywood had mentioned as well.

Judge Gordon eventually ruled that Stephen Hogg had to testify before a grand jury, and Hogg told reporters, "I'm not a witness. I'm a lawyer. But as much as I hate it, I follow what the judge says."

Ron Zonen told a reporter, "As to the conversation Hogg had with Hollywood, we need to know the specifics of that discussion. The information he has could be very important to the prosecution and should not be kept secret until the moment of trial for no better reason than that Mr. Hogg is inconvenienced or embarrassed."

Because of the comments between Jesse Hollywood and Stephen Hogg, the DA's office was not content to just prosecute Hoyt, Skidmore, Rugge and Pressley. They also wanted the person they deemed to be the mastermind behind the murder—Jesse James Hollywood. Of course, the first thing they had to do was catch him, and that was easier said than done.

11

REVELATIONS

There were many people who eventually testified before the grand jury, but amongst these Jack Hollywood, John Roberts and Michelle Lasher would give some of the most telling insights into Jesse James Hollywood's world. DDA Ron Zonen's questioning of Jack Hollywood before the grand jury was lengthy and detailed. Zonen did not always believe the answers he was getting from Jack Hollywood. In several instances the answers seemed to be in variance with what Zonen knew, or thought he knew. Nonetheless, the questions and answers shed new light on some of the events that had occurred.

Things kicked off by Ron Zonen saying, "Mr. Hollywood, good morning. You've just appeared before Judge Gordon, is that correct?"

"Yes, it is," Jack Hollywood replied.

"Judge Gordon—did he grant and convey upon you a grant of immunity?"

"Yes."

"And at this time, is it correct that you're prepared to testify and answer all questions?"

"Yes."

Ron Zonen had Jack testify about his phone conversation with Stephen Hogg at the Ventana Inn in Big Sur, his drive back to the L.A. area with his wife, Laurie, and his trying to page Jesse, but being unsuccessful. Zonen also asked him about John Roberts and what their plan was. Jack said, "I talked to Jesse, and Jesse said that they were just scared, but that the kid was okay and he was just hanging out at some house somewhere. I didn't know at the time which house it was, or whose house it was, or what city it was in."

"Did you ask him (Jesse) specifically to tell you where?"

"He was hesitant. I said, 'Who was with you?' and I started to say some names of kids that he hung out with, and he said, 'I don't want to say anything! I don't want to say anything! I'll find out where he is and then you can go and get him.'"

Zonen asked, "Do you know a Jesse Rugge?"

Jack answered, "Yes, I do."

"Do you know that he lives part-time in Santa Barbara, part-time in the Valley?"

"Yeah."

"At some point did it occur to you that might be the place that they would have taken this kid?"

"Not really. It didn't occur to me. No."

"Were you under the belief that at the time that you were having this conversation with your son at Michelle Lasher's home that this kid was still being detained, to some extent?"

"Yes."

"Did it concern you?"

"It did concern me, if he was being detained."

Many of Jack Hollywood's answers did not satisfy Zonen that Jack had done much of anything to make sure that the "detained kid" was set free. Zonen told him, "Mr. Hollywood, I'm having difficulty believing that this is true, that you had now spent about twelve to sixteen hours worrying about the fact that your son was involved in a kidnapping, and you finally had a conversation with the person who your son tells you was responsible for this kid's release, and you didn't bother to ask him (Ryan Hoyt) who this person (Nick) was."

Jack replied, "I may have, but I don't recall. I mean, to me, it wouldn't matter who it was, the important thing was to get him out of the situation he was in. And maybe I did ask, and maybe he told me, and it really didn't mean anything to me."

"Didn't it occur to you at some point that there may be some kid you knew, whose parents you knew? Did that cross your mind at any time during this twelve- to sixteen-hour period?"

"It may have."

"All right, when you asked him (Hoyt) the question, and he may have given an answer, do you remember if it was a name you recognized?"

"I'm just not sure if he gave me the answer, or if it was that important to me what the name of the kid was."

"You didn't have a discussion with your wife at any time while you were driving down from Big Sur? 'I wonder who this person is that they took and why they took him?'"

"At that point when I was driving from there, I didn't have that much information, and I didn't discuss it with my wife. I just said there was some kind of jam that these kids have gotten into and I want to find out what it was."

"While you were talking with your son Jesse, did you ask him who this kid was, and what the gripe was about?"

"I'm not sure if I did."

"You're not sure if you asked your son who the kid was?"

"I'm not sure if I asked that question. I mean, we can go

round and round, but I'm just telling you, I don't recall exactly if I knew what the kid's name was at that point. Maybe I did, and maybe I didn't. It didn't seem important to me. The thing that was important, if there was a kid, it didn't matter what his name was. [I was thinking,] 'Let's make sure that nothing happens to him.'"

"Were you kind of under the belief that this might have something to do with your son's drug dealing?"

"No."

"You were aware that your son was dealing drugs?"

"Yes."

"Your son owned a couple of homes, didn't he?"

"No, he owned one home."

"He owned a few cars at different times?"

"You know, reading the paper, it made it sound like he had millions of dollars. What he had was a 1986 Mercedes with about two hundred thousand miles on it that he bought for four thousand dollars."

"He also had a Honda that he insured for over thirty thousand dollars, didn't he?"

"Yeah. I can tell you about that car. I bought the car for him. And his hobby was fixing up cars, getting them painted, putting things on them and doing things. And over a two-year period, he got it fixed up and got it into a magazine. Then I guess he had it insured for a lot of money because it was a valuable car."

"And how long after he insured it, was it stolen?"

"I'm not sure."

"Were you aware of the fact that it was stolen?"

"Yes."

"Do you know if he collected on the insurance?"

"I think he said so, yes."

"Do you know if your son had any enemies?"

"Yeah."

"Do you know who they are?"

"The only one I can think of was Ben Markowitz."

"And what did you understand to be the nature of the friction between your son and Ben Markowitz?"

"I knew that Markowitz was always threatening him. I think Jesse felt that the guy killed his dog and broke windows and always called up and left threatening messages on his voice mail."

"Did you ever talk with your son specifically about the allegation that Ben killed his dog? I mean, it would seem to me to be a fairly serious matter, someone intentionally killing one's pet."

"Yes."

"What kind of dog was it?"

"It was a puppy. Pit bull puppy."

"How was the dog killed?"

"It was mysterious. I wasn't sure if the dog just caught his collar on the fence, or if it was choked, or if it was poisoned, or whatever. But, mysteriously, the dog was dead."

"How long prior to the incident that we're referring to here, was the death of the dog?"

"Probably three months."

"Now, assuming the dog was killed, the likely number one choice of who would have done it would have been Ben Markowitz, according to your son, is that right?"

"Right."

"Was there any other name that came up?"

"No."

"At some point in time, your son was actually friends with Ben Markowitz, wasn't he?"

"Right."

"Do you know when they were friends, what period of time that was?"

"Not very long, I don't think. Maybe four or five months."

"Do you know what ended their friendship?"

"I think from what I heard, that the guy (Ben) was always hanging around there, and then one day he just stole, well, one time Jesse wasn't home, and Markowitz found his wallet or something, grabbed a thousand bucks out of it and just disappeared. Everybody else that knew Jesse thought the guy was a scumbag and that he was a leech. A crack-smoking kind of guy."

"So Jesse told you that he believed Ben Markowitz stole about a thousand bucks from him?"

"Yeah."

"All right, so it was bad blood even before the dog died. When did you understand the broken-window incident to occur, and what do you understand that to be?"

"The broken-window incident—Jesse was going to move out of the house and go move into an apartment. Go back to school and get away from every problem he was having. And they (he and his friends) had already moved most of the stuff out of the house into a storage unit. They were just staying over for the last night to clear up the rest of the stuff, and then he was going to go out and start looking for another place to live. And, evidently, windows were smashed and another threatening message was left: 'This is just the beginning. It doesn't matter where you go, I'm going to get you!' Blah, blah, blah."

"So, again, during all of this period of time, the first name that comes up in Jesse's mind is Ben Markowitz, right?"

"Right."

"There's nobody else that you're aware of at this point, at least according to your son, who he believed posed a threat to him?"

"Well, I think he said that the guy (Ben) was involved in some kind of gang and had people posing some kind of threats. As soon as I saw that kid I said, 'Why is this guy always hanging around your house?' He was living in his house. Jesse was working, laying hardwood floor. He wasn't involved in a big giant drug scheme, like the paper said. He was working laying hardwood floor. His girlfriend was living there, and he was doing well for a kid his age. And then all of a sudden, this Markowitz kid showed up. When I saw that, I noticed a change in Jesse's personality, and I said, 'What's this guy doing? He's over there answering your phone all the time.' Next thing I know, Jesse's girlfriend is moving out. And Jesse got kind of mad at me and he said, 'Well, this guy is my friend. I don't need you telling me what's going on.' And after all of this stuff started happening, he was very hesitant to tell me about it. He didn't want to tell me because, kind of like, 'You were right about this guy and he's not a good guy.'"

"All right, let me ask you this—you were having a conversation with your son where you believed that he was involved in the abduction of some kid, to some extent—why didn't it occur to you that Ben Markowitz might have been involved in this?"

"I think it occurred to me."

"You think you might have known that it was Ben Markowitz's brother who was abducted at that point?"

"I may have."

"All right. Didn't that really change things rather significantly that you know the identity of the person who was taken up there? I mean, wouldn't it change your view very substantially at this point, as of the time of the second conversation the next day with John Roberts?"

"Change my view from what to what?" Jack asked.

"Well, did you make an effort to contact Ben Markowitz's parents?"

"I don't know them. No, I didn't."

"Did you know who they are?"

"No. I never met them. I didn't know where they lived. I didn't know anything about them."

"Did you ask your son anything about them?"

"No."

"Did you open up a telephone book and look up the name Markowitz?"

"No."

"Why not? You were concerned about locating him.

Wouldn't that be the obvious answer as to how to locate him?"

"No, that's . . . I didn't do that."

As for any questions that related to Stephen Hogg, according to Jack Hollywood, Hogg had given him permission to talk about the conversations that had taken place between himself and Hogg.

Zonen asked, "Then let me address that question right now. What specifically did Mr. Hogg tell you about the difficulties your son was having?"

Jack answered, "He didn't get specific about it. He just told me that Jesse was in some kind of jam, and that it was serious. And you know, that was pretty much all I remember."

"Did he tell you that your son asked him specifically what kind of consequence there was to what he did?"

"No."

"In other words, how much time potentially he could serve?"

"No, he didn't."

"Did Mr. Hogg tell you what the jam was?"

"Not specifically. He was very vague about it, but he sounded like it was serious."

"Did you ask him any questions along the lines of, has he hurt anybody? Did he steal something? Was he arrested? Did you ask questions along that line?"

"Not that I can recall."

"And why not? Wouldn't you have been interested as a parent?"

"I was interested, but I've known Mr. Hogg for a long time, and I knew by the tone of his voice, he didn't like to talk about things like that over the telephone, and that it was serious. And I told him, 'Okay, I'm going to come down and I'm going to find my son,' and that was it."

"Who called who [first]?"

"I called him regarding a case that I had in Ventura."

Jack Hollywood said the phone call had been made

from the Ventana Inn, and that it had been in the later part of the afternoon. Zonen wondered why Jack called Hogg at his home, and not his office, and Jack Hollywood said that he knew Hogg wouldn't be at his office around 3:00 or 4:00 P.M.

Zonen once again asked if Hogg had been more specific about Jesse rather than just saying the situation was "serious."

Jack Hollywood answered, "Steve said, 'He's okay, but this is serious.' And I said, 'Well, what's it about?' And he said, 'It's not something that we should discuss on the phone.' And I said, 'Okay, well, then, I'm going to be down tonight.'"

"Did you ask Mr. Hogg to call John Roberts?"

"I'm not sure if I initiated that. I might have," Jack answered.

"Why would you have asked Mr. Hogg to call John Roberts?"

"Well, because John is a close family friend and he was there, and if there was something that he could do before the eight hours, or seven hours, whatever it was going to take to drive down, he would be the one that I would have called."

"Did you ask Mr. Hogg to give more information to John Roberts than he gave to you?"

"No."

"Did you ask Mr. Hogg to meet with John Roberts?"

"I don't recall if I did or not."

"Did you feel that this was a problem that John Roberts could deal with?"

"I didn't know exactly what the problem was, but I just knew that John . . . well, if Jesse needed help with something, he was the guy that I would have got ahold of."

"You felt that John Roberts could remedy a problem that your son was having?"

"I don't think I would put it that way. I'd just put it that he's a good family friend."

"Okay, let me get back to the conversation that you had with Mr. Hoyt in the park. Tell me about your conversation with Mr. Hoyt. Did you ask him why this happened?"

"I don't think I did."

"Did you ask him what the nature of the event was? What happened?"

"He was evasive and vague and just seemed very rattled," Jack replied.

"Did you ask him where Ben Markowitz's brother was?"

"I think so."

"What did he tell you?"

"He said he didn't know. He didn't have any control of it. He said he'd see what he could find out."

"Did you ask him who else was involved in this?"

"I believe I did."

"What did he say?"

"He wouldn't give me any names."

"So, at the conclusion of your conversation with Mr. Hoyt, you had no reason to believe at that moment that Ben Markowitz's brother was safe?"

"Correct."

"You had a conversation with two people, one was your son and the other was a close friend of your son, and neither one of these two people, who you know intimately, were prepared to give you information at all, is that correct?"

"My son gave me the information that he was trying to get ahold of Nick. And that wherever he was, they probably let him go, and then he gave me Ryan's number. And then Ryan didn't indicate to me where he (Nick) was, or anything."

"How come you weren't more insistent in getting information from him?"

"I was getting nowhere with him. He wasn't acting like himself."

Jesse James Hollywood was an accused drug dealer who lived a wild life in southern California and bought his own home by the time he was nineteen years old. *(Mug shot)*

Ben Markowitz by his own admission dealt drugs for Hollywood. They were pals who shared the same residence for awhile.
(Mug shot)

Things went bad between Ben and Jesse when Ben could not repay a drug debt. Hollywood and his girlfriend Michelle went to this restaurant where Ben's girlfriend worked, had a meal, and left without paying the check.
(Author photo)

Ben's younger brother Nick was at Universal City Walk with some friends on the weekend before his abduction. *(Author photo)*

The victim, Nick Markowitz. *(Yearbook photo)*

Jesse and the others roughed up Nick Markowitz next to this wall.
(Author photo)

Jesse James Hollywood and his pals were going up to Santa Barbara at the time of the kidnapping for Fiesta Days. So they decided to take Nick along with them. Fiesta Days harkened back to the Spanish period around Mission Santa Barbara. *(Author photo)*

When Jesse Hollywood left Santa Barbara to go back to Los Angeles, he left Nick Markowitz in the care of Jesse Rugge. Over time, Jesse Rugge and Graham Pressley came to like Nick. Pressley even partied with Nick and two teenage girls at the Lemon Tree Inn in Santa Barbara. *(Author photo)*

Jesse Hollywood spoke with lawyer Stephen Hogg after the kidnapping. *(Courtesy of Santa Barbara News Press)*

The site of Markowitz's murder turned out to be an isolated area in the mountains northeast of Santa Barbara. *(Author photo)*

While Hoyt, Pressley, and Rugge took Nick up into the mountains to be murdered, Jesse Hollywood created an alibi by eating at this steakhouse with his girlfriend Michelle. *(Author photo)*

Hoyt forced Graham Pressley to dig a grave near this rock formation called the Lizard's Mouth.
(Author photo)

Detectives soon arrested Hoyt, Rugge, Pressley, and Skidmore on various charges, but Jesse James Hollywood proved to be more elusive and escaped capture.
(Courtesy of the Santa Barbara Sheriff's Office)

Hoyt, Rugge, and Pressley had their trials at one of America's most beautiful courthouse complexes in Santa Barbara.
(Author photo)

Ryan Hoyt was charged with first degree murder and kidnapping. Because of the enhanced charges, he was eligible for the death penalty. *(Mug shot)*

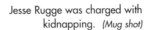

Jesse Rugge was charged with kidnapping. *(Mug shot)*

Graham Pressley, although only seventeen years old at the time, was charged as an adult and faced life in prison. *(Mug shot)*

At their arraignment in Santa Barbara (right to left), Pressley, Hoyt, Rugge, and Skidmore all pleaded not guilty. *(Courtesy of Santa Barbara News Press)*

Both Jeff and Susan Markowitz were crushed by the death of their fifteen-year-old son Nick. *(Courtesy of Santa Barbara News Press)*

Jeff Markowitz hugged a friend in court upon learning that Ryan Hoyt was found guilty of first degree murder and kidnapping. *(Courtesy of Santa Barbara News Press)*

Jesse Rugge was convicted of kidnapping in his trial. *(Courtesy of Santa Barbara News Press)*

Pressley was shown a TEC9 automatic, which he said was owned by Jesse James Hollywood and used by Ryan Hoyt to murder Nick Markowitz. *(Courtesy of Santa Barbara News Press)*

Ryan Hoyt at the moment he received the death penalty for the first degree murder of Nick. *(Courtesy of Santa Barbara News Press)*

Incredibly, in 2005, Jesse James Hollywood was tracked to Brazil by the FBI. He was arrested in a seaside resort on the Atlantic coast. *(Mug shot)*

The Santa Barbara Sheriff's Office created this photo to show that Jesse James Hollywood had finally been arrested after evading capture for five years. *(Courtesy of the Santa Barbara Sheriff's Office)*

Jesse James' dad, Jack Hollywood, had troubles of his own in 2005. He was arrested on drug related charges. *(Courtesy of Santa Barbara News Press)*

Judge Brian Hill began to preside over all affairs connected to the Jesse James Hollywood case. *(Author photo)*

Jesse Hollywood had a top notch team of defense lawyers. *(Author photo)*

Defense attorney James Blatt had been named Southern California defense attorney of the year in 2003. *(Author photo)*

The defense team fought tooth and nail for their client, including whether a jury would see Jesse wearing handcuffs and shackles at a trial. *(Author photo)*

By 2005, DDA Ron Zonen, who had been successful in prosecuting Hoyt, Rugge, and Pressley, became mired in controversy. *(Author photo)*

Veteran DDA Joyce Dudley, who might have taken over the Jesse James Hollywood case after Zonen, had troubles of her own. *(Author photo)*

Nick Markowitz is buried in a serene setting at Eden Memorial Park. Nearby several Hollywood celebrities, including Groucho Marx, are interred. *(Author photo)*

"Did you tell him you were going to the police if he didn't answer your question?"

"No."

"Why not?"

"I don't know. I wish I had."

"Did it occur to you to contact the police?"

"Yeah."

"So you made a conscious decision not to?"

"I was just in a really confused and worried state of mind." Jack added, "Everything was a blur from the day it hit the newspaper, and then a couple of days later, my son was wanted. And it was just the newspaper people all around, and police coming to my house. And I was in some kind of state of panic."

Zonen said, "Your life has been very different since that trip to Big Sur, hasn't it?"

Jack replied, "Yes."

Zonen questioned when the next time was that Jack had a conversation with his son, and Jack said it was after he'd learned that Nick Markowitz had been killed. "I was trying to get ahold of Jesse and find out what was going on. What had happened. And he was just avoiding me. He didn't want to talk about anything. I was calling his friends and asking them where I could find him. I never really had any conversation with him after that. I tried to get ahold of him, and I maybe touched base with him on the phone. I said, 'We need to get together.' And he always said, 'I have to do something.'"

Zonen replied, "From the time that you had the conversation with your son, the second conversation at Michelle Lasher's home, to the time that you discovered that there had been a killing in connection with this event, how many conversations did you have with your son?"

"I never had any conversations with him regarding what had happened. I just had tried to page him or track him somewhere and say, 'Let's get together and talk.' But he didn't want to talk about it."

"Did you try to contact anybody else who you knew to be friends of either your son or Ryan Hoyt?"

"I know I tried. I called friends of his to see where he was and tell him to call me."

"Was your son not staying at home during this time?"

"I think he was staying at Michelle's house."

"Did you still believe your son was in danger? That the activity that was the subject matter of your conversation with Mr. Hogg, something that Mr. Hogg convinced you was a serious matter—did you believe that it was any less serious after a number of days had gone by?"

"No."

"How did you learn that Nick Markowitz had been killed?"

"From the newspapers."

"When you saw the newspaper, did it have Nick Markowitz's picture?"

"Yes."

"Did you automatically assume that this was what this was all about?"

"Yes."

"What did you do?"

"I was just out of it. I just looked at it, and I knew my son's life could be over, for all intents and purposes. I was shocked," Jack admitted.

"Mr. Hollywood, I understand your reaction, but the question specifically is—what did you do? Did you call somebody?"

"I probably didn't do anything."

"Did you talk with your wife?"

"Yes, I think so."

"Were you, at the time, living with your wife?"

"No."

"Had the two of you been separated for some time prior to that?"

"Yes."

"Did you call her?"

"I think I was over there. I spent a lot of time over there because I have another son."

"Had you been keeping her advised of what was going on?"

"I think I was sheltering it from her."

"When you saw the article, what did you do, with regard to your wife?"

"I think we talked about it. That somehow our kid might have something to do with this stuff."

"Can I assume that she was as horrified as you were at that point?"

"Yes."

"And perhaps even more so, because she didn't really know what was happening, up to that point?"

"Right. She knew something was going on, but I don't think she wanted to deal with it."

Zonen took Jack back in time to the trip to Palm Springs, and Zonen asked if he had made any efforts to contact Jesse while he was there. Jack said no, that he didn't get to Palm Springs until around midnight, and then left again at 6:00 A.M., after only a few hours' sleep. Zonen asked if Jack had talked to his wife about anything that Jesse had told her, while in Palm Springs, and Jack answered, "She just indicated that he was very distressed and he wasn't himself. He was very upset."

"Did she tell you whether or not she had discussed these issues with your son? The issue specifically of Ben's missing brother?"

"She didn't indicate that she had."

"Did you ask her, why not?"

"I hadn't even really discussed it with her up to that point."

"You seemed not to be making a great big effort to see if you could resolve it. Why not?"

"Like I said, when this whole thing happened, it turned

my life upside down. I was worried about my son. I was worried about what could happen to this kid. And I didn't know what to do. I didn't know if there was anybody I could trust about anything. That I would implicate Jesse in it and would make the situation worse. I was just in a daze."

"Did you try to locate Michelle?"

"I wouldn't have known how. I had her number that one night, and I forgot where I had written it down. I know that I called up where they were staying (in Palm Springs) and I got no answer in the room where they were."

"Did you try to contact Michelle's parents?"

"No."

"Why not?"

"I don't know."

"How long do you believe Jesse stayed in Palm Springs?"

"Two or three days."

Zonen was very dubious that Jack never saw Jesse in person in Palm Springs, but Jack Hollywood remained adamant on this point. Zonen was also very dubious that Jesse's mother had not gotten any information out of Jesse, which she passed on to Jack.

Zonen asked, "Have you talked with your son Jesse since discovering about the homicide?"

"He called my cell phone after the homicide was discovered and he indicated that he was going to go to Colorado. He said Bill."

"Do you know who Bill is?"

"Yeah, Bill Jacques."

"Did you call Richard Dispenza after you learned that your son would be going to Colorado?"

"I'm not sure if I called him or he called me. I mean, by this time I was in a panic. I didn't know what was going on. I think I might have called and left a message where he worked or something, and then he called me back."

"When he called back, did he actually make contact with you?"

"Yeah."

"How many days after learning about the killing of Nicholas Markowitz was it that you had this conversation with Richard Dispenza?"

"I think three or four, but I'm not sure."

"What did you ask Mr. Dispenza . . . what did you tell him?"

"I said, 'I think my kid is in some kind of trouble. I'm not sure how involved he is or what's going on, but the last I heard, he was headed that way.'"

"Did you tell him he might be involved in a murder?"

"No."

"Why not?"

"Because I didn't . . . one, I didn't want to say something like that over a phone. I wasn't sure if Jesse was directly involved with it, and I didn't want to get specific with him about it."

"Did you ask Mr. Dispenza if he would call you if he had any contact with your son?"

"I think I did."

"And did he agree to do so?"

"Yeah."

"Did he then call you when he had contact with your son?"

"It wasn't for a couple of days that he called. He left a message on my home phone, or something like that. I didn't get a chance to talk to him directly."

"Did you hear what the message said?"

"Just, 'Call me back.' He wanted to talk to me. So I called back and I couldn't get ahold of him."

"Did you ever get ahold of him?"

"He got ahold of me, I guess after the FBI had showed up at his house, and he asked me what was going on. And I said, 'I'm not sure, but the kid is in trouble.'"

Zonen wanted to know if Jack had ever called Bill

Jacques in Colorado. Jack answered, "I called his mother, and I told her, 'I think my kid is in trouble. If he gets in contact with you, have him call me. We need to get him a lawyer. He needs to go and face this thing.' She (later) said, 'What's going on?' And I said, 'My kid's in some trouble.' And she said, 'Jesse called and he was, like, two hundred miles away and he asked where Bill was.' And I guess Bill wasn't around, because she said, 'Jesse sounded very upset. Like he was desperate.'"

Zonen asked if anyone else had contacted him about any of this, and Jack answered, "Chris (the man who had leased the Lincoln to Jesse) called me and said that this kid (Chas Saulsbury) had pulled up to his house and got out and said Jesse was in the car, and he wants to talk to his dad. And then he (not clear if it was Saulsbury or Chris) got ahold of me and said, 'We're going to meet Jesse at the Sage Brush Inn (in the Los Angeles area).' I went there and Jesse didn't show up.

"We (Jack and Chris) sat around there and he told me that the kid (Saulsbury) had come up and dropped him off, and then Chris's wife called him and said, 'Come over here.' And then she just said, 'Jesse's going to be at the Country Inn. He's at room 344 at the Country Inn in Calabasas.' So I went out and I called that room and nobody answered. I was kind of waiting at the Sagebrush, waiting around, and then driving around to his friends to see where he might have been, and up near Calabasas where Michelle lived. And I was in a panic. Then I got a call from John Roberts and he said, 'Come over.' I was, like, all the way in a different part of town. But I came over, and John told me, 'Jesse was just here and he wanted me to help him, and he wanted me to get him some ID or something.' And John told Jesse, 'Look, I can't help you. You need to get a lawyer and turn yourself in.' At that, Jesse got kind of upset and just walked out, and that was it. I left John's house and I drove around, looking for him, and the next thing I knew, the police were coming over every night."

"Have you learned of any individual who has been furnishing your son Jesse [with] money?"

"No."

"Do you know where Jesse is today?"

"No, I don't."

John Roberts also had some interesting things to tell the grand jury. Most of it was a recitation of his encounters with Stephen Hogg and Jack Hollywood, and the day that Jesse James Hollywood suddenly showed up at his door. Roberts, however, added a few new things. Roberts spoke of cleaning the white van out with bleach after it was returned by Jesse Rugge. And he also said, "I was interviewed by the FBI and they suggested that I turn my answering machine back on. They thought, perhaps, Jesse would call and I'd be able to figure out where he was calling from. He'd say something. But that has not happened." (Roberts had turned off his answering machine for a spell.)

Asked about Jesse's drug dealing in the San Fernando Valley, Roberts said that it wasn't a family enterprise. He claimed that Jack was not supplying Jesse with the marijuana. Roberts testified, "There was no collaboration that I'm aware of. His dad and I were involved together at one time. Sometime ago, but never in conjunction with Jesse. There are so many people out in the Valley that do this. But insofar as Jack and myself are concerned, we never had anything to do with that."

The most contentious testimony before the grand jury came from Jesse Hollywood's girlfriend, Michelle Lasher. On the drive to Colorado, she said of Jesse's behavior, "It was the same as it had always been. He was just acting normal." These were statements she would contradict later. When it came to their time in Colorado, she was very evasive.

Zonen: Did you meet a person by the name of Richard Dispenza?

Lasher: That name doesn't sound familiar.

Zonen: Somebody, perhaps, that Jesse might have identified to you as his godfather?

Lasher: I met an older man. I don't know who he was.

Zonen: Were you introduced as Sue to the older man?

Lasher: I think so.

Zonen: As of the time of your departure from Colorado, had Jesse discussed any of the events that had taken place in the San Fernando Valley or in Santa Barbara concerning the abduction and killing of Nicholas Markowitz?

Lasher: No.

Zonen: Miss Lasher, isn't it true that you were in Santa Barbara on the seventh of August at the time that Nicholas Markowitz was at Jesse Rugge's house?

Lasher: I don't remember what day it was.

Zonen: All right. Isn't it true that you were in Santa Barbara at the time that Nicholas Markowitz was at Jesse Rugge's house?

Lasher: I have never seen him (Nick), so I don't know.

Zonen: Do you remember driving up there to Santa Barbara?

Lasher: Yeah.

Zonen: Which vehicle were you driving in?

Lasher: I don't remember. I just remember going there. I don't remember the details. It didn't

Zonen: seem out of the ordinary. I've been there many times.

By "many times," how many times is many times?

Lasher: Probably three times before.

Zonen: All right. And how long did you stay in Santa Barbara on this last occasion?

Lasher: Probably a couple of hours. An hour.

Zonen wanted to know if Jesse Hollywood had been dealing drugs, and Michelle shrugged her shoulders. Irritated by this response, Zonen told her, "Miss Lasher, you understand that you have a grant of immunity. Did your attorney explain to you what that meant?"

She said that her lawyer had.

Zonen continued, "What did your attorney explain? What do you understand that to mean?"

She answered, "I have to tell the truth."

"And what happens if you don't tell the truth?"

"I'll get in trouble."

"Do you know to what extent?"

"I'll get arrested."

Zonen responded, "I asked you a question about whether you knew if Jesse Hollywood was dealing drugs, specifically marijuana, and you shrugged your shoulders. Was that the correct answer? Knowing the consequences of what might happen to you if you lie on the witness stand, was that the correct answer?"

"No."

"Okay, what did you understand to be Jesse Hollywood's involvement in the marijuana trade?"

"I don't know exactly. I wasn't involved with it."

"You knew he wasn't working, is that correct?"

"Yes, but he laid hardwood floors for a while."

"'For a while,' you mean what? It was measured more

in weeks or months rather than years during the three years you knew him, isn't that correct?"

"Yes."

"The overwhelming majority of time that you knew him, this three-year period of time that you were boyfriend and girlfriend, he was not working at any visible job that you could see. You can't tell me now it was more than a few months?"

"I don't know how long it was."

"You have a relationship with him that's close enough that you've put his name on your body tattoo, didn't you?"

"Yes," Michelle replied.

"Where is it on your body?"

"On my back."

"And how large a tattoo is it?"

"It's about this big."

"And you're holding your fingers, what, eight inches apart?" Zonen questioned.

"Yeah."

"And what's the name tattooed on your back?"

"It says, 'Jesse James.'"

"At the time you decided to put the tattoo on your back, you knew he was something of a gangster, didn't you?"

"I guess. I mean, I didn't consider it."

"Well, you understand that the name 'Jesse James' is the name most people associate with a man who was a famous outlaw?"

"Yes, but that's his name."

Zonen kept asking how much she knew about Hollywood's marijuana business, and Michelle kept claiming that she was in the dark about it. Zonen even brought up the fact that Jesse Hollywood had owned one home, and was renting another one in Reseda, in which he and Michelle had lived during 1998 and 1999. Jesse had a lot of money and expensive possessions for someone who worked just part-time.

The subject moved on to why Ben had been angry with

Jesse, but Michelle skirted that issue as well by saying that Ben had been angry with a lot of people. Zonen quizzed her on the time that she and Jesse had eaten at BJ's Microbrewery, where Ben's girlfriend had worked, and Jesse left without paying, as an insult to Ben. Michelle said that she understood that incident to be because Ben owed Jesse money.

Zonen asked, "When you were driving up to Santa Barbara on this last occasion, did Jesse mention anything to you about Nick Markowitz?"

"No."

Zonen replied, "I need to tell you something, Miss Lasher. We have now had two witnesses who have testified in this proceeding (Natasha Adams and Kelly Carpenter) that you were in Santa Barbara at Jesse Rugge's house at the time that Nick Markowitz was there. Two witnesses have testified that both of them were introduced to you. Both can give a graphic description of you, and you have to agree that description's easy to give. They both have a description of a brunette, pretty and petite. One of them said that she believed your name was Michelle. So, do you remember being introduced to two young women, both about the age of seventeen?"

Michelle answered that she recalled being introduced to "a bunch of girls" in Santa Barbara, but that she didn't recall the girls Zonen was talking about.

Zonen replied, "I'm finding it difficult to believe that Jesse Hollywood brought you to Jesse Rugge's house, after he had been instrumental in kidnapping Nicholas Markowitz, knowing that Nicholas Markowitz was there at Rugge's house, without telling you something about what was going on. Would you like to take a moment and talk with your attorney before you resume your testimony?"

Michelle said that she would, and conferred a short time with her lawyer. After she was through, Zonen asked, "During the time that you were at Jesse Rugge's house, did anybody talk to you about Nicholas Markowitz?"

"No."

"Would you have recognized the name?"

"Only as being the same last name as Ben's. I didn't know his brother."

"Are you being completely honest with us today?"

"Yes."

"During the time Jesse's been a fugitive, he hasn't contacted you?"

"No."

"Hasn't sent you any letters?"

"No."

"Nobody has contacted you and said that they've spoken to Jesse Hollywood and he wants to convey a message to you?"

"No."

"You made the statement at one point to officers who interviewed you about when you were in Colorado. You said, 'Jesse began to act like a shithead!' Do you remember that statement?"

"I make that statement a lot," Michelle replied.

"What is that in reference to?"

"He's an asshole!"

"In what fashion?"

"He would say mean things."

"Like what?"

"Putting me down."

"Tell us what you mean?"

"He would tell me I wasn't smart, sometimes."

"Regularly?"

"Yes."

"Do you consider him to be your boyfriend now?"

"No."

"What are you going to do with the tattoo?"

"Get it removed."

* * *

At the end of all the testimony, the grand jury found that evidence against the four individuals—William Skidmore, Jesse Rugge, Ryan Hoyt and Graham Pressley—was sufficient to send the cases directly to trial, skipping the preliminary hearing process. This meant that a judge could not reduce charges or dismiss them, nor could the defense attorneys question the witnesses that Ron Zonen had just questioned. Jesse Rugge's lawyer told a reporter, "It's unfortunate that in such a serious case that defendants, through their lawyers, were not able to examine the evidence." One thing that Crouter and the other defense lawyers didn't have to worry about was a rush to justice. Plenty of evidence was still being gathered, cataloged and analyzed. There wouldn't be any trials for almost a year.

12

LIFE IN HELL

From the moment Susan Markowitz knew Nick was dead, her whole world collapsed in, upon itself. Most mothers have a bond with their sons, but this was particularly true between Susan and Nick. She wandered around in a daze after his death—hours of complete numbness, followed by bursts of rage or crying, so violent, they left her drained.

For something to hang on to, Susan created a Web page entitled *Aching for Nick*. On it she wrote at various times about her emotions and the devastation of her life after Nick was murdered. In one section entitled "Denial," she spoke of hearing everything going on around her, but not wanting to participate. She could still smell the scent of his shirt and see the posters on his wall. At times it felt as if he weren't gone at all.

In another section entitled "Fading," she wrote that to be his mom was all she ever wanted. It seemed almost impossible to her that when graduation day came at his high school, he wouldn't be there to receive his diploma. Son, I miss you. I ache for you, and I cry for you. They have ripped out my heart and soul. I would have died for you.

Susan also had a message board on the Court TV Web page, where she created a timeline of everything that had happened starting on August 6, 2000, when Nick was kidnapped off the street. Susan included a graphic that stated: Wanted: Jesse James Hollywood. $$$$$ Please Help. Jesse James Hollywood is on the FBI and *America's Most Wanted* lists. Jesse is the coward that orchestrated the kidnap and execution of my son, Nick.

In one posting, Susan wrote: We are so going to get you Jesse James Hollywood. Big name for such a little boy. You can run, but you cannot hide. You have no idea. Smile for the camera cuz this mama is waiting to wipe that smile off your face!

People from around the nation wrote back to her, and one posting stated, I am praying so hard for this evil person to be found for you for Christmas. Another wrote, Maybe he (Jesse Hollywood) is reading this message board. Here is a message from me. "You are the scum of the earth. You have no right to the air you breathe. Why don't you just put a bullet in your head. You are DIRT!!!"

Someone else offered, I double ditto that. He is a scumbag and one day HE WILL BE FOUND.

Susan kept up the theme that someone, somewhere, would know where he was and post that they had seen Jesse James Hollywood. She wrote: Someone out there has to know where he is hiding out. I pray someone will turn him in! Has anyone heard anything new about him?

Others agreed with Susan on this theme, and one replied: I am so sorry you lost your son. Someone will know where this guy is and bring him to justice. There is always someone who knows something out there. I just hope he is caught soon so he can't harm anyone else and make more people grieve.

Yet, despite the posts and well wishes from hundreds of people, Susan was wrapped in a cloak of grief and depression.

She later told reporter Marianne McCarthy, "There are days I can't get out of bed. I see Nick everywhere—standing there, sitting here, playing outside with his dog, Zack."

McCarthy noticed that the house itself was a shrine to Nick. There were poster-sized photos of Nick in every room, and every room had some memento of Nick—personal items and his Bar Mitzvah gifts. Nick's room was exactly how he had left it on the morning of August 6, 2000, except Susan had added some of his baby things, which came out of storage.

Susan told the *Jewish Journal* that since Nick's murder, "You listen to everything differently. You smell things differently. There's nothing that isn't affected by Nick's death. I'll be talking, and then all of a sudden, I panic, remembering who I am. I don't want to be me."

There was also the deep resentment and anger at Ben that still filled Susan with bitterness. She admitted it was a problem that sometimes cropped up between herself and Jeff. Ben was, of course, Jeff's son, but she wanted nothing to do with Ben. She said, "Nick died for his brother, Ben. Nick did nothing to escape, because he felt his brother would come and save him. In my opinion Ben has done nothing in memory of that."

Susan later told *Dateline NBC* correspondent Chris Hansen, "I've been in the hospital twelve times. Something like that. I don't remember. I thought of suicide, pills, with drinking. And I cut my wrists."

In Susan's darkest hours complete strangers on the Internet wrote her not to give up hope. One person wrote: I understand your anguish, but please, please, please, try to think through your grief and not do anything that will jeopardize yourself and your family. You have suffered enough. That slime will get his due in prison. My prayers are with you and your family, as I know Nick would not want you to hurt yourself. Nick is safe from harm now. He would want you to be safe, too.

At least by August 5, 2001, Susan and Jeff Markowitz

could finally put a marker upon Nick's grave. There was a photo of Nick when he was fifteen years old on one side of the marker, plus a photo of Nick as a young boy kissing his mother, Susan. At the bottom of the marker were the lines *Nicholas Samuel Markowitz. Sept. 19, 1984–Aug. 9, 2000. Step softly, a dream lies here. Sweet dreams, Nick.*

In a short statement about the unveiling, Susan said, "Once again everyone gathered at the Groman-Eden Memorial Cemetery. It is a Jewish tradition that the families of loved ones wait about one year before placing the headstone. The ceremony was held Sunday, August 5, 2001. The fact that Nick is gone is no easier to accept now than it was a year ago. I imagine that is due to the nature of his death. I have lost relatives in the past, and, with a lot less pain, learned to accept the fact. Nick's fate will never be settled in not only my mind and heart, but all that knew him."

Susan also wrote poetry, to and from Nick. One poem was entitled "Letter from Heaven," and it was from Nick to his family. The poem concerned Nick arriving in Heaven and letting those who loved him know that he was okay. Nick said that in Heaven he dwelt with God, and there were no tears or sadness.

Another poem was almost a statement in non-rhyming meter. It was entitled "Drifting." Susan wrote that Nick was on her mind day and night. She begged God that there truly would be a Heaven for her only child who had been so senselessly murdered.

Despite the numbness, grief, turmoil and suicide attempts, Susan Markowitz did survive. In one of her postings on the Court TV Web site, she wrote: I have spent the past year in and out of the hospital for being suicidal. I almost gave up. However, something happened this past month and I have never felt stronger. I hope it lasts, I have so many things to fight for. I know Nick would want me to stay strong.

Susan said she had plans of making a memorial quilt out of Nick's clothes, including his karate uniform and

Shakespeare drama T-shirts. A person wrote back and said: I have missed your wonderful up-lifting words. Please remember, you are the wind beneath someone's wings every day. Bless you my dear.

Another wrote about Jesse James Hollywood, I know the little **** is sitting here right under our noses. He's gonna slip one day. Justice will be served. Peace and strength to you, my friend.

Because of the nature of the murder, where so many people had been witnesses to Nick's kidnapped status, but none of them contacted authorities, Jeff and Susan Marko-witz retained a lawyer and filed a civil lawsuit claiming "wrongful death." The period covered was from August 6 to August 9, 2000, and the list of defendants was immense:

Jesse James Hollywood and his parents, Jack and Laurie Hollywood

Jesse Rugge and his father, Baron Rugge

Graham Pressley and his parents, Charles and Christina Pressley

William Skidmore

Ryan Hoyt

Stephen Hogg

Natasha Adams and her mother, Allison Adams

Michelle Lasher and her parents, Douglas and Elaine Lasher

John Roberts

Richard Hoeflinger

Emilio Jerez

Kelly Carpenter

The Lemon Tree Inn

Casey Sheehan

Brian Affronti

Nathan Appleton

Gabriel Ibarra

Shauna Vasquez

Armen Tovmasya (who they said had given the TEC-9
    to Jesse Hollywood)

The City of Los Angeles

The Los Angeles Police Department

Navegar, Inc.—doing business as Intratec Firearms

The last listed, Navegar, Inc., of Florida, had created the
TEC-9, and the Markowitzes' lawyers argued that it had
been negligent in its business practices. They wrote: *They
built a weapon whose purpose is to kill people, marketed
it to criminals by touting its resistance to fingerprints
and failed to sell the gun exclusively to law enforcement
personnel.*

This section about the gun was an uphill fight, since the
California Supreme Court had recently ruled that a man-
ufacturer could not be held responsible for the actions of
a gunman.

On other points the lawsuit claimed that both Allison
Adams and Stephen Hogg, who were lawyers, were guilty
of negligence because they were aware that a teenager was
being held captive, but they failed to contact authorities.

The LAPD came in for special scorn from Jeff and
Susan Markowitz for their actions concerning the two 911
calls that were made shortly after Nick was grabbed off
the street. According to the lawsuit, Officers Rygh and
Lyons did not follow correct procedures when they failed
to investigate properly the whereabouts of the van used
in the kidnapping, nor did they alert other law enforcement agencies in the area.

The Lemon Tree Inn was part of the lawsuit as well because of the allegation of *operating a business that helped prolong the crime.* In this allegation there were points that the room should not have been obtained by Jesse Rugge, who was not twenty-one years old at the time, and that it was obvious that minors were accompanying him to the room.

One of the most contentious parts of the lawsuit sought to hold adults responsible for the actions of their children, especially the parents of Jesse Hollywood, Jesse Rugge and Graham Pressley.

With her thoughts never very far away from Nick, Susan braced herself for the first of the co-conspirators to be brought to trial, Ryan Hoyt. In some way it would be the hardest test of all for her. It was the gun in Hoyt's hand that had ended her son's life.

13

TRIGGERMAN

When Ryan Hoyt's trial finally got under way in 2001, DDA Ron Zonen's opening argument took the jurors back through the events of August 2000, and Zonen said that even though Ryan Hoyt was not part of the initial kidnapping of Nick Markowitz, once he joined the plot, he became part of the kidnapping. And even though it seemed at times that Nick could have simply walked away, this did not mitigate the fact that he had been kidnapped. Zonen also argued that Hoyt was now claiming amnesia about the interview he had with detectives where he admitted to shooting Nick. Zonen said this was all a scam on Hoyt's part to try and distance himself from the words he had uttered at that interview. Zonen stressed that Ryan Hoyt, by his own words, had admitted to being a killer.

Cheri Owen, Hoyt's lead attorney, in her own opening statements, said in part, "Mr. Hoyt was not telling the truth during his statement. Mr. Hoyt feels that he has to protect those people who gave him a sense of being in his lifetime." She also stated that Hoyt's claim of amnesia, where

the interview was concerned, was valid due to the immense
amount of stress he had suffered at that time.

The first witness for the prosecution was Jeffrey
Markowitz, Nick's father. Jeff identified for the jury a belt
buckle and ring that had belonged to Nick, as well as a
photo of Nick. Jeff spoke a little about Nick, but mostly
his testimony was used to get certain items into evidence.

Defense co-counsel Richard Crouter had no questions
for Jeffrey Markowitz, but he did tell him that he was
sorry for his loss.

Zonen then called Benjamin Markowitz to the stand, but
the trial day was almost over before Ben could be asked
many questions. There was a late start on the next day, and
a real problem occurred. Juror #10 did not show up for the
trial on time. Bailiff Roger Brenner phoned the juror's
home and the juror in question answered, saying, "I took
some drugs and had a bad reaction and might have to go to
the hospital." This brought everything to a screeching halt
as Judge Gordon went into chambers with the prosecution and defense. When they returned, Juror #10 was excused from the jury, and an alternate took his place.

The real news, however, was that Ron Zonen was nego-
tiating a plea bargain deal with William Skidmore. Obviously, what Skidmore had to say would be very damaging
to Ryan Hoyt. Zonen told the judge outside the presence
of the jury, "We are working very hard to resolve the case
with Mr. Skidmore." Also by bringing Skidmore in, in this
fashion, Zonen wanted both Rugge and Pressley's future
trials combined, since the witnesses and testimony were
expected to be the same for both. Judge Gordon, however,
had his doubts, and quipped, "Logistically, it will be very
difficult. Where are we going to do this? At the Earl

Warren Showgrounds?" Nonetheless, he took it under advisement.

After this matter was addressed, Zonen had Ben Markowitz return to the stand and tell of his life and his feud with Jesse James Hollywood, which had sparked the kidnapping of Nick. Through Ben, Zonen introduced photos of Jesse Rugge, William Skidmore and Jesse James Hollywood. Also introduced was a photo of the TEC-9 pistol that had allegedly been used by Ryan Hoyt to kill Nick Markowitz. Ben said that he knew the TEC-9 belonged to Jesse James Hollywood.

Because of sound problems of a videotape concerning Jesse James Hollywood and his buddies, on which Hollywood discussed Hoyt's $1,200 debt, Zonen was unable to play it at the moment, so Crouter cross-examined Ben Markowitz. He did get Ben to admit that Jesse Hollywood had often bossed Ryan Hoyt around and made fun of him. Ben said Hoyt was "the puppy dog of the group."

The next witness, Pauline Mahoney, laid the groundwork about the whole abduction scene on the corner of Platt and Ingomar Streets, and how she and her boys had chanted the license plate numbers on their way home so they would remember them. She also testified about photos of the white van she had seen.

Then Mahoney's 911 tape was introduced and played for the jury; followed, after lunch, by the videotape of Jesse James Hollywood and his buddies at a party in which Hollywood was spouting off and Hoyt was the cameraman. Halfway through the videotaping, Hollywood took the camera and asked Hoyt when he was going to pay his marijuana debt. The amount of $1,200 was mentioned.

Brian Affronti testified to events of August 6, 2000, when Jesse James Hollywood, Jesse Rugge and William

Skidmore had an unknown boy in Hollywood's van. Affronti originally thought the boy was their friend. Affronti retained that illusion until Jesse Hollywood made the comment that if Ben thought he was going to kill Hollywood's family, he had another thing coming, and basically lit into Nick.

Gabriel Ibarra followed, and a photo of the house on Modoc Road, in Santa Barbara, was introduced. It was there that Ibarra had witnessed a teenage boy trussed up with duct tape, in Richard Hoeflinger's bedroom. Ibarra repeated the comment that Jesse Hollywood had made to Jesse Rugge, "Shut the fuck up" about anything concerning Nick.

Richard Crouter had no questions of Ibarra.

Richard Hoeflinger was questioned by the prosecution about what he had seen when Rugge, Skidmore, Affronti and Hollywood arrived with an unknown boy at his residence. He told about how Hollywood was acting crazy in his house and threatened anyone who told about Nick being there.

Crouter's cross-examination was brief, to the point of lasting only one minute.

Next on the stand for the prosecution was Kelly Carpenter, who spoke of her days with Nick at Natasha Adams's house, at Jesse Rugge's house and at the Lemon Tree Inn. Among other things she spoke about the offer Jesse Rugge allegedly had been given by Jesse Hollywood to murder Nick, and Rugge turned it down. The amount was either stated as $2,000 or $2,500.

Since it was late in the day, court was recessed at 4:25 P.M., and Kelly began her testimony again the next day, at 10:45 A.M. Once again, cross-examination was fairly brief by the defense, since Kelly Carpenter didn't even know Ryan Hoyt, nor had she ever seen him at the Lemon Tree Inn.

* * *

Larz Wikstrom, who worked for the Santa Barbara sheriff's office, was the next witness, and he introduced a photo of the Lizard's Mouth area, and a photo of Nick's grave site, with the body present.

Natasha Adams, who was now Natasha Adams-Young, testified as to her recollections of the events of August 7, 8 and 9. Among other things she testified about someone coming up from the Los Angeles area on the night of August 8, although she didn't actually see who the person was.

Once again cross-examination was short by the defense, since Natasha did not know, nor had she met, Ryan Hoyt. Defense counsel Richard Crouter added one more thing, however—he would be the only defense counsel for the rest of the day, because he said Cheri Owen was ill and would not return until the next day.

Detective Albert Lafferty, like Larz Wikstrom, introduced several photos of the crime scene, including photos of the Lizard's Mouth area as seen from a helicopter, an overall view of the West Camino Cielo Road, the grave site location, bullet strike marks on a rock and the TEC-9 pistol in the grave.

Ron Zonen had Detective David Danielson introduce a photo of a sock with duct tape on it, which was used to gag Nick at one point, and he had David Barber, of the California Department of Justice, testify about the TEC-9 pistol.

The fourth day of trial brought Stephen Hogg to the witness stand for a short recitation of what had transpired between himself and Jesse James Hollywood in August 2000. Jack Hollywood's testimony followed, and was much longer and far-ranging, covering everything from the boys he had coached in baseball, to his son's life, to the actual days of trying to find out what had happened and where the kidnapped boy was being held.

Crouter, on cross, asked Jack Hollywood if his actions had been self-serving, and he admitted they had been.

Crouter asked, "Were you doing them to protect your son?"

Jack answered, "Yes."

"Did you go to the police?"

"No. But now I wish I had."

After Jack Hollywood testified, Casey Sheehan took the stand. He spoke of seeing Ryan Hoyt buy new clothes after August 9, 2000, even though Hoyt was normally broke. And Sheehan spoke of Hoyt coming up to him and saying, "They picked the boy up at a hotel, and they shot him and put him in a ditch, somewhere up there around Santa Barbara." It wasn't absolutely clear if the word "they" indicated Ryan Hoyt as well, though Sheehan thought that it did.

Day five of the trial brought Sheehan back on the stand, to identify photos of his car, which had been used by Jesse Hollywood, and then transferred to Ryan Hoyt so that he could drive up to Santa Barbara to "take care of Nick." Unlike some of the other testimony, which had been short in nature, Cheri Owen cross-examined Casey Sheehan more extensively.

Next in line was Michelle Lasher. Like Sheehan, she corroborated that Jesse Hollywood was with her at an Outback Steakhouse on the night Nick was murdered, and Hollywood spent the night at her house. This proved the prosecution's argument that Jesse Hollywood could not have been the triggerman who killed Nick, and Hoyt had been the one who actually pulled the trigger. Of course, the prosecution was contending that Hoyt killed Nick on Jesse Hollywood's behest.

It could not have been easy for Susan and Jeff Marko-witz to listen to Dr. George Sterbenz, forensic pathologist, who described the many wounds that Nick suffered. During Sterbenz's testimony an X-ray of Nick's skull and an X-ray of his chest were admitted into evidence. One by one, the bullet wounds were talked about, analyzed and brought into evidence.

Darla Gacek was on the stand a short while, testifying to how she and the others found Nick's body only partially buried on August 12, 2000. Then it was Detective Cornell's turn, followed by Detective Mike West.

One of the most damning things of all against Ryan Hoyt, of course, was the videotape of Hoyt being interviewed by the detectives. During this video Ryan said at one point, "I didn't dig the grave! All I did was kill the kid!" Now Cheri Owen attempted to undo the damage that had already been done by comments such as those to the detectives back in August 2000. She got Hoyt on the stand to testify as to why he had said such things and led him through his claims that he didn't recall now what he had said during that interview at all. In fact, Hoyt now claimed to have amnesia about almost everything from the time of his arrest until a week thereafter, due to the stress and trauma of the event.

On the stand Hoyt testified that he did vaguely recall talking to his mother by telephone before going to the interview room, but he could not remember what he'd said to her. Having listened to that tape of the phone conversation with his mother, in the courtroom, he acknowledged it was his voice, but still didn't recall saying anything that was on the tape. He added, "It gave me a different perspective on my mother," and he agreed with her that he might have been guilty of some things by association. "I mean, I'm guilty because I'm associated with those who are."

Owen told Hoyt, "On the tape your mother stated that she wanted you to find Jesse Hollywood and turn him in, and quit being a cannibal for his crimes. How did you feel about Jesse Hollywood at the time you were arrested?"

"He was still a friend."

"And even after you were arrested, would you have preferred to go home or to protect Jesse Hollywood?"

"I wanted to go home, but I felt really bad because, I mean, whether I knew it or not, I believe I brought the means to that child's end up to Santa Barbara that evening."

"So you felt that by taking the duffel bag to Santa Barbara that you were the means to Nicholas Markowitz's death?"

"Yes, ma'am."

When asked if he remembered talking to the detectives, or recalled what he'd obviously said on the tape, Ryan said that he didn't. Owen stated, "I'm going to ask you to explain to the ladies and gentlemen of the jury, after hearing these statements being made, what would be the reason for saying, 'I killed him! I killed him!'"

Ryan answered that he probably said that because he felt guilty for bringing a gun in a bag up to Santa Barbara, where someone else killed Nick Markowitz. He implied that Jesse Rugge or Graham Pressley must have done the actual killing, because now he was claiming he had never been up to Lizard's Mouth, nor had he even seen Nick Markowitz when he went up to Santa Barbara on the night of August 8 with a duffel bag that Jesse Hollywood had given him. Hoyt claimed that he never laid eyes on Nick Markowitz there, and that he thought at the time he was just delivering a "brick" of marijuana to Jesse Rugge. Delivering dope for Hollywood was something he had done in the past, and it didn't seem out of the ordinary to him that he was doing it on a trip to Santa Barbara.

Hoyt claimed he had no idea that there was a gun in the duffel bag.

Owen asked him, "You saw on the tape where the detectives asked you, 'You know where you are now, right?' And you answered, 'Yeah, behind bars for life. If I wind up behind bars for life, I can't be behind bars for life as a rat.' Do you remember making that statement when you saw the videotape?"

"Wait!" Judge Gordon interjected. "You're saying, does he remember seeing that on the videotape, that's the question?"

Owen answered, "Yes, Your Honor."

Hoyt answered he remembered seeing it on the videotape in court, but he didn't recall saying it in the interview, because he really couldn't remember anything he said during the interview.

Judge Gordon and all the attorneys started having a a real problem on their hands, which was becoming a catch-22 for Cheri Owen and Ryan Hoyt. If she asked him specific questions about whether statements he made to detectives in the interview were true or false, how could he answer her questions? Supposedly he couldn't recall what he'd said back then. Judge Gordon finally told her, "He says he doesn't remember the interview at all, and to ask him what he meant by something in the interview he doesn't remember calls for speculation." Finally a sidebar had to be called for, out of the hearing of the jury.

Crouter tried to clear things up by saying to Judge Gordon, "It's not asking him about what somebody else might have meant by those words. He can tell us what he means by those words in general."

Zonen chimed in and said, "I think it's irrelevant how he uses the words."

Judge Gordon agreed and responded, "That's what I think. I mean, I assumed you were going to go through this and when you got into portions where he incriminated himself, ask him if those were true statements. But I didn't think we were going to go through this and ask him what he meant by each word when he doesn't even remember the interview."

Crouter replied, "She can ask him what the word means to him, because we know he used it."

Judge Gordon responded, "I'll let you do that. But I'm going to be very careful about this, and this is the last sidebar we're going to have on this subject."

Cheri Owen wanted to be clear on this important point and asked the judge, "Can I ask him, 'Well, for what reason can you give this jury why you would say something like that, when it isn't true?'"

Gordon's answer was "It's hard for me to bridge that gap, since he doesn't even remember saying it at all. You ask the questions, and I'll simply rule on it, question by question. That's all I can do."

When Owen finally asked Hoyt what he meant by the word "rat," Ryan responded, "Those are people who wind up as somebody's kid or dead."

Owen asked if it was a true statement when Detective Reinstadler asked him what he did with Ben's brother, and Hoyt said, "Kill him."

Owen asked, "Is that a true statement?"

Hoyt replied, "Oh, no, I did not kill Ben Markowitz! Or anybody. Excuse me." It was odd, indeed, that Hoyt said the name of Ben Markowitz instead of Nick's name.

Owen continued, "Sergeant Reinstadler said, 'You buried the kid.' Is that a true statement?"

"No, it is not."

"Sergeant Reinstadler said, 'Jesse Rugge said you put the duct tape on him.' And you responded, 'The only thing I did was kill him.' Was that a true statement?"

"No, it is not."

"Sergeant Reinstadler asked you, 'I just can't help but wonder if there was ever a time when right before you pulled the trigger, that you just thought, you know, "I shouldn't do this. This is wrong."' And you answered, 'Hell yes! Right before.' Is that a true statement?"

"No, it is not."

"Why would you say it?"

"You know, I've been sitting, thinking about this for the past year, and the only thing I can think of would be to protect Jesse Hollywood and those involved."

"Would you protect Jesse Hollywood at the expense of going to prison for the rest of your life?"

"Would I have? Yes."

"Was Jesse Hollywood more of a family to you than your own family was?"

"Yes, he was."

"And did you have anything to do with the kidnapping of Nicholas Markowitz?"

"No, I did not."

"Did you ever see him at the Lemon Tree Inn when you went there?"

"No, I did not see him at all. Period."

Ron Zonen was skeptical about almost everything Ryan Hoyt had just said on the stand. Zonen began his counteroffensive against Hoyt's comments by asking why Hoyt would risk going to prison for Jesse Hollywood, since Hollywood had used him as a virtual slave at his residence. Zonen declared, "This is the same Hollywood who on a regular basis would make you go out in the backyard and pick up beer cans after there would be a party. The same Jesse Hollywood who would have you sand down his front fence in front of all your collective friends and tease you about it afterward. This was all a business arrangement, wasn't it?"

Ryan replied, "How do you mean 'business arrangement,' sir?"

"Well, were you being paid for that work?"

"No, I was not."

"It was for a reduction of your debt, is that correct?"

"That is correct."

"Whatever he ordered, you did. Is that correct?"

"Concerning his backyard, yes."

"And did it also concern the killing of Nicholas Markowitz? He ordered it, and you did it?"

"No, sir."

Zonen asked Hoyt about the segment on the videotape where Jesse Hollywood operated the camera, and asked Hoyt how much the debt was at that time. Hoyt agreed that the debt then was $1,200. Zonen also got into the area of the interview that Hoyt had with detectives in August 2000, where he admitted to killing Nick. Hoyt now claimed he recalled seeing the video in court, but he could not remember the initial interview or talking to the detectives in 2000. Nor could he remember the phone call to his mother, prior to the interview. In fact, Hoyt now said that from the time he was arrested near the pay phone booth, to an indeterminate time in the jail cell, he had almost no recollection of the events that had occurred. He said he couldn't recall being in the police car on the trip up to Santa Barbara or the booking process.

As to why Jesse James Hollywood had given Hoyt $400 at his birthday party, Zonen asked, "Did you ever think it was strange that Jesse Hollywood could, on one hand, be such a generous, giving, kind person, and—on the other hand—torment and humiliate you in front of his friends?"

"Looking back, sir, he was a very erratic person."

"Did you ever talk to him about that?"

"It wasn't my place to."

"What do you mean it wasn't your place to? Weren't you friends?"

"Yes."

"Well, why can't a friend talk to another friend about his behavior? About how he treats you?"

"As I stated. He was a very erratic person. Why piss him off?"

Zonen asked why Hoyt allowed Hollywood to keep increasing his debt at incredible rates, when Hoyt couldn't pay it down, and why Hoyt didn't argue about that. Hoyt answered, "Look how he was treating me at the time. How would he treat me if I told him—excuse my language—to fuck off."

"Well, why did you think that friendship was so valuable? Why didn't you just walk away from it?"

"I had known Jesse Hollywood for a long, long period of time. I was friends with his family. I'm friends with his father and mother. I babysat his brother."

Zonen then asked if Ryan Hoyt had ever been in any fights before the events of August 2000, and Ryan said that he had, and he knew how to take care of himself. Zonen's next question was "Is it safe to say that during this eight-month period of the time you were indentured to Jesse Hollywood—that during that period of time you were not scared of him physically?"

"I believe I was. I don't think I would have fought him. I don't particularly fight friends. And if he would have fought me, he wouldn't have fought me by himself."

"Were you scared if you didn't pick up beer cans in his backyard, he would fight you with any of his friends?"

"Yes, sir. I believe at one point, before I started working in his backyard, he said, 'You want an ass kicking?'"

Zonen asked why in the period of time from when he was seventeen years old until he was twenty-one, Hoyt had worked only four months.

Hoyt said, "Laziness."

Zonen replied, "So, during that period of time, your preference was to drink beer, smoke dope and hang out with Jesse Hollywood?"

Hoyt replied, "That is a fair statement."

Zonen then asked, "Mr. Hoyt, during this time that you were working fairly rigorously for Jesse Hollywood, almost daily cleaning up and going to work around the house, did it occur to you that you could pay off this debt a lot quicker if you simply had a job?"

"Yes, sir. But as I've stated, if I did not show up at his house, my grandparents would receive harassing phone calls."

Zonen wanted to know at what point had Hoyt lost his memory, and when had he regained it.

Hoyt said he lost it at the time of his arrest, and began to remember things again on Sunday, August 20. Someone had slipped a newspaper under his cell door about the murder of Nick Markowitz on that date and he started to recall things around that time period. Hoyt said that he had no recollection of the events of August 17, 18 or 19, nor did he remember the first attorney who had come to speak with him, a man named Bill Duval. In fact, he said he couldn't even remember the arraignment process with Richard Crouter, except for seeing a photo of that event in a newspaper later on.

Zonen asked, "So, hearing yourself talk (on the videotape) about how you killed Nick Markowitz doesn't spark any recollection?"

Hoyt replied, "No, sir, it does not."

And then even Zonen was stunned by the lack of time Hoyt said that he had prepared with his lawyers for the trial. Zonen asked, "How many hours in preparation for your testimony today did you put in with your lawyers?"

"Just one night, and that was last night. That was for a period of an hour and a half."

"For one hour and a half?"

"Maybe two hours."

This was incredible, since Ryan Hoyt was on trial for his life.

Zonen wanted to know if Hoyt ever had "situational amnesia" before, where he couldn't remember specific periods of time.

Hoyt said, "Yes, sir. And usually I was drinking."

Zonen countered that Hoyt hadn't been drinking in jail, and Hoyt agreed.

"Did you ever have occasion where you had a complete blackout after drinking, a complete failure of recollection of the order of what you're telling us happened during the course of this interview, where there was a whole period of a number of days that are a complete mystery to you? Has that ever happened before?"

"No, sir. It hasn't."

"Did you ever have instances of emotional trauma-induced amnesia—in other words, where you see something or experience an event that has nothing to do with alcohol at all that caused you to forget the event itself?"

"If there was, I do not remember it."

"So, to the best of your knowledge, this particular occasion would have been the very first time in your life where you ever had a period of profound amnesia. A complete lack of any recall at all."

"I would have to say yes, sir."

Once again Zonen asked, "You have no recollection of ever sitting in the room where these two detectives were interviewing you?"

"No, sir."

"Then, how did you know that there had been a grave dug?"

"I don't recall."

"Your memory is actually fairly good prior to your arrest, is that right?"

"As good as can be expected for somebody who was always on drugs," Hoyt answered.

"Prior to your arrest, how many people did you have conversations with about this murder?"

"I believe I asked Mr. Sheehan, 'Do you think that they killed him?'"

"Did Mr. Sheehan tell you something about a grave being dug?"

"Not that I can recall, sir."

"Did you ask Jack Hollywood anything about a grave being dug?"

"I don't believe Jack Hollywood knew anything. No, I didn't."

Zonen said that Hoyt had mentioned talking to William Skidmore about the murder, and then Zonen asked what Skidmore had told him.

Hoyt replied, "I can't recall exactly, but the gist of the conversation was that Ben's brother had been killed."

"Mr. Hoyt, you were just told that the younger brother of somebody that your good friend was at war with had just been murdered, is that correct?"

"Yes."

Zonen wanted to know why Hoyt hadn't asked more questions of Skidmore about the circumstances, and Hoyt said it didn't occur to him to do so at the time.

Zonen also got into Hoyt's relationship with Jack and Laurie Hollywood. Hoyt said they treated him decently and even let him stay over the house on occasion. "They let me sleep on the couch. They were kind to me. They fed me."

Since Ryan was so close to Jack Hollywood, Zonen asked if Jack had ever told Ryan that he was a dealer of marijuana. Ryan replied, "Didn't know, and didn't care."

"The whole time that you were close friends with Jack Hollywood, you never asked him why he always had such large amounts of marijuana available?"

"The least I knew, the better, [that] was the way I looked at it."

"Was there anything unique about the week following your trip to Santa Barbara that was different from any other week in terms of your drug use?"

"Yes. Mass consumption. It was my birthday. My twenty-first birthday. So it was kind of made a big deal of, and I did a lot of stuff."

"Does that include the night you went up to Santa Barbara?"

"I smoked weed and had a little bit of cocaine with me."

"Okay, so let me be real clear. Or perhaps you can be real clear on exactly what Jesse Hollywood's involvement was the night that you went up to Santa Barbara. He gave you a package to take up to Santa Barbara?"

"A duffel bag."

"You then took the duffel bag and put it into the car? Or did he?"

"I did."

"Was it your assumption that Mr. Hollywood was not going to be coming to Santa Barbara, and that's why he was asking you to run that chore?"

"Yes, that was my assumption."

"You were up in Santa Barbara for a number of hours, weren't you?"

"Yeah. In the hotel mostly."

"When you got to the hotel, did you meet with Jesse Rugge outside the hotel or inside the hotel?"

"I walked up to the room, and he opened the door for me."

Zonen asked Hoyt a series of questions about his time in Santa Barbara, and Hoyt's answers were at variance with what Jesse Rugge and Graham Pressley had said, or even what Ryan told detectives in 2000. Hoyt now related that the bag he carried to Santa Barbara was heavy, but not too heavy. He didn't know there was a gun inside. Instead, he thought he was delivering a "brick" of marijuana to Rugge for distribution in the area. Hoyt said the item in the soft duffel bag did not feel like a gun, but rather "it felt soft. I just assumed he had covered it (the brick) with clothes or something." Hoyt said he never unzipped the bag to see what was inside.

Hoyt added that he was surprised to see another person in the room at the Lemon Tree Inn when he got there. This other person was introduced to him as Graham. Hoyt also claimed that he never saw Nick Markowitz in the room or anywhere else in Santa Barbara. According to Hoyt, Jesse

Rugge borrowed Casey Sheehan's car from him, and Rugge went with Graham, leaving Hoyt in the room alone. Hoyt said that Rugge "told me he had to run some errands, and I assume he took the bag with him." After a while, Hoyt said, he got hungry, so he walked down the street to a Jack in the Box for some fast food. He said it was a long walk, which took him about twenty-five to thirty minutes.

Zonen asked if the appearance of Jesse Rugge and Graham Pressley was different when they came back to the hotel, as opposed to when they had left.

Hoyt answered, "I didn't pay much attention to them."

Zonen wanted to know if Hoyt had any other conversations with Jack Hollywood after their meeting in the park, and Hoyt said that he hadn't. Zonen then asked, "Twenty-four hours after your conversation with Jack Hollywood, you were in the same home as his son, the person he's concerned about. Did you go up to Jesse Hollywood and say, 'What's going on with Ben's younger brother?' Did you say that to him?"

Hoyt replied, "No, I don't believe I did. I can't recall. I was asking around. I was asking Mr. Sheehan. Obviously, I spoke with Mr. Skidmore."

"Was it your belief that the kidnapping or grabbing of Ben Markowitz's younger brother had something to do with Ben Markowitz breaking out Jesse Hollywood's windows?"

"That could have been—how do you say it?—the blow that broke the back, so to speak."

"So when you learned that Ben's younger brother had been killed, conceivably related to something Jesse Hollywood did, weren't you curious in knowing any of the facts?"

"I made no further inquiries. I distanced myself from the whole situation."

Once, when Zonen asked a question that Hoyt thought had been asked before, he got irritated and answered, "For the third time, sir, I don't recall the conversation."

Judge Gordon admonished Hoyt sternly. "You just answer the question. If I think he's asking you the same question too many times, I'll tell you that."

Hoyt meekly replied, "Yes, Your Honor."

Hoyt also testified that the second time he discussed the topic of the murder with Casey Sheehan was on their trip to Sheehan's father's residence in Malibu, and Hoyt had a different take on matters than Sheehan's testimony. Hoyt related that he'd been snorting coke the night before and he'd only slept a couple of hours. On the drive over, Sheehan supposedly asked Ryan about Skidmore's comments, and Hoyt reiterated that Skidmore had said that Nick had been murdered. Hoyt denied that he told Sheehan that he'd been the gunman or even been up to the area where the body had been discovered.

Zonen said that since they'd been talking about the murder all during the trial, could Hoyt now remember anything more about his interview with detectives? In other words, had all the testimony in court jogged his memory? Hoyt answered that none of it had. Zonen added, "So nothing that happened yesterday, nor spending the night thinking about it, has refreshed your recollection in any way about this interview?"

"I believe I spent the past year thinking about it."

"As you sit here today, you still have no recollection of anything in that interview?"

"That is a fair statement."

Cheri Owen took another shot in testimony with Ryan Hoyt on the stand to try and make the jurors believe he suffered from total amnesia when it came to the interview with detectives on August 17, 2000. Owen asked Hoyt if after he incurred his debt, if he'd ever entertained thoughts of crossing Jesse James Hollywood.

Hoyt replied, "No, I would not. He usually got back at those who would, one way or another."

Owen asked, "Back in August 2000, when you were arrested, would you have been willing to go to prison for life for Jesse Hollywood?"

"Yes, I would have."

"Has the arrest been the most emotional, traumatic experience of your life?"

"Yes, ma'am. By far."

"After that point, did your memory start to fade?"

"Yes, ma'am."

After Hoyt's testimony, both the prosecution and defense had experts testify to Ryan Hoyt's state of mind and his mental capacity. Neither one said Hoyt suffered from "profound" mental illness, but they both said he suffered from a personality disorder. This personality disorder was characterized as the need to depend upon others for approval because of low self-esteem. Hoyt was constantly in fear of their rejection and did things to please them. The real crunch came as to whether Ryan Hoyt suffered from amnesia regarding the actual events of Nick Markowitz's murder. The psychologist for the defense, Dr. Michael Kania, said that Hoyt's claims were credible and that his confession to detectives could have been fabricated in a misguided attempt to be seen as a "tough guy" by Jesse James Hollywood and the others. And it was also a misguided attempt to please Jesse Hollywood.

Dr. David Glaser, on the other hand, stated that Ryan Hoyt's claims of amnesia were not credible. Glaser, the prosecution's expert, saw these as being a ruse to evade a conviction, and it was no more than a ploy to try and distance himself from the statements he had made to police back in August 2000.

There were very few witnesses for the defense, and many were surprised by the seemingly lackluster case put on by Cheri Owen. Some witnesses would claim later that they were surprised on being called at the last minute to the stand by the defense, and they weren't prepared.

In closing arguments Ron Zonen told the jurors that Jesse James Hollywood was a "minor league drug lord" who approached Ryan Hoyt with an offer—if Hoyt would kill Nick Markowitz, Jesse Hollywood would forgive Ryan's drug debt, Zonen said. "The logical explanation for what happened here is that Jesse Hollywood wanted Nicholas killed, and Mr. Hoyt was the guy who said he'd do it." Zonen added that Ryan Hoyt's own confession to detectives, and the things Casey Sheehan had to say, backed up this contention.

Cheri Owen, on the other hand, told the jurors that the case boiled down to two questions: Did Ryan Hoyt kidnap Nick Markowitz? And did he pull the trigger? Owen stated that there was no evidence from anyone that Ryan Hoyt had grabbed Nick Markowitz off a street in West Hills on August 6, 2000. And she said since there was no physical evidence that linked Ryan Hoyt to the killing of Nick at Lizard's Mouth, his admission to the detectives that he did so was just Ryan living in a fantasy world. Ryan Hoyt had said those things out of a misguided allegiance to Jesse James Hollywood.

Owen pronounced, "You're gonna believe that someone, with no history of violence, murdered someone for such little money? I find that very hard to believe!"

Ron Zonen had a last crack at the jurors in a rebuttal, and he argued that if Hoyt joined in anywhere and at any time during the illegal holding of Nick Markowitz, then he was guilty of kidnapping. And Zonen added that Hoyt, even by his own admission, said that he'd delivered a package from Jesse Hollywood to Santa Barbara. The package, according to Ron Zonen, was of course the TEC-9 pistol.

As far as Hoyt's claims of amnesia about his admission of guilt during an interview with detectives, Zonen argued, "The fact that Mr. Hoyt recalls details before and after his talk with detectives proves he lied on the stand. What caused the so-called amnesia was a conscious decision on how to deal with the confession. Mr. Hoyt was a drug-addicted, alcoholic slacker who didn't need a violent streak to kill someone."

During the jury deliberations the jurors sent notes to the judge asking two interesting questions. One stated, *We would like to request a transcript of Casey Sheehan and Natasha Adams so that we can pause portions of the video*. In other words, the jurors wanted to compare and contrast the statements Ryan Hoyt made as opposed to those of Casey Sheehan and Natasha Adams. The second note read: *Is the kidnapping a continuous single event?* They, in essence, wanted to know if the kidnapping started in West Hills and never ended, even though Ryan Hoyt had not been part of grabbing Nick off the street, and it often seemed as if no one was guarding Nick at certain times and he could have walked away.

Apparently, the jurors got the answers they needed, and for a case that was so convoluted, with so many characters involved, it only took the jury of seven women and five men a short time to come back with a decision. When they pronounced a verdict of guilty, Ryan Hoyt showed no emotion at all as he was led from the courtroom.

Susan Markowitz, however, was very emotional. She held a jacket that had belonged to Nick next to her as she told reporters outside the courtroom that she was pleased by the verdict, and she planned to take the stand during the sentencing phase.

Jeff Markowitz added, "There is no joy in the fact that he was convicted of first-degree murder. It won't bring our son back. Still, an eye for an eye."

The sentencing phase began on November 26, 2001, and Susan Markowitz had a statement to read before the court. She started off by saying, *"I know that Nick's death has touched many hearts around the world and I pray that I have the strength to eventually thank everyone that has been so supportive, including over 400 that attended his services that brought cards, flowers, plants, love and prayers."*

Susan spoke of how before his murder, Nick had planned to make a positive difference in the world. At his Bar Mitzvah, he'd read from the Torah and his topic had been about justice. He'd said that he knew right from wrong, and in one of his entries in a journal that he and Susan kept, there was a signature of "Rabbi Nick." She pondered if maybe someday he would have become a rabbi, but that was all just speculation now.

Nick had looked forward to getting his driver's license, graduating from high school and had hopes for the future that included the possibility of working for his dad, or as an actor or being a psychologist. Susan said he was great with others and would have made a good psychologist. Friends had loved Nick for his qualities of confidence, humor and strength. And Susan brought up the fact that Nick always had a positive outlook on things, and he'd spoken to one of the girls at his kidnapping that it would all be an interesting story he would one day tell his grandchildren.

Susan related that Nick was planning to get together with his first true love, Jeannie, on the day after he was released. She imagined Nick trying to be strong and waiting out the kidnapping, because he wanted to help his brother, Ben. Susan wondered if Nick ever did truly understand all the danger he was in.

She said that Nick had become lost while riding his bike, six months prior to the abduction, and added that he'd been very shaken by the incident. She wondered how much worse it must have been to be "lost" in Santa Barbara with no sense of direction home, and now he was indeed lost forever.

Susan noted that her husband, Jeff, loved all his children—Ben, Leah and Nick—but it was very hard for her to forgive Ben or to be around him. As far as Jeff went, she said, *"That I have lost my only child compounds his loss, and looking into each other's eyes and seeing the pain is tearing us apart."*

Susan told the jury that Nick's whole life had come down to a single moment, when Ryan Hoyt held Nick's life in his hands. *"He did not even know the name of my son when he shot my child in the face."* She turned directly to Ryan Hoyt in court and said defiantly, *"His name was Nicholas Samuel Markowitz!"*

Susan said that grandmothers, grandfathers, aunts, uncles, cousins and friends had all been devastated by the murder. In fact, her mother had suffered a heart attack in Colorado when listening to the testimony of Richard Dispenza at his hearing. One of Nick's uncles spent every moment that he could creating and running a Web site in remembrance of Nick. The holidays and get-togethers with relatives had been altered forever. Even though people on those occasions tried not to think of Nick, there was no way of getting around it. She said there wouldn't be any more holidays without tears.

Even Nick's friends at El Camino Real High School were deeply affected. Their sense of a safe environment at school and in the community had been shattered. Many still had nightmares about Nick's death. Susan said if Nick had lived, she could imagine him crossing the stage at his graduation, smiling and giving her and Jeff a glance, embarrassed because she would have gone there with horns and holding a hundred balloons to let him know how proud she was of him.

"There are no words to express my loss. I can only imagine Nick's last breaths that were spent trying to plead for his life through the duct tape that muffled his cries. Hunting and killing game receive more dignity in their death than Nicholas did. This vision has haunted me every minute."

Susan said that she may not have been shot, but she also died on August 9, 2000. She'd attempted suicide twice and had a hospital bill of over $20,000. She still felt at times that she would receive a telephone call and be able to pay a ransom to get him back, and then she'd remember the reality of the situation.

She noted that there were three more trials to go through (Skidmore being in the process of making a plea deal), and she said "three" because she felt in her heart that Jesse James Hollywood would be captured, and there would be one for him someday. She added, *"You can die of a broken heart, and if I do not take my life before that happens, it is what will consume me."*

Susan said that Nick died the worst type of death, knowing that he did not have a chance to say good-bye to those he loved. Susan added that she and Jeff would have gladly given their own lives for his, but for some reason they were doomed to still be alive and suffer upon earth. *"We have dug to the depths of nausea and envy the people that had a moment to say goodbye. We honestly believe that our son, Nicholas Samuel Markowitz, would have wanted at least a hug, a kiss and a tearful 'I love you.' He deserved so much more. I will be with you soon, son. Love, Mom."*

After Susan spoke, Victoria Hoyt was called by the defense to make her pleas for leniency for Ryan. She spoke of the chaotic life he had suffered as a child and the abuse by Ryan's dad. Victoria added how Ryan would often take the blame for something that his siblings did so that they would not be punished.

After Victoria, however, there was a whirlwind of defense witnesses: Ryan's aunt Anne Stendel Thomas speaking for five minutes, and his grandmother Carol Stendel speaking for fifteen minutes.

The same held true for the second day of the sentencing phase. Ryan's father, James David Hoyt, was only on the stand for five minutes during the defense phase. Jonathon David Hoyt, Ryan's brother, was on for a little longer, around twenty minutes. And a friend, Jane Elizabeth Bright, was on for eight minutes.

It was Ryan's younger brother, Jonathon, who affected Ryan the most emotionally. Since Jonathon was serving a sentence in a prison for armed robbery, a crime for which he had been incarcerated as an adult, he was in handcuffs during his testimony. Jonathon said that he and Ryan had often been kicked and punched by their father. Jonathon said that in one incident his father became so angry at him that he picked him up and threw him across the room, leaving a hole in the wall. Jonathon said that he thought Ryan might have suffered the same treatment from his dad.

During this testimony Ryan sat next to his lawyers, blinking back tears. He was so upset, in fact, that after Jonathon was done, Ryan was excused from the courtroom.

Cheri Owen did not call Ryan Hoyt to the stand to plead with the jury during this all-important death penalty phase. Whatever he might have planned to tell them was never known.

Before the sentence was read, Judge Gordon warned everyone in the gallery that he would not allow any kind of outburst when the verdict was read. The courtroom was absolutely silent as a court clerk began reading the verdict, with the final three fatal words from the jurors: *"Sentenced to death."*

After the courtroom cleared, Ryan's aunt collapsed on the shoulder of a friend in the hallway, sobbing. There were also tears in Jeff and Susan Markowitz's eyes as they left the courtroom. Susan told a reporter, "We agree with the jury's decision, but this is not a sweet victory. It doesn't bring us any joy."

Outside the courtroom Hoyt's defense attorneys, Richard Crouter and Cheri Owen, were clearly stunned. They agreed it was a difficult case, because of Ryan's taped confession, but Richard Crouter believed the mitigating factors should have led the jury to a sentence of life without parole. He cited the mitigating factors of Ryan's age, abusive family history and lack of any previous arrests. Crouter said, "It was just not the sort of heinous crime reserved for the death penalty."

Ron Zonen disagreed, however, saying, "It's nothing for anybody to be happy about, putting someone to death. But it is the case that justice was done. The defendant is quite deserving of the verdict that he got."

After the proceedings were over, Jeff Markowitz announced to the reporters that the reward leading to the arrest of Jesse James Hollywood was going up from $30,000 to $50,000.

Miles away from Santa Barbara, another important hearing was taking place, and it involved a Los Angeles Police Department Board of Rights panel looking into allegations that LAPD officers had mishandled the initial 911 call about Nick Markowitz's kidnapping on August 6, 2000. When Officer Brent Rygh, an eight-year veteran in 2000, and Officer Donovan Lyons, a seven-year veteran in 2000, arrived on the scene at Platt and Ingomar, in West

Hills, there was no fight in progress, or boys or van to be seen. Officer Rygh told the panel, "I thought it was some high-school kids just slap fighting, or horsing around, the way high-school students tend to do."

Officer Lyons told the panel, which included two LAPD captains and one civilian, "There was a lack of witnesses, lack of suspects, lack of blood. There was overwhelming evidence for lack of a follow-up."

One of the panelists asked the officers why they did not visit the 911 caller, Pauline Mahoney, in person. Officer Rygh answered that he had called her on his personal cell phone and believed that he had gathered enough information. Panelists also asked why the officers didn't believe a kidnapping was in progress. The officers said they thought that Nick had been released down the block. As to Officer Rygh's cell phone call to Pauline Mahoney, board member Xavier Hermosillo said, "While you acted properly, it should have gone further. You weren't wrong in anything you did, you just weren't right enough. There is no margin for error in this department."

Adding to the mistakes had been the fact that the second 911 call had been mishandled by the dispatcher and labeled as an "information-only broadcast." Panelist member Sergeant John Mumma said it should have been labeled a "kidnapping report." Since the officers never received this second 911 call, they had no way of knowing that a kidnapping was still in progress.

Officer Rygh did run the van's license plate number, which Pauline Mahoney had given him, but he mistakenly thought the address of the van's owner was a long distance away, when, in fact, it was close by. The officers did not visit the registered van's owner, John Roberts, or file a crime report.

The panel reviewed what they had heard for a few hours, and then returned with a finding: Officer Rygh and Officer Lyons were guilty of a minor breach of policy. Both officers received only a written reprimand, rather than much harsher penalties ranging from suspension to termination. Board chairman Captain Gary Williams told the officers, "Although a more thorough investigation should have taken place, it would not have prevented Nicholas Markowitz's tragic death."

The panel may have seen things in that light, but Jeff and Susan Markowitz did not. Both officers and the LAPD were definitely named, along with many others, by the Markowitzes in a lawsuit for wrongful death. Just how that would play out remained to be seen, as well as the fates of Jesse Rugge and Graham Pressley. William Skidmore was not going to trial—he pled guilty to kidnapping and robbery, and received nine years in state prison.

14

FALLOUT

In a February 2002 hearing, Richard Crouter started a process of appeal to try and overturn the sentencing decision concerning Ryan Hoyt. He addressed factors of aggravation and mitigation, noting that the jury had already rejected the special circumstance of kidnapping for extortion and found that the killing had occurred during a "simple kidnapping."

Crouter stated that the killing had not been "particularly egregious" in that it wasn't prolonged, nor had Nick been tortured before being killed. Crouter admitted that any murder was morally wrong, but compared to many murders that had been seen in court, this particular killing had not been prolonged or as brutal as some that had gone through the Santa Barbara County judicial system.

A mitigating factor, according to Crouter, was that Hoyt had been under extreme mental and emotional disturbance at the time of the crime. From evidence presented during trial, Crouter related that it had been proven that Hoyt suffered from a dependent personality disorder with an avoidant personality component. Even the prosecution's psychologist had admitted to the same thing. Because of these disorders, Crouter alleged, Hoyt had been dominated by Jesse James Hollywood and followed his orders without hesitation. Crouter argued, "Witnesses agreed that Mr. Hoyt had a mild-mannered personality which caused him to attempt mediation rather than violence in conflicted circumstances. Circumstantially, Mr. Hoyt was led to the killing here by his dependence on Jesse Hollywood for acceptance and recognition."

In her argument against the death sentence, Cheri Owen even put forth some of Ron Zonen's own words spoken to the grand jury in 2000. "What about the fact," Ron Zonen had said, "that for a period of time their security wasn't really security. I mean, could Nick have walked away at different times? Certainly. the two hours that he was over at Natasha Adams's house, Rugge wasn't even there for much of that time. None of the original kidnappers were there, he was in that house, he elected to go with everybody else back to Rugge's house."

Owen got into the particulars of the interrogation of Ryan Hoyt on August 17, 2000, and said that after Hoyt repeated that he didn't know who brought the gun to Santa Barbara, and he told the detectives he wanted to "stop there, for now." Owen said at that point Hoyt had invoked his right to remain silent and the interrogation should have ended, but didn't. Soon after that, Hoyt asked for another request to remain silent when he wanted to take a break, but he wasn't allowed to do so, according to Owen.

Owen argued, "After this request to remain silent, the detectives 'felt' that Hoyt wanted to keep talking, and kept interrogating him. Only until Hoyt made further incriminating statements against himself and asked, once again, that he wanted to stop talking, did the detectives

finally feel that the interview of Hoyt was to be concluded."

Owen also argued that the entire indictment should have
been thrown out because the deputy district attorney failed
to present relevant exculpatory information to the grand
jury. Chief among these was whether Jesse James Hollywood coerced Hoyt into playing a role in the crime.

This was Cheri Owen's "last hurrah" for her client,
however. Soon she would be in plenty of trouble herself.

It all began when Robert Sanger became the new attorney for Ryan Hoyt, on Hoyt's request. Sanger told a judge
that he'd requested documents from Cheri Owen, and "it
has been two weeks since I substituted in as attorney of
record for Ryan Hoyt and I have not been able to obtain
either Cheri Owen's or Richard Crouter's file. I am simply
unable to move forward without the files, materials and
transcripts."

Sanger was absolutely stunned when he discovered
from Richard Crouter that even Crouter was not able to get
in touch with Cheri Owen anymore. Tara Haaland, an attorney who was an associate of Sanger's, tried phoning the
number given for Cheri Owen and the phone number had
been disconnected. Haaland phoned the California State
Bar Association, and they had no new phone number
listed for Owen.

Then Sanger discussed something else. Sanger told the
judge, "On February 12, 2002, Cheri Owen, along with
paralegal Gloria Pernell, met with Ryan Hoyt at the Santa
Barbara County Jail. It appears that Ms. Owen's visit to
meet with Mr. Hoyt was for the sole purpose of obtaining
Ryan's signature on two relatively unprofessional documents which purported to have Ryan Hoyt convey any and
all rights, including literary rights, to Ms. Owen. First he
signed a waiver of attorney client privilege, and the second
document Mr. Hoyt signed was entitled 'Unconditional

Grant of Rights.'" This last document concerned all rights pertaining to literary and media concerning the case.

As to the last part, about literary and film rights, it was more than just pie in the sky. There was already talk floating about that people in the film industry were interested in making a movie about the events of August 2000. Sanger argued that these documents created a "conflict of interest" between Cheri Owen and her client.

Then Sanger blasted Owen on a much more serious matter in his presentation to the judge. He claimed that Ryan Hoyt's elderly grandmother had initially sought Owen's services to represent Ryan on the death penalty case, when, in fact, Owen had no expertise in that area and was in way over her head. Sanger blasted Owen with the statement, "Ms. Owen was an ambitious, quite frankly greedy lawyer who talked her elderly receptionist (Hoyt's grandmother) into paying a sizeable retainer consisting of her entire retirement and savings, on behalf of her grandson. Ms. Owen accepted the money and the case, knowing that she did not have the training or experience to handle such a serious and specialized manner. But Ms. Owen did not stop there. She took part of the money paid to her by the grandmother and used it to pay off accounts with an investigator for work done on other cases. Greed and ambition."

Sanger went on to say that Owen had treated the case as a media opportunity from the very start, never objecting to cameras in the courtroom, although she did try to keep Hoyt's police interview tape out. Sanger said that Owen actually encouraged filming in the courtroom because she hoped for a book deal and movie rights later on.

Sanger then argued that Owen didn't even have the minimum experience and training needed to handle a capital case. Sanger noted that there was a new proposal in the *California Rules of Court* to have an attorney who handled capital cases be an active trial practitioner for ten years in the field of criminal law, and to have had experience in at least ten prior serious or violent felony jury trials. At the time Cheri Owen took on Hoyt's case, she had been practicing law for fourteen months and didn't even come close to those standards.

Backing up Sanger's statements was Anne Stendel, Ryan Hoyt's maternal aunt. In a declaration to the court, Stendel stated that she had only spoken to Owen's investigator, George Zeliff, briefly in 2000, and to Investigator Danny Davis for maybe twenty minutes. According to Stendel, Cheri Owen had told her numerous times that she would not be testifying in the penalty phase and not to worry because "Ryan will be home by Christmas."

Then the penalty phase arrived, and Stendel was suddenly called on to testify. Stendel said it had happened so suddenly that she had not dressed properly, she was on medication that day and not clearheaded, and she had trouble recalling certain incidents because of the medication. If she had been properly aware that she was going to testify, Stendel said, she would have told the jurors all the mental-health issues that Ryan's mother, grandfather, niece and aunt had suffered from. Stendel noted, "I spent a lot of time with Ryan while he was growing up, and witnessed firsthand his day-to-day life and the struggles he went through with the abuse and the chaotic family setting he was forced to deal with on a daily basis." She added that she had wanted to tell the jury what a loving and caring person Ryan was, and how he adored his brothers, sisters, nieces and nephews, but she had not been asked any questions related to that.

Anne Stendel, the sister of Ryan's mother, Victoria Hoyt, had some new things to add about Victoria and Ryan's chaotic childhood. She related to the judge that she thought her family was extremely dysfunctional. She said that her father suffered from depression for many years and was suicidal for most of his life, and added that Victoria (Ryan's mother) had been diagnosed with mental illness when she was sixteen years old. Anne declared,

"Vicki still experiences outrageous behavior and violent outbursts, but is not currently seeking treatment. She would often take any drugs that were prescription and is an alcoholic."

Anne related that when Vicki got married to Jim Hoyt, things only got worse for her. "He had a very bad temper. There was violence and fighting. Jim would hit Vicki and then say, 'What happened?' as if he'd blacked out. The fights occurred frequently in front of Ryan, Jonathon and Kristina."

Regarding Kristina, Ryan's sister, Anne said that the girl would "play house" at the age of three and pretend to be smoking crack cocaine. Kristina ran away from home at the age of thirteen and "turned to drugs. She was found begging in front of a McDonald's in Hollywood, which soon led to prostitution."

To say that young Ryan Hoyt's home life was chaotic was a vast understatement. His grandmother Carol Stendel related to Sanger that "Ryan told me that he was never given a fair chance in life and he never felt wanted." Perhaps the only place he got that feeling was at the Hollywood household. Carol Stendel said, "Jack Hollywood made Ryan feel as if he was part of that family."

Carol added that Jesse James Hollywood took advantage of Ryan and dominated him. She said if the phone rang and it was Jesse, Ryan would drop everything and go do whatever errand Hollywood wanted him to perform. According to Carol, Jesse Hollywood got food poisoning one time, and instead of having his parents take him to the hospital, he made Ryan drive him there.

Anne Stendel also had some very damaging things to say about Cheri Owen. She related that her family had paid Owen close to $100,000—her mother alone having taken $60,000 out of a retirement account to help in the defense of Ryan. Anne Stendel had paid Owen close to $15,000, and added that Owen kept asking during the trial for more money. According to Stendel, Owen told her, "The Rugges mortgaged their home, why can't you?"

She also said that Owen would sit in a hotel for hours speaking with attorneys regarding a lawsuit against Owen at the time, rather than prepping for Ryan's upcoming trial. During the trial, Anne related, "Cheri Owen would drink a lot of wine in the evenings after trial. On one occasion when we were sharing a room at a hotel, she drank so much it resulted in her passing out on the bed."

One of Stendel's most damning comments was "On the afternoon of October 31, 2001, Cheri Owen left the court early, informing the judge that she was sick. I drove Cheri Owen to a hotel and then she had me drop her off so that she could go shopping. After she returned from shopping, she spent the rest of the afternoon on the telephone with her lawyer, Joanne Robbins, discussing her case with the state bar."

As if things weren't murky enough, court documents came to light that showed exactly what had been distracting Cheri Owen so greatly while she was supposed to be putting on a defense for Ryan Hoyt. Owen was embroiled in a civil suit against a corporation called American Justice Publications Inc. Its primary business was the publication of a magazine for lawyers. This magazine was distributed to inmates in prisons around California, and they, in turn, could contact attorneys who advertised in the magazine. Catrina Carruth was the president of American Justice Publications.

Professional Account Services (PAS) was an organization that supposedly dealt with accounting, bookkeeping and a collection service for *American Justice.* Catrina Carruth just happened to be an executive in PAS, and her mother, Terry, also had some title within the corporation. In the summer of 1999, Cheri Owen submitted her résumé after reading an ad in the *Daily Journal* that stated: *Criminal attorneys wanted . . . flexible hours . . .*

good pay. Owen eventually met with Brent Carruth, father of Catrina and husband of Terry.

According to Owen, once she got there, she wasn't offered a job, but rather services in how to develop a criminal practice. Specifically, the Carruths said that they sold advertisement space in *American Justice* magazine, which was distributed to potential clients in prisons. In the process, these clients would have their families contact PAS, send money to that organization, and PAS would credit money to the attorney's account, and allow the attorney to practice law without having to handle all the bookkeeping.

Owen signed an agreement to advertise in *American Justice* and paid them for the services. Owen later said this worked satisfactorily for a while. Then sometime in 2000, PAS requested that Owen give them her court calendar so they could determine her availability for new clients. Owen did so, and after this point things began to turn sour. She said that new information on clients was incomplete, inaccurate and sometimes completely missing. Owen added that she would be contacted by PAS about a certain client that she had never heard of, and be told that the person in question had been assigned to her. Owen stated, "This situation typically came to light when a court appearance for the client had been missed, and the client had called PAS to complain." All money from clients and their families was going to PAS before Cheri Owen saw any of it.

Because of all these problems, clients and their families began to complain to the state bar and file small claims against Cheri Owen. Owen said as she became aware of all the problems, she began to request that PAS return money to certain clients, and PAS refused.

Then in the summer of 2000, Owen learned that Brent Carruth was a disbarred attorney who had a shady past. In response she severed all ties with PAS and *American Justice* magazine, but the damage had already been done. Owen now went into such a state of "emotional shock," as she put it, that she sought help from physicians and therapists, and for a time was unable to attend the daily affairs of her practice. It was a nightmare that just wouldn't go away, however.

Owen learned that PAS was still trying to collect fees from people who were not her clients anymore. This went on even after she had severed her ties with PAS. When certain of these clients asked PAS about Cheri Owen, she claimed, PAS replied that she was "stealing from defendants, been fired by defendants, was incompetent, and similar false allegations." In response, Cheri Owen began suing *American Justice* and PAS for fraud, defamation and negligence. She was seeking $1 million in damages, but by now her practice was in real jeopardy. With all of this going on, it may have been the reason she took on Ryan Hoyt as a client, even when she had no experience in defending a person in a capital case. The allure of a possible book or movie deal about the case might have been a factor. At least that's what Ryan Hoyt's new attorney, Robert Sanger, thought.

Things for Cheri Owen only got worse when George Zeliff, her former investigator on the Hoyt case, chimed in, in support of Sanger's contentions. Zeliff wrote a declaration to a judge that he had been hired by Owen for $30,000, but all she ever paid him was $4,500 for services rendered. Zeliff wrote: *On several occasions, I told Ms. Owen that I needed to go to Santa Barbara to discuss the case with Mr. Hoyt. Ms. Owen instructed me to not talk with Mr. Hoyt and told me that she did not want me speaking with him or contacting him in any way. In my experience in dealing with capital cases, one of the first and most important steps of investigation is to contact the client for complete details.* Zeliff wondered much later if he was told not to speak with Ryan Hoyt because Cheri

Owen did not want anyone else to have information from him that she could use in a book or movie deal.

Zeliff had made up a list of witnesses he wanted to talk to, but according to him, Owen only let him interview certain people. Then Zeliff wrote that he had asked Owen what should be done with the $25,500 that had not been used on Hoyt's case. According to Zeliff, she told him to use that money on other cases she was handling. Zeliff eventually spent the money on two other cases he was working on for her. After about four months on Hoyt's case, Owen quit returning Zeliff's phone calls, letters and e-mails.

Roger Best, who was an investigator, was assigned by Sanger to look into all the allegations concerning Cheri Owen and the defense of Ryan Hoyt. Best made a declaration to the judge that he was "diligently investigating the case," and noted that preceding counsel Cheri Owen should have retained a criminalist or a forensic specialist to review the physical evidence supposedly tying Ryan Hoyt to the murder. Best talked with Investigator Zeliff and found out that Zeliff had been instructed not to talk to these witnesses. Best noted, *This type of instruction, to Mr. Zeliff, by counsel, is unheard of in a capital or any major case. Who knows better what happened than the client?*

Best claimed that he would have interviewed as many witnesses as possible, and these would have led him to other witnesses. Best also started interviewing Danny Davis, an investigator that Cheri Owen had hired at one point. Davis told Best that he had worked with Owen for a year on Hoyt's case, and no one had been able to contact Cheri Owen since the trial ended with Hoyt's death penalty conviction. She would not answer her telephone, cell phone or her door. The only way to still reach her was by her message machine.

Davis added that during his initial investigation, even when he met in person with Cheri Owen, he rarely received written instructions from her, as if she didn't want a paper trail. Davis told Best he wasn't even sure if he'd ever been given a witness list by Owen. Davis added that no attorney he'd worked for on a death penalty case had ever gone about it the way Cheri Owen had. "In the end I knew it was going to come back and bite her in the butt," he said.

Davis did interview Hoyt's mom, grandparents and a neighbor or two, but when he was on the road to Reno to interview Ryan's father and stepmother, Owen phoned him and told him to cancel the trip. Davis had visited the crime scene area briefly, but only took photos of the nearby road, and not the actual murder location near Lizard's Mouth. Davis added that he had tried to locate an alibi for Ryan Hoyt, but he had not been successful in that regard.

Even more important, Best identified another witness, Ernest Seymour, mentioned in an early police report. Seymour had been a guest in the room next to Jesse Rugge, Nick Markowitz, Graham Pressley, Kelly Carpenter and Natasha Adams at the Lemon Tree Inn. Seymour was later shown photographs of several people and he indicated that he recognized Jesse Rugge and Jesse James Hollywood as being at the room. He did not recognize Ryan Hoyt as being there. In September 2002, Best was able to interview Seymour, who added some things not mentioned in previous reports. Seymour said while on the balcony he had actually spoken with Jesse James Hollywood. Hollywood introduced himself as Jesse James, and Seymour spoke with him for about twenty minutes. (Though Seymour's description of Jesse James Hollywood as being six feet tall did not jibe with the reality of Jesse being five-four. He may have mistaken the name "Jesse" as being for Jesse James Hollywood instead of Jesse Rugge.) Seymour believed there were about six other people in the room next to his and they were having a party.

Seymour told Best that after he went to sleep, he was awakened by "banging and scuffling" sounds. He came out of a deep sleep, heard more sounds and thought someone was banging on his door. He said, "Who is it?" and opened the door. No one was out there. Seymour returned to bed and started to go back to sleep. He was drifting in and out of sleep when he heard more banging and scuffling sounds. He said that a person inside that room was screaming in a muffled tone, as if there was a "hand or something else over his mouth." Seymour did not get out of bed this time to investigate and after a while the noises stopped and Seymour went back to sleep.

When asked about it by Best, Seymour said he believed it was Nick Markowitz who was making the noise at the time by having duct tape placed over his mouth and wrists. He felt bad that he had not intervened that time, because there might have been a different outcome than what happened next.

Seymour added that a person identifying himself as an LAPD police officer wanted to meet with him soon thereafter. Seymour was afraid that he was being set up to be killed, however, by some of the suspects or their friends, and he refused to meet anyone outside a police station. The interview with the supposed LAPD officer never occurred.

Also weighing in on the issue of Cheri Owen's possible negligence in the case was Robin Hoyt, Ryan's stepmother. She said that George Zeliff had interviewed her for only fifteen minutes, and Danny Davis, Cheri Owen and Richard Crouter never contacted her at all. Robin said, "I was extremely disappointed that no one ever contacted Ryan's stepbrothers Ben and Tim Deschaine or followed up with me in regard to Ryan. Had Ben and Tim been contacted, they could have given valuable information with regard to Ryan."

Robin said that Ryan had lived with them from the time he was six years old, and she considered him a "loving and compassionate child." Robin added that Ryan had wanted to join the navy after high school but was unable to do so when he tested positive for marijuana. Robin brought up the chaos with Ryan's sister, Kristina, and how the family had spent $25,000 in drug rehabilitation for her. There was a separation between James, Ryan's father, and Robin for fifteen months, and James lived with Ryan and Jonathon. Robin said, "James did hit the kids, and probably hit them more than necessary." She spoke of James hitting Ryan in the head and kicking him in the stomach.

Despite a lot of negative things having been said about her, Vicki, Ryan's mother, made a declaration to the judge as well. She said that she'd been interviewed briefly by George Zeliff and by Danny Davis for about twenty minutes. She also spoke briefly with Dr. Kania. Vicki wrote: *I attended the trial everyday, but at one point Cheri Owen told me that I was not allowed to return. Two days before I testified, I was served a subpoena by someone identifying himself as a friend of Danny Davis. It was 11 P.M. and the man had no information for me and could not answer questions. No one ever contacted me to tell me what was expected of me or gave me any idea what would be required of me in court. I had repeatedly been told by Cheri Owen that I would not testify. I was not prepared to speak on Ryan's behalf and feel that there were many issues that were never addressed. No one ever discussed with me, nor did I ever have an opportunity to tell the jury about Ryan's good character.*

In the bitter end Cheri Owen signed a form to the Supreme Court of California, tendering her resignation from the state bar and her ability to practice law. The form read in part: *The voluntary resignation of Cheri Ann Owen, as a member of the State Bar of California, is accepted without prejudice to further proceedings.* Of course, this was much too late for Ryan Hoyt, who now sat on San Quentin State Prison's death row.

Many people, besides Ryan Hoyt, argued that Cheri Owen's defense of him had been a disaster. And in some ways, Owen was the latest "victim" of the events that had occurred on August 6, 2000. The kidnapping and murder of Nick Markowitz seemed to spread out in waves from the initial event, an event that Jesse James Hollywood set in motion.

15

A Tale of Two Trials

The first order of business for Graham Pressley's lawyer, Michael Ganschow, was to get his client's trial severed from that of Jesse Rugge. Right from the start, Ganschow pointed out that Pressley had not been part of the original group in the van that had abducted Nick Markowitz. Ganschow noted that on a page in the prosecution's original statements, there was a "false" declaration that "both [Rugge and Pressley] were dealing drugs for Jesse Hollywood. Both were involved in kidnapping Nicholas Markowitz from early stages of the offense."

Ganschow argued before Judge Gordon that "this fanciful version of events of August 6 through August 8, 2000, illustrates that the prosecution is seeking the unitary trial specifically for the purpose of confusing the juries by introducing facts applicable only to defendant Rugge, but then arguing its application to both, by smearing defendant Pressley by virtue of his association with defendant Rugge."

Ganschow said that Pressley had not sold drugs for

Jesse Hollywood, and he cited several sources to prove it. Casey Sheehan had said that Ryan Hoyt and Jesse Rugge sold marijuana for Hollywood, but Sheehan didn't even know who Graham Pressley was when shown a photo lineup. Brian Affronti and Chas Saulsbury made similar statements.

Ganschow noted that when Pressley visited his friend Jesse Rugge's residence on August 7, it was the first time he had ever seen Nick Markowitz. Originally, Pressley had thought that Nick was one of Rugge's friends. Later, when Pressley joined Rugge, Nick, Natasha and Kelly at the Lemon Tree Inn, he was on friendly terms with Nick, and even went swimming with him in the motel pool. By lumping Rugge and Pressley together, Ganschow said, it was akin to saying, "Barry Bonds and Michael Ganschow hit seventy-three home runs last year."

Ganschow went on that Pressley had not been part of any of the decision making, as far as a conspiracy went. In essence, he had stumbled into something he barely understood. Jesse James Hollywood had masterminded most of the events, according to Ganschow—and even Zonen— and Ryan Hoyt had carried out the actual murder. Since Pressley had nothing to do with the early stages of the kidnapping, Ganschow said, the jurors who listened to that part of the testimony would have to be excused for long periods of time while the witnesses testified about Rugge. In Ganschow's estimation Rugge and Pressley had no business in being tried together.

Michael Ganschow didn't have to go any farther than Santa Barbara County to point out the problems surrounding trials that involved multiple situations. Ganschow pointed out that in 1987, none other than Ron Zonen had been the prosecutor in such a case before Judge Gordon. At that time a Mr. Morsette was being tried for raping three women in three separate cases. The defendant sought three separate trials involving each alleged victim, because circumstances had been different in each case. Zonen had written up a memo to the judge, just as he was now doing, to keep the trials together, and he stated topics similar to the ones now being put forth about Rugge and Pressley. The cases were kept together and Morsette was found guilty of the charges. A court of appeals, however, looked at the verdicts and decided, *The jury was confused by the accounts of separate victims.* The court of appeals reversed the convictions on all counts and ordered new trials. Ganschow knew that judges hated having verdicts overturned by appeals courts and banked on that fact in helping sever his client's case from that of Jesse Rugge.

In the end Ganschow's wish came true. Two separate trials were ordered by Judge Gordon, and Jesse Rugge's would be the first to occur.

In his opening arguments at Jesse Rugge's trial, Ron Zonen told the jurors that Jesse Rugge was a key player in the kidnapping and murder of Nick Markowitz. Rugge helped Jesse Hollywood and William Skidmore grab and beat up Nick on a sidewalk in West Hills and throw him into the white van. Then Rugge had been the driver of the van all the way up to Santa Barbara. During August 6, through the early hours of August 9, Rugge was the guy Hollywood told to keep Nick from leaving. And, most important, from the murder aspect of the charges, Jesse Rugge had walked Nick up to his place of execution. Even though Zonen admitted that Nick had plenty of opportunities to escape, those opportunities did not mean that the kidnapping had ever ended.

Rugge's lawyer, Michael Carty, on the other hand, argued of the kidnapping that it was a "spontaneous, unexplained, nonconspiracy coincidence, and Mr. Rugge never wanted to be a part of it. At no time did he have intentions to harm Nicholas Markowitz." Carty argued that during his days with Nick in Santa Barbara, Rugge treated Nick the same way he treated Graham Pressley and Natasha Adams.

Rugge had even offered Nick money so that he could go back home, and it was Nick who decided not to leave. Even when Ryan Hoyt came to the Lemon Tree Inn, with a gun, Rugge really did not believe that Nick would be killed. Rather, he thought that the gun was there only for show, to keep Nick quiet.

There were many witnesses back on the stand, who had been in Ryan Hoyt's trial. Most of these repeated what they had said at that trial.

During the defense phase, Jesse Rugge testified, and many of the things he had to say now were at variance with what he'd told detectives after his arrest in mid-August 2000. The real fireworks came during the cross-examination, and Ron Zonen came right out of the gate with a hard-hitting question. "Mr. Rugge, why in the world would Ryan Hoyt bring two witnesses to a murder?"

This brought an immediate objection from Carty. "Argumentative!" he said.

"Sustained," Judge Gordon replied.

Zonen took a different tack. "Isn't it true that Ryan Hoyt's reputation among your group of friends with Jesse Hollywood is something of a buffoon?"

"Not a buffoon."

"Isn't it true that Ryan Hoyt's job around Jesse Hollywood's house was picking up dog poop?"

"That's correct, sir."

"He would pick up beer cans and litter that was in Jesse Hollywood's backyard, is that right?"

"That's correct, sir."

"And people made fun of him for doing that, isn't that right?"

"No, it isn't."

"You knew Nick Markowitz, didn't you?"

"I'd met him a few times."

"You once drank a beer with him?"

"Yes, at Justin Orenstein's house."

"So you knew Ben Markowitz's younger brother, right?"

"Yes, through Justin Orenstein's house, when I met Susan and Jeff there. Same evening." This was a new wrinkle. The standard way of thinking had been that Jesse Rugge had never laid eyes on Nick Markowitz until the morning of August 6, 2000.

Of the initial kidnapping, Zonen asked, "In the drive to Brian Affronti's house, if you had stopped at any time, taken the key out of the ignition, and said to Nick Markowitz, 'You better leave the van right now, and I'm leaving,' do you feel you would have died if you had done that?"

"No, sir. I don't think I would have died at that moment."

"So while you were driving, up until Affronti's house, there was nothing that would have stopped you from pulling the van over, in terms of a life-threatening immediate danger, is that right?"

"I can't tell you, sir. It was just a fear factor, the man (Hollywood) sitting next to me with a gun."

"Mr. Rugge, that wasn't an unusual event, sitting next to Jesse Hollywood while he had his gun, was it?"

"In this situation, to me, it was."

"There was a witness who testified to seeing you wipe prints off Nick's wallet, is that true?"

"That didn't happen."

"And you never called Emilio Jerez and asked him if he had a closet big enough to put a person in?"

"That's not true."

Switching to the night at the Lemon Tree Inn, Zonen asked, "When you saw Ryan Hoyt show up at the door and you saw the blue bag, what did you think at that point?"

"I couldn't even tell you, man!"

"Well, were you thinking that your life was in danger as soon as he showed up at the door?"

"I thought all of our lives were in danger."

"Did you believe at that moment he would kill you?"

"I couldn't tell you that."

"All right, you didn't know what the contents of that bag was at that time, though?"

"I did. Because I had seen that blue bag at Jesse Hollywood's, carrying the TEC-9."

Moving on to the scene in the bathroom, Zonen said, "So you understood when Hoyt talked about how much you screwed up, that it was in reference to your treatment of Nick Markowitz, is that right?"

"I believe so."

"And exactly at that moment he pulls out the gun?"

"Yes."

"Now, isn't it true that you believed that the gun was going to be used to kill Nick Markowitz?"

"No."

"However, you just told the jury that when the door opened and you saw Hoyt there, you believed the gun was going to kill you?"

"All possibilities ran through my mind, sir."

"Why would he kill you, a friend of his since elementary school, and not kill Nick Markowitz?"

"You misunderstood me. I was not a friend of his."

"Did you ask him, 'Ryan, what are you doing here with a gun?'"

"Yeah, I asked him, but he shined me on."

"Did he ask you who Graham Pressley was?"

"Yes, sir."

"What did you tell him?"

"He's a friend of mine."

"Is it true that you're the connection between Graham Pressley and your Los Angeles friends?"

"My connection?"

"Yes," the attorney confirmed.

"He would get his pot from somebody else as well, but he got his pot from me, too."

"Had he met Jesse Hollywood before?"

"Yes."

"Did he know what Jesse Hollywood's association to you was?"

"Yes."

"So Graham Pressley saw the gun when Hoyt was there?"

"That is correct."

Moving on to the time frame when Hoyt and Rugge walked out the door, leaving Pressley and Nick in the room, Zonen asked, "Why didn't you run?"

"I was scared."

"For doing nothing more than running, you were afraid you would die in the hallway of that hotel from the submachine gun, is that right?"

"Yes."

"Did you tell Graham Pressley—as you were leaving the hotel to go to your house with Mr. Hoyt—did you tell Graham, 'Now is a good time to leave. Just get out of here'?"

"No, sir."

"In the car, is it your testimony, Mr. Rugge, that you believed that if you jumped out of that car and ran at the stop sign or stoplight, that he would have jumped out of the car and shot you with that assault weapon?"

"I believe so, yes."

As to the shovels, Zonen said, "Mr. Rugge, you didn't think he was going to garden with those shovels, did you?"

"That's correct."

"The purpose he had in mind with those shovels was something very bad, is that right?"

"I believe so."

"You believed he was going to do something very, very bad with those shovels?"

"I thought it was just to scare us at first."

Zonen pointed out that when Ryan Hoyt went to get the

shovels, he was on the side of Rugge's house and could not have seen Rugge for a number of minutes. Rugge agreed. Zonen then asked, "You could have run at that point, isn't that right?"

Rugge replied, "I could have."

"At some point, did you tell him what he was doing is wrong?"

"I didn't want to even question him, man."

When they got back to the hotel, after getting the shovels, Zonen wanted to know if Rugge was concerned about Nick's well-being, and Rugge answered, "Yes, sir."

Asked if he thought Nick was going to die that night, Rugge responded, "I believed all of us could have died that night."

"You, more than Nick Markowitz?"

"No."

"Nick Markowitz, more than you?"

"I thought about the same."

"So, at the hotel, you believe if you'd yelled out for help that Ryan Hoyt would have killed you right there?"

"I believe so."

Rugge added that Hoyt made Graham Pressley go with him almost as soon as he and Hoyt got back to the room after getting the shovels. Nick was still asleep at the time, according to Rugge. Zonen asked if Hoyt had a conversation in the room with Pressley about finding a nice dark isolated spot, and Rugge said that didn't happen in his presence. As to Pressley and Hoyt leaving the room, Zonen asked, "Did Hoyt say to you, 'You better be here when I get back'?"

Rugge said that he hadn't. Zonen then asked, "Mr. Rugge, you did not at that moment grab Nick Markowitz and leave the room, did you?"

"No, sir."

"You did not go to the telephone and call the police at that point, did you?"

"No, sir."

"You did not go knock on your neighbor's door, the one that you shared a blunt with, did you?"

"No, sir."

Rugge agreed with Zonen that Hoyt and Pressley were gone from an hour and a half to two hours, and yet he never tried to escape with Nick, even though he thought something bad might happen. Asked why, Rugge responded that he was scared. Questioned about what he did during that time, Rugge replied, "I was drinking Jack Daniel's straight. I was numbing myself."

Zonen responded to that by saying, "You were numbing yourself because you knew something very bad was going to happen, didn't you?"

"No, I did not, sir."

"Why did you even think it was a problem to stay in the hotel room? Why not go home?"

"The fear factor. It just wasn't real. I thought he was just playing us. Like trying to scare us."

"If you thought he was playing a game, why not just go home at that time? Why take the chance that he wasn't playing a game?"

"I don't know. I can't tell you that."

"Could the answer be that you were part of it?"

"No, sir."

"You were under orders from Jesse Hollywood, weren't you?"

"No, sir."

"But when you were holding Nick Markowitz for that entire sixty-hour period of time, you were following directions of Jesse Hollywood, weren't you?"

"I wasn't holding him."

"What? Did you think you had any culpability in Nick's abduction?"

"I didn't think I committed a crime at all. I didn't know what was going on."

"You were just taking him for a drive?"

"Like I said, I didn't know what was going on."

"On the sixth of August, after you abducted Nicholas Markowitz, did you come to believe that the defiance of Jesse Hollywood would result in your death?"

"I couldn't tell you. I don't know."

"Mr. Rugge, that two-hour period of time that you were in the hotel room waiting for Pressley and Hoyt to return, did you think about calling anybody—anybody at all—your father, the police, anybody at all?"

"No. I was scared of the situation. I didn't know if he was going to hurt or just scare us."

When it came to the part about walking up the trail toward the Lizard's Mouth, Zonen wanted to know if Rugge thought they might be heading toward a grave site. He answered, "It crossed my mind." Zonen then asked if anything else crossed his mind, and Rugge replied that he still didn't know if the shovels and hole and gun were just a way of keeping Nick quiet about everything that had happened. On the darkened trail up to Lizard's Mouth, Zonen asked why Rugge didn't just jump Hoyt. Rugge replied, "Would you jump a man with an automatic gun?"

"But it was in a bag. How was he going to use it in a bag?"

"He was already crazy enough to walk down the hallway of the hotel with a TEC-9. I wasn't going to jump a man with a TEC-9," Rugge reiterated.

"But you had two allies there, why didn't all three of you jump him?"

"I was not going to jump a man with a gun, sir."

Zonen wanted to know if there was any other lighting up there, except the flashlight that Hoyt had. Rugge answered, "Yeah. It was bright outside. I mean there were the moon and stars."

Rugge explained about the two people up near Lizard's Mouth, who seemed to be cuddling and then these people walked away, right past them on the trail, saying good-bye to them. It was after they were gone that Hoyt, according to Rugge, taped up Nick with duct tape and marched him forward toward the hole. Rugge once again stated that he did not get up off a rock and seemed to be almost frozen into place. Then he heard what sounded like a shovel being struck against Nick, and Hoyt dragging him to the hole. A moment later there was a series of gunshots. Rugge said, "They were deafening."

Rugge now denied putting even a single shovelful of dirt on Nick's body. He said, "I took off running. I was scared of the whole thing and how it went down. It crossed my mind that Hoyt might kill me. There was a point where I tripped on a rock. And I got sick and I was on my hands and knees throwing up. Dry heaving. And that's when Mr. Hoyt came up with the flashlight and he pointed it at me and chuckled."

Zonen asked Rugge who had carried the shovels back to the car, and he said that Hoyt carried everything—the blue bag and the shovels. Rugge also said he didn't know if the gun was in the bag at that time, but he presumed that it was. Asked if it was a surprise to see Graham Pressley still sitting at the car after all the gunshots, Rugge answered, "The whole situation was a big surprise."

Carty had a few questions on redirect, and he asked Jesse Rugge, "Since you've been in custody, has Hoyt threatened your life?"

"Numerous times."

"In front of witnesses?"

"Yes. People, cops."

"Are you still afraid of Hoyt today?"

"Yes."

"Did you intend to hurt Nick Markowitz at any time?"

"No."

"Mr. Rugge, is there anything you did at that scene that

was done with the intent of assisting Mr. Hoyt to shoot Nick Markowitz?"

"No."

After Rugge's testimony Ron Zonen played an audiotape for the jurors in which Jesse Rugge spoke to Detectives Reinstadler and West during his interview of August 16, 2000. On the tape there were many discrepancies as to what Rugge was now saying on the stand. And to one question by a detective, as to whether he was afraid of Jesse James Hollywood, Rugge had answered, "No."

During closing arguments Ron Zonen told the jurors that Jesse Rugge should be found guilty of both murder and kidnapping. In fact, Zonen stated that the plot actually began on August 5, 2000, when Jesse Hollywood came to Rugge's home in Santa Barbara and they made plans for a retaliation against Ben Markowitz. Rugge went to Los Angeles with Hollywod to exact some kind of revenge on Ben, and in the process stumbled upon Nick Markowitz. Zonen said that the kidnapping was continuous from the time Nick was grabbed off the street and shoved into a van, until he was murdered near Lizard's Mouth. Zonen agreed that the security for Nick was almost nonexistent at times, but he argued, "There were many occasions when Nick could have made his escape, but that does not mean the kidnapping ended."

As far as the murder went, Zonen argued that by going with Hoyt up the hill with Nick to Lizard's Mouth in the early-morning hours of August 9, 2000, Jesse Rugge was helping make sure that Nick did not escape at the last minute. Zonen claimed, "Why in the world would Mr. Hoyt bring two witnesses to a murder? It doesn't make sense. It only makes sense when you understand that Mr. Hoyt was in league with Mr. Rugge and Mr. Pressley."

* * *

Michael Carty, on the other hand, told the jurors that Jesse Rugge had befriended Nick Markowitz in Santa Barbara and even offered to help him return to West Hills. As far as the kidnapping went, Carty said that Rugge was guilty of simple kidnapping and not kidnapping for ransom. And when Jesse Hollywood offered Rugge $2,500 to kill Nick, Rugge turned him down. "The purpose for this kidnapping was not for ransom or extortion. It had to do with the windows being broken and threats from Ben Markowitz."

As far as the kidnapping progressing continuously up to the time of the murder, Carty declared, "No one used force to keep Nick there. He was treated like one of the group." Carty claimed that since the kidnapping was no longer in progress, Rugge could not be held responsible for the murder of Nick Markowitz. That was Jesse James Hollywood's doing, and Ryan Hoyt's as well. Carty argued, "It's not a crime to be too afraid to stop a crime from happening."

The jurors debated the guilt and innocence of Jesse Rugge on the murder charge and kidnapping charge for two days. Then the jury of seven women and five men handed down a split verdict: not guilty for first-degree murder, but guilty of kidnapping. When Rugge heard "not guilty," on the murder charge, he put his head down, grabbed his head and cried.

After the verdict was rendered, none of the jurors chose to talk with reporters, honoring a pact they had made not to speak to the media. And not unlike them, Jesse Rugge's father would not say anything as well. When approached by reporters outside the courtroom, he muttered an expletive and gestured to be left alone.

* * *

Michael Carty, however, was more than willing to talk, and he said that he was pleased with the verdict of not guilty on the murder charge, but disappointed about the kidnapping charge of kidnapping for ransom. He stated that Jesse Rugge should have been charged only with simple kidnapping, and not the more aggravated kidnapping charge. Carty said he planned to appeal the decision, citing that he still believed the trial should have taken place outside of Santa Barbara County, because of all the publicity surrounding the case.

Carty told reporters that Rugge's parents "were disappointed in the kidnapping verdict, but very pleased with everything else. Jesse Rugge was not someone who wanted Nicholas harmed." Attempting to explain why he thought the jurors acquitted Rugge of murder, Carty said, "They felt that Nick was no longer being held against his will. The jury worked hard with the evidence."

Ron Zonen told reporters he could live with the verdict. "It's disappointing they didn't convict him of murder, but it's gratifying they did convict him of aggravated kidnapping, which carries a life sentence."

Stunned by the decision of acquittal on the murder charge, Jeff and Susan Markowitz did not talk to a reporter until nearly an hour after the verdict. Jeff Markowitz then said that the jury left a message of "hang around with a bad crowd when the worst thing happens, and you can get away with it. Whether Mr. Rugge had compassion at any moment he was with Nicholas doesn't matter. He picked him up and delivered him on a silver platter to Mr. Hoyt. Mr. Rugge got away with murder."

* * *

Before Graham Pressley's trial even got under way, his attorney, Michael Ganschow, tried to convince the judge that Pressley's statements in his interview with law enforcement "were the product of Jesse Rugge's *coerced statements.*" In other words, Ganschow was saying that Pressley's interview had to be thrown out, because it stemmed from things Rugge had said under duress. It was all fruit of the poisoned tree in his estimation. The exact portion of Rugge's statements to detectives were the following:

Reinstadler:	This is a capital murder case. Do you understand what that means?
Rugge:	I don't know, sir.
Reinstadler:	That means you could be sentenced to death. Unless we start gettin' information better than it looks. You took him (Nick) up the hill and you killed him. You put him in his own grave. You shot him multiple times with an automatic weapon while he was trussed up. So it isn't gonna matter who you're afraid of. I'd be afraid of the needle.

Ganschow claimed it was only when Rugge was faced with the death penalty that he mentioned Graham Pressley as being the one who had helped Hoyt dig a grave for Nick Markowitz:

Reinstadler:	Who dug the hole?
Rugge:	Graham dug the hole, but didn't kill the kid.

Ganschow related, "It was precisely that statement by Jesse Rugge that Graham Pressley dug Nick Markowitz's grave which formed the focus of interrogation of Graham Pressley on August sixteenth." Even Detective Cornell and polygrapher Smith admitted that it was these statements by Rugge that led them to question Pressley the way they did on August 16, 2000.

In the end Judge Gordon did not believe that Graham Pressley had been brought into an illegal situation because of statements Jesse Rugge had made. Pressley's trial would go on as planned.

At the beginning of Graham Pressley's trial, DDA Ron Zonen told the jurors in opening arguments that Graham had been on a downward spiral that summer, smoking a lot of dope to the point where he was in debt. It was that debt, Zonen contended, and not fear, that motivated Pressley to show Ryan Hoyt a route up to Lizard's Mouth and to dig a hole that would become Nick Markowitz's grave. Zonen also said that Pressley wanted to please Hoyt, because he knew that Hoyt worked for Hollywood, and this might help Pressley in the drug trade.

Pressley's attorney, Michael Ganschow, argued, however, that Pressley had been in fear of his life the moment that Ryan Hoyt showed up in Santa Barbara with a gun. Ganschow asked rhetorically, "Is Graham Pressley a kidnapper, a murderer, or is he a surviving victim of that senseless slaughter?" Ganschow answered his own question by saying that Pressley was a victim.

Ganschow argued that after digging the hole up at Lizard's Mouth, Pressley believed he might be shot by Ryan Hoyt to eliminate him as a witness. "Graham had no motive to murder or even harm Nicholas Markowitz. Mr. Pressley wasn't part of the group of young men that dealt marijuana for Mr. Hollywood, and he was actually much like Nicholas. His friends, teachers and coaches will testify that he was a gentle, thoughtful and peaceful young man who wouldn't hurt a fly. He and Nick were close in age and had become friends, smoked pot and talked about sports and girls in the two days before Nicholas was killed. The night of the murder, Mr. Pressley was just trying to survive."

There was a repeat of many witnesses who had been in Hoyt and Rugge's trials, but Natasha Adams and Kelly Carpenter had a few new tidbits to add to their previous testimony. Natasha, who was now nineteen-year-old Natasha Adams-Young, said she had told Pressley at one point, "We need to say something to somebody. A lawyer, the police." According to Natasha, Pressley assured her that Nick was not going to be harmed, and, in consequence, no lawyer or police were contacted.

Kelly Carpenter spoke of her last words with Nick on the night of August 8. She said that she hugged him, told him good-bye and wished that they had met under better circumstances. When he was released in West Hills, she said, he should come back to Santa Barbara someday and look her up.

During the defense part of the trial, Ganschow brought forward a string of character witnesses—friends, coaches and teachers who had known Pressley. Ganschow even had Pressley's former Boy Scout leader, Paul Tumbleson, on the stand. Tumbleson testified that when he found out what Pressley was being charged with, "I was astonished, amazed and shocked. It didn't fit his character to be involved in something like this."

Zonen, on cross, got Tumbleson to admit that he hadn't seen Pressley in years. Zonen asked, "Did you know that Mr. Pressley was expelled from high school at fifteen because of drug use?" Tumbleson answered that he didn't know that.

* * *

One of Ganschow's most effective witnesses to prove that Pressley was not part of Jesse James Hollywood's crowd was Hollywood's old buddy who had driven him home from Colorado—Chas Saulsbury. While Hollywood was in Colorado, he read a news article about the four who had been arrested in Santa Barbara, including Graham Pressley. Hollywood told Saulsbury, "Who is this kid? What is he doing there? I don't even know him!"

It wasn't certain at first that Ganschow would put Pressley on the stand, but then he reasoned that Pressley's chances were better with the jury if he did. On direct Pressley retold all the events at Natasha Adams's house and at Rugge's house as well. Then he added a few things about their time at the Lemon Tree Inn. Pressley said that he and Nick went swimming and used the hot tub for about an hour while the others stayed in the room. "He was a nice guy. We hit it off. Then we spent a lot of time smoking marijuana and drinking. I was beginning to nod out. Then about eleven-fifteen P.M. there was knock at the door."

Pressley said a guy came in who he had never seen before, carrying a duffel bag. "The guy kind of did a double take when he saw me. A critical glance." Pressley said that the unknown person carried the duffel bag into the bathroom, but he left the door ajar. When Pressley went to get a drink from a nearby faucet, he saw the barrel of a gun sticking out of the duffel bag and the person was wiping down the gun's ammunition magazine. Pressley said, "I was absolutely not expecting to see that. You don't expect to see someone you never knew in a hotel room with a gun. I just remembered feeling scared." One thing Pressley didn't do at the time was tell either Jesse Rugge or Nick Markowitz about what he had just seen. As to why he didn't, he said he was too afraid to do anything at all.

After this episode, according to Pressley, Ryan Hoyt

came out of the bathroom and motioned for Jesse Rugge to follow him outside. According to Pressley, they stayed out there for about twenty minutes. Pressley added, "I didn't want to know what they were doing."

When the two came back inside, Rugge immediately asked Pressley if he knew where Lizard's Mouth was in the Santa Ynez Mountains. Pressley said that he did, and Rugge told him to go there with Hoyt. Pressley added, "The way he said it was like a demand, but a reassuring one, like, 'You need to do this.'"

Pressley said he did as instructed, and when they arrived at a pullout near the trailhead to Lizard's Mouth, Hoyt pulled two shovels out of the trunk, gave Pressley one and said, "Let's go." Once they went up the trail, according to Pressley, "He told me, 'I want a hole seven feet by two feet, and as deep as you can dig it. Just dig, if you know what's good for you.'"

Pressley did start digging, and said that all the time he was wondering if the hole was meant for him. "I wondered if I would ever see the light of day. I thought it was my grave."

After about twenty minutes of digging, the hole was nowhere near seven feet long by two feet wide, nor was it very deep. Hoyt, however, was tired of Pressley's digging attempts and suddenly said, "That's enough! That's enough! Let's go."

Pressley testified that on the way back down to the car, he felt a sense of tremendous relief. "I thought that maybe he had just been trying to scare me."

As far as the second trip up to Lizard's Mouth went, Pressley admitted on that ride he believed Nick would be killed, and he also admitted to walking partway up the trail with Hoyt, Rugge and Nick. Before he went very far, however, Pressley said that he sat down on a rock and refused to go any farther. The others left him there and he waited passively until he heard gunshots, and only Hoyt and Rugge returned.

At this point on the stand, Pressley broke down and

started crying, acknowledging the things he had failed to do led to Nick Markowitz's execution. "I was just ashamed," he said, referring to why he had originally lied to his friends, his parents and authorities about his role in the affair. "Ashamed because I did dig the grave, because I didn't tell Nick about the gun, I didn't say anything on the ride up there, I didn't do anything but sit there when they took him away. I felt absolutely responsible for what happened. I didn't want to believe because of my cowardice, Nick was dead."

On cross-examination Ron Zonen took Pressley through many of the aspects of his two days with Nick and the others. Zonen asked if Pressley had lied to authorities when they began questioning him about the events. Pressley admitted that he had, but that he'd done so because he was scared of Hoyt and Hollywood, and was confused. "I lied about a lot of things. All those half-truths and lies were for the reason that I knew if I said what really happened, and walked out of there, they (Hoyt and Hollywood) were going to find me. I was just afraid for my life, period."

Asked why he hadn't informed Nick at the Lemon Tree Inn of the imminent danger, Pressley said, "I was scared and confused about what was going to happen. Things just didn't make sense that night."

Pressley could have added that things didn't make much sense from the moment Nick Markowitz was grabbed off the street on August 6 in West Hills.

In his closing argument to the jurors, Ganschow portrayed Graham Pressley as being a victim in his own way. Ganschow told the jurors, "Graham Pressley never intended to do anything bad. He's not the sort of person who would willingly and knowingly ever do anything remotely resembling these charges. He was seventeen years old at the time. He has repeatedly said that he was scared, he was petrified, he was frozen. Absolutely, he was in fear for his life. Graham Pressley is not a ruthless, cold-blooded murderer. He is not a kidnapper who would harm anybody, much less Nicholas Markowitz."

In his closing arguments Zonen painted a very different portrait of Graham Pressley as a stoner who was in league with Jesse Rugge and Ryan Hoyt. "Graham Pressley is a pathological liar who hid the truth from his friends, from his parents and from the police. He directed Ryan Hoyt and Jesse Rugge to the grave site. He absoltuely had to have done that. That's the only way it could have been, because of the difficulty of getting there in the darkness. Mr. Pressley was motivated in a desire to maintain his extensive narcotics dealings and drug use through his friendship with Mr. Rugge and the connections to Mr. Hollywood's drug business. His association with Mr. Hollywood is much greater than he lets on. If he hadn't been doing dope, he wouldn't have been involved in this murder."

Zonen pointed out that though Pressley claimed to be afraid of Ryan Hoyt, he made no attempt to flee or seek help when he was left alone in the car for nearly twenty minutes after the first trip up to Lizard's Mouth. All during that time, the weapon he was so afraid of was in the trunk of the car. As far as never warning Nick of the danger, Zonen asked, "Why? The answer is, he was a part of this."

Jury deliberation went on for four days. When the jury of seven men and five women came back, they acquitted Graham Pressley of kidnapping, but were unable to agree if Pressley was guilty of murder. Judge Gordon had the jurors polled individually, and they all said that they could not see any hope of them coming to a unanimous decision.

With that, Judge Gordon announced, "It appears the jury is hopelessly deadlocked." He declared a mistrial and gave the prosecution until August 15, 2002, to decide whether to retry Pressley.

On hearing this decision, Graham Pressley lowered his head and wiped tears from his eyes with a tissue, while his mother, Christina, wept quietly in the gallery. Jeff and Susan Markowitz appeared to be stunned, and then angry at the decision. Outside the courtroom Susan told reporters, "I don't know what happened. I'm still confused. Now what? I don't want to go through this again! I'm so tired."

Jeff Markowitz told a reporter, "This kid chose those guys over our son's life. If he was truly not guilty, he would have come forward immediately and told someone about the killing, instead of waiting a week to be identified and located by detectives. I guess if you don't pull the trigger, you can do whatever you want."

Christina Pressley only had a short comment outside the courtroom. "We're grieved for the Markowitzes. And we know Graham is innocent. That's about all I can say."

Michael Ganschow told reporters, "Even though Mr. Pressley was acquitted of the kidnapping charge, it's not a victory. It's sad we couldn't come to a resolution on the murder count. I have no idea what Mr. Zonen is going to do now."

What Mr. Zonen was going to do was mull things over for a while and then press forward. In the end there would be another trial for Graham Pressley in the murder of Nicholas Markowitz.

16

SECOND SHOT

As soon as Ron Zonen let Judge Gordon know that the prosecution would seek another trial of Graham Pressley, Michael Ganschow put forth arguments as to why a second trial should not take place. Ganschow said, in part, "In his opening argument the prosecutor claimed that he would establish that Graham Pressley was an agent of Jesse James Hollywood. Specifically, he expected to prove that Graham Pressley bought drugs from Jesse James Hollywood, and that he participated in the conspiracy to kidnap and kill Nicholas Markowitz at the behest of Hollywood. The district attorney said that he would establish the connection between Mr. Pressley and Mr. Hollywood through evidence of subpoenaed phone and pager records. However, at the conclusion of evidence, the connection could not be made.

"Given the irrational thinking that motivated the original kidnapping of Nick as retaliation for his brother's drug debt, Pressley could only speculate as to what the killer had in mind and believed that he, too, was about to be killed for having witnessed the captivity of Markowitz. All of his actions were guided by this anxiety, because he had been told, 'Keep your mouth shut, if you know what's good for you! We know where you and your family live.' He did not come forward and inform law enforcement of what he knew for that reason."

In conclusion of his statements, Ganschow told Judge Gordon, "A retrial would be a severe hardship for the defendant and waste of resources. Nothing can ever repair the terrible hurt and pain the Markowitz family has endured as a result of the senseless murder of their son. But a retrial of this case is not the solution to obviate their pain."

Lending weight to Ganschow's arguments was a juror from the trial that had just concluded, who was a graduate student of the University of California, Santa Barbara. In a three-page letter to Judge Gordon, concerning the advisability of a new trial, the former juror was decidedly against it. He started off by saying that he did not take illegal drugs and believed that all people had to be held responsible for their actions. That being said, he explained his own theory of what might have happened on the night of August 8 and early-morning hours of August 9, 2000. This former juror believed Graham Pressley was never part of the plan to kill Nick Markowitz, and, in fact, had been surprised when Ryan Hoyt showed up with a gun at the Lemon Tree Inn and began cleaning ammunition in the bathroom. From that point on, the former juror said, 130-pound Graham Pressley did everything he could to not anger the much heavier, six-three Ryan Hoyt. Hoyt obviously had a weapon that could be used on anyone, including Pressley.

The juror expressed, *As the events of the night unfolded and it became obvious that Mr. Hoyt was planning to use the gun, I believe Mr. Pressley entered a state of denial and clung to the hope that everything would turn out fine.* In hindsight, that might have been irrational, but the juror said that nothing was rational about anything that had happened. On top of that, Pressley could not believe that his friend Jesse Rugge would be involved in a killing of Nick. Rugge and Pressley had been partying with Nick for the past two days, and if nothing had happened to him yet, then chances must have seemed slim to Pressley that something bad would happen now, at least according to this former juror.

The juror also said that eight out of the twelve jurors did not believe Pressley knew he was digging a grave for Nick Markowitz. In fact, the former juror said, they soon by-passed that issue and focused on Pressley's second trip up to Lizard's Mouth with Rugge, Nick and Hoyt. It even came up by a few jurors that Pressley might have been a prisoner of Rugge—and especially of Hoyt—on this second trip. As far as Pressley's actions, or lack of action at the parking lot of the Lemon Tree, when Hoyt left him in the car alone, they surmised this was not part of aiding and abetting, but rather passive in nature, which did not add to the plot to kill Nick Markowitz.

As to the prosecution's contentions that Pressley will-ingly showed Ryan Hoyt the trail again, on the second trip up to Lizard's Mouth, the juror said that many believed if Pressley had shown the trail part of the way, it was be-cause he had been threatened by Hoyt. The juror added, *I believe at that point Mr. Pressley's only reasonable course of action was to passively obey the orders of the man with the gun. Any other action would have resulted in two bodies buried at the site.*

Another juror, also from the first trial, wrote to Judge Gordon, and in part of her statement, she expressed, *I do not believe there is conclusive evidence of his guilt. I think a second jury will reach the same conclusion we did. Jus-tice has been served. I do not believe that in the two and a half days he knew Mr. Markowitz, Mr. Pressley really un-derstood what was happening.*

Not all jurors from the first trial, however, agreed with this assessment. One juror wrote the judge saying that he believed Graham Pressley was guilty of first-degree murder. This juror claimed, *The jury was completely dysfunctional. At best, only one or two hours of our deliberation involved any discussion of the evidence, and in fact, most jurors seemed pretty uninterested in that topic.* This juror added that some of the jurors would have liked to have looked at the evidence more, but they couldn't get a word in past the talkative jurors more interested in relating their life experiences. And then, this former juror really slammed his fellow jurors: *Since Pressley hasn't yet had a real jury, he has not yet had a real trial!*

Judge Gordon took all of these statements under advisement, and in the end he decided that there were grounds for a new trial. The second trial would not have any special circumstances, as far as kidnapping went. That was no longer an issue. This second trial would solely be on a count of first-degree murder against Graham Pressley.

So, in November 2002, both Ron Zonen and Michael Ganschow were back at it once again in front of a new jury. They basically had the same opening statements, with a few new wrinkles, but the issues of the timeline and accounts of the co-conspirators were basically the same. Graham Pressley also took the stand again and he reiterated the conversation he'd had with Jesse Rugge, on the afternoon of August 8. Pressley stated, "Jesse Rugge said that he'd been offered money from Jesse Hollywood to kill Nick. Then he said, 'But that's not going to happen.' He said that's never going to happen. After that, I think all of us were a bit more at ease."

As to why he didn't go to the police after speaking with Natasha Adams about the situation, Pressley testified, "I basically said we shouldn't get involved in this because we could potentially be in danger ourselves."

When it came to why he had at first lied to detectives, Pressley answered, "I doubted they would believe me if I told them the truth. They wouldn't have believed I was forced to dig the hole and that I thought I was going to die."

Ron Zonen, however, kept claiming that Pressley was in on the plot to kill Nick all along, and he'd had plenty of opportunities to just walk away from the others, including Ryan Hoyt. Even if Pressley hadn't told Nick of what was going to occur, he could have simply left the car at the Lemon Tree Inn when Hoyt went up to get Rugge and Nick, after the hole had already been dug. That he didn't, in Zonen's mind, proved that Pressley was on board with the scheme and knew that he was going to show Hoyt the way back up the trail to the hole that was dug near the Lizard's Mouth.

There was once again a parade of witnesses on the stand, many of them who had been in Hoyt's trial, Rugge's trial and Graham Pressley's first trial. During closing arguments Michael Ganschow told the jurors, "There is no evidence that Mr. Pressley intentionally aided Ryan Hoyt. What we really have here is a tale of two teenage boys, Nicholas Markowitz and Graham Pressley. One did not return, and was brutally murdered, and one survived."

In his closing arguments Zonen stated, "Digging the grave of Nicholas Markowitz wasn't the worst thing Graham Pressley did to aid the murder of Nicholas Markowitz. The most significant act was leading Nick Markowitz to his grave. Ryan Hoyt could not have found his way back to that grave site. The trail forks eleven times before reaching that spot. The reasonable explanation is that Pressley was escorting them up there to accomplish his crime. The unreasonable explanation is that he was an unwilling participant. He wasn't acting like someone who was scared. He behaved like a full-fledged member of the enterprise. He was not experiencing fear, except perhaps the fear of getting caught."

The jury of eight men and four women deliberated three days before coming to a verdict: a conviction of second-degree murder for Graham Pressley. Christina Pressley burst into tears and exclaimed, "Oh, my God! Why didn't he run away? Why didn't he leave?" It wasn't apparent if she was talking about Nick or Graham.

The jurors quickly walked out of the courthouse, and had nothing to say to reporters about their decision. Naturally, Michael Ganschow was upset by this ruling in the second trial for his client. He said of this set of jurors, "I have no idea where they thought the evidence was. Juries do anything they damn well please! We ran into a very cold group of fish. If Mr. Pressley is sent to prison, it will be the equivalent of a death sentence. He's a pretty boy and will be targeted by the other inmates."

Ron Zonen, on the other hand, was pleased with the decision and told reporters, "I never believed Mr. Pressley was forced to do what he did, and it doesn't appear that the jury believed it, either."

Along with Zonen, Jeff Markowitz was heartened by the decision of the second trial. "My only surprise was getting twelve jurors to agree to something this monumental," he said. "There were too many holes in Mr. Pressley's testimony and statements to county sheriff's detectives for jurors to acquit him of being a willing participant in the execution-style murder."

Susan Markowitz told reporters, "I wouldn't have wanted to be one of those jurors. It was a very tough job." She was less pleased, however, with Judge Gordon's ruling, that Graham Pressley would be out on bail until sentencing. Susan related, "Because Mr. Pressley was found guilty, he should be behind bars until he's sentenced. I thought letting him be out is wrong."

* * *

Before the sentencing of Graham Pressley, there was a full-court press by both Ganschow and Zonen to sway Judge Gordon in the matter. The defense wrote a document: "Upon a Showing of Good Cause a Person Who Is in Custody May Be Retained in Juvenile Hall After He Becomes 18 Years of Age." The whole point of the document was to keep Pressley in juvenile hall, and not to be sent to an adult prison after sentencing. Ganschow argued that Pressley could continue his education at juvenile hall, which he had been doing over the previous year via the Internet with Santa Barbara City College while in jail. Ganschow stated, "It is in his interest to develop as an educated member of society and to build credentials toward being a productive member of society."

To back up these contentions, Ganschow submitted letters written by various college professors, juvenile facility workers, friends and family members who knew Pressley. James Chesher, a philosophy professor at Santa Barbara City College, wrote Judge Gordon a letter stating that Pressley in his philosophy course read on issues of moral theories in Western thought. These included works by Plato, Aristotle, Hobbes and Kant.

In Pressley's case Chesher wrote: *I strongly urge that a decision be made in favor of enlightenment. The one thing that philosophers of every tradition have agreed upon is this: the single greatest cause of human suffering is ignorance, the only remedy is education. As Graham's future unfolds, let it be shaped by education, so that he can become the man that he is struggling to be.*

Ken Kuroda, an instructor at the La Posada School in the juvenile hall, wrote that he'd been working closely with Graham Pressley while Pressley was incarcerated there. Kuroda stated: *The other students here look up to Graham, and Graham has been a positive role model for them. It's not simply his hard work in academics, but more importantly he has modeled responsibility, kindness, cooperation, politeness, as well as positive proactive speech to them.* Kuroda said that taking Pressley out of the juvenile hall would result in a reversion of gang leaders becoming the role models for younger boys in the facility, who currently looked to Pressley for guidance.

Along with academic instructors, Ganschow had friends of Graham Pressley and church members who knew him send letters to Judge Gordon, speaking of his good qualities. Among these was a letter by Alissa Wuertz, a missionary to Madagascar, who wrote that she had once been caught up in the *fast life of drugs and other illegal activities.* Since that time she had turned her life around and gone on to serve others. She wrote, *Like myself, Graham Pressley has become a Christian and has experienced God's grace and eternal forgiveness in his life. God has given Graham a second chance; I humbly ask you to do the same.*

Fourteen-year-old Katie Alexander, who had transverse myelitis, which made her walk with a brace and crutches, wrote, *Graham is a big help to me. I think God gave Graham to me to help me not get sad and discouraged. Please do what you can to help him stay here and be my friend.*

Perhaps the strongest and most heartfelt letter came from Graham's mother, Christina Pressley. She said that she had sat in court during both trials, and *when the jury convicted Graham of a most heinous crime that he is not capable of committing, my very soul was pierced.* She added that Graham now lived for two people—himself, and to make things up for Nick Markowitz.

Christina said that she wished she could bring back the events of the day when Nick and Graham had been in her car as she drove them to the Lemon Tree Inn, and she added that she would live with that guilt for the rest of her life. She was perplexed by the fact that so many adults—like John Roberts, Jack Hollywood and Michelle

Lasher—had been granted immunity, when they had, in her estimation, helped Jesse James Hollywood escape punishment. She also believed that if the TEC-9 pistol had not jammed, Ryan Hoyt would have killed Jesse Rugge and her son, to get rid of all witnesses.

Christina ended by writing, *Please, I beg for my son's life. Please don't send Graham to prison. I know that he has tremendous potential to help others. Together, with his sister, we will be on a crusade to never let Nick's memory be forgotten.*

The letters in favor of leniency for Graham Pressley were all profound and poignant, but so were the letters in favor of sending Pressley to an adult prison. Jaime Brooke Ashmore, a friend of the Markowitz family, said that people were responsible for their own actions. She wrote, *One of the most amazing people I have ever known was taken out of my life and many others, for no reason. Please do not let this crime go unpunished. Graham Pressley dug and walked Nick Markowitz to his death bed. I'm sure Nick wished for mercy when being sentenced, but he didn't get it, and Mr. Pressley doesn't deserve it.*

Caren Auchman, who was about the same age as Pressley, wrote that Graham might have just been following orders: *But the Nazi soldiers in the Nuremberg trials said they killed millions of Jewish people because they were following orders. They were still guilty of murders because they did not stop it. Is this not the same case with Mr. Pressley?*

As Christina Pressley's letter, asking for leniency, had been one of the most powerful to Judge Gordon, the letters of Jeff and Susan Markowitz to the judge asking for a stern sentence were just as powerful. Jeff started his letter by saying that three thousand years in the past, Moses had given a farewell speech to the Jewish people by stating that as they entered the Promised Land, justice had to be followed with fair trials and witnesses speaking out for the accused and witnesses for the victim. In fact, Nick had read this very passage in Deuteronomy during his Bar Mitzvah.

Jeff wrote that they were all faced with a similar situation at the present time in Graham Pressley's trial and sentencing. The jurors knew that Pressley had not pulled the trigger that ended Nick's life, but without his participation this event would have been much harder to accomplish. In the last few hours of his life, Jeff wrote, Nick had been surrounded by pretty girls, a party atmosphere at the Lemon Tree Inn, where Pressley told him that everything would be okay. Pressley and Nick even went swimming together at the motel pool, but not once did Pressley tell Nick that Jesse James Hollywood had already offered money to Jesse Rugge to kill him. Later, when Ryan Hoyt showed up, Pressley saw a gun in a gym bag, and Hoyt cleaning a clip of ammunition, and still he did not warn Nick of impending danger.

Once Pressley had taken Hoyt up to Lizard's Mouth, Jeff said, Pressley did not show him a spot near the rock where it would have been hard to dig a hole. Instead, he took him to a place where the ground was soft enough to dig a grave. When they got back to the Lemon Tree, Hoyt didn't tell Pressley to come up to the room, but instead went up there himself and left the TEC-9 in the trunk of the car with Pressley. Pressley did not run away or tell anyone what was happening, he merely stayed in the car. Jeff said that even if someone was scared or stupid, no one would have stayed in that car unless they were involved.

Jeff even quoted from a transcript of Pressley's interview with detectives, when Graham spoke with his mother:

Christina: So you dug it (the grave) and went back to the car, and when you got to the car they took the boy?

Graham: There were two trips up there. One

                    trip to dig, and then we went back down
                    and got the kid.

Christina: That makes it worse.

Graham: I was held at gunpoint.

Christina: If you were held at gunpoint the whole
                    time, why did they take you up there
                    and make you do that, and then just let
                    you go the next morning?

In fact, Jeff wrote, soon after the murder, Jesse Rugge
invited Pressley to a barbecue and Pressley willingly went
along. In conclusion Jeff Markowitz wrote, *I have thought
about what Ryan Hoyt did, and how menacing he must
have looked and how heartless he was. But I ask you now,
what is worse, a heartless monster or a meek-looking de-
ceitful person that lures you to imminent danger and ultimately to your death? Which is more premeditated?*

Susan Markowitz's letter to Judge Gordon was absolutely heart-wrenching. She began by saying, *I am the
lost, broken and suicidal mother of kidnapped and executed Nicholas Samuel Markowitz. I am still unsure of how
I am going to get through tomorrow without Nick, my only
child. I was a housewife, blessed to be a stay-at-home
mother. Nick, being my only child, makes me wonder if I
am still a Mom. Losing two pregnancies after Nick made
him that much more special. Nick was my life. I ache for
him every minute of every day. The thought of him not
coming home, 860 days later, still panics me.*

Susan told of how Nick's death had been so senseless
and had utterly destroyed her. She used to be an outgo-
ing person who entertained, but now she didn't answer the
phone or the doorbell. Friends and family members didn't
know what to say to her, so they avoided her, and even the
ones who tried to help, she kept at arm's length. She no
longer went to Bar Mitzvahs, birthdays and weddings, because she knew how much they would make her cry and

spoil the occasion for others. She said she was sentenced to her own prison, without hope of a pardon or parole.

She spoke of Nick's best friend, who cried on each of his birthdays because of the loss of Nick. Nick had planned to make a difference in the world, and he loved drama and computers. He had a talent in drawing; he was funny and made her constantly laugh. Susan wrote that everyone made choices, every minute of every day, and Graham Pressley had chosen to participate in the kidnapping and murder of Nick. She said she knew beyond a doubt that if Darla Gacek and the others had not found Nick's body, Graham Pressley would never have come forward to confess about himself or the others. Susan ended by writing, *I beg you to give Graham Pressley the leniency he gave Nick, which is none.*

In the end Judge Gordon was as lenient as Graham Pressley could have hoped for. He sentenced Pressley to five years at a California Youth Authority facility.

17

HOLLYWOOD MEETS HOLLYWOOD

On the two-year anniversary of the date on which Nick Markowitz had been kidnapped in West Hills, a reporter for the *Santa Barbara News-Press* spoke with various people connected to the events of August 2000. Jeff Markowitz told him that he and Nick used to go to the movies almost every weekend when Nick was a boy. It took Jeff two years to go back into a movie theater by himself. He related to the reporter, "Sitting in the theater, I cried uncontrollably, knowing Nick would never see this or any other movie again. Of course, the list of things he will never do is endless."

The situation was no better for Susan Markowitz. Often she sat by a window, staring outside, wishing she could catch sight of Nick returning home one more time. She told the reporter, "I'm dead. I'm an empty shell. I view life as if through a lens. It's like having tunnel vision."

Susan slept in Nick's bed several times a week, and she

had tried committing suicide twice by that point. She tried therapy, but nothing seemed to work. To the efficacy of therapy, she stated, "I've decided no one can help me. Nick was my only child, and I lost him in the most barbaric way."

Before Nick's murder she used to take pride in decorating the house, hand-painting porcelain dolls and gardening. Now all these activities had ceased and she found it hard to even drag herself out of bed. Susan told the reporter, no matter what occurred in the future, she and Jeff would never give up until Jesse James Hollywood was caught. She spoke of Jesse Hollywood as a ball and chain around both of their ankles.

That Jesse James Hollywood would ever be caught seemed to be more and more of a remote possibility as time passed. In fact, by 2003, the clues leading to possible sightings of Hollywood in Canada had grown cold. Even though he'd been featured a half-dozen times on *America's Most Wanted* and on *Unsolved Mysteries* and *Dateline,* no new important clues of his whereabouts had surfaced.

Speaking about how criminals of Jesse's caliber, and those who might help him, managed to elude law enforcement, Chief Deputy Bruce Cornell said, "They know we monitor their pager and cell phone activity, that we do wiretaps and monitor money transactions. The difference between Jesse James Hollywood and the average fugitive is that he has had mentoring about law enforcement capabilities."

The case had thirty detectives working on it in 2000; by 2003, there were only two. They did keep in touch with the FBI, and looked at all new leads, but as Lieutenant Jeff Klapakis said, "Obviously, we haven't gotten a good one yet."

Klapakis still held out hope for Jesse James Hollywood's capture, however. He said that Hollywood was not sophisticated, and sooner or later he would make a mistake. One big factor that had helped Jesse Hollywood was that he'd had access to quite a bit of money, and there were still contentions by law enforcement that his father was still clandestinely helping him with money. Even so, Klapakis predicted that "he's going to make a mistake at some point."

The FBI in the case was innovative in its approach. They held an online chat on the Internet about Jesse Hollywood, asking for tips from anyone who might have seen him recently. Tips came in from as far away as Finland. The chats were a tool developed by an FBI unit called the Fugitive Publicity Unit. One participating Internet user asked why the FBI had chosen Jesse James Hollywood for that particular chat. The response was Because of the violent nature and gruesome way the victim was killed in the crime. The FBI feels the public may be able to assist in his apprehension.

A participant from Boston asked, What is the state Jesse James Hollywood is most likely hiding in?

The FBI responded that he'd been sighted in a number of states, including Colorado, and might be as far north as Canada.

A person from Woodland Hills, California, asked, Why is the FBI having such a difficult time finding a 21-year-old kid?

The response was that with his money and possibly changed appearance, Jesse James Hollywood was able to blend in wherever he'd gone.

A chat respondent from North Carolina asked, It would seem as if someone this violent and this young would get tired of a constant life on the run. Do you have experiences where people such as Jesse turn themselves in because so much effort is being made to capture them?

The answer was That happened on numerous occasions and we encourage Hollywood to turn himself in, as he is postponing the inevitable.

The inevitability of his capture, however, seemed as elusive as ever by 2003, and chats or not, Jesse James Hollywood did not turn himself in to authorities.

* * *

There had been plenty of publicity on the various cases surrounding the murder of Nick Markowitz, and the story was so compelling that it seemed almost a natural for the film industry of Hollywood, California, to make a movie about the events. Nick Cassavetes, son of famed director John Cassavetes, started thinking of making a feature-length movie of the individuals involved, and he turned to his longtime friend Michael Mehas, attorney and aspiring screenwriter, to obtain information about the cases. With a great deal of energy and gusto, Mehas waded into the thousands upon thousands of pages of transcripts, files and documents of the events.

Mehas and Cassavetes had gone to school together and even played on the same basketball team that had made it to the national championships. In the early 1980s, Mehas tried landing roles in film projects with little success, though he did manage to become an extra in the infamous Michael Jackson Pepsi commercial, where Jackson's hair caught on fire. During his high-school years, Mehas became very close to John Cassavetes and thought of a career in the film industry. Cassavetes, however, gave him advice that he should "write from what you've lived first. Go out and get experience in life."

Mehas became a defense lawyer in the late 1980s, but he still had a yen to one day become a screenwriter. When the Jesse James Hollywood case came along, it appeared that his big chance had finally arrived.

Throwing himself into the project, Mehas looked at grand jury transcripts, police reports and interviewed people who were close to the case, including Ben Marko-witz. Through Ben, Mehas began to have a real sense of how things had spiraled out of control with Jesse James Hollywood. Originally, Jesse Hollywood thought it would be a good idea to have someone as tough as Ben on his side in the world of drug dealing in the San Fernando

Valley. Ben, however, was a volatile two-edged sword, often barely able to control his temper. As Jack Hollywood had told the grand jury, "My son didn't want to tell me much about what was going on with him and that kid (Ben)." And Michelle Lasher called Ben "a crazy psychopath."

Even though Ben did live with Jesse Hollywood for a while—partying, lifting weights and selling dope—things would not remain on a friendly basis. When Ben took that trip to San Diego, on Hollywood's behest, and failed to collect all of the $2,000, he set in motion the tragedy that followed.

As the movie project got off the ground, both Mehas and Cassavetes were sure they had a winner on their hands. By July 2003, the *Santa Barbara News-Press* was reporting that Tobey Maguire and Leonardo DiCaprio would become producers and help with financing, while Kevin Connolly would direct. Nick Cassavetes, who was helping to write the screenplay, met with Susan Markowitz and talked with her about the film project. She told a reporter at the time, "I am very, very thankful and gratified that the movie will be done. I really think it will help with the hunt for Mr. Hollywood."

Nick Cassavetes said, "I've been thinking about writing this story for a long time." In fact, Cassavetes had a teenage daughter who had attended El Camino Real High School, where both Nick Markowitz and Jesse James Hollywood had once gone to school. Cassavetes told a reporter, "It's surprising when a story like this happens so close to you. It was in my backyard."

Even Ron Zonen was excited about the project, and said, "I think it's a wonderful idea if this movie reaches a lot of people and can give us some leads on where to find Jesse James Hollywood. If it results in somebody recognizing him, it could be a great thing."

* * *

Mike Mehas noted later that he first spoke with Ron Zonen in April 2003, and over the next several months, "Ron Zonen basically gave me access to all his files dealing with Jesse James Hollywood's codefendants. In July 2003, I spoke with Jack Hollywood for the first of many times. To my recollection, he never said anything inconsistent with statements attributed to him in reports I had read. In April 2004, I spoke with Detective Mike West, and in November with Ben Markowitz and Michelle Lasher."

By 2004, Nick Cassavetes became director of the movie project, instead of Connolly, and the casting of the film was well under way, with Emile Hirsch as a fictionalized Jesse James Hollywood and singer Justin Timberlake as a fictionalized Jesse Rugge. Sharon Stone would play a character based on Susan Markowitz and Bruce Willis, a character based on Jack Hollywood. Filming began in October 2004 at locations around Los Angeles and Las Vegas. By this point Sidney Kimmel Entertainment of Beverly Hills was producing the film, along with A-Mark Entertainment.

Yet, all was not peaches and cream, by 2004, on a movie that was to be entitled *Alpha Dog*. Jeff and Susan Markowitz learned that the film might not even mention Jesse James Hollywood's name. A publicist told reporters that this could happen because "the film is loosely based on his life, but isn't a true biography." In fact, the movie would eventually change Jesse Hollywood's name to Johnny Truelove, and all the other individuals tied to the abduction and murder would have their names changed as well in the film.

Susan told a reporter for the *Santa Barbara News-Press,* "How can they do a movie about someone on the Most Wanted list and not mention his name?" Jeff added, "That doesn't do us any good at all! We want to put his face out there. We want the reward put out there. Otherwise, what's the point? What are we getting out of it?"

The Markowitzes' main concern was that the film would glorify Jesse James Hollywood and his lifestyle. Jeff said, "It's painful to know they're doing a movie about this Hollywood guy, and maybe are going to turn him into some kind of folk hero."

Around this same time Nick Cassavetes added something that would be very prophetic. He said, "Should Mr. Hollywood be captured before the film hits the big screen, then I'll have another chapter to write." Unknown to Cassavetes at the time, everyone—including the film industry, law enforcement and the judiciary—would be writing many more chapters in the Jesse James Hollywood saga.

Mehas was busy amassing thousands upon thousands of pages of documents on the various aspects of the case, including material pertaining to Hoyt, Rugge, Skidmore, Pressley and all the others. He immersed himself in Jesse Hollywood's world and told a *Ventura County Reporter* journalist his take on Hollywood. "Jesse is a sharp, smart-ass, tough little alpha dog. He's quick-witted, he's sharp, he's got a funny sense of humor."

As the film project progressed, New Line Cinema had its own take on what the film was going to be all about. In their press release they wrote: *Inspired by actual events,* Alpha Dog *revolves around a mid-level drug dealer from the San Gabriel Valley whose thirst for power led him to become at 19, the youngest man ever to appear on the FBI's Most Wanted list. Emile Hirsch stars as a teenage suburban drug dealer Johnny Truelove, an ambitious young man whose lifestyle is a Mecca for guns, sex and drugs.* The release went on to say that when a drug deal went bad with a client, Truelove and his buddies kidnap the client's younger brother. It wasn't a typical kidnapping—the crew begins to like the boy and everyone becomes caught up in *the dangerous and violent world they once idealized.*

And so the film project carried on through 2004 and early 2005. Unbeknownst to Nick Cassavetes, events had come to a point where he was going to be forced to write that new chapter he'd once talked about.

18

THE MAN FROM BRAZIL

"Michael Costa Giroux" was living quietly in Saquarema, Brazil, on its Atlantic coast, along with his girlfriend, Marcia. Not a native Brazilian, Giroux spoke English and made money by teaching that language, and taking care of people's dogs. He was handsome, tanned and had a certain confident air about him. The city was a lovely beachside resort that catered to many people from Rio de Janeiro who came to the coast for relaxation and to escape city life.

Giroux and his seven months pregnant girlfriend lived in a yellow house with a high fence around it, and they mostly kept to themselves. Neighbor Walma Lindberg da Silva said that Giroux "always had his head down, and wore caps, even inside his house. I told my husband I thought there was something wrong with him." Giroux could often be seen jogging along the beach with his two pet pit bulls. He never seemed to work very much, rather he jogged around with his pit bull dogs, and could be seen lifting weights and generally taking it easy.

Even though Giroux tried keeping a low profile, he

seemed to have an explosive temper, and he would sometimes argue with bar owners over his bar tab. He just couldn't seem to let even insignificant things go, if he felt slighted or taken advantage of. Giroux went from bar to bar, and at a bar near his house, he seemed to be the most talkative and expansive. One patron later said, "We kidded him. Are you Mike, like in Mike Tyson?"

Giroux responded, "No, Mike Tyson uses his fists to defeat his opponents. I use a baseball bat to defeat mine."

Mike seemed to like hanging out in bars a lot. In fact, Mike had met his girlfriend, Marcia Reis, at a singles bar in Rio de Janeiro. She was more than ten years older, but he seemed to be attracted to her from the start. She recalled, "When I met him, I thought he was very young. I thought he was a little lost. He had a lot to drink." When she asked him why he had come to Brazil, he answered that he'd come there to study. Mike had apparently come to Brazil from Canada.

March 8, 2005, was just like any other day in Saquarema—soft breezes blew off the Atlantic, and the surf boomed on the shoreline. Giroux and his girlfriend, Marcia, were sitting at an outdoor table at a shopping mall in the city, enjoying a quiet morning. A woman walked toward them, smiling, and called out Giroux's name. As he stood to greet her, the woman unexpectedly told him that she was an undercover policewoman.

Suddenly, without any warning, men in sunglasses and suits walked up and, without any preamble, told Giroux that he was under arrest. As they led him away in handcuffs, the woman shouted, "My son! My son! I have a son with him!" But, in fact, there was no Michael Costa Giroux—that was only an alias for Jesse James Hollywood, who had been hiding out in Saquarema for years.

Marcia Reis later told *Dateline NBC,* "With me, he was wonderful. He was very sweet and tender. He was very caring, attentive. Everything I wanted, he would get. He was always with me, kissing my feet, my hands."

At the moment, however, there was no hand kissing. Jesse James Hollywood was escorted in a police vehicle to Rio de Janeiro, where it was obvious he only had a limited speaking ability of Portuguese. Even though he still tried to claim that he was Michael Giroux, the detectives confirmed that his identification card was a fake. After about two hours of interrogation, he finally admitted that he was, indeed, Jesse James Hollywood.

Just how the authorities knew that Jesse Hollywood was there was its own lengthy and byzantine tale. The FBI had been monitoring phone calls from Jesse's parents for years, and by the middle of 2002, they were fairly sure that Jesse was in Brazil, due to a fluky incident that had occurred concerning one of Jesse's relatives who had just happened to pick Brazil as a vacation spot, not knowing that Jesse was hiding out there. The FBI sent photos and video images of Jesse to Brazilian authorities, and these authorities started keeping an eye out for him. As luck would have it, they did discover Jesse James Hollywood in Brazil.

As time went on, according to law enforcement reports, there were more phone calls from Hollywood's family to Jesse, which were monitored. It was also learned that Jack Hollywood was sending his son $1,200 a month. That was an ironic amount to say the least, since it had been a $1,200 debt by Ryan Hoyt that had turned him into a killer. A sting operation was set up with Brazilian authorities wherein Jesse's cousin was supposed to meet him at an outdoor mall in Saquarema. Marcia Reis said later that Jesse got a phone call from a female cousin he hadn't seen in years, and she would be visiting Brazil and "Mike" decided to meet her at the small seaside café. In fact, there would be no meeting of cousins, only a team of law enforcement ready to nab him.

Brazilian agent Kelly Bernardo, the woman decoy, later

told *Dateline NBC,* "At first, when I approached him, he got up as if he knew me. He was surprised as I approached him, and as authorities told him he was under arrest. He kept saying he was someone else. Michael Giroux."

Jesse Hollywood might have thought he was safe in Brazil, because they had no extradition treaty with the United States, but he was not quite as clever as he thought. The thing that tripped him up was that he was in Brazil using false identification, and since he was in the country illegally, that was grounds for extradition. He'd even supposedly been told (source not revealed) to follow in the footsteps of train robber Ronnie Biggs and have a child by a Brazilian woman. That way he couldn't be deported, if caught. At least that's what Jesse Hollywood thought. But even this ploy did not work. Deported to the United States, Jesse Hollywood was immediately arrested at the Los Angeles International Airport on the warrant that had been written in August 2000.

On the same day that Jesse Hollywood was arrested, his father was also arrested on suspicion of possessing an illegal substance. Not only was Jack Hollywood in trouble in Los Angeles County, but in Arizona as well, and that incident was going to be a lot more troublesome for Jack in the days to come than the California problem.

Within a very short time period, Jesse Hollywood had obtained the services of defense lawyer James Blatt. The same James Blatt who had been Jack Hollywood's lawyer when Jack spoke to the grand jury in 2000. In Jesse Hollywood's arraignment at Santa Barbara Superior Court—where Hoyt, Rugge, Skidmore and Pressley had been before him at their arraignments—Jesse Hollywood wore an orange jail jumpsuit. Two of the people in court to see him were Jeff and Susan Markowitz. Susan told reporters, "I would like to have gotten a closer look at him. You would hope by looking at our faces, there would be some pain in his heart and some stirring of emotions, but I doubt it."

James Blatt also made a short statement to reporters: "Like any other criminal defendant facing the possibility of a death penalty, he's very concerned. I'm not saying anything at this time in reference to the case, except that perceptions could be misleading. It's clear that Mr. Hollywood was not the shooter. He was not present at the scene. So the key determination is whether he gave the instructions for this unfortunate murder."

Jesse James Hollywood for his part pled "not guilty" at his arraignment. He maintained his innocence in the whole affair and put out the perception that Ryan Hoyt was a loose cannon who had instigated the murder on his own behalf in a misguided attempt to please Hollywood and gain status.

Just where Jesse had been living for years was soon portrayed in a *Santa Barbara News-Press* article by Hildy Medina. She noted that Saquarema was a city of fifty thousand people on the coast, about fifty miles from Rio de Janeiro—blessed with exotic beaches, and popular with surfers who held major surfing competitions there each year. A prime getaway spot for Rio de Janeiro citizens, tour guide Rafael Torres Lopes described it as "a very beautiful and wild locale. You can compare it to the beaches in Sydney, Australia. It's very European and modern. It's a perfect getaway from the hassles of city living."

Many Rio residents had second homes in Saquarema, and real estate was very affordable. A modern three-bedroom home near the beach with a swimming pool could be had for $400 to $500 a month. Since Jack Hollywood was allegedly sending Jesse $1,200 a month, he could have lived very well off that amount. Jesse was teaching English in Saquarema, and he had a usable amount of Portuguese. Torres said that with the amount of money Jesse had, "he could have lived like a millionaire in Saquarema."

Jack Hollywood's own problems mushroomed by the spring of 2005. LAPD officers, state drug enforcement agents and a fugitive warrant team barged their way into his Sherman Oaks residence and arrested him that spring, and he was booked into the Los Angeles County Jail for intent to manufacture methamphetamine. However, charges weren't strong enough at that time, so prosecutors did not charge him.

There were other things in the works against him, however, and Jack was facing an indictment from Arizona that alleged he was into drug smuggling. During the grand jury hearing of 2000, Ron Zonen had called Jack Hollywood a "mobster" and "big-time San Fernando Valley drug dealer." According to newspaper accounts the indictment in Arizona concerned the allegation that Jack Hollywood had tried shipping several pounds of marijuana to that state via FedEx. Richard Wintory, an assistant Pima County attorney, said, "It's not a huge amount of pot, but it's enough to trigger mandatory prison time." All of this came about because an Arizona narcotics enforcement task force, nicknamed the "Box Squad," found two FedEx boxes stuffed with marijuana allegedly sent by Jack Hollywood to someone in that state. When Jack was arrested, agents discovered that he had packing slips connected to those two boxes.

By 2005, Jack Hollywood said that he was an automobile wholesaler, as well as someone who ran a baseball card shop and restaurant. He had recently been divorced from Laurie, and said that he presently had no income. Jack was not in custody at Jesse's arraignment, so he went to court with his ex-wife, Laurie. Across the aisle Jeff and Susan Markowitz sat with Nick's half sister, Leah. As they waited for Jesse Hollywood to appear and enter a plea,

Jeff Markowitz leaned across the aisle and whispered to Jack, "I thought you were in jail!" Jack Hollywood did not respond.

An interesting article about Jack Hollywood also came out in the *Santa Barbara News-Press* by journalist Scott Hadley, who had been reporting on all the main characters of the Jesse James Hollywood saga for years. Hadley spoke of Jack playing a "cat and mouse" game with detectives ever since August 2000. According to Hadley, law enforcement and drug agents had tailed Jack Hollywood, monitored his e-mails and tapped his phones. But Jack would go out one door of a building, circle around and go another way before getting in his car. At other times he would go into a covered parking garage, slip into another vehicle than the one he had driven into the garage, then drive away undetected.

Jack was tracked to an overlook of the San Fernando Valley on one occasion, but he had a dozen prepaid digital phones in his car, making calls difficult to track. According to a law enforcement source, Jack would make calls to arrange shipments of marijuana from British Columbia to airports around the Los Angeles region.

When Hadley spoke with Jack Hollywood about Jesse, Jack told him, "He's generous and a good person. He did not kill that kid."

Defense lawyer James Blatt was Jesse Hollywood's one big hope to evade Ryan Hoyt's fate in a first-degree murder trial—in other words, the death penalty. Blatt had received his B.A. degree from UCLA in 1970, and a Juris Doctor degree from Loyola University in 1973. He was named "Lawyer of the Year for Southern California," and his Web site was named *Raising the Standard in Criminal Defense.*

If the previous trials had gone fairly smoothly for the prosecution, that would not be the case with anything concerning the trial of Jesse James Hollywood. For one thing, the FBI and the Santa Barbara Regional Narcotics Enforcement Team (SBRNET) were refusing to give up key documents to the prosecution about individuals who were involved in the surveillance of and arrest of Jesse Hollywood in Brazil. The FBI and SBRNET claimed that to do so would endanger their sources.

Ron Zonen, on the other hand, said that it was vital to have this information before a jury to show how and why Jesse had been collared in Brazil, and how he had been supported there illegally by his father, Jack. Zonen noted that when Jesse was arrested in Brazil, he'd answered to a different name, had Brazilian identification in that name, along with a photo, and spoke Portuguese. Zonen stated, "The people intend to introduce evidence of defendant Hollywood's flight to Brazil and the extraordinary efforts made by him to reinvent himself as a Brazilian, including his acquisition of a new identity and a facility in a new language."

Zonen said that SBRNET could redact portions of documents that concerned confidential sources. Zonen added that SBRNET detective Mark Valencia had taken photos of the identification card that Jesse had while in Brazil, and Zonen was worried that Brazilian authorities may have destroyed the original identifications since the arrest. Zonen once again said that the source who had helped supply information on Jesse Hollywood would not be revealed, but "the People seek to introduce into evidence the photos of the identification documents. Therefore, the circumstances of his arrest will be relevant to the issue of the admissibility of the photographs."

One thing hurting Ron Zonen's cause by this point, however, was the fact that Mike Mehas and Nick Cassavetes, in their quest to gather information about the upcoming film *Alpha Dog,* received some documents from Ron Zonen that should have remained sealed, and not been turned over to individuals who were not in law enforcement. Perhaps already knowing of this aspect, Detective Mark Valencia, who was a member of SBRNET, was totally against any information from his team being handed over to Ron Zonen.

Detective Valencia did note that in May 2004, he had been assigned to assist in the Jesse Hollywood investigation, particularly on his whereabouts at the time. Valencia related to a judge that "as a result of my investigation, information was obtained which relates to ongoing investigations into criminal conduct which are continuing to be pursued by various law enforcement agencies. There are outstanding suspects in those cases, and to disclose any information would allow those cases to be compromised, and suspects may seek to evade apprehension."

Detective Valencia added that confidential witnesses could be placed in danger if the information that Zonen requested was granted. One informant had already been the subject of a death threat. Detective Valencia said that all the information concerning Jesse James Hollywood in the documents was "intertwined" with other cases, and those familiar with those cases could piece together information and deduce "identities of informants and suspects."

The county counsel for SBRNET got involved in this matter and wrote up a document requesting that the judge not grant Zonen's request. This document stated: *The identity of informants are privileged from disclosure and neither party is entitled to records of an un-related on-going investigation.* It also stated, *The prosecution had made an inadequate showing for the requested information.*

While all this played out, there were problems with the film *Alpha Dog,* and those problems were coming back to haunt DDA Ron Zonen. *Alpha Dog* was heading for the Sundance Film Festival in Utah, and in its progress the *New York Times* noted that *Mr. Cassavetes tossed several days and about $500,000 worth of film, and added some* *more, to tailor his thinly veiled story—about a tough-talking marijuana dealer named Johnny Truelove, played by Emile Hirsch—to the newly changing facts.* A big problem had been that Jesse James Hollywood was no longer in hiding, he was in jail awaiting trial and had a defense lawyer. The ending of the film *Alpha Dog* had to be revised.

Because of all the publicity surrounding the making of *Alpha Dog,* and DDA Zonen's cooperation with the filmmakers, there now began a war of words between James Blatt and Ron Zonen, with profound legal implications on the case concerning Jesse James Hollywood. Blatt declared before Judge Brian Hill, who was handling Jesse Hollywood's case, that an investigation was in progress against his client, and that it was necessary for him to have discovery rights of all that material. Blatt got to the heart of the matter by saying that he'd recently had a telephone conversation with Nick Cassavetes, on June 15, 2005, and Cassavetes told him that he was a screenwriter and director of the movie and that filming had been completed and postproduction was done as well. Cassavetes hoped for the movie to be released in theaters by December 2005 or January 2006.

Cassavetes then told Blatt that he'd talked with Jesse Rugge, William Skidmore and Graham Pressley, and had received letters from Ryan Hoyt. Cassavetes had also met with numerous witnesses in the case and spoken with them. Cassavetes said that back in April 2003 he'd met with Ron Zonen and asked him for material concerning the case. Zonen and certain law enforcement officers had even gone with Cassavetes up to Lizard's Mouth to view the killing and burial site of Nick Markowitz. Cassavetes then gave Blatt seventeen audiotapes that had been turned over by Zonen to coscreenwriter Michael Mehas.

Wanting to know exactly what Mehas's role was in all of this, Blatt met with him, and Mehas said that he'd talked in person to Ron Zonen in April 2003. At that meeting Zonen handed over trial transcripts, all of which were public record. From June 2003 through February 2005, a month before Jesse James Hollywood's arrest, Mehas had met with Zonen on a regular basis.

Blatt told Judge Hill, "The researcher (Mehas) advised me that during the time referenced, the researcher obtained access to the entire Santa Barbara Deputy District Attorney's Office file in this prosecution, and further stated he had been informed by Mr. Zonen that this access was made with Santa Barbara County district attorney Tom Sneddon's knowledge. The researcher (Mehas) described his access, with permission, to the Santa Barbara District Attorney's Office file room, where all the case materials were located. The researcher stated he was provided access to computer disks, photographs, audio recordings, video recordings, still photographs, law enforcement reports, psychological evaluations, probation reports and criminal history reports. The researcher stated these items of evidence were stored in boxes, which he was permitted to remove without supervision from the Santa Barbara District Attorney's Office."

According to Blatt, it wasn't until February 2005 that Ron Zonen requested that Mehas return all the material. Among the material Mehas had were law enforcement investigative reports, photos of the removal of Nick Markowitz's body and videos of "strip searches" of Hoyt, Rugge and Skidmore. This kind of material was not usually granted to journalists. Mehas also had a copy of Ron Zonen's trial notebook, which was another item not usually granted to the view of journalists. Blatt stated, "The researcher advised me that in addition to his access to prosecution files, there occurred numerous discussions between the researcher and Mr. Zonen regarding witness and codefendant character, motivation and demeanor."

Blatt declared that he was going to serve Nick Cassavetes and Michael Mehas with subpoenas for them to appear in a court hearing to tell of these serious matters. Blatt also let it be known that he wanted Ron Zonen removed from the case for what he deemed as overstepping the bounds of what a DDA could do.

Ron Zonen argued back to Judge Hill that he had initially been approached by Nick Cassavetes, who was making a film based on the Jesse James Hollywood case, and that Cassavetes wanted material that would help in making the film. Zonen said he met in person with Cassavetes three times and spoke with him on the phone a half-dozen times. Zonen also stated that Detective Mike West took Cassavetes and Mehas up to Lizard's Mouth, but according to Zonen, he did not do a crime reenactment, as Blatt claimed they had done. Then Zonen said, "Unlike the defendant's father, Jack Hollywood, who consulted on the same film for money, I did not request, accept or receive any compensation for my consultation. I asked only that Jesse Hollywood's picture be shown at the conclusion of the film, along with a phone number to call with information as to his whereabouts. I asked that the audience be told that Hollywood remained a fugitive and that there was a reward for his arrest."

The news media picked up on this new angle in the Jesse James Hollywood story, and the *Santa Barbara News-Press* reported James Blatt as saying: *"We're very concerned about what happened. We don't feel it is appropriate for the District Attorney's Office to be involved in creating a major motion picture on a pending capital murder case. I'm not aware of this ever happening before."*

Prior to a hearing on these matters, Jack Hollywood pled guilty on drug charges in Tucson, Arizona. Pima County Superior Court judge Howard Hantman asked Jack Hollywood if he understood what he was admitting to, and he said that he did. The judge then asked him to describe what it was that he had done. Jack said he'd

driven to Tucson in July 2003 to meet a man, whose name
he didn't know; the man took his car and later returned
with marijuana in the car. Jack paid the man for the marijuana and planned to sell and distribute it later. Judge
Hantman agreed to delay the start of Jack's prison term
so that he could spend Thanksgiving with his family and
attend a hearing in Jesse James Hollywood's case in
Santa Barbara.

Looking tired and dejected, Jack Hollywood told reporters outside the courtroom in Tucson, "I guess I'm
going to be here for a while." Looking further into the
charges against Jack, a reporter discovered that the indictment stated that Jack Hollywood had tried to smuggle
fifty pounds of marijuana and had been stopped by the
California Highway Patrol (CHP) right after he crossed
the Arizona/California state line. The CHP officers had responded to a request by California narcotics officers who
had placed a tracking device on Jack Hollywood's car.

Before the upcoming hearings about the film *Alpha
Dog,* Nick Cassavetes and Mike Mehas quit their collaboration with James Blatt. Mehas related later that he didn't
want Ron Zonen to get into trouble because of the research
he had been doing. Cassavetes told a reporter, "Mr. Mehas
indicated to me he is reluctant to continue to cooperate
with Jesse James Hollywood's attorney, James Blatt, due
to his fear that such cooperation may lead to criminal
charges filed against Mr. Zonen." This noncooperation
with James Blatt, however, was about to cause its own
set of problems for the filmmakers and Ron Zonen.

By this point Zonen conceded that he may have inadvertently shared information that he shouldn't have, including rap sheets, witnesses' phone numbers and
probation reports. Zonen said he didn't know that material
was in the boxes that contained files and documents that
were not okay for Mehas and Cassavetes to review.

Zonen admitted to possibly an error in judgment, but nothing criminal to the extent that he should be recused from the case.

Whether they liked it or not, however, both Cassavetes and Mehas were now a part of the legal process in a case that they were depicting on film. Both had to cite their involvement with Ron Zonen, and Cassavetes made a lengthy declaration before the court. He stated how he, Michael Mehas and Kevin Connolly, the film's original director, had met with Zonen to discuss making a movie about the events surrounding Nick Markowitz's death. Cassavetes said he asked Zonen for information about the homicide, and that Zonen would provide them with transcripts from the trials and other material they could use in researching the case for the film.

Once the project got under way, Zonen took Mehas, Kevin Connolly, Heather Wahlquist, Chuck Pacheco and Nick Cassavetes up to the Lizard's Mouth area and showed them the location of where the events had taken place. Cassavetes and the others started to videotape the area, but halfway through the process, the camera's batteries no longer worked. Cassavetes explained that Zonen described the killing while at Lizard's Mouth, but it was not a reenactment. Cassavetes talked to Zonen there, while Mehas spoke with Detective West. As far as the district attorney's files went, Cassavetes said that Mehas was excited about the amount and quality of the materials they had received.

Cassavetes related that he did remember seeing photos of Nick Markowitz's body and some people who had no clothes on, and these may have been "strip search photos" of Hoyt, Skidmore and Rugge. Zonen had discussed with Cassavetes about Ryan Hoyt's family life. Cassavetes asked Zonen about his feelings for the case in general, and according to Cassavetes, Zonen told him, "These were a bunch of stoned, dumb guys."

Nick Cassavetes did say that he was never aware whether Ron Zonen had told District Attorney Sneddon about the material he was giving to Mehas and himself. And Cassavetes added that even though he tried talking to sheriff's deputies about the case, they were much more closemouthed about the events of the murder. Cassavetes acknowledged that Zonen's cooperation was what he would describe as "enthusiastic."

Nick Cassavetes admitted that the movie *Alpha Dog* could have been made without Zonen's help, but that it "would have been worse." It would have taken a lot more time to dig up the information, and the final cut would have been very different. Cassavetes said he was comfortable with bringing the film to Santa Barbara and showing it to whoever needed to see it.

One of the more interesting comments Nick Cassavetes made to the court was when he said that Mehas had spoken to Zonen, who had expressed concern that his involvement in the movie might get him prosecuted. Mehas said he didn't want to deal with Hollywood's attorneys if it was going to cause that kind of trouble for anyone.

This last statement generated a whole new problem for the court, Ron Zonen and James Blatt—Michael Mehas legally could not withhold information that was relevant to Blatt's defense of Jesse James Hollywood. To put up a defense for Hollywood, Blatt needed to know just how far the situation had gone between Zonen and Mehas, and exactly what material had been handed over to Mehas.

James Blatt was less than pleased with this new revelation and stated that on October 13, 2005, he received a digital video disc from Heather Wahlquist, who was an assistant in the creation of *Alpha Dog*. Wahlquist had made this video while accompanying Zonen, Detective West, Nick Cassavetes, Michael Mehas and Chuck Pacheco in Santa Barbara. The initial scenes on the video disc were of these people up at and around Lizard's Mouth. Zonen could be seen on the video discussing his theories about how Nick Markowitz was brought up there, the position of

Nick's body, how he was hit with a shovel and how he was shot. Zonen spoke of Hoyt having an IQ in the 70s.

On the video Zonen also discussed his trial and retrial strategy for Graham Pressley's trials, aspects of various witnesses, his opinion of lawyer Stephen Hogg and speculation about how the feud between Ben Markowitz and Jesse James Hollywood had incited the kidnapping. Zonen also discussed aspects of Jack Hollywood and efforts to apprehend Jesse James Hollywood. At the very end of the video were images of Cassavetes and Mehas taking material from the district attorney's office, and they seemed to be very pleased. In fact, Cassavetes can be heard saying on the disc, "The guy (Zonen) said anything we needed. . . . Boy, I shouldn't be saying this on tape . . . anything we needed he would give us, but we have to say, 'We had to talk to the Markowitz woman first,' and if anything came out, I just have to say, 'The Markowitz woman told me.'"

This was a very important point—one way of interpreting this was to think that Ron Zonen had told Cassavetes to lie if ever asked how he had obtained so much information. The other way of looking at it was that Zonen had said this was a way of giving credit to Susan Markowitz, and not himself, and nothing illegal had taken place in this exchange.

Within days Blatt put forward a motion with Judge Hill to recuse Ron Zonen from prosecuting the case against Jesse James Hollywood, but Zonen wasn't taking it lying down. Zonen stated why he had initially been so enthusiastic about a film being produced on the case, and added that Jack Hollywood had been vital in helping Jesse escape and had been under intense surveillance in that regard. In fact, Zonen said, Jack's activities had helped Jesse stay underground for years, making it very hard to apprehend him. Jack often engaged in countersurveillance tactics, such as driving forward and backward, going around the block a few times and making frequent turns. According to Zonen, detectives spent countless hours contacting various people, checking phone numbers and driving around certain areas when rumors surfaced that Jesse Hollywood was back in town. Jack's phones were tapped, but he bought disposable cell phones with prepaid minutes to get around this. The FBI had to employ special equipment to identify just what phones Jack was using. In fact, on one given day, Jack used three separate phones. Wiretaps did give useful information about Jack's drug dealing, according to Zonen, but not to the whereabouts of Jesse Hollywood. Zonen said, "I saw this as the last opportunity to get the kind of widespread publicity necessary to locate defendant Hollywood and bring him to justice."

Zonen brought up another interesting point. He said that after September 11, 2001, much of the FBI's surveillance turned to counterterrorist operations, and he could no longer count on the amount of time spent by the FBI in helping him on the Jesse Hollywood matter. Zonen added that DA Sneddon did not know about his dealings with Cassavetes and Mehas.

When Ron Zonen actually attended a viewing of *Alpha Dog,* he said, "The film opens with a deluge of profanity, alcohol, drugs and rap music, and follows that format until the end. They affect the type of dialogue one would expect from stoned, uneducated, unemployable losers. The movie will have no appeal to the forty-and-over audience who make up the majority of our venue (for prospective jurors)."

Zonen added that the movie followed events of the actual case in only the most general way, and everyone's name had been changed, as well as locations. Most of the events in the film took place in and around Palm Springs, substituting it for the real locations in Santa Barbara. When the Jesse Hollywood–type character runs from the area, he goes to see a friend in New Mexico, not Colorado. Zonen also noted the fictional aspects in the film of the Nick Markowitz character having sex in a pool with two young women, and the Ben character beating up a whole room of thugs. These events had never occurred in real life. Zonen said that from what he saw in the movie, all the facts could have been gained from public documents that were down at the courthouse. Nothing in the film, according to Zonen, was either prejudicial or gathered from material that was off-limits. At the end of the film was a disclaimer: *For the purpose of dramatization, names, locations and the circumstances of the events have been changed, modified and created and dialogue invented.*

As far as Pressley and Rugge being caught on videotape in what Cassavetes termed a "strip search," that is not what occurred, according to Zonen. He said at the end of their interviews, these two changed from street clothing into jail clothing. Supposedly, both Rugge and Pressley kept their underwear on during this process, and it was not a strip search at all.

Zonen added that no original exhibits or actual evidence items were ever given to the filmmakers, and they received only copies of reports, transcripts, photos and tapes. Zonen noted that James Blatt had also seen a version of *Alpha Dog,* and knew that no names of the participants, including Jesse James Hollywood, were mentioned in the film. Nothing new was revealed that hadn't already been in the area newspapers and on television. And as far as Zonen perhaps writing a book about the case one day, that was not prejudicial, he said. He also said he thought about writing a book about the David Anderson case—the murder of a Montecito millionaire whose skeleton was found in the mountains near Ojai, and he even thought of writing a book about his experiences in the Michael Jackson trial.

* * *

Judge Hill eventually heard testimony by Nick Cassavetes and Mike Mehas in a hearing on the matter, and ruled that Ron Zonen had not overstepped his bounds as a prosecutor, and that Jesse James Hollywood could still get a fair trial in Santa Barbara County. Judge Hill added that he couldn't find any evidence that Ron Zonen had done anything that amounted to a conflict of interest. Judge Hill stated, "I do not find a scintilla of evidence that he (Zonen) had a financial stake or improperly utilized a criminal proceeding."

After this hearing, however, it was plain that both James Blatt, and cocounsel Alex Kessel were not giving up on this issue. Blatt told reporters, "Sometimes it's not the crime, but the cover-up." Blatt said that all of this was more than just Mehas not wanting to talk to him. According to Blatt, it was that Mehas had quit talking to him because that's what Ron Zonen wanted. At least this was Blatt's take on matters.

And now things wandered into First Amendment rights versus rights to a fair trial. Michael Mehas was ordered to testify on the stand and possibly give up his notes on what had occurred. He vigorously objected to this, saying that everything he had gathered was a part of his "work product" and guaranteed privacy.

Since Ron Zonen was under a cloud at this point, Senior Deputy District Attorney Joyce Dudley was handling the prosecution's side of this argument. The defense kept insisting there was wrongdoing by Zonen, who they claimed forced Mehas to quit cooperating with the defense as far as discovery material was concerned. Jesse James Hollywood's defense team was about to seek higher authority on the rulings, and they went to an appellate court. If need be, they were determined to go all the way to the state supreme court or even to the United States Supreme Court.

19

HOLLYWOOD HELL

To what extent all these proceedings had spiraled out of control was captured in an article in the *Santa Barbara Independent* aptly entitled HOLLYWOOD HELL. In part it stated: *Jesse James Hollywood's defense team is fighting tooth and nail to get veteran Santa Barbara prosecutor Ron Zonen removed from its client's case.* It was a wise move by the defense to try and get Zonen removed—a defense attorney named Sam Eaton told the *Independent,* "He's really good at his job. After one case I tried against Zonen, the defendant's mother said to me, 'I don't think even God could get him off now.'"

"The defense team fighting tooth and nail" was an accurate assessment. Even when the California State Attorney General's Office appeared to be disinclined to remove Ron Zonen from the case, James Blatt persisted. He wrote a memorandum of points and authorities to Judge Hill for an evidentiary hearing, asserting, *An evidentiary hearing must be conducted to resolve the inconsistencies and to discover with certainty Deputy District Attorney Zonen's motivation for his conduct as consultant to the filmmakers.*

Blatt said it was disingenuous of Zonen to say he wasn't aware of laws prohibiting the release of certain material, and noted that Zonen was a knowledgeable prosecutor with many years' experience in practicing law. Blatt stated that he was skeptical about Zonen's claim that he only helped the filmmakers because he'd run out of options in trying to discover the whereabouts of Jesse James Hollywood.

Now Blatt went even further, he wanted the whole Santa Barbara District Attorney's Office taken off the case. Blatt said he found it impossible to believe that Ron Zonen hadn't told DA Sneddon what he was doing, as far as the filmmakers were concerned. On this issue Blatt noted that Sneddon and all other DDAs had remained silent as to whether they knew what Zonen was up to or not.

Blatt finally claimed that because of Ron Zonen's conduct, Mike Mehas had quit cooperating with him (Blatt) on discovery issues, and that was a violation of the law and made it impossible for his client to have a fair trial. Blatt declared, "Mr. Mehas is the most critical witness in these recusal proceedings. Deputy District Attorney Zonen's communications with Mr. Mehas are not consistent with innocent behavior. To the contrary, his actions are more akin to those that represent consciousness of guilt."

Eventually Michael Mehas was compelled to testify on the stand in November 2005, in a hearing on this recusal issue. The *Ventura County Reporter* ran an article on the battle of wills between Mehas and defense counsel Alex Kessel, once Mehas was on the stand. Kessel asked Mehas where an audiotape was of an interview Mehas had conducted with Ben Markowitz. The newspaper reported: *Seemingly flustered by the amount of annoyance in the attorney's voice, Mehas mutters something about having handed the tape over to his own lawyer. The questioning continues like this for what seems like an eternity. As sexy as this case is—full of drugs, guns and an international manhunt and characters' names ripped from a 1950s potboiler—this particular hearing is excruciatingly boring.* The reporter called it two hours of semantic hairsplitting.

One thing very detrimental to the prosecution, and Zonen in particular, was a comment that Mehas made on the stand at that hearing. He said that he saw Zonen's presentation of the murder, and that of witnesses he had talked to, as being inconsistent. In other words, Mehas seemed to indicate that certain witnesses had not told investigators or Zonen the truth, but rather they told them things the investigators wanted to hear about Jesse James Hollywood. Mehas indicated that these witnesses told him things that differed from what they had told law enforcement and the DA's office earlier. With that said, Blatt and Kessel wanted all material that Mehas had gleaned to be turned over to them. Mehas initially refused because he termed this his "work product," but Judge Hill so ordered, and Mehas would have faced jail time if he didn't comply.

Judge Hill did decree that Mehas didn't have to surrender any written work to the court at the present time, but he did have to try and recall what his conversation had been with Christina Pressley when he had interviewed her, and get back to the court with that information within a month. And when he gave the material to the court, the contents would not be released to the public.

Mike Mehas testified to one more important thing from the stand—just where he stood on his feelings about Jesse James Hollywood and the case in general. Mehas said, "Nick Cassavetes and I feel a heavy pathos for our involvement. I've had a tremendous amount of it. I tried to be as truthful as I could. I dramatized a couple of things, but I tried to bring the truth of what happened, so we can present this story in as full [detail] as we could, so if it teaches somebody a lesson about how to take care of their

kid and not let their kid get in this kind of situation, then
at least we've benefited that one person. But in this process,
I'm going to tell a lot of stuff that's probably going to
create a negative impression on Jesse James Hollywood in
front of his day in court. It was through that feeling that I
felt I could help save his life by at least enlightening the defense on these issues. I don't want him to die."

Mehas had a very interesting thing to say to the *Ventura
County Reporter* journalist in the days after the hearing:
*The one man who I probably have the greatest relation-
ship with there (in court), and I've never met or spoken to
him in my life, is Jesse James Hollywood. I make eye contact with him, and that eye contact is so powerful to me.
He smiled to me, I smiled back at him, and it just reminded me that this young kid is out there with a heart,
and he probably knows whatever he did are mistakes, and
he's battling for his life.*

Everything was a quagmire now, as far as *Alpha Dog*
went. The film was slated for the Sundance Film Festival
in Park City, Utah, in early 2006, but its general release
was in a legal no-man's-land. The *New York Times* stated
that it gave *new meaning to postproduction snags.* Even
though Nick Cassavetes said he was not worried about the
film release date, and thought that James Blatt did not
have legal grounds to enjoin a movie, it still was a huge
headache for him and everyone else connected to the
movie.

The film *Alpha Dog* aired at the Prospector Square
Theater in Park City, Utah, on January 27, 2006. While reviews were mixed, one thing that many critics agreed
upon was the fine acting done by Justin Timberlake.

The film did well at the Sundance Festival and some
moviegoers had to be turned away at the door for lack of
space. It closed the festival at the large Rose Wagner
Performing Arts Center in Salt Lake City.

An MTV reporter concluded in a piece about *Alpha Dog:* "Now the stars are looking forward to the film's April general release." That optimism of an April 2006 release date was going to be a lot more wishful thinking than they imagined at the time.

Jesse James Hollywood was going through his own brand of troubles during this time period. He complained of an injury to his right thumb and soreness in his hand, and for that reason, he said, it was painful to wear handcuffs while in court. To counter this, Lieutenant Julian Villarreal Jr. wrote a report stating, *Inmate Hollywood refused to go to sick call on December 14, 2005 to see a doctor about his right hand. Handcuffs may be properly applied to the hands of Inmate Hollywood, including his right wrist, despite his claimed injuries to his right thumb.*

Prison Health Services noted that as far back as March 2005, Jesse Hollywood had been complaining about problems with his right thumb. In April 2005, a hand surgeon specialist from the County Clinic X-rayed him. It was noted that the base of Hollywood's right thumb had minor soft tissue, but, otherwise, it was normal and no treatment was recommended.

Of greater concern for the prosecution was Jesse James Hollywood's propensity for trying to escape, especially one event in June 2005. A report stated that he'd fashioned a sixteen-foot-long length of rope and had acquired contraband material, including cutting tools and weapons. To the officers it definitely looked like Jesse was planning to escape from the jail. He'd already proven that he could get away to a foreign country and stay there for a long period of time. If he escaped again, he just might make it to a country that did not have any kind of extradition treaty with the United States. Finally the report stated: *Given Defendant Hollywood's history of*

*escape risk and physical resistance, the Sheriff's Depart-
ment asserts that Defendant Hollywood's hands and feet
must be restrained at courtroom pre-trial proceedings in
order to control the significant risk of courtroom escape
and/or a courtroom assault.*

In another report an officer wrote, *During count, Hollywood was disrespectful and non-compliant. When removing him from his cell, he became combative.* It was noted
that Jesse had in his cell, a weight bag, two razors, three
altered razors, a manufactured rope from sheets, ten extra
socks, three extra jumpsuits, two extra boxers, four extra
towels and six extra shirts. Just where he had obtained all
these items was not noted.

In February 2006, the defense team for Jesse Hollywood got what they were looking for. The state supreme
court ordered the Second District Court of Appeal in Ventura County to take another look at Ron Zonen's conduct
in his cooperation with the filmmakers. They did not elab-
orate on their reasons, but one of Jesse's lawyers, Michael
Raab, told reporters, "We believe strongly that this was
unprecedented." (They were referencing the actions Zonen
had taken.)

If all the problems with *Alpha Dog* weren't enough for
the Santa Barbara District Attorney's Office, that same
April they had a new serious problem on their hands.
DDA Joyce Dudley, who could have stepped into Ron
Zonen's shoes if he was recused on the Hollywood case,
suddenly was in hot water for very similar reasons. She
had just written a fictional mystery novel, *Intoxicating
Agent,* but the plot was very similar to a case that she was
prosecuting that had not yet gone to trial. This was the
Massey Haraguchi case, and the similarities between it
and *Intoxicating Agent* were striking.

What caught the defense attorney's eye in that particular
instance was a name that Dudley cited in her Acknowledg-

ments section in the book—Judge George Eskin, who helped her in editing the book. In the Acknowledgments, Dudley wrote, *I don't believe anyone can write a trustworthy novel without the help and support of friends and colleagues who are willing to read and criticize their work.* Among the people she thanked was Judge George Eskin, who just happened to be the presiding judge in the upcoming Hara-guchi case.

Defense attorney Bob Sanger wanted to disqualify the judge in the case, because he had "helped" Dudley on the book. Sanger said, "*Intoxicating Agent* portrays the prosecution as brave, physically attractive, brilliant and always right. The book describes the defendant and defense lawyers as unethical, corrupt and vile."

Judge Eskin replied to the motion by saying that he'd helped Dudley in spelling, punctuation and inconsistencies, and nothing more. "To characterize me as having collaborated in writing the novel is, speaking plainly, ridiculous." Nonetheless, Sanger wanted Judge Eskin and Joyce Dudley recused from the Haraguchi case.

The Jesse James Hollywood trial should have been in progress by the summer of 2006. Instead, legal matters now shifted from Santa Barbara Superior Court to the Second District Court of Appeal in Ventura County. Former state supreme court justice Armand Arabian, who was on Jesse James Hollywood's side, told the court that Ron Zonen should be recused from the case because of his dealings with the filmmakers. Arabian said that by his actions Zonen had tainted potential jurors in the case. In florid language Arabian declared, "Justice stands here insulted, her blindfold askew, her scales unbalanced."

On October 6, 2006, the Second District Court of Appeal handed Jesse James Hollywood and his lawyers exactly what they were looking for: DDA Ron Zonen was tossed off the case. The ruling was seventeen pages in length, and it began with a recitation of the facts in the cases involving Jesse Rugge, Ryan Hoyt, Graham Pressley and then on to Jesse James Hollywood. It then told of Zonen's cooperation with Cassavetes and Mehas, James Blatt's viewing of the film *Alpha Dog,* and Mehas's refusal to cooperate any longer with the defense attorneys.

Of the damning accusation by James Blatt—that Zonen had told the filmmakers to "lie" if they ever had to go to court and explain where they had obtained the information by saying it had come from Susan Markowitz—the court found, *The trial court asked Zonen to explain the film-maker's comment. Zonen said, "I don't remember a conversation where we talked about crediting information to Susan Markowitz. However, if there's information that could have come from both of us, I could very well have said, 'Credit it to Susan Markowitz. I prefer not being quoted.'"*

The court basically believed Ron Zonen on this matter, and focused on whether Zonen had improperly influenced Michael Mehas to stop talking to the defense. The court said this raised concerns and they did see a pattern from Zonen that was troubling. Finally the Second District Court of Appeal stated why they ordered the recusal of Ron Zonen in the Jesse James Hollywood case. This was a death penalty case, and in striking a balance between the state and the defendant, it was necessary to protect the rights of the defendant: *A prosecutor in a death penalty case had to be held to the highest standards. Prosecutors should try their cases in the courtrooms, not in the newspapers, television or in the movies. As far as we know, no prosecutor has ever been a consultant (even without pay) to a film director on a pending criminal case that he or she is prosecuting. To say that Zonen went too far in his attempt to apprehend petitioner is an understatement.*

The court did note that Zonen had been motivated, not by money or fame, but by a wish to have Jesse James Hollywood apprehended. Nonetheless, he had given out private documents to persons who were not at liberty to have them. And in a double whammy, the Second District Court of Appeal that same day ruled on the matter with Joyce Dudley in the Haraguchi case. They addressed many of the same issues, recused her from that case and went one step further. The court had found Zonen's motivation to be meritorious, unlike *the situation in Haraguchi where the prosecutor was motivated by a desire for literary fame and fortune.*

The appeals court noted that in her book Dudley had referred to the defendant as a *"dirt bag, despicable, felony ugly, a pig and heartless bastard."* The justices noted: *These stereotypical generalizations have no place in a current public prosecutor's thinking, and there is a reasonable possibility that Dudley's perspective of the criminal justice system, like Danner's (her fictional heroine), is so one-sided that she may not exercise her discretionary functions in an even-handed manner.*

So there it was—the prosecutor Ron Zonen, who had successfully brought juvenile hall time for Pressley, prison time for Skidmore and Rugge, and the death penalty for Hoyt, was now off the Jesse James Hollywood case, and the person most likely to replace him had troubles of her own. The only silver lining for the Santa Barbara District Attorney's Office was the Second District Court of Appeal's decision not to throw the entire DA's office off the case. They said in part: *We do not see the especially persuasive showing of a casual connection between Zonen's conduct, the former elected district attorney, and the remainder of the deputies in that office.*

Just how far the news of this recusal process spread could be ascertained by an article from Russia's *Pravda* with a piece entitled: DEPUTY DA REMOVED FROM JESSE JAMES HOLLYWOOD CASE. If this was news in Russia, it could only be imagined what impact this had back in Santa Barbara.

* * *

Even after this victory, the defense was not ready to rest on its laurels. They went ahead with their plans to kick the entire Santa Barbara County DA's Office off the case. Arabian told reporters, "That office is too tainted with Mr. Zonen's terrible deeds, which can't simply be eliminated by removing Zonen, the lead prosecutor. The court of appeal ruling gave the defense half the apple, but the entire apple would keep the system of jurisprudence clean in the state of California."

And so it went, on into the autumn of 2006, the defense not only trying to get the district attorney's office off the case, but still trying to block the national release of the movie *Alpha Dog* as well. By now, James Blatt was arguing this latter issue in United States District Court in Los Angeles, saying a film release would "irreparably poison viewers' minds about the capital case and make it virtually impossible for Jesse James Hollywood to receive a fair trial anywhere in the country." He said that what had happened with this case was the prosecution joining up in a partnership with a major motion picture company to produce a film according to the prosecution's version of events. And he added that the movie depicted Hollywood as responsible for the murder. "Think of the public policy poison that is created here, if we are to allow prosecutors and defense attorneys to create their own motion picture divulging their files to control or change the jury pool." This United States District Court case had the unusual title of *Hollywood* v. *Universal Studios* (Hollywood being Jesse James and not the city). In fact, some pundits called the situation "*Hollywood* v. *Hollywood.*"

Universal Studios, a major motion picture company, was not taking this lying down. There had been a lot of money invested in *Alpha Dog,* and now it was almost a year later than its planned release date. If Jesse James Hollywood's defense team had their way, the film would not be shown in theaters until after the trial, and God only knew when that would be. This was squarely a case of freedom of the press (and films) versus the rights of the accused.

Several experts in the field of these issues spoke to reporters, and entertainment lawyer Rex Heinke told Dawn Hobbs, of the *Santa Barbara Press-News*. "The courts have repeatedly held there are all sorts of ways to ensure you get a fair trial that doesn't involve enjoining the broadcast," Heinke said.

Another First Amendment lawyer said, "I think the likelihood that the court would approve the injunction preventing the release of the movie is next to none. No matter how big the counsel happens to think this case is, it ain't bigger than O.J. And we all know what happened in O.J." In other words, O.J. was found not guilty despite the huge amount of pretrial publicity.

Ultimately, these two attorneys were correct—the U.S. court did not block the release of *Alpha Dog,* and finally, on January 7, 2007, it was released in theaters all across the nation. It was temperately received in most cities, to mixed reviews, but that was not the case in Santa Barbara. Perhaps the defense team's worst nightmares came true—the public in Santa Barbara lined up in droves to see a movie that was based on a case that they'd been reading about and watching on television news for six years.

The *Santa Barbara Independent* reported that a representative for the Metropolitan Cinema said the film was doing very well. The *Independent* reviewer gave the movie high marks, and called particular attention to how the Markowitz murder was a real event that affected real lives.

For the screenwriter Michael Mehas, there was a "surreal" quality to the premiere of the movie in Los Angeles. When he stood with Susan Markowitz outside the theater, and Sharon Stone, who played Mrs. Markowitz in the movie, came up and gave Susan a hug, Mehas told a reporter, "It was the greatest scene to see Susan and Jeff there. Sharon was honoring them that night."

Mehas added one more thing, and it probably did not

sit well with Jeff or Susan Markowitz. Mehas told the reporter, "Without me, without this movie, Jesse Hollywood would have already been steamrolled and sitting on death row. I don't want him to die."

After viewing the movie, Jeff Markowitz told a reporter for the *Jewish Journal* that the film was "poor, not entertaining and depressing." Because all the names of individuals had been changed, in fact, Nick Markowitz to Zack Mazursky, and Jesse Hollywood to Johnny Truelove, Jeff was very irritated that Jesse Hollywood's name wasn't mentioned at all in the movie. Jeff said that while he sat in the theater, he wanted to scream out Nick's real name so that the audience would know. On other issues he called Ron Zonen, "Nick's champion," and was very angry about the whole situation of Zonen being kicked off the case, because of his interaction with the filmmakers. Jeff saved his angriest comments for Jack Hollywood, however. He said that Jack Hollywood "was a cancer in our neighborhood. I don't think he's ever taken responsibility."

The *Los Angeles Times* was less kind to the film than the *Santa Barbara Independent* had been. It stated, Alpha Dog *digs into the sordid world of Jesse James Hollywood but comes up rather empty.* In one portion of the article, it referred to the movie as a *moral doughnut of a movie with an equally empty dramatic center. In turning the real-life tragedy of wasted young lives into cinematic narrative, Cassavetes applies plenty of gritty style, but is unable to make any of it very compelling.*

However, the *Los Angeles Times,* like many other media outlets, had great praise for Justin Timberlake's acting abilities. It wrote: *Timberlake turns in* Alpha Dog*'s most nuanced performance. In a film with several over-the-top characters bordering on camp, Timberlake's Frankie is the only one who approaches three dimensions, adept at convincingly dishing out some of the movie's disturbing violence as well as registering subtle shifts in Frankie's allegiance.*

Yet, by the spring of 2007, Timberlake's performance

was perhaps the only bright spot in what the *Los Angeles Times* had called, "the real-life tragedy" of "wasted" lives. Whether Jesse James Hollywood's own life would ever be one where he could live outside of prison walls remained to be seen.

20

TWELVE CITIZENS

The Santa Barbara DA's Office got exactly what it hoped for on August 11, 2008. The Supreme Court of the United States, in a lengthy statement, ruled that the Santa Barbara County DA's Office would not be pulled off the Jesse James Hollywood case, as the defense had hoped for. The Supreme Court justices admitted that this case was unprecedented and breaking new ground in the rules of law. Their decision stated, *No federal or state court previously has addressed a scenario remotely resembling the circumstances here.* That being said, the justices ruled that Ron Zonen may have made errors in judgment, he did not taint the entire Santa Barbara DA's Office. That office could now prosecute Jesse James Hollywood in their county.

The jury selection process, when it finally began in April 2009, was intense by both the prosecution and defense. There was a jury pool of literally hundreds of people, and many of them would rather have been anywhere else than facing the prospect of sitting on a jury for two months or more. Many did have legitimate excuses for not serving, either for hardship reasons or prior commitments that fell into the days that the trial was expected to last.

Most of the people excluded from jury duty fell into the "hardship" category, because of financial reasons. Their employers would only pay them for a few days of service or wouldn't compensate them at all. In fact, one man was let off because he was the entire workforce at his business. He was owner, employee and secretary all rolled into one. Another man let off was a fisherman, who could not afford to be away from the ocean for so long a period of time. Another group of people let off were students at nearby colleges and universities, and finals were only days away.

And so it went, hour after hour, day after day, in a lengthy and tedious process of elimination. Even Jesse James Hollywood seemed bored at times as he sat at the defense table. More than once he stifled a huge yawn behind his right hand as the questions from both defense and prosecution droned on. One major reason for exclusion was that a prospective juror was just too far at one end of the spectrum when it came to the death penalty question. One person said, "I'm not God. Only God can take a life." Another answered that all murderers should be put to death, despite mitigating circumstances. Another knew Ron Zonen, and was excluded, while another knew a detective who had been to the Lizard's Mouth murder scene. To try and make the process go more quickly, Judge Hill constantly kept trying to make the lawyers move along from prospective jurors who had little chance of being empaneled. Hill kept saying, "We have to be pragmatic about this."

Once in a while there was a very unusual reason that someone would be excluded. One person had plane tickets to the Philippines to celebrate the recent win of a boxing match. And in another case, one of the prospective jurors had actually been a student of DDA Hans Almgren. In his questioning Blatt facetiously asked Almgren if the young woman had received an A in his class. Almgren shot back, "All my students are A students." There was even a big laugh by one and all when one person stated on the questionnaire in big bold letters at the end, *Please don't pick me!*

One of the most unexpected people in the jury pool was a middle-age woman. Alex Kessel asked her with a great deal of irony if she was glad to be sitting where she was, knowing that the overwhelming majority of people were not. The woman answered, "Yes."

"You are?" Kessel asked in surprise. "Why?"

The woman replied, "Because it's nice and cool in here."

Outside on the streets of Santa Barbara, it was a very warm day, and the courtroom was one of the coolest places in town.

Oddly enough, if most prospective jurors did not want to be on a jury for six to eight weeks, there were a few who looked forward to the experience. They had the time and inclination to sit on a death penalty case. And eventually all those who were picked fell into the middle ground on the death penalty issue. They agreed that they would keep it open as an option, and follow all the instructions that Judge Hill would give them.

Ever since 2005, when Jesse James Hollywood had been captured in Brazil, there had been one delay after another as his case headed to trial. The largest delay, of course, stemmed from the movie *Alpha Dog*. By May 2009, it looked as if all the delays were finally over. And yet, there was one more huge delay that no one could have foreseen. It wasn't caused by prosecutors, defense lawyers or filmmakers. It was caused by Mother Nature, and in its fury, it not only disrupted the trial, it threatened to wipe out the city of Santa Barbara.

It was learned later that the fire had been started by someone actually trying to trim back brush along a trail in San Roque Canyon above Santa Barbara, at about 1:40 P.M. on May 5, 2009. By 4:30 P.M., the fire had burned 150 acres, and there were seventy engines on scene, along with fourteen strike teams. Things were fairly well in hand at that point, but there were fears for the next day when afternoon winds were expected to kick up.

The fears were more than justified. The winds didn't just "kick up," they roared down from the mountains with near hurricane force. At around 3:35 P.M. on May 6, while the prosecutors and defense were still arguing issues before Judge Hill, the lights suddenly dimmed in the courtroom. When everyone stepped outside the courthouse, they were amazed to see that the fire, which had been thin wisps of gray smoke in the mountains, had suddenly blown up into a raging inferno. Thick clouds of black smoke rose above the city, like a malignant genie released from a bottle, and flames shot one hundred feet high into the air.

By 4:15 P.M., Santa Barbara Fire Department spokesperson John Ahlman told reporters, "This thing is out of control. All we can do now is try to save homes."

By the evening of May 7, twenty-four thousand Santa Barbarans had evacuated their homes, some in mandatory evacuation zones, and others in precautionary zones. The courthouse, where the Jesse James trial was to take place, was only a couple of blocks from the mandatory evacuation zone. By now, one spokesperson told of upper Santa Barbara being a "ghost town." Once again, by evening, "sundowner winds" kicked up, and flames leapt one hundred feet into the air. May 8 was much the same, with heroic efforts by firefighters to save homes surrounded by walls of flame.

In the end, though, it was the cool moist air of May 9

that more than anything allowed the firefighters to get a handle on the fire. It was their first break in four days. By the time it was over, the "Jesusita Fire" had consumed more than nine thousand acres, destroyed eighty homes and injured twenty-nine firefighters. At its peak, 4,200 firefighters had battled the blaze along with 428 engines. The firefighters not only saved Santa Barbara, they saved the Jesse James trial from moving out of town—a matter that the prosecution had been fighting ever since 2005.

Even before the fire was fully contained, prospective jurors were filing back into the courtroom on Monday, May 11. One by one, a juror was selected to sit on the jury, while nearly one hundred others crammed every seat available in the courtroom gallery.

One thing was certain, both William Blatt and Alex Kessel were as thorough and efficient as Cheri Owen had been careless in her pretrial jury selection. And on May 11, Blatt sprang a huge issue before Judge Hill. Kessel stated that both Graham Pressley and Jesse Rugge were slated to be witnesses for the prosecution, and that they had better have their lawyers consulted. The reason was, both Blatt and Kessel were going to impeach Pressley's and Rugge's prior testimony, saying that they had lied to the police and on the witness stand in previous trials. And if they lied in this forthcoming trial, and it led to a death penalty conviction of Jesse James Hollywood—it was actually Pressley and Rugge who could receive a death penalty for lying in the trial. Kessel stated, "Even Ron Zonen called Jesse Rugge a liar when he was on the stand in his own trial."

This was, of course, a huge risk for both Pressley and Rugge, who might not want to testify at all. And it was a major concern for the prosecution. Both Pressley and Rugge were key witnesses in the prosecution's theory of the case against Jesse James Hollywood as the "mastermind" of the murder of Nick Markowitz. It was Pressley who had supposedly told Natasha Adams and Kelly Carpenter that Jesse Hollywood had offered Rugge money to kill Nick.

And it was Jesse Rugge who supposedly confirmed this to the two girls on August 8, 2000. If the jurors never heard this from Pressley's and Rugge's own lips on the witness stand, the prosecution's case would be diminished exponentially.

This was also a big issue for Judge Hill to decide upon, and he said to Kessel, "You've had the prosecution witness list for over a month. Why is this coming up now?"

Kessel agreed that he and Blatt did have the witness list for that period of time, but all during that period, they had been dealing with other issues in court. Then Kessel said, "I don't know of any prosecutor who has ever put on the stand, witnesses they know who have perjured themselves in other trials."

The new prosecutor, Joshua Lynn, was beside himself with this latest revelation by the defense, just before trial was to begin. Even Judge Hill seemed none too pleased by this latest development in the proceedings. He did agree, however, that it was a problem that needed to be addressed. Before anything went any further in this area, he said, he had to read statements that Pressley and Rugge had made in those other trials.

When Judge Hill finally ruled on these motions, he told the defense that Joshua Lynn and Hans Almgren were not asking Pressley and Rugge to lie on the stand now. If they had done so in previous trials, that was a different issue. "It does not exclude them from being witnesses now," Hill declared.

The defense strongly disagreed, and said that it put the defense at a huge disadvantage, knowing that "two liars will be on the stand." Judge Hill responded, "Even if they lied in some portions of former trials, they didn't lie throughout." One thing was for certain, after four years of delays, Judge Hill was not going to let this latest issue derail the trial, which was now set only days away.

Hill said, "Opening statements are going to be on Friday, May fifteenth." Barring another disastrous fire, flash flood, earthquake, the trial of Jesse James Hollywood was finally going to begin.

21

AT LAST

At 10 A.M., on Friday, May 15, the jurors filed to their assigned seats in the jury box, and Judge Hill spent twenty minutes giving them instructions. After he was through, DDA Joshua Lynn approached a lectern and began his opening arguments. Lynn immediately pointed at Jesse James Hollywood, at the defense table, and said, "Jesse James Hollywood murdered Nicholas Markowitz as if he pulled the trigger himself. It was Jesse James Hollywood who had his crew put Nick into a shallow grave."

Lynn then held up a large photo of Nick and said that his murder to Hollywood was "just business." Pointing at Jesse Hollywood again, Lynn declared, "He is a ruthless coward."

Lynn began presenting the complex case by showing the jurors poster boards with large photos of the "main players" in the events of August 2000. On the board were photos of Jesse James Hollywood, William Skidmore, Jesse Rugge, Graham Pressley, Ben Markowitz and, right in the middle of the board, Nick Markowitz. Lynn also presented a large timeline chart of the days of August 5, 2000, to late in August of that year.

Speaking of Jesse Hollywood's lifestyle in 2000, Lynn said that he was a major marijuana dealer in the San Fernando Valley. Lynn declared, "He had lots of dope and he had lots of guns. He had a house by the time he was twenty. What he didn't have was a job."

Lynn spoke of the feud between Jesse Hollywood and Ben Markowitz that led up to the kidnapping of Nick on August 6, 2000. Agreeing that the initial taking of Nick had been "spontaneous and irrational," Lynn asserted that it was a kidnapping nonetheless. Lynn said that on many occasions on the ride up to Santa Barbara in the van, Jesse Hollywood threatened Nick with bodily harm. Once they reached Richard Hoeflinger's house, Hollywood ordered the others to bind Nick with duct tape, and he even wanted to shove him into a closet. Lynn said, "Jesse Hollywood was walking around that house like he owned it. And he had a gun with him. Richard Hoeflinger was so rattled by this, he left his own house just to get out of there."

Joshua Lynn's timeline was helpful in pinning down the varied, and often confusing, events of August 6, 7, 8 and 9, 2000. And Lynn stressed that Jesse Hollywood and Michelle Lasher came up to Santa Barbara on August 7, and had lunch with Jesse Rugge. According to Lynn, it was then that Hollywood offered Rugge $2,000 to kill Nick Markowitz. (By now, the amount of $2,500 or $2,000 became interchangeable, depending upon who was discussing the matter.)

When it came to August 8, and Nick was hanging out with Rugge, Pressley, Adams and Carpenter, Lynn claimed that Jesse Hollywood was clearing out his bank accounts. He accumulated nearly $25,000 in cash that day, because, according to Lynn, he was going to eliminate Nick Markowitz and go on the run. It was the afternoon of August 8, according to Lynn, that a crucial event took place. Jesse James Hollywood went to see lawyer Stephen Hogg, who told him that kidnapping could get a person life in prison once and for all. It was that revelation that made Jesse Hollywood decide to kill Nick Markowitz, Lynn stated.

Lynn declared, "While the others were partying at the Lemon Tree Inn, Jesse James Hollywood showed up at his friend Casey Sheehan's house to borrow his car. Why? Jesse owned a tricked-out Honda at that point, and his girlfriend had a BMW." Lynn answered his own question by saying that Jesse Hollywood wanted a vehicle that could not be connected directly to him. A vehicle he was going to let Ryan Hoyt use in the mission to kill Nick Markowitz.

"It had to be Jesse Hollywood who told Ryan Hoyt to go to the Lemon Tree Inn," Lynn declared. "Hoyt had never been there before." Then Lynn told the jurors about Hoyt's trip up to Santa Barbara with Hollywood's TEC-9, Hoyt forcing Graham Pressley to dig a grave near the Lizard's Mouth, and Nick Markowitz's fatal ride up to that location. "And all while this was going on, Jesse James Hollywood, Michelle Lasher and Casey Sheehan were eating at an Outback Steakhouse miles away so that Hollywood could create an alibi. Jesse Hollywood paid with a credit card, when he usually paid cash, so that he could create a paper trail as to where he was at that time."

On Wednesday, August 9, Lynn declared, Jesse Hollywood sold his Mercedes and leased a new Lincoln Town Car. Then he went to Ryan Hoyt's birthday party at Casey Sheehan's house and forgave the rest of Hoyt's debt. Lynn said, "On August eleventh, Jesse Hollywood was running all over the place, collecting money so that he could make his getaway. He went to Palm Springs, where Michelle Lasher was, and when the news about Nick Markowitz being murdered came out in a Santa Barbara newspaper, Jesse Hollywood collected a further five thousand in cash from a bank account."

Lynn told of Jesse Hollywood and Michelle Lasher driving from Palm Springs, via Las Vegas to Colorado

Springs, Colorado, and their time there. Lynn also spoke of Jesse Hollywood's interactions with his old friends Chas Saulsbury and William Jacques, and Hollywood trying to trade his guns for fake IDs. Then Lynn spoke of Jesse Hollywood's ride back with Chas Saulsbury to Las Vegas and the Los Angeles area, and that on the way, Hollywood told Saulsbury that he'd had Nick Markowitz killed, because he'd learned from his lawyer, "Steve," that kidnapping could get him life in prison. Once Jesse Hollywood reached John Roberts's house, that was the last anyone saw of him, until he was arrested in Brazil, in March 2005.

Joshua Lynn told the jurors, "The evidence will show that Jesse James Hollywood is like an offensive coordinator in an NFL game." Lynn said that Hollywood stayed up in a luxury box, while using his friends like pawns, down on the playing field. They were the ones who got hurt, while Jesse stayed in his comfortable box, high above the fray.

Lynn held up a photo of Jesse James Hollywood, showing how Hollywood looked in the summer of 2000. He noted that the sedate-looking man at the defense table looked nothing like that "gangster image"of back then. Lynn said to the jurors, "I'd like to ask you to show the bravery that Jesse James Hollywood lacked, and come back with a verdict of guilty."

A break was taken, and when the jurors came back, James Blatt began his opening statement. Blatt called Joshua Lynn's timeline, "only a road map, which is not written in stone." And then Blatt said he would refute many things that Lynn claimed to be true, and the refutation would come through questioning the prosecution's own witnesses. In fact, most of the defense case would be challenging what the prosecution witnesses had to say.

Blatt stated, "Mr. Lynn called Jesse Hollywood a thug

and a coward. But just attaching labels is not helpful in this case." Then Blatt said that both the Hollywood and Markowitz families were dysfunctional in the year 2000. Blatt zeroed in on all the problems that Ben Markowitz caused for himself, his family and those around him. Blatt said that even though Ben Markowtiz was Jewish, he associated with neo-Nazi gang members. Ben even had a swastika tattooed on his own body.

Moving on to Nick Markowitz, Blatt claimed that Nick had his own problems in 2000, and was using drugs and even selling drugs. "If Jesse Hollywood was selling drugs, Nick was doing the same thing. Jesse Hollywood was never a big-time drug dealer. In an area of three million people in the San Fernando Valley, Jesse Hollywood could not be considered a big-time marijuana dealer, a drug that has practically been legalized in this state."

Getting back to the topic of labels, Blatt declared that the prosecution always referred to his client as Jesse James Hollywood. But up until the events of 2000, Jesse always went by the name Jesse Hollywood. There was no "Jesse James" involved in the way he was referred to by others, according to Blatt. As to the movie *Alpha Dog,* which Blatt disdained, he said that the movie referred to Jesse as "some kind of animal."

As far as any anti-Semitism on Jesse Hollywood's part, Blatt said, there wasn't any. In fact, Jesse's girlfriend Michelle Lasher was Jewish. Jesse went over to her family's house on Jewish holidays, and she came over to his family's house on Christmas. There was no "gangster lifestyle," according to Blatt. Jesse did not buy Michelle expensive gifts; he didn't wear flashy gold jewelry or exotic clothing. And when it came to Ryan Hoyt keeping Jesse Hollywood's house clean, Blatt said, Jesse, Michelle and the others also did house cleaning. "Jesse Hollywood is not some kind of Mansonesque person," Blatt declared. But Blatt did call Ryan Hoyt "a loose cannon."

Blatt said that Hoyt always craved attention, and he

made outlandish claims to his friends. At one point Hoyt said that he was a Navy SEAL, and at another time he claimed that he was a film actor. Neither one was true.

Blatt really kept pounding home that the debt between Ben Markowitz and Jesse James Hollywood was not the pivotal event that eventually sparked the kidnapping of Nick Markowitz. Blatt said that this debt happened six months or more before the incident of August 6, 2000. Blatt may have been making this point to distance Jesse Hollywood from any kidnapping for financial gain or extortion. It was going to be hard to prove that Jesse Hollywood was not part of the kidnapping, but if it had not been done for financial gain and extortion, then it was only a "simple kidnapping," and that would not get his client life in prison. Also, Blatt noted, not once after Nick had been taken did Jesse Hollywood, or his friends, ever contact Ben Markowitz or Nick's parents and demand money from them for the release of Nick.

Blatt noted that Ben was a "hothead," and may have killed one of Jesse Hollywood's dogs. Ben certainly broke the windows in Jesse's home. In fact, Blatt stated, Jesse Hollywood was moving out of his house to let things cool off. Jesse and Michelle Lasher were going to move to Malibu and not tell anyone where they were residing. It was in light of the broken windows, and the sudden spotting of Nick Markowitz on the street, that Jesse had Rugge pull the van over. "It was impulse, not premeditation," Blatt declared.

Blatt stressed that by August 7, 2000, the kidnapping was definitely over, and on many occasions, Nick could have simply walked away. Blatt stated, "He was not tied up and no one was even guarding him. Not one person will say that there was ever a ransom or extortion at any time."

By August 8, Blatt contended, Jesse Hollywood was trying to defuse the situation, and that was the reason he went to see Stephen Hogg. When Hogg told him that whoever had the "kid" needed to let him go, that was what

Jesse Hollywood tried to do by sending Ryan Hoyt to Santa Barbara. According to Blatt, it never occurred to Jesse Hollywood that Ryan Hoyt would take it into his own head to kill Nick Markowitz in some misguided attempt to impress Jesse Hollywood and the others. Blatt said that Jesse Hollywood's conversation with Casey Sheehan at the Outback Steakhouse on the evening of August 8, 2000, proved it. According to Blatt, Jesse told Sheehan, "Nick is coming home."

Blatt stressed that it was Ryan Hoyt who had the TEC-9, and he had been keeping it over his grandmother's house for months prior to August 2000. In fact, Blatt said, the first time Jesse Hollywood suspected anything like the murder of Nick was when he saw Hoyt on August 9 at Casey Sheehan's house. Hoyt apparently told Jesse Hollywood for the first time what he had done, and Sheehan recalled Hollywood having a huge argument with Hoyt. Sheehan would even say that Hollywood yelled at Hoyt, "How could you fuckin' have done that!"

Blatt said that from that point on, when Jesse Hollywood first learned that Ryan Hoyt murdered Nick Markowitz on his own initiative, Jesse began acting very differently. Michelle Lasher would attest to how upset he was, and the great change in his demeanor.

Blatt stressed over and over, "Not one person will come here and state that Jesse James Hollywood ordered anyone to kill Nick Markowitz! The decision to kill Nick was made by Mr. Hoyt, Mr. Rugge and Mr. Pressley. That Hoyt once lived with Ben Markowitz and had a falling-out with him is a factor in all of this. That Hoyt's sister had once gone out with Ben, and broken up with him, is another factor. In a misguided loyalty to Jesse Hollywood, Ryan Hoyt decided to kill Ben's brother, Nick."

James Blatt ended his opening argument by making his own sports analogy. Blatt referred to a statement that football legend Johnny Unitas had once uttered before a game: "Talk is cheap." Blatt made a connection between Unitas's statements and those of the prosecution. Blatt said that in the end, the facts, not labels, would prove that his client did not kidnap Nick Markowitz for financial gain or extortion, and he did not order that he be murdered.

On Monday, May 18, 2009, the trial's first witness, Jeff Markowitz, took the stand and spoke about his family and all the problems Ben caused. Jeff spoke ruefully of August 5 and 6, 2000, saying that he was supposed to participate in a martial arts tournament with Nick then, but he was too busy that weekend. Jeff related, "It would have been a good idea if I had."

Jeff also told the jurors about his and Susan's confrontation with Nick on the night of August 5, when Nick came home and seemed to be stoned. Jeff related that the next morning he and Susan were going to talk to Nick about the situation, but Nick had slipped out of the house. In relation to Nick being gone, Jeff stated that he was not too concerned at first, thinking that Nick had only gone to Ben's residence once again. But as the hours went by, and Nick did not come home, he and Susan became more and more worried.

Jeff spoke of all Nick's friends they contacted, and Susan constantly paging him, with no return message. This really concerned them, because Nick loved his pager and knew that it would be taken away by his parents if he did not return their pages. When Ben came home, both he and Jeff tried tracking Nick down, to no avail. At the end of Joshua Lynn's questioning, he asked, "When did your efforts to find Nick cease?"

In a quiet voice Jeff said, "At six A.M. on August 14, 2000, we had the window open and were listening for Nick's footsteps. But detectives walked up to the house, instead. Even before they said anything, we knew what had happened."

James Blatt, on cross-examination, had to walk a thin

line. He knew that if he seemed to be badgering Nick's father, it could backfire with the jury. But to give his client a chance, he also couldn't give Jeff Markowitz a free ride. Blatt asked, "If Valium and marijuana came from Ben to Nick, that would have been a betrayal of the family?"

"Yes," Jeff replied.

"What was Nick's attitude toward you and your wife at that time?"

Jeff answered, "There were bumpy roads. But Nick loved his mother."

"Did you strongly advise Nick not to go down the road that Ben had?"

Jeff declared, "I didn't put my finger in his face and say you can't be around Ben."

Blatt got into Nick's rebellious attitude in the year 2000, and the fact that he was dabbling in drugs. And then Blatt asked why Jeff waited so long before calling the police after Nick went missing. Jeff replied, "Ben and I were on a search-and-find mission. In retrospect, I wish I had done a lot more earlier."

Blatt asked why Jeff thought it was important that he and Ben go on the "search-and-find mission" instead of the police. Jeff said, "Nick had brought some new friends over to the house the week before, and I didn't know them. There was one kid who had come over, and I was not able to track him down. I just kept thinking that Nick had to be with someone new. Something different had to have happened."

Blatt asked, "Did you ask Ben if he had any enemies that could have caused this?"

Jeff answered, "Yes."

"Did he give you a number of names?"

"Yes."

"Was one of the names Henry Chang?"

"Yes."

Blatt ended his questioning by saying, "Did anyone ever contact you asking for a ransom?"

Jeff answered, "No."

* * *

. The next witness was Jennifer Michelle Cundip, who
had been Jennifer Markowitz, Nick's cousin. She was
three years older than Nick had been in 2000, and she had
been riding in her father's car that Sunday, August 6. As
her father's car approached the corner of Ingomar and
Platt, around noon on August 6, they spotted Nick walking toward his home. Jennifer's father pulled the car over
and she asked Nick if he wanted a ride home. He said no,
since he was so close to home at the time. Asked by Lynn
how Nick had looked at the time, Jennifer replied, "He
looked like a normal fifteen-year-old."

Joshua Lynn showed Jennifer a photo of the corner
of Ingomar and Platt, and asked her if she recognized
the area. Jennifer said, "Yes, that's where Nick was kidnapped."

She didn't say it, but many in the courtroom wondered
how different things might have been if Nick had climbed
into his uncle's car that Sunday instead of continuing to
walk home. From Jennifer's timeline, Nick must have
been kidnapped shortly after his uncle's car drove away.

After Jennifer Cundip, Pauline Mahoney took the stand
and told of her drive back from church on Sunday, August
6, 2000, with her two boys and one of their friends. Her
words to this jury were "I was coming up on Ingomar and
there was a boy on the ground. He was being beaten up
horribly. Then they picked him up and threw him into
a van."

Mahoney recalled what she saw of the white van, and
how she and the boys repeated the van's license plate
number until she got home and called 911. Joshua Lynn
then played the 911 audiotape, and Mahoney's voice from
nine years before filled the courtroom. Everyone listened

very attentively to the audiotape, including Jesse James Hollywood at the defense table.

On cross-examination Blatt got Mahoney to admit that she didn't know if three or four young men were beating up the boy on the sidewalk. And she also admitted that she thought the boy being beaten up had bleached-blond hair, when, in fact, Nick had dark brown hair.

Now it was time for one of Jesse Hollywood's former buddies to take the stand. Brian Affronti no longer looked like the tough teenage punk with cropped hair and a sullen attitude. Instead, he wore a business suit and appeared to be a young businessman. Asked what he did for a living, he said that he managed a nightclub. Affronti said that he had been friends with Jesse James Hollywood for about four months in the year 2000, but he had been friends with William Skidmore for twelve years by that point.

Affronti said that on August 6, 2000, Jesse Hollywood arrived at his house in a white van, and Affronti took off for Santa Barbara's Fiesta Days with the others. Affronti retold his story of the ride there, as he had done in the other trials, and added little new information. One thing he did say was that Hoyt seemed to be a virtual slave around Jesse Hollywood's house, "picking up dog shit and having to paint the fence."

Joshua Lynn asked if Affronti was worried about what he had seen in the van and at Richard Hoeflinger's house, in relation to any threats against him by Jesse Hollywood. Affronti replied that Skidmore had told him that Jesse Hollywood had said in the days after August 6, "Brian is the weak link, and he might have to be taken care of." And Affronti added, "I told my sister that if I should disappear— well, I gave her a list of people I had been with. Mainly, it was Jesse Hollywood and Jesse Rugge."

* * *

It was on cross-examination that Brian Affronti was grilled. In fact, it was the cross-examination of prosecution witnesses that *was* the defense case. And if James Blatt portrayed the "good cop" in the defense routine, then Alex Kessel was the "bad cop" in the questioning of witnesses. Kessel zeroed in on witnesses' prior statements to police, and in Hoyt's and Rugge's trials, and Kessel grilled the witnesses now with hard questions, often in a combative manner.

Right off the bat, Kessel asked Affronti, "In testimony you just gave, did you lie or fudge a little bit?"

Affronti replied, "Everything I told you was the truth."

"Are you sure?" Kessel said with scorn. "You never reviewed your audiotape from the police interview?"

Affronti said that he had not done so.

So Alex Kessel started in on what would be a theme with Affronti and many other prosecution witnesses: arguing how what they said in *this* trial differed from what they had said before. Affronti had indicated in the present trial that Jesse James Hollywood was having Nick held until Ben repaid his debt. But Kessel asked Affronti, "Did you ever hear Jesse Hollywood say, 'Hey, until your brother pays, you're not going home'?"

Affronti replied, "No, sir."

"Was Nick Markowitz unrestrained on the couch and playing video games with Jesse Hollywood at Richard Hoeflinger's house?"

"Yes."

"At this trial, have you tried to minimize anything that you did?"

"No."

To counter this, Kessel showed Affronti prior testimony where he said he had dealt marijuana for Jesse James Hollywood, and that he was more implicated with Hollywood than he was letting on. Kessel also showed Affronti where he had lied about this to the police.

Kessel asked, "That is totally inconsistent with your testimony to this jury. So what's the truth?"

Affronti replied, "What I testified to now."

Another thing Kessel got Affronti to admit was that when he saw Nick in the van on August 6, 2000, he didn't see any scratches, cuts or bruises on him.

Kessel said, "In the time you knew Jesse James Hollywood, did you ever see him use violence against anybody?"

"No," Affronti replied.

"Ever know him to ask his friends to use violence on anyone?"

"No."

Kessel even got Affronti to admit that the TEC-9 was what he termed a "floater." In other words, a gun that was passed around between Jesse Hollywood's friends, and could have been used by different people at different times. And Kessel even got Affronti to admit that Jesse Hollywood had said to Nick at one point, "Oh, dude, don't worry about this. Just tell your parents you ran away for a couple of days." The implication was that Jesse Hollywood was going to send Nick home.

On redirect Joshua Lynn said to Affronti, "You know you can go to prison for life if you lie in this court?"

"Yes," Affronti replied.

"So, isn't it true, you heard, in the van ride to Santa Barbara, Jesse Hollywood say to Nick Markowitz, 'Your brother is gonna pay me that money'?"

"Yes."

"And in a transcript you said, 'Ryan Hoyt was a slave of Jesse Hollywood.' Do you remember saying that?"

"Yes."

Regarding seeing any injuries that Nick might have incurred from being beaten, Lynn asked if Affronti had ever seen Nick with his shirt off, his shoes off or his pants off. Affronti answered no to each question.

And for the TEC-9, Lynn got Affronti to admit that he never said the gun was "passed around." He had said it was "passed down" to the others, meaning that Jesse Hollywood passed his TEC-9 to them.

Chas Saulsbury had been a good witness for the prosecution at Rugge's and Hoyt's trials. And in the current trial, he repeated most of what he had said before. And then— most of the way through his testimony in Jesse James Hollywood's trial—Saulsbury dropped a bombshell. He not only said that Jesse Hollywood told him that a lawyer named Stephen had told him to "get rid of the kid," Chas now claimed that Hollywood said that this lawyer had told him, "Kill the kid and bury him in a deep hole."

James Blatt, on cross, took a page out of Alex Kessel's book; he bombarded the witness with a series of rapid-fire questions. And under this bombardment Chas Saulsbury was about to crack. Blatt, in fact, before long, got Chas to admit that he had lied on several key points to detectives during his first interview in August 2000. During that interview Chas said that he didn't know why Jesse Hollywood was on the run, and that was part of the reason he helped him. Blatt asked, "Did you lie just to make yourself look better to the detectives?"

Chas said, "Yes."

Chas had also testified before that he had not looked at any news concerning Jesse Hollywood while in Colorado. But now he admitted to Blatt that he and Jesse had both done so on a computer while in Colorado. They had seen a Santa Barbara newspaper story about the killing of Nick Markowitz, and about Jesse being on the run. The questions came at Chas from all directions, and he seemed flustered and almost in tears by the end of the first day of questioning.

* * *

On the next day of trial, James Blatt asked Chas if he had left the courtroom the day before in an upset mood. Chas said that he had, and Blatt apologized to him. But if Chas Saulsbury thought this day would be any easier on him, he was sadly mistaken. The questioning from Blatt was just as vigorous and rough at times.

Blatt asked at one point, "Didn't you think you were assisting Jesse in escaping?"

Saulsbury replied, "Yes."

"Didn't you know that was a crime?"

"Not at the time," Saulsbury replied.

And yet, Blatt zeroed in on this statement as well, proving that Saulsbury had phoned a lawyer before leaving Colorado Springs, and another lawyer between Las Vegas and Los Angeles, just to see how much trouble he was in. In fact, Saulsbury finally admitted that the second lawyer told him, "What the hell are you doing? You need to get the fuck away from Jesse!"

By this point Chas was rattled on the stand—his eyes were wild at times, and he appeared to be sweating. And the questions kept coming at him from every direction. Blatt asked, "During the police interview, weren't you told that an omission was the same as a lie?"

Chas responded, "Yes."

Often in answers to questions, Chas seemed to be ducking responsibility by answering, "I can't remember" or "I don't recollect." It got to the point where Blatt asked him, "Did smoking high-grade marijuana between Colorado Springs and Los Angeles impair your memory?"

Chas said, "Not that I recall," which brought a round of laughter in the courtroom.

Blatt particularly zeroed in on the comment that Chas had made on direct about a lawyer named Steve, who supposedly told Jesse Hollywood to "kill and bury" the boy. Blatt asked Chas, "You don't remember at what point on that trip Jesse Hollywood told this to you, do you?"

Chas replied that Hollywood had said that to him, but he couldn't remember exactly where. Chas added that he hadn't been looking at road signs along the highway.

Then Blatt asked him, "Did Jesse Hollywood offer you any money for assistance?"

"Not that I recall," Chas replied. "Jesse just wanted me to go with him to Canada or Mexico. He wanted me to run along with him forever."

Blatt asked if Chas had seen the movie *Alpha Dog,* and Chas said that he had several times.

So Blatt asked, "Did the movie disturb you?"

"No," Chas responded.

"Were you saddened by the movie?"

"Yes."

"Did you see yourself in that movie?"

"Yes. I spoke with director Nick Cassavetes before it was made. I think actor Michael Moriarty played me."

"Did you get paid for your cooperation?"

Chas's answer momentarily stunned James Blatt. Chas replied, "Yes. It was an insult. Three thousand dollars."

When Blatt recovered from his surprise, he asked with scorn, "You think that being paid three thousand dollars for that was an insult?"

Now it was Chas's turn to be momentarily speechless, perhaps realizing how ill-advised his comment had been. Finally he said, "It was an insult because I was trying to forget the whole situation."

By now, Chas was getting very agitated, and he constantly squirmed around in the witness chair. At times he looked on the verge of crying, and at other times he appeared to be very angry. When Blatt asked him, "On direct you said that Jesse Hollywood wanted to trade guns for fake IDs, but you didn't tell the police that. Why?"

In an angry tone of voice, Chas said, "That was my impression. I'm not just pulling that out of my ass!"

Judge Hill was having none of that, and he sternly told Saulsbury, "That is not proper language in this court-room."

Chas meekly stated that he would not respond in such a manner again. By now, he seemed on the verge of completely breaking down. It got to the point where he seemed to be answering questions in the way he perceived that Blatt wanted them answered, if only it would help him get out of the witness chair.

Blatt asked, "You were going to do whatever it took to make a deal with the prosecution, weren't you?"

"Yes," Chas said.

Blatt even brought up the fact that in front of a grand jury in 2000, Chas had said to Ron Zonen that it was Jesse Hollywood's friends who had come up with the idea to kill Nick, and Chas didn't think Hollywood had anything to do with it.

Blatt asked, "Not one time did Jesse Hollywood ever tell you he had ordered the kid killed, did he?"

"Correct."

"Jesse, at different times on that road trip, looked sad and remorseful?"

"Correct."

"Even suicidal?"

"Yes."

"Did Jesse tell you he wished that this thing never happened?"

"Yes."

Blatt asked, "Why didn't you tell the police about the lawyer supposedly saying, 'Kill the boy and bury him in a deep hole'?"

Chas replied, "Because I was trying to protect Jesse."

"Oh, really?" Blatt asked in mock surprise. "Weren't you really just trying to protect yourself?"

Thoroughly browbeaten by this point, Chas answered, "Yes."

"So, have you been lying to this jury?"

"No," Chas said.

"What? But you just lied to this jury a moment ago when you said you were trying to protect Jesse, when you were really trying to protect yourself."

Confused and extremely rattled, Chas replied, "That was a mistake."

Finally, near the end of the questioning, Blatt asked, "Did you have a moral duty to tell the police what you've now told this jury?"

"Yes," Chas replied quietly.

"But did you?"

"No," he responded.

When James Blatt ended his questioning, he said, "Mr. Saulsbury, thank you very much."

Chas said not a word in reply. He just glared at Blatt. Rarely had a witness, who had done so well for the prosecution in other trials, been so thoroughly demolished in another trial.

Joshua Lynn had an almost impossible task in trying to restore Chas Saulsbury's credibility in the jurors' eyes. But Lynn gamely made a good attempt at it on redirect. Lynn said to Chas, "Mr. Blatt asked you a lot of questions very quickly. Were you confused."

In a vast understatement Chas replied, "I guess a little bit."

Then Chas teared up and added, "I just wanted to get out of here!"

Lynn wondered, "Was it your intention at any time to see Jesse James Hollywood convicted of capital murder so you could get out of whatever trouble you were in?"

"No!"

"Are you doing that now?"

"No."

"Are you lying to this jury about the fact that Jesse Hollywood, Jesse Rugge and Ryan Hoyt planned to have Nick Markowitz killed?"

"No."

"Did anyone ever tell you that if you don't help the prosecution in convicting Jesse James Hollywood, you're going to prison?"

"No."

"Were you trying to frame Jesse James Hollywood so that you could get out of trouble?"

"No."

Chas Saulsbury must have hoped that he would be released from being a witness after Joshua Lynn's redirect, but that was not the case. He still had to endure many more questions by James Blatt. At times he looked like a boxer who was holding on to the ropes, still in the ring, but barely on his feet. Perhaps in a show of contempt for the defense, and his anger at still coming back for another day, Chas wore flip-flops and board shorts to court on Friday, May 22.

Despite his casual attire, it wasn't long before Chas looked uncomfortable and irritated, once more. He twisted and turned on his chair so often, Judge Hill quipped to a bailiff, "Do we have a chair that doesn't swivel?" This brought a round of laughter in the courtroom, and even to Jesse Hollywood, who was obviously enjoying watching his former friend squirm on the witness stand.

Blatt kept pounding on one theme, that Chas had never seen Jesse with a TEC-9, but rather had only read about it in newspapers. But Chas stuck by his story that he had seen Jesse with a TEC-9, the same kind of gun deposited in Nick's grave.

When Joshua Lynn had his turn once more with Saulsbury, Lynn proved that Chas could not have known about the TEC-9 through newspapers when he had his early interviews with detectives. That early on, the only mention was of a "gun" linked to the murder of Nick Markowitz; there was not yet anything in the newspapers about a TEC-9.

Lynn also got Chas to reveal one more startling thing. Since he had been on the stand, Chas learned that his dog back in Colorado had been poisoned. The symptoms were consistent with rat poison.

Chas testified, "She's bleeding internally. There's so much blood, it's coming from her eyes. When I go home, I'm going to say good-bye to her and then put her down."

It was no big leap to infer that someone considered Chas to be a "rat," and had dealt with his dog according to that belief.

Unlike Chas Saulsbury, Kelly Carpenter kept her poise throughout her questioning. She exuded confidence and clarity as she retold things she had already said in Hoyt's and Rugge's trials, especially about hearing from Graham Pressley that Jesse James Hollywood had offered Jesse Rugge money to kill Nick Markowitz.

Alex Kessel, on cross, got Kelly to admit that everyone at the Lemon Tree Inn, including Nick Markowitz, was smoking marijuana. She also admitted that when she left the Lemon Tree, around 10:30 P.M. on August 8, 2000, Nick seemed to be fine and not in any danger. She also never saw Ryan Hoyt arrive at the Lemon Tree Inn, and certainly never saw Jesse James Hollywood there.

Kelly Carpenter had done a good job on the stand, and both the prosecution and defense scored points off her testimony. But the "truce" upon witnesses soon ended when Richard Hoeflinger took the stand, and the defense was once again on the attack as far as what Hoeflinger had to say.

It started out well enough for the prosecution with Hoeflinger. He related, "When Jesse Rugge and his friends came over on August 6, 2000, it wasn't long before Jesse Hollywood was acting like he was in charge. He was ordering the others around. I started to go to my room, and I saw Jesse Hollywood with a gun under his shirt. It scared me. I wondered what was going on. I went to my room, and Nick, Rugge and Skidmore were in there. Nick was sitting on the edge of the bed, and his legs were straight out in front of him. There was duct tape on his ankles. Will Skidmore had duct taped his hands. Nick was quiet and still. I looked at this, and Jesse Hollywood told me, 'Just be cool.' I didn't say anything back. I was scared for my life. I believed that if I called the police, he would have me or my cousin killed."

Then Joshua Lynn took Hoeflinger to a different time and area, by having him talk about his first meeting with Jesse James Hollywood, sometime in the spring of 2000.

Hoeflinger said, "I went with William Skidmore to Jesse James Hollywood's house in West Hills. Ryan Hoyt was protecting the front door. When we came in, he had a MAC-10 pointed in our direction. Jesse James Hollywood came into the front room, and Jesse Rugge introduced me to Hollywood. We hung around, waiting for a half pound of marijuana to arrive. We ended up getting a quarter pound of that, and it was about twelve hundred dollars. It was given to Rugge on consignment."

Because of this initial meeting with Jesse Hollywood, Hoeflinger said, Jesse got ahold of him a few months later to make a dope transaction. Hoeflinger took his girlfriend to an Embassy Suites hotel in the area, where they met Jesse Hollywood and Michelle Lasher in a room. Hoeflinger said he bought some dope from Hollywood, and he also contended that Michelle Lasher knew all about Jesse Hollywood's marijuana dealing, something she always firmly denied.

After the lunch break, Alex Kessel went right at Hoeflinger's testimony. As he had done with Chas Saulsbury,

Kessel got Hoeflinger to admit that he'd omitted things while talking to the police detectives in August 2000.

Kessel asked, "Did you knowingly tell falsehoods to the police back then?"

"Yes," Hoeflinger replied. "I was scared."

"Did you lie at any of the other trials?"

"Possibly."

Scornfully Kessel asked, "What do you mean 'pos-sibly'?"

Hoeflinger replied, "I don't recall if I lied or not."

Then Kessel said that in none of the police reports had Hoeflinger ever spoken of Jesse James Hollywood barking out orders to Rugge and Skidmore. Kessel wanted to know why Hoeflinger was saying that now.

Hoeflinger replied, "I remembered it later."

Kessel declared about Hoeflinger's house, on August 6, 2000, "At the grand jury you told Ron Zonen, 'I didn't see Jesse Hollywood speak at all when he was there.' Was that a truthful answer?"

"No."

"Why not?"

"I was scared of Jesse James Hollywood then."

"So why did you lie so often before?"

"I don't know," Hoeflinger answered.

"Then why are you supposedly telling the truth now?"

"Because it's time for the blame to be put where it should be."

"At Rugge's trial you were asked if you ever saw Nick wrapped up with duct tape. And you answered, 'No.' So, is that another lie?"

Hoeflinger responded, "It's all kind of fuzzy."

"So you sit here now, you can't recall any duct tape being on Nick, correct?"

Hoeflinger answered, "True."

Jaymi Dickensheet had also been at Richard Hoeflinger's house on August 6, 2000. She was a friend of

Richard Hoeflinger's cousin, Shauna Vasquez. Jaymi testified now that she had been introduced to a "tall Jesse" (Rugge) and a "short Jesse" (Hollywood), on August 6, and that's how she remembered them now. She pointed to Jesse Hollywood at the defense table and said he was who she remembered as "short Jesse." Of his demeanor at Richard Hoeflinger's house on August 6, 2000, she said, "He was agitated. He was on a mission. Hurried and busy. I remember of short Jesse, he said at one point, 'Nick is going to show me respect!'"

After the barbecue that she and Hoeflinger and Vasquez went to, Jaymi said they returned to find Nick Markowitz sitting on the couch. Nick told her that he was trying to help his brother. Jaymi added, "He didn't seem to be stressed or worried at that point. He was just hanging out. But he did ask permission of tall Jesse, if he could go to the bathroom."

Asked by Hans Almgren why she didn't go to the police after Nick and the others had left, Jaymi said, "I was in fear for Ricky. I knew from Shauna that they had been holding the kid. I didn't call the police because of the danger to me and Shauna."

James Blatt got Jaymi Dickensheet to admit on cross that her memory of August 6, 2000, "was jumbled as to the sequence of events." And then she added that since she had learned of Nick's murder, she had been prone to "night terrors." Jaymi said that she constantly had nightmares where she would see Nick's face; she had gone to a psychiatrist about this problem.

Blatt was as quiet in tone and reserved with Jaymi Dickensheet as Kessel had been loud and demonstrative with Saulsbury and Hoeflinger. Blatt got Jaymi to admit that she'd had at least ten beers on August 6, 2000, and when asked if it clouded her memory, she said, "Possibly."

Jaymi also admitted that Nick went outside on numerous

occasions to smoke cigarettes that evening, August 6, and "he could have left at any time."

Shauna Vasquez, on direct, was one of the few witnesses for the prosecution to tell of Nick's condition right after his ride in the van to Santa Barbara and at Hoeflinger's house. Shauna said that Nick's shirt was torn in front, and he was holding it together with his hands. Eventually Shauna asked Richard Hoeflinger to give Nick a shirt, and Richard gave him a white T-shirt to wear.

Shauna was also a good prosecution witness because she had actually gone into Richard Hoeflinger's bedroom and seen Nick sitting on the bed. Shaua related, "Short Jesse (Hollywood) and the others were in the bedroom. And I needed a mirror for makeup. But Richard was taking a shower in the bathroom. So I went into Richard's room to use a mirror, and Nick was sitting on the bed. His hands were duct taped. It was kind of a silver-colored duct tape. I went over and did my makeup. I freaked out a little bit and wanted to leave immediately. I didn't know what was going on. Everyone was talking at once, and short Jesse was asking the kid if he knew how to get ahold of his brother."

Later on, while sitting on the couch before going to the barbecue, she asked "short Jesse" what was going on. According to Shauna, "He told me, 'Nicholas's brother owes me money.'"

This was very important for the prosecution. Shauna was one of the few outside of Jesse James Hollywood's buddies who ever heard Hollywood say that the holding of Nick had to do with any money. If the jury believed Shauna on this, it could move matters from a "simple kidnapping" to "kidnapping for ransom," and that could get Jesse Hollywood a sentence of life in prison. Or if it was in conjunction with murder, it could get him the death penalty.

* * *

Alex Kessel on cross was definitely quieter and gentler with Shauna Vasquez than he had been with Richard Hoeflinger. In an exchange with Shauna, he asked, "Did you see anybody threaten Nick?"

"No," she replied.

"Did you see any injuries on him?"

"No."

"Did he ever complain about being held?"

"No."

"Did you ever see Jesse Hollywood with a weapon?"

"No."

"Did any of these guys tell you, 'Hey, we're gonna fool Nick into thinking he's going home'?"

"No."

Gabriel Ibarra had been a friend of Richard Hoeflinger's for thirteen years by the year 2000, and he was a supervisor at a local Kentucky Fried Chicken outlet at the time.

On the stand Ibarra recalled, "The guys all kind of filed in and went back to Richard's bedroom. Then Rick came out and sat down on the couch, where I was. He just sat there and stared at the wall. He appeared to be very shaken and nervous. The short guy named Jesse came out of Rick's bedroom and he went toward the kitchen. I went outside to smoke a cigarette and he soon joined me there to smoke a cigarette. He was very nervous and rattled, and kind of dramatic. He was very antsy.

"A little later, Emilio Jerez, who had been in the bathroom, went toward his room, and then he came out into the living room. I was still on the couch watching TV, and Emilio came toward me, looking shocked, angry and upset. He said to me, 'What the hell's going on here?'

"I said, 'What do you mean?'

"'Come and look!' he said to me.

"So we went to the hallway and I looked into Richard's room. The door was cracked open a bit. I looked in and saw a kid with his wrists and his ankles duct taped. He was sitting on the edge of the bed. Rugge and Skidmore were in there, too, and there was a sock over the kid's eyes. It was kind of a blindfold.

"After I saw that, I went back to the couch. I sat down and tried to figure out what was going on. I was freaked out. Short Jesse was pacing around a lot. I just wanted to get out of there at that point, but I was concerned about my friend Ricky.

"I asked Jesse Rugge when he came out of the bedroom, 'What the hell is going on?' He was really skittish. He kept saying, 'Hollywood is trippin'. Hollywood is trippin'.'

"Short Jesse came over and wanted to know what Jesse Rugge was saying to me. Short Jesse said, 'What are you saying? Shut the fuck up! Don't say anything!'"

Joshua Lynn asked Ibarra if he noticed anything strange around "short Jesse's" waistband.

Ibarra answered, "It appeared that there was a bulge in his waistband. It got my attention. It was on his left side."

"What did you think the bulge was?" Lynn asked.

Ibarra replied, "A gun."

Alex Kessel, on cross, asked Ibarra that if he was so scared of Jesse James Hollywood, then why did he go back to Richard Hoeflinger's house after he got off work at Kentucky Fried Chicken that evening? Ibarra answered that he did so because he was worried about his friend Hoeflinger.

"If you were so worried for him, did you ever call the police?"

"No."

"Why not?"

"I was scared of Jesse Hollywood."

Emilio Jerez must have cursed his rotten luck for having moved into his friend Richard Hoeflinger's house just a week before the incident of August 6, 2000. Emilio testified, "Jesse Rugge phoned and asked if there was a room or a closet for a person. I think I did say there was a closet big enough for someone, but that Richard wasn't home right then and he needed to call back. Then I got ready to go to a barbecue."

After taking a shower, Jerez was walking to his room when he looked into Hoeflinger's bedroom because the door was cracked open. What he saw there stunned him. Jerez said, "These guys were in there doing something pretty crazy. Fear ran through me. On the way out the door later, Rugge grabbed me and told me not to say anything."

Lynn asked Jerez why he hadn't told the police detectives all he had seen on August 6, 2000.

Jerez said, "At the first interview I had a fear of what happened to the kid could happen to me. I already knew about the murder by then. I mean, Jesse Hollywood was still a fugitive."

Once again, on cross, Kessel jumped on a prosecution witness by saying that he had committed perjury in previous trials, if what he was saying now was the truth.

Kessel asked, "Why did you lie about things in Jesse Rugge's trial?"

Jerez answered, "I was scared to tell the truth then. Scared for my life."

Kessel asked, "What were you scared of?"

Without batting an eyelid, Jerez said, "Your client."

Kessel pointed out that in Rugge's trial, Jerez spoke of Nick sitting on the bed, and Skidmore and Rugge were standing near him. But not once in that trial did Jerez ever say anything about duct tape or a sock over Nick's eyes.

And another thing not helping Jerez now was his concept of the timeline of the events of August 6, 2000. Jerez thought he saw things occur in the Hoeflinger house about noon, when, in fact, Nick was being kidnapped in West

Hills around that time. All the others had said that the
events had occurred at Hoeflinger's house between 3:00
and 4:00 P.M.

The next witness was Annie Blackford, a raven-haired
young woman who had been seventeen years old in 2000.
Blackford had known Jesse Rugge and William Skidmore
through her friend Jesse Hollywood. She spoke of the
atmosphere at Jesse Hollywood's house as being one continuous party in the summer of 2000. She said, "There was
a lot of smoking of marijuana and drinking there that
summer. I saw guns there at the house. Several different
kinds. I remember a large gun on the front couch near the
door. There were guns in Jesse's bedroom." She, in fact,
knew about Jesse's bedroom, because she admitted that
she had "casual sex with Jesse during that time."

About Ben Markowitz, Blackford said, "When I saw
him, he was acting crazy. Everyone knew him. I just kind
of stayed away from him. Later, Jesse (Hollywood) told me
that Ben had ripped him off and that he really hated Ben."

On cross-examination James Blatt had Annie Blackford
speak more about Ben Markowitz and all the trouble he
had caused. Blackford said, "Ben started a lot of fights.
He seemed like he was under the influence a lot. Drugs
and alcohol. I didn't want to get involved with his drama.
I considered him a very violent person. A lot of people
were afraid of him."

As far as Jesse James Hollywood went, Blackford said,
"I enjoyed his company. He was funny. He was respectful
to me. I liked being around him."

Then Blatt wanted to know who else had been sitting
outside the courtroom while Annie Blackford was waiting
to testify as a witness. Blackford said that Jesse James

Hollywood's old girlfriend, Michelle Lasher, had been in the same small room adjacent to the courtroom.

Blatt hinted at machinations by the prosecution for having both young women there at the same time. Certainly, Michelle Lasher could not have been too pleased if she knew that Annie Blackford had "casual sex," as she put it, with Jesse Hollywood during the time that Michelle and Jesse were still girlfriend and boyfriend.

On redirect Almgren asked Blackford, "Did we ever tell you to strike up a conversation with Michelle (Lasher) while she was in the waiting room?"

"No," Annie replied.

Right after Annie Blackford's testimony, it was Michelle Lasher's turn. Twenty-eight years old now, she still had girlish good looks, with dark hair and dark eyes. When she sat down at the witness stand, everyone in the courtroom could see just how petite she was. The top of Michelle's head barely showed above the lectern in front of her.

Lasher began by talking about speaking with detectives in the year 2000, her testimony at the grand jury and at Jesse Rugge's trial. Michelle mentioned that she had not testified at either Hoyt's or Pressley's trial. As far as guns went, Michelle admitted, Jesse Hollywood kept a shotgun under their bed at the Reseda home, but she claimed it had been there because it was a bad neighborhood, and not for protecting his marijuana operations. In fact, Michelle declared, as she had done since the year 2000, when first spoken to by detectives, she had never seen Jesse Hollywood dealing drugs, and hadn't known about that aspect of his life.

Shown the TEC-9 that had been used to murder Nick Markowitz, Michelle was asked if that was the same weapon that Jesse Hollywood had owned. She replied, "It looks similar."

Almgren asked, "Did they (Jesse and his friends) all handle it?"

Michelle threw him a curveball by saying, "I saw that TEC-9 in Hoyt's grandparents' garage."

"What?"Almgren responded. "That TEC-9 wasn't underneath your bed at the Cohasset Street home?"

"No."

The topic of guns went around and around, Almgren obviously not believing much of what Michelle was now saying. She became so upset that she was on the edge of tears, and declared loudly, "I never saw him (Jesse Hollywood) with that gun." This was at variance with what she had just said a few minutes before, concerning Jesse and all his friends handling guns.

Asked about meeting Richard Hoeflinger and his girlfriend at the Embassy Suites, in one of Jesse Hollywood's drug deals, Michelle firmly denied ever having been at that meeting. Asked if she loved Jesse Hollywood in the year 2000, Michelle answered, "Yes, and I'm still in love with him!"

Michelle became more and more upset as Almgren's questions covered the crucial days of August 6, 2000, into later August 2000. She often replied to questions by saying, "I don't recall" or "I don't remember." Almgren asked her more than once if she knew the penalty to her if she lied or was deceptive on the stand. Michelle answered that she did.

Asked about meeting Jesse Rugge for lunch in Santa Barbara, on August 7, 2000, where Jesse Hollywood allegedly approached Rugge with an offer of money to kill Nick Markowitz, Michelle said she didn't recall that lunch at all. And when asked about seeing Nick at Jesse Rugge's house after the alleged lunch, Michelle kept repeating that she hadn't seen Nick there. In exasperation, after being asked about this several times, she said in a very loud voice, "I don't know Nick! I've never seen him!"

Almgren was more than a little bit skeptical, and said,

"So you don't remember a remark by Jesse Hollywood that day, 'Let's just tie the kid up, throw him in the trunk and go to dinner'?"

"No!" Michelle said with heat and anger.

"When did you arrive at Casey Sheehan's house on August eighth?"Almgren asked.

"About six or seven P.M."

"Did Jesse Hollywood make a phone call from there?"

"I don't remember."

"Why did Jesse borrow Casey Sheehan's car?"

"He told Casey that he was going home to take a shower and change."

"Then why didn't he just borrow your car?"

"I don't know."

"How long was Jesse Hollywood gone from Casey Sheehan's house?"

"Maybe about a half hour or forty-five minutes."

"Did Mr. Hollywood tell you at any time that Mr. Sheehan's car was involved in a murder?"

"I don't remember."

Asked about her birthday dinner at the Outback Steakhouse, Michelle said that she, Jesse Hollywood and Casey Sheehan arrived there about 7:30 or 8:00 P.M. on August 8.

Almgren asked, "What, if anything, did Jesse Hollywood tell Casey Sheehan about the situation regarding Nick Markowitz?"

Michelle replied, "He said that the situation had 'become unwound.'"

This, of course, had two different connotations, depending upon how you looked at it. In one sense "unwound" meant that the whole situation had gone out of control. In the other point of view, it meant that things had been all wound up, but now they were "unwound" and better.

Michelle spoke of getting ready to go to Palm Springs, and of being with Jesse on August 10, when he leased a Lincoln Town Car. Later that day, Michelle said, she took off with her friends Joy and Edie, who were going to a modeling convention in Palm Springs. According to Michelle, Jesse Hollywood drove his new Lincoln down to Palm Springs on August 11, and she and Jesse spent the night in the motel room with her friends. Since it was so crowded in there, Michelle said, she and Jesse moved to the Palm Springs Hilton on August 12. Asked about Jesse Hollywood's demeanor in Palm Springs, she said, "He was acting kind of panicky. I asked why he was so upset. He wouldn't say. But he was upset the whole time there."

Regarding their sudden trip to Las Vegas, Michelle said that she didn't know why they were going there, other than Jesse was very agitated, and had threatened to leave her off in a bad part of town if she didn't go along with him on the journey. As far as who paid for the room at the Bellagio in Las Vegas, Michelle said that Jesse gave her cash, but she was the one who went to the front desk and showed them her credit card for security.

This theme of paying for hotel rooms also included Colorado. Michelle admitted that she was the one who went to the front desk at the hotel in Colorado, while Jesse stayed in the car. She even said that she put the room under a fake name of Sue Michelle, said that the car she was in was a blue Cadillac and gave a false home address.

Hans Almgren was very skeptical that on a ride of 800 miles to Colorado Springs from Palm Springs, Jesse Hollywood had not *once* told her the reason for their sudden and unexpected journey. But Michelle stuck to her claims that he never did tell her the real reason. She said, "I asked him what was wrong, but he wouldn't tell me. I wasn't going to push him."

Michelle admitted to lying to her parents that she had gone to Colorado with Jesse. Instead, she told them she had gone to San Diego with her girlfriends. Asked why she had done this, Michelle said, "Because I didn't think they would be comfortable with my going that far away."

As soon as Michelle flew back home, she was, of course,

met by police detectives at her parents' home. Yet, even there she admitted to giving out a string of lies to the detectives in the initial interview with them. She told them she had just gotten back from a trip with her girlfriends to San Diego. Asked by them why she was coming home in a taxi, she lied and said that her friend's car had broken down near Highway 101 and Interstate 405. Michelle added, "I was afraid of the police." And then she admitted, "I was also protecting Jesse."

By now, Michelle was speaking through tears with an often quavering voice. Her moods swung from agitated to mournful to angry. When asked, "Did you want Jesse to escape capture?" she replied, "Yes!" Then she added, "I would rather have lied to the police than help them capture him, no matter what he had done."

Michelle even admitted that she had gone with Jesse Hollywood when he went to see Stephen Hogg on the afternoon of August 8. But she declared she had not gotten out of the car, and didn't overhear what Jesse and Stephen Hogg had said. Asked if Jesse told her later in the car what had occurred, she replied that he hadn't.

One thing Michelle did testify to was that on leaving Colorado, Jesse had given her a blue accordion-type folder filled with documents that she was supposed to give to Stephen Hogg when she got back to California. She never got an opportunity to do so. The blue folder was seized, along with her luggage, when she got to her parents' home on August 17.

It wasn't until August 18 that Michelle said that she phoned the police department and started telling them some of the truth. She told them that Jesse Hollywood had a Lincoln Town Car—though she lied about the color being blue instead of white—and that it was a rental.

When James Blatt began questioning Michelle on cross, that was when she calmed down. But her moments of calm were short-lived. When asked what it was like when the police first contacted her on August 17, Michelle said through tears, "They started accusing me of things. And accusing Jesse of murder. They said it was all his fault. They said they were just going to shoot him if they saw him!"

It wasn't until August 18, 2000, Michelle declared, that she started realizing the gravity of the situation. It was at that point that she started telling detectives some of the truth. After that experience, Michelle declared, "I didn't get out of my bed for a week. I was absolutely traumatized."

To allay rumors that Jesse Hollywood might have had Nick killed because he was Jewish—and Jesse was a racist—Michelle said that she herself was Jewish. She stated that not once had she ever heard Jesse Hollywood say anything derogatory about Jews.

Of Ryan Hoyt, Michelle said, "Ryan was always making up stories to try and impress people. He just didn't have any stability in his life. He would just hang around on the couch, doing nothing. He messed up anything he ever tried. He would go away for days and then come back and say he was being chased by gang members. You could not count on him for anything."

Michelle said that she moved out of Jesse Hollywood's house after Ben Markowtiz started hanging around all the time. Michelle related, "He was constantly selling drugs, and I felt like I was in danger there. I was afraid of him because he was crazy. He put everyone in dangerous situations. I knew through other people that Ben was ripping off drug dealers."

Of Ben's phone message threats, Michelle testified, "He left one message where he said to Jesse, 'I'm going to kill you, your family and your girlfriend! You'd better keep a gun with you!'"

Michelle added, "Because of all the threats, we were going to move to Malibu. Just Jesse and me, and not tell anyone our new address."

Asked by Blatt about Nick Markowitz, Michelle claimed—as she had with the prosecution—that she had never met Nick. In fact, she now said, "I didn't even know that Ben had a little brother."

As far as knowing something was wrong between Jesse Hollywood and Ryan Hoyt, Michelle said, she first got an inkling of this at Casey Sheehan's house on August 10, 2000. And she said it was in the afternoon and not at Ryan Hoyt's birthday party, which, she claimed, she did not attend. Michelle stated that on August 10 she was talking with Casey Sheehan when she suddenly heard Jesse cussing out Ryan Hoyt. Michelle said she heard Jesse Hollywood say, "Are you crazy!"

Michelle added, "It was at that point that Jesse panicked. He was from like zero to a hundred from that point on. The blood vessels on his eyes got red. I didn't want to know what it was all about. I didn't want to push him over the edge."

And then in a moment of absolute unexpected vehemence and anger, Michelle pointed at Hans Almgren and DA investigator Paul Kimes, and declared, "They told me if I didn't get up here and lie, they would charge me with murder!"

Michelle could not have started a buzz more powerful than if she had just swatted a hornet's nest. To accuse Almgren and Kimes of telling her to lie on the stand was akin to a declaration of war. Such acts could not only cost them their jobs, but put them in the way of prison time. But if these words were a new set of lies, then she was in more jeopardy than she may have realized.

Even James Blatt seemed stunned by what had just come out of Michelle Lasher's mouth, and for a moment he was at a loss for words. Perhaps realizing that any more unexpected "revelations" could hurt Michelle Lasher's credibility even more, Blatt soon rested on cross-examination.

22

A BUMPY ROAD

To say that Hans Almgren was "steamed" on redirect did not do justice to the word. But it was a kind of slow-burn steam, and he began his questioning by asking Michelle Lasher, "Who was there at that meeting on Friday with you?" (The meeting, just before she was to take the stand happened only a few days previously.)

Michelle stated that it was herself, her attorney, Hans Almgren and Investigator Paul Kimes.

Almgren asked, "What was one of the first things I told you at that meeting?"

"I can't recall," Michelle replied.

"Do you remember me telling you to tell the truth?"

"You had me confused," she responded.

"I brought the immunity papers there and you were extremely upset with me. And we spoke for about five minutes. When you walked out, you were extremely angry with me. Correct?"

Michelle said, "I was very nervous. And I was confused

as to what you were saying to me because I thought, you thought, I was refusing to testify."

Almgren then had Michelle read the paper she had signed. After she was done, he asked, "You were very agitated with me then?"

"Yes. I was afraid you were going to do a psychological attack on me."

"Didn't I ask you to slow down and read it? And you signed the immunity paper and threw it back at me. I told you then it was for your own protection. Didn't I tell you in front of Mr. Gregory (her lawyer) and Mr. Kimes that I was concerned about you lying in front of this jury?"

Michelle spit words back at Almgren. "What I heard you do was tell me to lie!"

"I told you to lie?" Almgren asked with disbelief.

In an almost hysterical, shrill voice, Michelle replied, "Yes! I was threatened by Ron Zonen in 2000. My rights were not given to me. I was threatened by lawyers! I'm so traumatized, I'll never be the same! I've been through so much, I'll never be the same!"

Even Judge Hill's admonition for Michelle to calm down and compose herself fell on deaf ears. By now, she was hysterical, and without any question pending, Michelle blurted out, with a mixture of tears, anger and emotion, "I'm very afraid! I'm just sitting here to tell the truth! I'm scared!"

Finally Judge Hill sent the jury out as Michelle Lasher had a breakdown on the witness stand. Her body shook with convulsive sobs and she buried her face in her hands. For many veteran court observers, they had never seen a witness have such a complete meltdown.

On the morning of Tuesday, June 2, 2009, Michelle Lasher was back on the witness stand, and more composed. But she was definitely not happy to be there. When Judge

Hill addressed her and said, "Good morning, Ms. Lasher," her reply to him was "Hey."

It took less than ten minutes for Michelle's composure to erode. To a question about the police first speaking with her, she said once again, "They told me if they found Jesse, they would shoot him down like a dog!"

And then in a panicked voice, Michelle added, "I can't do this all day again, today! I've been harassed for nine years. I can't do this again!"

Judge Hill responded, "Ms. Lasher, you have to take a deep breath. But you have to answer questions."

Even as she answered new questions, Michelle's hand fluttered around above her head like a distressed bird. It appeared that at any moment she might jump out of her chair.

Asked about the detectives she dealt with in August 2000, Michelle said, "I spoke with a female detective and a male detective. I was sitting in a room and a lot of people were coming and going. The interview lasted for eight hours."

By that point Michelle was practically spitting her words at Hans Almgren, and Judge Hill leaned over toward her and said, "Ms. Lasher, we are not going to have you behave in an insolent manner, or we'll have to bring you back tomorrow."

Almgren asked, "Would you consider yourself to be Jesse Hollywood's girlfriend to this day?"

Michelle responded, "Yes."

"Did you ever call any police and say that Santa Barbara Sheriff's Office deputies had threatened to shoot Jesse Hollywood?"

In a very loud tone, Michelle replied, "No! I was afraid of the police!"

Judge Hill had Almgren move on to a different topic, since Michelle was nearly becoming unglued by that point.

Almgren asked, "What was in that blue accordion-type envelope that Jesse gave you in Colorado?"

"I don't know," she said. "I didn't look inside."

At one point Almgren asked if Michelle was suffering from post-traumatic stress disorder (PTSD). Before he went any further, Judge Hill spoke up and said, "Are you sure you want to go down this road about PTSD?"

Almgren looked momentarily surprised, then answered, "Your Honor, it sounds like I don't."

This was greeted by laughter in the gallery, and even among some of the members of the jury.

Almgren moved on to a different area of questioning, but like a recalcitrant child, Michelle crossed her arms and refused to answer the question before her. Instead, she said, "By now, my brain is dead, sir!"

Almgren just shook his head and asked, "Have any police agencies, besides the one you mentioned, threatened you?"

"Yes!" Michelle nearly shouted. "When they were at my house with a search warrant!"

James Blatt started on recross to explore this area of alleged threats by police officers upon Michelle Lasher. Blatt asked, "Tell me about the search-warrant search at your parents' house."

By now, Michelle was crying without cease. "They pulled me naked out of bed! And they had a gun to my head!"

At that point she completely broke down, sobbing and wailing. Even Judge Hill could see that asking her further questions was useless. Finally after days of grueling, and often frustrating and chaotic questioning, Michelle Lasher was through as a witness.

Since Michelle Lasher had accused Hans Almgren and Investigator Paul Kimes of telling her to lie to the jury,

Almgren had Kimes on the stand as his next witness. Almgren got Kimes to speak about the meeting with Lasher just before she was a witness in the present trial.

Almgren asked Kimes, "Did I ask her any questions about this case?"

"No," Kimes replied.

"Is it true you didn't appreciate her throwing the immunity document and pen at me?"

"Yes."

Alex Kessel asked Kimes on cross, "Did you take any notes at that meeting?"

He answered that he hadn't.

"Did anyone ask if she understood what she was signing?"

Kimes replied, "She was asked if she wanted to talk to her lawyer before signing the document, and she said no."

"Was she told that if she lied to this jury, she was in a lot of trouble?"

Kimes said, "She was told that if she lied, she would be charged."

"How did she react to that?"

"She was upset."

At least the next regular witness after Michelle Lasher was as composed as Lasher had been erratic and emotional. The witness was Jesse Hollywood's old Colorado boyhood friend William Jacques. He told the prosecution of how Jesse Hollywood suddenly showed up in August 2000, and related what happened then. Almgren asked Jacques, "Would you say that Jesse Hollywood was a follower or a leader?"

Jacques replied, "A leader."

"Why?"

"Because people would follow him. Even on the baseball field, he was a leader."

Stephen Hogg was a very important witness for both the defense and prosecution. It was the prosecution's theory of the case that Jesse Hollywood decided to have Nick Markowitz murdered after he learned from Hogg that kidnapping for ransom could get a person life in prison.

Hogg began by testifying that even before the important meeting of August 8, 2000, Jesse Hollywood had come to see him concerning all the problems he was having with Ben Markowitz. Jesse often referred to Ben in that meeting as "Bugsy," modeled after the name of Jewish gangster Bugsy Siegel.

Hogg said, "Jesse spoke with a lot of fear about Ben. He said this guy was crazy. A gang member. He'd damaged Jesse's property and killed one of his dogs. Jesse didn't want his parents to know about all of this, because his younger brother was scheduled for heart surgery. I agreed with Jesse that it was a good idea for him to move. After that meeting I didn't suggest that he go to the police about Ben. I've learned over the years that restraining orders aren't worth the paper they're written on.

"Then on August 8, 2000, in the afternoon, Jesse was suddenly at my door. We went in the backyard and he said, 'Friends of mine have snatched Bugsy's brother. They have him far away from where we are.'

"Jesse didn't say where they had the boy. I asked him a series of questions, but he wouldn't really answer. So I didn't press him. One of my questions was 'Is he tied up?' Jesse said no. He didn't give me any specifics, but everything he said was [as] if it was currently going on. He didn't tell me the person's name, but he seemed to know who the person was.

"Jesse did say that after the initial kidnapping, the boy

was smoking pot and playing video games with the others. He was partying with these guys. Even with that, I thought the situation could become serious. Something might change these guys' attitude, and that Jesse's mere presence could get him indicted.

"When kids tell you that their friends are doing something, there's a good chance that they are involved as well. In my mind I thought this was a possibility with Jesse. At the moment I was just factoring in what he said.

"I suggested that Jesse should go with me to contact the police. He said, 'No, they'll kill my family.' By this, I thought he meant Bugsy and his friends.

"Jesse was very agitated. He would sit down and then stand up. He smoked three cigarettes while he was there. And he was only there for ten to fifteen minutes. Because of what Jesse said about the kid smoking pot and partying with the others, I didn't think he was in grave danger at the moment. I'd never heard of a kid being kidnapped and partying with his kidnappers.

"I started questioning Jesse very specifically about what he had communicated to the other people. I didn't ask specifically if he had been at the initial kidnapping, but I got the idea that he had been. I told him, 'If your friends hurt this kid, or ask for money to release him, they could get life.' I was trying to stress to him how his friends could be in serious, serious trouble."

At this point Jesse Hollywood did not take off in a hurry, according to Hogg now. This was in variance to what Ron Zonen and others had been stating as a fact, for years.

Instead of running off, Hogg said, Jesse Hollywood was still agitated, but talking to him at that point. Hogg said, "We were sitting there, and I told him again that it would be best if we went to the police. Once again he said, 'Don't you understand? They'll kill my parents.'"

Then Hogg added, "Just before he left, Jesse said to me, 'I'm going to make those guys take him back, or put him back.'"

Joshua Lynn said, "Why are you bringing that up for the first time now? That comment has never come up before."

Hogg said that it had, and that he'd mentioned that comment from Jesse to one of the DA investigators in the spring of 2009.

Lynn asked, "Did Jesse Hollywood tell you why these people took Bugsy's brother?"

Hogg replied, "I didn't ask."

This was important. If Hogg had said that Jesse told him that the "others" had taken the kid because of a debt owed by Ben Markowitz, then that was kidnapping for ransom. And it was almost a foregone conclusion by now that the jury would realize that Jesse Hollywood had been part of the initial kidnapping. Any mention of a debt being owed would have placed Jesse Hollywood right in the middle of a kidnapping for ransom, and it could cost him the life in prison that he had been so worried about in his conversation with Stephen Hogg on August 8, 2000.

As to what Hogg did after Jesse Hollywood left that day, Hogg said that either he contacted Jack Hollywood, or Jack Hollywood contacted him. He couldn't remember the exact sequence of events on that score. But Hogg said that he realized how serious the situation could be, and he tried paging Jesse four or so more times. Hogg said, "Jesse had never failed to answer my pages before. But he did this time. I quit paging him around seven P.M."

Lynn asked, "After you quit paging him, did you call the police?"

Hogg responded, "No."

On cross, asked if it was Jesse Hollywood who brought up the possible sentencing for aggravated kidnapping, Hogg replied, "No, I was the one who brought it up."

"You weren't advising him because the boy was being held for money?"

"No. I was just trying to show Jesse the seriousness of the problem."

"When you told Jesse about the penalty, how did he react?"

"He really didn't react at all right then. The reaction was later."

Once again, this went against the common perception in the newspapers and on television news that once Jesse Hollywood heard about the possible sentence for aggravated kidnapping, he split right away. That scenario was certainly what Chas Saulsbury had indicated.

To counteract Saulsbury's further claims of wrongdoing, Kessel asked Hogg, "Did you ever advise Jesse that because he was in trouble, he should kill the kid?"

Hogg emphatically answered, "I did not!"

"Did you ever advise him to commit a crime or further a crime?"

"No."

Lynn asked Hogg numerous questions on redirect, and there was one objection after another from the defense table.

Lynn started to ask, "Extortion is the same as asking for ransom, isn't that—"

Another objection came, and Lynn snapped, "Can I finish just one question, Your Honor!"

Judge Hill told the defense to wait until Lynn had made complete and full questions before objecting.

So Lynn asked Hogg, "If you had told the police about the situation that you've described to us here, you don't think they would have done anything?"

Hogg replied, "I don't know what they could have done. I didn't know where the boy was."

Since Jesse Rugge and Ryan Hoyt were not going to testify, and Chas Saulsbury, Brian Affronti and Richard

Hoeflinger had been beaten up pretty badly by the defense, the prosecution hoped that Graham Pressley would be their star witness. In the end they would get more than they had hoped for from Graham. No longer the geeky-looking "pothead," of August 2000, Graham now looked like a young, albeit thin, Johnny Depp. With his curly dark hair, stylish clothes, and aviator sunglasses dangling from his collar, Graham exuded a "Hollywood-like aura" that many of the other witnesses had lacked.

Pressley also exuded a calm confidence, so lacking in Saulsbury. Graham started off by saying that he hadn't known Jesse Hollywood before the summer of 2000. It was that year that Graham said he started hanging out a lot with Jesse Rugge and smoking marijuana every day. Most of the information Pressley gave about the crucial days of August 7, 8 and 9, 2000, was not new, except to this jury, who was hearing it for the first time. Pressley's delivery was both calm and convincing.

Graham spoke of the important topic of Jesse Rugge telling him that Jesse Hollywood had offered Rugge money to kill Nick Markowitz. And, of course, as he'd revealed before, Pressley had passed that information on to Kelly Carpenter and Natasha Adams. In this version Graham said that "Natasha immediately confronted Rugge. She wasn't crying or argumentative, but she was very serious when she confronted him.

"Rugge said, 'Yeah, I've had it! I'm putting Nick on a bus or a train.'

"After this, everyone heaved a collective sigh of relief. Things went back to normal."

Lynn asked, "Why didn't you go to the police then?"

Graham replied, "It was because at the time I was engaged in illegal activities. I avoided law enforcement like the plague."

Pressley spoke of how he, Rugge, the two girls and Nathan Appleton went to the Lemon Tree Inn and added,

"It wasn't unusual then for us to rent a motel room, party and go swimming in the pool."

Pressley testified to smoking marijuana with the others at the room and going swimming with Nick. Asked about this, Graham said that he and Nick met some girls there and joined them in the Jacuzzi. Asked why he and Nick went back to the room, Pressley said, "No more girls."

As to why Graham Pressley stayed at the Lemon Tree Inn, when Kelly Carpenter, Natasha Adams and Nathan Appleton left at about 10:30 P.M. on August 8, Graham said, "Rugge turned to me and said, 'Hey, why don't you stick around. We'll smoke some more weed.'"

For Graham Pressley, the decision to smoke more weed was the costliest of his life. It still haunted him nine years later.

Pressley answered questions about Hoyt coming to the Lemon Tree, and seeing Hoyt there with a gun in a blue duffel bag. Once again, as he had done in other trials, Graham spoke of being ordered to go with Hoyt up to Lizard's Mouth and ordered to dig a hole there. He repeated about Hoyt telling him to do it quickly, "or else." And once again, Pressley spoke of Nick's last ride up to Lizard's Mouth, and being walked up the trail by Rugge, Hoyt and himself. What varied from his previous testimony was Pressley's very detailed account of walking up the trail until they heard a young man and woman coming down the trail. These two were in good spirits, and as they passed the four young men, who had moved off the trail to let them by, the couple said "good-bye"as they passed. Pressley said that he had been sitting on a rock, and at that moment "I lost it. I refused to go any farther. I knew what was going to happen." According to Graham, the others moved on, and he could see the beam of Hoyt's flashlight as they moved up the trail. And then they were lost in the darkness. Fifteen minutes after they left him, Pressley heard a quick succession of gunshots.

Lynn asked Pressley what he did in the days after the

murder of Nick Markowitz. Graham said, "I smoked a lot of weed after Nick was killed. I lied when I saw Kelly Carpenter and Natasha Adams. I lied about what had happened. I told them Nick was okay. That he was still alive. I was afraid that if I told the truth, they would come after me. I knew these guys could easily find out where I lived."

Asked who "they" were, Pressley answered, "Hoyt and Hollywood."

Then he testified, "Three or four days after I left the Lemon Tree, I saw Jesse Rugge. I can't remember everything about which day that was because it was such a blur. Rugge invited me to a barbecue, and Nick's body hadn't been found yet. The barbecue was at the same park where I had talked to Natasha and Kelly. I went there and found out from Rugge where I fit in with his friends Ryan Hoyt and Jesse Hollywood. He told me that I would be in danger from them if I told anyone about what had happened.

"Rugge gave me some details about the killing of Nick at that time. He was very nervous, very intoxicated, but very clear. Then Rugge asked me if I was going to be cool about all of this. If I wasn't, then I might become a liability."

Because Judge Hill had let in some information from Graham Pressley to the jury that Alex Kessel thought was not appropriate, Kessel, on cross, asked for a mistrial. Kessel said, "Mr. Hollywood cannot get a fair trial." This motion was summarily dismissed by Judge Hill, and Kessel continued his cross-examination of Pressley. In his usual style Kessel began firing off a rapid succession of questions.

Kessel: Did you lie at your other trials?
Pressley: No.

Kessel:	Did you ever intend to kill Nick?
Pressley:	No.
Kessel:	You were afraid of Hoyt and Hollywood. Correct?
Pressley:	Yes.
Kessel:	And you were so terrified that you said you weren't going to tell anyone?
Pressley:	Yes.
Kessel:	Then you just lied to this jury?
Pressley:	No.
Kessel:	Oh? You told Kelly and Natasha about them after Nick was dead.
Pressley:	I didn't say anything incriminating about them.
Kessel:	Didn't you tell them that Jesse James Hollywood came up to the Lemon Tree Inn? You said that in your other trial. You said he came there with his TEC-9 and started slapping Nick around.
Pressley:	I don't recall saying that.

Kessel's rapid-fire questions had turned Chas Saulsbury into a rattled, quivering witness. It got to a point where it seemed that Chas would answer almost anything in the way he perceived Kessel wanted it answered, just to get off the witness stand. But this tactic did not work with Graham Pressley. Despite Kessel's animated nature, Pressley stood his ground, and he calmly answered each and every question. The person who seemed to become visibly upset as this went on was Judge Hill. Numerous times he told Alex Kessel to keep his voice down. In fact, it got so bad that at one point Kessel was practically shouting at Pressley, Lynn was shouting at Kessel, and Judge Hill had enough. He cautioned both lawyers that they were out of line, and to keep their voices down.

Despite all this heated testimony, Lynn had to have been glad at the way Graham Pressley was conducting himself. Perhaps originally, Chas Saulsbury was to have been the prosecution's star witness. But in the end it was Pressley who filled that role.

Even by the third day of testimony, Kessel could not sway Pressley's resolve or calm demeanor. When Kessel said to Pressley, "You probably watched Hoyt pull the trigger, didn't you?"

Pressley replied, "No, I didn't. I stand by what I've always said."

Not as crucial as Pressley had been, or subjected to the same barrage of questioning, Natasha Adams-Young had few new things to add to what she already had testified to in other trials. She did, however, stick to her story of talking with both Graham Pressley and Jesse Rugge on August 8, 2000, and said that Rugge had told her about being offered $2,500 from Jesse Hollywood to kill Nick Markowitz.

By the time Ben Markowitz was called as a witness, the courtroom was packed in anticipation of not only what he might say, but how he might act. And they had a lot to ponder, when it was learned, outside the presence of the jury, that Ben had contacted Jack Hollywood on the day before he was to testify. The defense was furious about this, and they wanted Ben severely reprimanded by Judge Hill.

Hill did tell Ben not to contact any members of the Holly-wood family, and Ben said that he would follow the judge's orders. When the jurors finally did see Ben Markowitz, he looked nothing like the intimidating skinhead of the year 2000. Wearing blue jeans and a sports jacket, he conducted himself with restraint on the stand. Speaking of the way he used to be, Ben said, "I was a dickhead back then. I walked around with a chip on my shoulder, and if you looked at me sideways, I'd kick your ass."

Unlike many others, Ben said that Jesse Hollywood got his marijuana from his father, Jack. Ben declared that Jack Hollywood supplied Jesse with "good-quality bud." And as far as the situation that started the feud between himself and Jesse, Ben now said that he didn't drive down alone to San Diego to get money owed to Jesse Hollywood. Ben said that Jesse accompanied him and they took guns and baseball bats. Ben added that the person in San Diego was actually one of his friends, so he tried defusing the situation. Ben declared that this friend told them he knew someone who sold Ecstasy, and he gave them information who the guy was, in exchange for being let off the hook as far as his debt went. Ben then added that he and Jesse cooked up a plan to rob the dealer of his Ecstasy.

In carrying out that plan, they met the Ecstasy dealer, took the pills, then "scrammed" without paying him. It was at that point that Ben got greedy. He said that instead of just handing the pills over to Jesse, worth about $2,000, Ben decided to try and sell them himself. He expected to make $4,000—$2,000, which he would give to Jesse, and $2,000, which he could keep himself. Much to Ben's surprise, however, the pills turned out to be fakes, and now he owed Jesse Hollywood $2,000.

As in his past renditions, Ben told of giving Jesse Hollywood $600, which he had on hand, borrowed $200 more from his dad, and gave that to Jesse, and still owed him $1,200. Ben said he had every intention of paying Jesse the rest, until Jesse and Michelle Lasher showed up at the restaurant where Ben's girlfriend worked, and stiffed her on the bill. "It all went sour from there," Ben said.

Ben admitted that he left several threatening phone messages with Hollywood, including one where he said, "You're a fucking little punk, and you're not gonna get a dime from me!"

Then something else new came up. Ben said that after this phone call, he returned from work one day to see Jesse Hollywood and Ryan Hoyt standing outside his apartment building. Knowing that Jesse often traveled around with a gun, Ben took off without returning home. Within a day he moved out of that apartment. He also did one more thing—he bought himself a gun. Then he left a message with Jesse Hollywood, "I know where you live. I know where your family lives. Two can play this game!"

Some new information came up as well. Ben said that after Nick was murdered, he kept on living his wild lifestyle. After the murder he committed a robbery on a couple, was caught and convicted, and served a year in prison. Not long after he got out, he said, he assaulted Casey Sheehan for being part of the group that had killed his brother.

On cross-examination Blatt got to the robbery incident that had occurred in December 2000. Blatt asked Ben if he'd drawn a gun on the people, and he said that he had. Then Blatt asked, "Did you make that couple take off their clothes?"

"Yes," Ben replied. "But I stole drugs from them, not money."

"Why did you have them take off their clothes?"

"I did it to embarrass them."

"Oh, it wasn't enough to just take their drugs? You wanted to beat them down, didn't you?"

"Yes," Ben replied.

As far as the TEC-9 went, Blatt wanted to know why Ben said in one of the previous trials that he had seen that gun at Ryan Hoyt's grandparents' house. Now he was claiming he never saw it there. Ben said that his recollection of things about the year 2000 was better now than it had been during that trial.

All in all, Ben had conducted himself with restraint on the stand. There were none of the crazy and dangerous antics that he was known for in his previous years.

Casey Sheehan was a witness important to both sides. Sheehan testified that he remembered Jesse Hollywood and Michelle Lasher coming to his house on the afternoon of August 8, 2000. Asked if he knew who Hollywood loaned his Honda Accord to that evening, Sheehan said no. He didn't learn about who had it until later, he declared. As far as comments Hollywood made at the Outback Steakhouse later that evening, Sheehan said that Jesse talked a little about Nick Markowitz being in Santa Barbara and the situation there. And then, according to Sheehan, Jesse Hollywood said, "Everything with Nick is good. The situation has been taken care of." This comment came sometime between 10:00 P.M. and midnight, when Nick was still alive.

Joshua Lynn got Sheehan to admit that he saw three guns at Jesse Hollywood's house, and one of them was a TEC-9. (Yet, during the defense phase, Sheehan contradicted this statement and said that he only saw a gun bag there.) Once it was time for Lynn to ask questions on redirect, he wanted to know why Sheehan had changed his story. Finally Lynn got Sheehan to admit, once again, that he had seen guns at Jesse Hollywood's house, and not just a gun bag.

In fact, Sheehan seemed to be so "pro–Jesse Hollywood" that Lynn got Judge Hill to categorize him as an "adverse witness."

Kessel asked what Sheehan recalled of Jesse Hollywood blowing up at Ryan Hoyt on August 9, 2000. Sheehan said that he remembered Hoyt saying, "We fucked up!" And by that, Sheehan thought that Hoyt meant himself and Jesse

Rugge. The statement, according to Sheehan, did not include Jesse Hollywood.

Kessel asked, "Did anyone ever tell you that Jesse Hollywood ordered either Jesse Rugge or Ryan Hoyt to kill Nick Markowitz?"

"No," Sheehan replied.

Done with Hollywood's friends and associates on the witness stand, Joshau Lynn next questioned Lisa Hemman, a crime scene investigator for the Santa Barbara County Sheriff's Department. She had not only helped uncover Nick's body, but had taken numerous photographs of the crime scene as well. Hemman spoke of recovering a TEC-9 semiautomatic pistol from beneath the boy's body. She was also allowed to show some photos of a deceased Nick, despite the strong objections from both Blatt and Kessel.

Next was Marilyn Harris, a forensic investigator for JPMorgan Chase & Company. Harris testified that Jesse Hollywood had closed out six accounts on August 8, 2000, for the amount of $25,250. He eventually wrote two checks for a lease on a new Lincoln Town Car. Lynn made a point that all this activity took place just before, and just after, Nick Markowitz died. Lynn suggested that it was done by Jesse Hollywood because he was already thinking about fleeing the area.

Dr. Robert Anthony, a forensic pathologist from Santa Barbara County, spoke of all the wounds that Nick Markowitz had received. Using a prop, where the bullets had entered Nick's body, Anthony showed the jurors the angle each bullet had taken. He also pointed out numerous wounds that would have been fatal to Nick.

Scott Perry was the next witness on the stand. He was general manager of the Lemon Tree Inn. Perry testified that it was Jesse Rugge who registered at the Lemon Tree on August 8, 2000, and paid $152 for the room. Perry also noted that between 6:01 and 9:55 P.M. on that date, there had been sixteen phone calls made from the room.

With the conclusion of Scott Perry's testimony, the prosecution was done with its lengthy witness list. It had indeed been a mixed bag for them. Many witnesses had done credible jobs, Chas Saulsbury had been a disaster, but Michelle Lasher, as an "adverse witness," had actually helped them, but not in the way she might have hoped.

Rumors were rife before the defense called a single witness that movie stars would be taking the stand. James Blatt let it be known to Judge Hill that he wanted to call not only Nick Cassavetes as a witness, but Justin Timberlake and other actors as well, who had been in the movie *Alpha Dog*. In the case of Timberlake, Blatt noted that Timberlake had gone to see Jesse Rugge in prison before the filming of the movie began, and Timberlake had talked to Rugge there. Judge Hill took this under advisement and then ruled that he didn't see the relevance of either Nick Cassavetes or Justin Timberlake testifying.

Thwarted in this area, the defense next wanted to put Jesse Hollywood's seventy-year-old second cousin, Jerry Hollywood, on the stand. But because of some new information that Jerry Hollywood supposedly had to tell, he was questioned first outside the hearing of the jurors.

Jerry Hollywood had been a real estate agent in August 2000, and Jesse Hollywood came over to his office to sign some papers concerning his house on Cohasset Street on August 8, 2000. (This occurred before Jesse's meeting with Stephen Hogg that day.) The real point of contention now was that Jerry Hollywood said that Jesse told him a little bit about some friends who had kidnapped a boy. Joshua Lynn asked if Jesse had told him that story, why hadn't Jerry phoned the police? Jerry answered that the details were vague, and "I wasn't in his (Jesse's) world."

Jerry continued that on the night of August 8, Jesse phoned him about the Cohasset Street house once again, and Jerry asked how the situation was with the kidnapped boy. According to Jerry, Jesse told him that the situation had been resolved. The boy was going home.

Looking into this matter, Joshua Lynn told Judge Hill that the defense investigator had "helped" Jerry Hollywood remember this alleged phone call. Jerry Hollywood admitted that statements he made concerning August 8 were accurate in a report, "but they just weren't my own words."

Judge Hill finally said that he would let the jury hear what Jerry Hollywood had to say, and they could decide if he was telling the truth or not. Before Jerry Hollywood got to testify, however, Joshua Lynn questioned defense investigator Ashley Fauria. Lynn was very dubious that Fauria had only "helped" Jerry Hollywood "recall" events of August 8, 2000. Lynn was adamant that Fauria had essentially put ideas into Jerry Hollywood's head about his interactions with Jesse Hollywood on that key date. Fauria, however, said that the only thing used to jolt Jerry Hollywood's memory was mentioning the date of August 8, 2000.

Once Jerry Hollywood actually testified, he said that at 10:22 P.M. on August 8, 2000, he received a phone call from Jesse Hollywood. Jesse was calm at the time, and asking some more questions about his house. Jerry asked Jesse if he'd heard any more about the situation in Santa Barbara with the boy who had been taken. According to Jerry, "Jesse said yes. 'Someone is taking the boy home.'"

This was the strongest statement so far by any witness that at a time when Nick Markowitz was alive and at the Lemon Tree Inn, Jesse Hollywood told a person that "someone is taking the boy home."

* * *

After Jerry Hollywood testified, many in the gallery were stretching and talking during a break, with the jury out of the courtroom. There seemed to be some confusion at the defense table as to who would be their next witness. One of the court observers, who had been at the trial every day, was named Jennifer. She was talking to her friend Rene when Blatt indicated who the next witness would be. Jennifer said later, "We heard who Mr. Blatt said he was putting on the stand and we couldn't believe our ears. It was going to be Jesse Hollywood!"

Dressed in a black suit, dark tie and gray shirt, Jesse Hollywood looked nothing like the photo that Joshua Lynn kept showing the jurors earlier of how Jesse Hollywood looked in 2000. Jesse started off by telling of his feud with Ben Markowitz in the year 2000. Getting to the part about the abduction of Nick on August 6, 2000, Jesse, in essence, admitted to kidnapping by saying, "I jumped out of the van, pinned Nick against a tree and yelled at him, 'Where's your brother? Where's your brother?'" Then Jesse said that he and William Skidmore "ushered" Nick into the van.

Jesse claimed that he never once told Nick that he would be held until his brother, Ben, paid a debt. Rather, Jesse said, the taking of Nick took place because he was so angry at Ben breaking out his windows and threatening him and his family. On the ride up to Santa Barbara, Jesse said that neither he nor anyone else laid a finger on Nick. And when he discovered that William Skidmore had placed duct tape on Nick, at Richard Hoeflinger's house, Jesse said that he made Skidmore take the duct tape off. In fact, Jesse said, Nick was soon free to walk around the house, and that he and Nick sat on the couch, playing video games.

Jesse declared that to defuse the situation even further, he sent Brian Affronti and William Skidmore back in the van to Los Angeles. This left him without a ride, and he made several phone calls from Hoeflinger's, trying to get a ride back home for himself. Jesse eventually declared that he got a ride home with a friend with the last name of Green.

As far as August 7, 2000, went, Jesse said that he came up to Santa Barbara with Michelle Lasher to pick up $500 that Rugge owed him for marijuana. Jesse did not mention going out to lunch with Jesse, as Rugge had claimed, and Jesse adamantly denied ever offering Rugge money to kill Nick. In fact, Jesse claimed, "At that point I didn't believe there was any danger to Nick."

Jesse then spoke of meeting with Jerry Hollywood before noon on August 8, to sign some papers about his house on Cohasset Street. And he admitted to going to see Stephen Hogg that afternoon. But Jesse declared that it was only to "seek advice" from Hogg, and that he did not make plans to have Nick killed after hearing that the kidnapping could get a person life in prison.

Jesse said of the meeting with Hogg, "My attorney advised me to take the guy home and go to the police. I wasn't going to call the police because of my business. But I was going to get the kid home!"

Asked about all the phone calls between himself and Jesse Rugge on August 8, 2000, Hollywood said that Rugge wanted a ride back to the Los Angeles area, since Rugge had a suspended driver's license. Jesse claimed that because he and Michelle were going out to dinner that night, to celebrate her birthday, he borrowed Casey Sheehan's car, and sent Ryan Hoyt up to Santa Barbara to get Rugge. Jesse added, "Hoyt was supposed to bring Rugge and Nick back to Los Angeles. He was going to take the kid home."

Hollywood testified that he went by Casey Sheehan's house at about 4:30 P.M., along with Michelle. Since Ryan Hoyt was boxing up items at Jesse's Cohasset Street home, Jesse said, he went by there to check on how it was going. When he got there, Jesse said, he asked Hoyt to drive up to Santa Barbara, and gave him the keys to Casey Sheehan's car. Once again, Jesse declared, "I told Ryan to take Nick home. Hoyt agreed and said that was fine."

Jesse claimed that he had no idea on August 9 that Ryan Hoyt had actually murdered Nick Markowitz. In fact, Jesse said that he assumed that Nick was back home by then. He did admit that he leased a new Lincoln Town Car, but that was because his old car had been in and out of the shop so much recently.

Jesse stated, "I had a brief phone conversation with Ryan Hoyt that day about the situation in Santa Barbara. He told me everything was fine. It wasn't until later, just before his birthday at Casey Sheehan's house, that Ryan came up to me and said, 'We fucked up!'

"I asked him what he meant, and he said that they had killed Nick.

"I said to him, 'Are you kidding!'

"He said he wasn't kidding."

Jesse declared that after that pivotal moment, "I was stressed out and worried and very concerned that what he told me was true and whether this was going to turn into something very bad." Jesse said he wasn't sure if it was true or not, because Hoyt was always coming up with wild stories.

Hollywood said that on August 11 he went to see his mother, because of what Ryan Hoyt had told him. If it was true, Jesse said, "I wanted to see my mom, because it might be the last time I saw her for a long time."

Jesse drove to Palm Springs in his Lincoln, with his mother as a passenger, and they met up with Michelle Lasher there. Jesse claimed that he did not discuss with his mother anything about the kidnapping of Nick, or the supposed murder of Nick by Hoyt.

Jesse's recollections of the next couple of days were not exact, and said that they were kind of a blur now. He did say that after Palm Springs he and Michelle went back to the Los Angeles area. It was probably on August 13 that he and Michelle were over at William Skidmore's house. Skidmore had just read a newspaper about Nick's body being discovered and told Jesse about it. Hollywood said that at that moment he knew that what Ryan Hoyt had told him was true.

Jesse testified, "At that point our little world became everyone's world. It dawned on me there was going to be trouble, for sure. I told Skidmore, 'I'm ghost.'"

Asked what he meant by that term, Jesse said he meant that he was leaving town in a hurry.

Jesse basically reiterated what Michelle Lasher had said about their journey to Las Vegas and Colorado. He spoke of visiting Coach Richard Dispenza there, and his friends William Jacques and Chas Saulsbury. After putting Michelle on the plane back to Burbank, Jesse said that he hung out with his friends. He did change one detail, however.

The common perception had been that Jesse had left Coach's house to get a pack of cigarettes, and when he walked back toward the house, he saw police cars there, and just walked away. Jesse now said that he was in a motel room when Coach phoned him and told him there were cops at his house, and not to come over. Jesse said at that point he just walked away from the motel and his new leased car, and began trekking down the road. It was a road that eventually led him to Chas Saulsbury's house.

Then Jesse added another new revelation. He said that Chas didn't drive him to Los Angeles out of loyalty. Jesse said that Chas drove him there after demanding $3,000, which Jesse gave him. On the way to Los Angeles, Jesse said, Chas called a lawyer, and found out from that person that the authorities were already declaring they were going to seek the death penalty against Jesse Hollywood, and they were calling him a "child killer."

Of this latest revelation, Jesse said that he was extremely

scared on the way back to Los Angeles. "I was definitely praying, crossing myself and asking God for help. I thought I had lost my life."

Jesse then spoke of the failed attempt to meet up with his father in Calabasas, and being driven to John Roberts's house by Chas. Jesse added that as soon as he was out of Chas Saulsbury's view, Chas took off, along with $8,000 that Jesse still had in Chas's car.

Jesse agreed with John Roberts's story that he'd turned Jesse down when he'd asked for help in getting a passport and fake ID. And Jesse also said that Roberts told him to turn himself in to the police. What Jesse added now, which had not come up before, was that Roberts gave him a manila envelope with $10,000 inside.

Instead of turning himself in to the police, Jesse said that he contacted a friend named Donner, who lived out in the middle of the Mojave Desert. According to Jesse, this friend took him out to his trailer there, a place so isolated and rough, Jesse testified, "the post office wouldn't even deliver the mail there." Jesse claimed that he spent the next two weeks surviving on "frozen dinners, cigarettes and beer." Then he added that he watched television in the trailer and repeatedly saw himself on the news and even on *America's Most Wanted.*

Of this news coverage, Jesse said, "I felt that the media had already convicted me. I was scared to death."

One of the most bizarre incidents while Jesse stayed there was watching on television the SWAT team bombard John Roberts's house with tear gas. The authorities, of course, thought Jesse was inside that house. Instead, he was out in the Mojave Desert watching the incident on television, drinking beer and smoking cigarettes.

After two weeks in the desert, Jesse said, he decided to catch a plane to Seattle, Washington. Even after all the news coverage about him, Jesse stated that it was fairly easy going through security at Los Angeles International

Airport and catching a flight. This was, of course, before the tightened security after 9/11.

Jesse testified to staying two weeks in Seattle before bribing someone to take him by boat to Canada. For the next six months, he bounced all over Canada—from Vancouver to Quebec, then to Calgary, Montreal and back to Vancouver. Jesse added that he was astonished when he turned on the television one day in Canada and saw himself on *America's Most Wanted* up there. He had no idea that Canadian television ran that program.

Then one day he watched a movie called *Blame It on Rio.* Jesse claimed, "The idea just popped into my head to go to Brazil." It was the ultimate irony of Jesse Hollywood, emulating Hollywood. After obtaining a very good fake passport for $1,000, Jesse said, he flew from Canada down to Cancun, Mexico. He spent two days there, and then got a flight to Rio de Janeiro. Once in Brazil, he learned enough Portuguese to get by, and even got a job in an office. It was in Rio de Janeiro that he met Marcia Reis. Despite their age difference, they began dating, and then she moved into a house with him in Saquarema, on the Atlantic coast. Of his time with her, Jesse said, "The relationship was a good one." He now referred to her as his wife.

Joshua Lynn had plenty of questions of Jesse Hollywood on cross-examination, and it was obvious that he believed very little of what Jesse had just testified to on the witness stand. Lynn began by showing Jesse a photo of Nick Markowitz and asked Jesse if he knew who that was.

Jesse replied, "Yes."

Then Lynn asked, "Do you know what you're on trial for?"

Jesse replied, "Because I'm accused of a serious crime."

"Do you think you did anything wrong?"

Jesse responded, "I do, and I feel terrible. It was wrong

to push Nick up against a tree and take him away from his home." Jesse would not admit to kidnapping for extortion, or having anything to do with the murder of Nick Markowitz.

Lynn was less than enthused by Jesse's answers, and he asked him point-blank, "Why did you have Nick Markowitz killed?"

"I didn't," Jesse replied.

If Lynn hoped that his questions would rattle Jesse Hollywood, the way Chas Saulsbury had been rattled on the stand, it didn't work. Jesse often answered, in a low, measured voice, "Yes, sir," and "No, sir" to Lynn's questions. After a while, Lynn was calling Jesse "sir" as well. It was almost as if there was a duel to see who could sound more polite.

By the second day on the stand, Jesse was still holding up under a barrage of questions. Jesse was very restrained in his answers, until the questioning got around to his marijuana business. Even now, he sounded proud of what he had accomplished by the age of nineteen. He boasted that he had an excellent credit score of 780 back then, and he was making $7,000 to $8,000 a month. He said that he didn't sell low-grade, hamburger-type marijuana. He sold "New York steak."

Trying to trip Jesse up, Lynn, out of the blue, asked, "Why did you offer Jesse Rugge two thousand dollars to kill Nick?"

Jesse calmly replied, "I didn't."

"That never happened?" Lynn asked with skepticism.

"Never, sir," Jesse responded.

One area of testimony that differed greatly from what Casey Sheehan and Michelle Lasher had said concerned their time at the Outback Steakhouse on the evening of August 8, 2000. During that dinner, Sheehan testified, Jesse had told him about what was happening in Santa Barbara. Sheehan related that Jesse said, "The situation with Nick has been taken care of." And Michelle had testified that Jesse said, "The situation became unwound."

Jesse now said that he never mentioned Nick or Santa Barbara at all, while at the Outback Steakhouse. And he also disagreed about what Chas Saulsbury had testified to concerning the gun that had been found in Nick's grave as a TEC-9. Jesse said that Chas must have read that in a newspaper, because he claimed he didn't have a TEC-9 in August 2000. Jesse added that he had deposited the TEC-9 over at Hoyt's grandparents' house in 1999. The reason he did so, Jesse claimed, was because he and Hoyt and Ben Markowitz had fired that fully automatic weapon at a firing range one day in 1999. An employee there told them that an altered fully automatic weapon could get them arrested, so Jesse decided to get the gun out of his house, and Hoyt took it.

But Lynn was able to prove that newspapers only referred to a "gun" being found in Nick's grave when Chas first spoke to authorities. And Lynn also brought up the fact that even Jesse's friend Casey Sheehan testified to seeing the TEC-9 at Jesse Hollywood's house in March 2000.

As to why Jesse Hollywood had gone to see lawyer Stephen Hogg on the afternoon of August 8, 2000, Jesse said that he had done so because he considered Hogg to be a "wise man," and he only went there for advice.

Lynn retorted, "If Hogg was such a wise man, why didn't you answer any of his pages that evening?"

As many witnesses had done before him, Jesse uttered the words "Because I was scared."

Jesse also had no concrete reason as to why Ryan Hoyt, who was chronically broke, suddenly had enough money to buy new clothes at the 118 Board Shop the day after Nick was murdered.

Getting to Hollywood's time in Brazil, Lynn asked, "Had you heard that if you had a child by a woman in Brazil, you couldn't be extradited?"

"I had heard that," Jesse answered. And then he added

about his wife and their son, whom he named John Paul, that he loved them.

Court observer Jennifer glanced over at Susan Markowitz at that moment. Jennifer said later, "When Jesse mentioned the name of his son, named after a pope, Susan shot daggers at him from her eyes."

By day three of testimony, Joshua Lynn and Jesse Hollywood were still verbally sparring. But it wasn't the raucous, often cantankerous sparring of Lynn versus Lasher, or Saulsbury versus Kessel. Many answers Jesse gave were either "Yes, sir" or "No, sir."

Lynn kept pounding on Jesse's meeting with lawyer Stephen Hogg on the afternoon of August 8, 2000. Lynn asked, "Did you tell Chas Saulsbury the ramifications of that meeting?"

"No, sir," Jesse replied.

"Didn't you tell Chas Saulsbury the things you had done might get you a life [sentence] in prison?"

"No, sir."

"Didn't you tell Chas Saulsbury that you ordered Ryan Hoyt to kill and bury the boy?"

In a strong and loud voice, Jesse answered, "No, sir, Mr. Lynn. I never did!"

"So what is your responsibility for this situation?"

"I feel moral responsibility for this situation. But I did not have Nick Markowitz killed."

"When did your responsibility end?"

Jesse replied, "Nick was free to go when I left Richard Hoeflinger's on August 6, 2000."

"So when you left Richard Hoeflinger's house, your responsibility ended?"

"Yes. When I left Richard Hoeflinger's, Nick was safe."

It seemed that Lynn was almost done, and then he asked, "Why did you sign some letters from jail after you were arrested, 'Alpha Dog'?"

Before Jesse could answer, James Blatt objected, and it was sustained.

There was only one person left that the defense called as a witness, Investigator Paul Kimes. To a bombardment of questions from Alex Kessel about pages and phone numbers, and as to whether he had contacted those people, Kimes answered to most questions, "No."

Asked why not, Kimes replied they either weren't relevant, detectives had contacted those people, or they just plain couldn't be found.

And to the all-important alleged conversation between Jesse Rugge and Graham Pressley, when Rugge first told Pressley that Jesse Hollywood had offered him money to kill Nick, Kessel wanted to know when and where this had supposedly taken place.

Kimes looked at his notes and said that it had occurred on August 7, 2000, in Jesse Rugge's kitchen.

Kessel then asked, "Did you ever contact Jerry Hollywood about the phone call he received from Jesse at ten twenty-two P.M. on August 8, 2000?"

"No," Kimes responded.

By this point Alex Kessel was getting so worked up that his voice became louder and louder. Judge Hill finally said, "Whoa! Wait a minute! You have to keep your voice down!"

Kessel did for a short period of time, but before long he was just as animated as before. Paul Kimes seemed to be amused by the constant reminders from Judge Hill to Alex Kessel to lower his voice. In response to the wry smile on Kimes's lips, Kessel suddenly said, "Do you think it's funny that my client is on trial for his life?"

Kimes said he didn't think it was funny, but the wry smile stayed on his lips nonetheless.

* * *

By the end of June 2009, the long parade of witnesses was over. Closing arguments by both the prosecution and the defense did not differ radically from their opening arguments—except to highlight the statements of witnesses who had been good to their cause, and brand as "liars" those witnesses who had not been favorable.

Joshua Lynn told the jurors, "There is a mountain of evidence against Mr. Hollywood and justice has waited nine years. When Jesse Hollywood testified, he looked you in the eye and lied to your faces."

As to the large number of witnesses who had spoken for the prosecution, Lynn asked why all of them would put themselves in jeopardy by lying. Lynn said, "What would be the motive for everyone to get on the stand and lie? Jesse James Hollywood is as guilty as sin! I would urge you to usher Mr. Hollywood into his new status as a convicted kidnapper and child killer. Convict him."

At the end of his argument, Lynn showed the jurors three photos of Nick lying in a shallow grave near the Lizard's Mouth. Nick's body was riddled with bullets. Lynn declared, "Look at Nick Markowitz. That is what is left of Nick."

Alex Kessel countered in closing arguments, "What the prosecution told you is not credible. It doesn't even rise to the level of thinking about it." Kessel argued that both Chas Saulsbury and Graham Pressley lied to detectives to make themselves look less involved than they were. Kessel then asked why his client, who was a bright individual, would have Nick Markowitz killed, after so many people had seen himself and Nick together in Santa Barbara. It didn't make sense, Kessel argued, as he argued that Jesse Hollywood was a rational, organized person.

The one person who was not rational or organized, Kessel said, was Ryan Hoyt. According to Kessel, on August 8, 2000, Hollywood sent Ryan Hoyt up to Santa

Barbara to pick up Nick and bring him back home. Instead, Hoyt got some crazy idea into his head that he could gain status by killing Nick. It was Hoyt's own illogical reasoning that led to the murder of Nick, and it had nothing to do with his client.

Kessel said of the prosecution, "They're trying to take a square peg and fit it into a round hole. You can't let emotion drive your decisions. You can't fill the voids of the people's case with pictures of Nick Markowitz in his grave."

23

DAY OF RECKONING

From the end of closing arguments, until 2:30 P.M. on July 8, the jurors debated, argued and looked over material concerning the case. When the Markowitz and Hollywood families heard there was a verdict, they hurried back to the courtroom, along with reporters and interested citizens. As soon as the verdict was read, Jack Hollywood was stunned. Jesse James Hollywood was found guilty of first-degree murder and kidnapping. He was now a candidate for the death penalty.

Jesse Hollywood's expression on hearing the verdict was more sedate than his father's had been. He sat at the defense table with an expressionless look. Soon after the verdict was rendered, Jesse was whisked away by some of the seventeen deputies who had been stationed around the courtroom to make sure there were no outbursts when the verdict was read.

Even though there was still a gag order in effect, Jack Hollywood told reporters outside the courthouse, "I can't believe they found him guilty of murder! It was not a just verdict."

Jeff and Susan Markowitz, naturally, had a much different opinion about the verdict that had just been rendered. Jeff said, "Now we can focus on Nick." Jeff knew that in the next phase, he and Susan would be talking to the jurors about Nick and all his good qualities.

Susan was less adamant about the finality of what had just happened. She said, "It will never be over." But at least she was happy that this important stage had been passed—a verdict she had been waiting for since August 2000.

Even Ben Markowitz had a few things to say to reporters. Ben declared, "I'm definitely happy about the verdict. It's a big relief. The last thing I wanted was for Jesse Hollywood to be free. It was such a senseless and stupid crime."

Now it remained to be seen if Jesse Hollywood, like Ryan Hoyt, would pay with his life for the senseless and stupid crime of August 2000.

On July 14, 2009, the sentencing phase began with families, friends and attorneys speaking both for and against the death penalty. Judge Hill allowed Joshua Lynn to play a small segment of the audio and video portion of Nick at his Bar Mitzvah. In that segment Nick's voice rang out in the courtroom for the first and last time. Nick said, "The golden rule of Judaism is treat other people as you would like to be treated." The jurors were not allowed to hear the rest of his speech about Moses and fair trials.

Jeff Markowitz related to the jurors about what he missed about his son. Jeff spoke of wanting to see Nick grow up and eventually have a family, as many of his childhood friends now had.

Susan Markowitz expressed many of the same thoughts of all the things she missed, and that would never occur in

Nick's life, once it had been cut short. Susan also spoke of the moment the detectives walked up to her house, a little after 6:00 A.M., all those years ago. She said, "They had that look in their eyes and the smell of death. I know at that moment, I died. Nick died a month shy of his sixteenth birthday. Instead of a car, he got a coffin."

Just as strongly as Jeff and Susan Markowitz had spoken of Nick, Jesse Hollywood's mom, Laurie Haynes, who was now remarried, spoke of Jesse's good qualities. She said, "I think every human being has value, my son included." She related how everyone loved watching him as a happy young boy on the baseball field. And then she added that many people didn't know that after a game Jesse would take groceries to one of his aunts, who was sick.

Laurie also spoke of Jesse now being a father. She said, "It would be a great injustice to deprive a son of his father, and to deprive the rest of the family of having any more interaction with him."

Even a jail nurse, Laura Hanan, spoke up for Jesse Hollywood. She said that he always treated her with respect and wasn't violent around anyone. Hanan said she decided to testify to let the jurors learn about the person she had come to know. She told them, "I see a loving father. I see a friend."

Joshua Lynn spoke once again of all the details of the kidnapping and murder of Nick Markowitz. Then he declared, "Jesse Hollywood is a killer of the worst kind. He executed an innocent, uninvolved fifteen-year-old boy to avoid a life sentence."

Lynn stated it was fear of a life sentence that had driven Jesse to murder. Lynn also spoke of Jesse Hollywood moving to Brazil and impregnating a woman there in the belief that if he did so, he could not be extradited. When Lynn started talking about this aspect of Jesse Hollywood's life, Michelle Lasher, who was sitting in the gallery, suddenly rose, stalked out of the courtroom and slammed the door behind her.

Lynn once again showed the jurors photos of Nick's bullet-riddled body as it lay in a shallow grave near the Lizard's Mouth. Lynn said, "This is the hole left by Jesse Hollywood. It's that simple. The appropriate sentence is death."

In some ways the sentencing phase became a forum of dueling images. Alex Kessel showed the jurors photos of Jesse Hollywood as a smiling young boy. And while Lynn's sole aggravating circumstances for death rested on the kidnapping charge and Jesse Hollywood's meeting with Stephen Hogg, where he learned what the consequences for his actions would be, Kessel had a list of mitigating circumstances. Kessel noted that the jurors had already acquitted Jesse of kidnapping for ransom or extortion, and said "the prosecution's assertion that Jesse had Nick killed to cover up a kidnapping never occurred." Then Kessel said that Jesse had a lack of prior criminal conduct, had behaved well in jail—and testimony by friends and family proved he was *not* a violent person. Kessel stated that Jesse didn't even come close to being the "worst kind of criminal," as Lynn had asserted.

Kessel hit hard on just what a verdict of death would mean. He said that in Utah a person could be executed by firing squad, and that one member of the firing squad always had a blank in his rifle. Just which rifleman had the blank, none knew, so that the executioners could always believe that they had not killed anyone. But Kessel said that if a juror voted for death in Jesse's case, that person would always know that he or she killed someone. Kessel stated,

"When you vote for death, it is *your* decision. That is something you're going to have to live with for the rest of your life."

Then Kessel said, "If you vote for life without parole, he is never getting out. That's a hard thing for the rest of your life. It's real punishment."

Outside the presence of the jury, the defense had one more thing to present to Judge Hill, and it was staggering. The defense once again asked for a mistrial, and this time they had a very good chance that it would occur. Alex Kessel let Judge Hill know that prior to the verdict in the guilt phase, one of the jurors had made a tasteless joke to another juror about Jesse Hollywood being electrocuted. The woman who heard the joke became so upset by it that she told her husband about it. Eventually this husband told Jack Hollywood of the situation, and Jack passed it on to the defense team.

Two things were now in play. One was that the juror who had told the joke might have "prejudged" Jesse Hollywood's guilt before all the evidence was in. The second thing was that despite all Judge Hill's admonitions not to tell anyone what was occurring at trial, the juror who had heard the joke told her husband about it. This was such a serious matter that Judge Hill had Jurors #3, #5 and #12 come in and talk about the incident. Juror #5 admitted to making the joke, but said she had not prejudged Jesse Hollywood when she did so.

Both the defense and prosecution argued vigorously about this incident. If the defense got its way, then more than six weeks of testimony were down the drain, and the trial would have to start once again, with a whole new set of jurors.

Judge Hill mulled all of this over and finally ruled, "Although the joke was crass, it did not necessarily constitute prejudgment. Any claim that Juror five prejudged the case is pure speculation. It appears that people in the jury room who had strongly held views that Mr. Hollywood was guilty tried to convince Juror three. But it did not go beyond that."

Once again, a case that had seen its ups and downs, twists and turns—for nine years—dodged a bullet at the very end. The jurors would now decide if Jesse James Hollywood would spend the rest of his life in prison, or receive the death penalty.

When the decision came, it came very quickly. After only three hours of deliberation, the jury of nine women and three men filed back into the courtroom. It was such a short period of time that very few ordinary citizens of Santa Barbara, who had filled the courtroom on prior occasions, even knew that it was happening. The courtroom was mostly empty, except for the Markowitz family, Hollywood family and reporters.

Once the jurors filled the jury box, the court clerk read in a clear voice that rang out in the absolutely quiet courtroom: Jesse Hollywood was sentenced to a life term in prison without the possibility of parole.

Alex Kessel swiveled in his chair, and mouthed the words to the jury, "Thank you."

Judge Hill thanked the jurors for their duty, and then quickly had the courtroom cleared. And just as after the Jesse Rugge trial, not one of the jurors chose to speak with the reporters waiting outside or to the lawyers.

Since Judge Hill had lifted the gag order, family, friends and attorneys did talk to the press. Speaking about the silence of the jurors, James Blatt said, "Some of the jurors are deeply troubled about something that happened in this trial. We're going to find out what that is." And then Blatt contended that Juror #3 had been "bullied" by the others during the guilt phase.

Blatt also, once again, blasted the movie *Alpha Dog* and the negative image that was portrayed of Jesse Hollywood in that movie. Blatt said that the movie put the defense in a bad position even before the trial began. And Blatt had a very negative opinion of many of the rulings that Judge Hill had made throughout the trial. Blatt said that the jury instructions were "confusing," and that Judge Hill should have ruled, as Judge Gordon had done in Jesse Rugge's trial, that the kidnapping had ceased at some point in Santa Barbara. In Judge Hill's ruling, the kidnapping never did cease until Nick was murdered.

Blatt declared, "I think if the judge had used the appropriate ruling, there would have been a very different outcome with the jury" (in the penalty phase).

Nonetheless, both Blatt and Kessel were pleased that the jurors had voted for life without parole, rather than death. Jack Hollywood was happy on that point as well, but he was still bitter about the first-degree murder verdict. Jack told reporters, "Jesse is not a killer. There were a lot of unfortunate rulings from the judge."

Joshua Lynn was more reserved in his comments to the press. He basically thanked the jurors, the Markowitz family and his cocounsel, Hans Almgren. Then Lynn expressed that he was glad that this long ordeal was finally over.

An "ordeal" is certainly what it had been. It began with all the missed opportunities to bring Nick Markowitz back home safe, starting on August 6, 2000. If any of the people who knew or suspected that Nick had been abducted on that date had told just one law enforcement officer, things might have turned out very differently for all involved. The opportunities to capture Jesse James Hollywood in the days after the murder were numerous in their own right. It would take countless days of phone surveillance, lengthy detective work and just plain luck to bring Hollywood back from Brazil to stand trial. Even Mother Nature in the Jesusita firestorm delayed the road to trial.

Jeff Markowitz told the gathered journalists that he could live with the verdict that had been handed down. He said, "Another son dying won't bring Nick back." Then Jeff added, "But let it be said that murder for hire is just as serious as pulling the trigger. If Jesse Hollywood had made a better choice, Nick would be alive, and Hollywood wouldn't be going to prison for the rest of his life."

Susan Markowitz agreed with Jeff that Jesse Hollywood dying would not bring Nick back. She said, "As a mother I would not be thrilled or relieved that he receive the death penalty."

More than anyone else, it was Susan Markowitz who best summed up everything that had occurred since the fatal meeting of her son, Nick, and Jesse James Hollywood on the corner of Ingomar and Platt, on the morning of August 6, 2000.

Gracious as always, Susan let the people of Santa Barbara know just how she felt in a letter to the editor of the *News-Press*. Susan explained that she hoped one day she could "look at your beautiful community and not link it to Nick's death."

Susan thanked all the detectives, prosecutors and everyone who had worked on the cases against Ryan Hoyt, Jesse Rugge, Graham Pressley and Jesse James Hollywood. She said that their kindness made her no longer fear being in a courthouse. Even the media came in for her praise. She said that she'd heard horror stories about how the media treated the parents of murdered children. Susan related that those types of things never occurred with her or her family. She wrote about the media, "You have never been any of that to me." She thanked the reporters and court observers for the compassion they always showed her.

Finally, Susan wrote, "Nick, thank you for your surprises. It was an honor to be your mother. We must never forget. We are all losers here. Some lose more than others. None more than Nick."

MORE SHOCKING TRUE CRIME
FROM PINNACLE

Lethal Embrace   0-7860-1785-6 $6.99/$9.99
Robert Mladinich and Michael Benson

Love Me or I'll Kill You   0-7860-1778-3 $6.99/$9.99
Lee Butcher

Precious Blood   0-7860-1849-6 $6.99/$9.99
Sam Adams

Baby-Faced Butchers   0-7860-1803-8 $6.99/$9.99
Stella Sands

Hooked Up for Murder   0-7860-1865-8 $6.99/$9.99
Robert Mladinich and Michael Benson

Available Wherever Books Are Sold!

Visit our website at **www.kensingtonbooks.com**